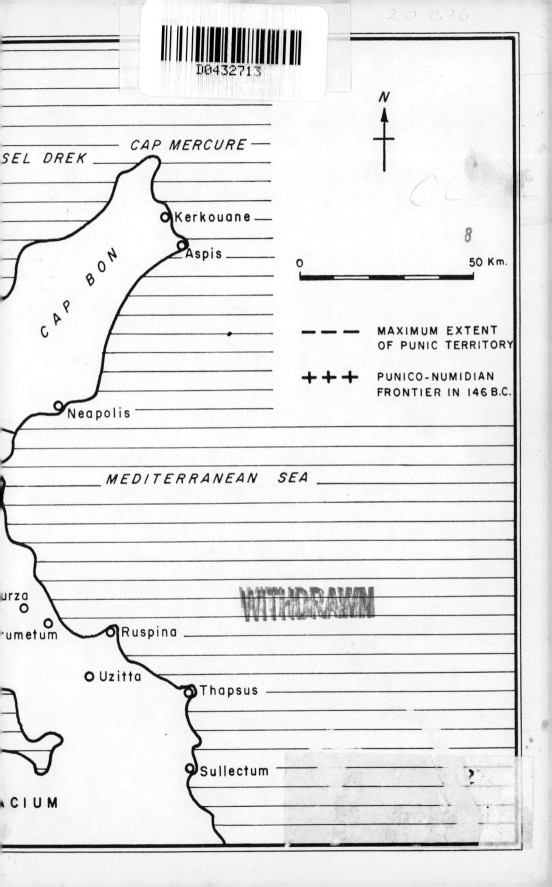

N

SEL DREK _____ CAP MERCURE ___

CAP BON

○ Kerkouane ___

○ Aspis

0 _____ 50 Km.

_ _ _ _   MAXIMUM EXTENT
          OF PUNIC TERRITORY

+ + +   PUNICO-NUMIDIAN
          FRONTIER IN 146 B.C.

○ Neapolis ___

MEDITERRANEAN   SEA _____

urza
○

umetum
○   ○ Ruspina _____

○ Uzitta

○ Thapsus _____

○ Sullectum _____

ACIUM

CARTHAGE

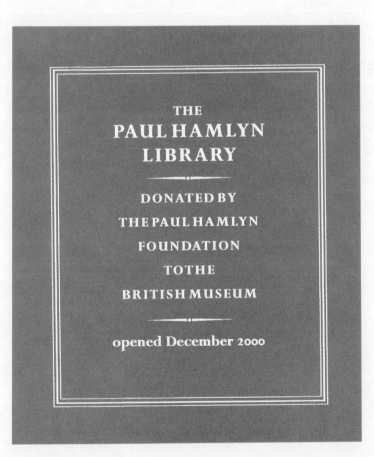

CARTHAGE

*A survey of Punic history and
culture from its birth to
the final tragedy*

by

GILBERT CHARLES PICARD

*Emeritus Professor of Roman Archaeology at the
Sorbonne and former Director of
Antiquities at Tunis*

and

COLETTE PICARD

Doctor in History

Translated from the French by
DOMINIQUE COLLON

SIDGWICK & JACKSON
LONDON

This edition first published in Great Britain
in 1987 by Sidgwick and Jackson Limited
Original edition published in Great Britain
in 1968

Copyright © 1968 and 1987 by
Gilbert Charles Picard and Colette Picard

Copyright in this translation © 1968 and 1987
by Sidgwick and Jackson Limited

ISBN 0-283-99532-7

Printed in Hong Kong
for Sidgwick & Jackson Limited
1 Tavistock Chambers, Bloomsbury Way
London WC1A 2SG

Contents

Introduction

MOST historians of Carthage have generally agreed that Western Phoenician society evolved remarkably little during the six or seven centuries of its existence. Gsell, in his *magnum opus* which, until recent years, was the definitive work on the subject, also held this view, and it has coloured all his writing as it has that of many other authors. These first record and discuss the various traditions relating to Tyrian colonization but then study separately the Internal and External Affairs of Carthage. According to them, only the latter are worthy of attention on purely historical grounds, while the former are arranged in an unchanging pattern. They use all the information which the writers of Antiquity have left to us, regardless of date, and attempt to bring this varied material together into a coherent whole, regardless of the many difficulties which they come across. This criticism also applies to customs, religious beliefs and even to economic life. Even where evolution is undeniable, it is discussed completely independently of any other section of the book. The historian attempts to minimize the importance of any change or evolution, in fact. In just such a way Gsell, and more recently Warmington, have tried to show that the magistracy of the *suffetes* dates back to the earliest Carthage, whereas we have definite information on this subject from only the last two centuries of the city's existence. Evidence of the cult of Tanit is equally late, but she is often considered to be a barely modified avatar of a Cypro–Phoenician Mother–Goddess which Dido would have introduced.

The present volume has been envisaged differently. Use has been made of material which the author had already brought together in a previous volume but in a simplified version and with many errors.[1] The history of Carthage has been divided into chronological sections and in each of these it has been studied within the framework of the Phoenician community in Africa,

I

with an attempt to prove its dependence on such a community. During the Magonid Period (*c.* 550–396 B.C.), for instance, Carthage was in open conflict with the Greeks over the control of the Western Mediterranean, and instituted an essentially militarist monarchy. In a further attempt to confine Hellenic expansion, she formed an alliance with the Etruscans and close cultural links were thus forged between the two peoples – links which Pallotino's extraordinary discoveries at Pyrgi have recently emphasized.

The 'monolithic' conception of Punic history was based on an implicit claim, namely that Punic is a Semitic language akin to Hebrew, that the Hebrews and Arabs both have a very intense religious life and are very conservative, and that therefore the same bold generalization and principles can be applied to all those speaking a language belonging to this group. Although it is certain that the 'People of the Book' try to follow its dictates as closely as possible and are often liable to regard innovations as sins, yet, in spite of any resemblances between the Hebrew and Phoenician religions, it seems as though the legalistic tendency was less developed in the latter than in the former. Furthermore, Punic economy looked seawards and was based on trade, and therefore differed fundamentally from that of Israel, and still more from the pastoral and nomadic way of life which was prevalent in Arabia then as now. From this point of view, the Carthaginians were far closer to the Greeks than were the other Semites; Aristotle studied their 'politeia', using information which is no longer available to us, and concluded it was very close to that of several Greek cities.

Nothing in the traditions of Antiquity can justify a theory of Punic immutability. Certainly Classical authors noted the persistence, at Carthage, of certain customs which seemed extremely archaic – for instance, human sacrifice. In several societies, however, the same fossilization, restricted to a well-defined field of activity, can be studied, while the structure of the same society has, itself, changed completely. Rome was celebrated for its religious conservatism and this opinion, as expressed by the Ancients, has been strengthened by Dumézil's discovery of a basis for Latin society which goes back to the most ancient Indo-European groupings; this did not prevent the Romans from being

2

the first, in the Mediterranean World, to progress from City to State.

In fact, it is the scarcity of material and information to have come down to us concerning the Carthaginians, which has led us, hitherto, to consider that the contemporaries of Hannibal must have lived and thought essentially as the companions of Dido did. With the sole exception of Aristotle, the authors of Antiquity were only interested in Carthage as far as her relations with the Greeks and the Romans were concerned. It is only in parenthesis, as it were, that they give us some information about their laws and customs. The picture we obtain when we gather together these scattered items, is full of lacunae and present-day authors have naturally attempted to fill these gaps by presupposing that what was true for one period could also be applied to another unless the contrary were actually stated.

For the last half-century, however, our knowledge has been substantially increased by the contributions of Archaeology. When Gsell was publishing his great work (1913–29), the only Punic remains which were known were the tombs, and the methods for classifying the material which they contained were far from perfect. Our approach to a great many problems has been altered by such discoveries, to name but a few, as that of the 'topheth' of Salammbo (excavated between 1921 and 1949), the excavation of houses and temples in Carthage itself, the exploration of a city of the third and second centuries B.C. at Dar es Safi near Kerkouane on the Cap Bon peninsula, and the work of Italian archaeologists in Sicily, Sardinia, and Malta. For example, the date of 814 B.C. for the foundation of Carthage was based on a study of ancient texts and was generally accepted, but the archaeological material so far discovered on the site is no earlier than the second half of the eighth century. The study of ex-votos from the topheth (the excavations have not yet been fully published, unfortunately) proves that the religious life of Carthage was convulsed by radical reforms, and there is general agreement that the most important of these, the elevation of Tanit to the rank of 'Lady of Carthage', happened in conjunction with a political revolution which put the aristocracy in power. Finally, the recent excavations at Pyrgi have brought to light inscriptions dedicated to Ashtart by the Etruscan king Thefarie Veliunas which give us an unexpected insight into the practically insoluble problems of Punico–Etruscan relations, and of the date of the first treaty between Rome and Carthage.

This new evidence has induced us to reconsider old problems. Gsell and Beloch disagreed, at the beginning of this century, on the question of Carthaginian monarchy. The Frenchman's greater knowledge triumphed but his students and the abbreviators of his work did not take into account the reservations which he had made. We shall see, further on, the reasons which make it necessary to reconsider Beloch's theory.

It is, indeed, regrettable that it is not possible, in this book, to give as precise an idea of Carthage as has been given of Greece and Rome in companion volumes in this series. In spite of the progress which has been made, Punic history remains extremely problematic. Some will, no doubt, be surprised or even gleeful to find that the present author has several times reached a different conclusion from that which he had been led to adopt in the past. It is to be hoped that either he, or his successors, will be able, in a not too distant future, to reconsider several points in this provisional picture. We shall only be able to reconstruct the past by constant dialectic; it is rare indeed, for an investigator to be able to solve a problem by discovering an absolute truth, and should he do so, it will be found to be a small point with but limited repercussions. It therefore becomes a necessity to undertake historical syntheses (for otherwise history would become a study for the initiated alone) but it must be made clear to the reader that such syntheses have a purely hypothetical and temporary character.

Reference

1. *Le Monde de Carthage*, Paris 1956: English edition under the title *Carthage*, London 1964; and cf. the review by B. H. Warmington, *J.R.S.*, LV (1965), p. 262.

Chronology

5

DATE B.C.	EVENTS
	Necho's Phoenician sailors circumnavigate the African continent
591	The Carthaginians colonize Ibiza
	Built tombs of Carthage and Utica; ex-votos in the shape of sarcophagi or chests in the topheth of Salammbo; first appearance of limestone stelae and female masks; large quantity of imported Corinthian pottery in Carthage
580	Foundation of Agrigentum
	Pentathlus attempts to settle Lilybaeum
559–530	Reign of Cyrus
c. 550–530	**Reign of Mago** (?)
	Conquest of Sardinia by the Carthaginians
	The Carthaginians lords of Motya
535	Battle of Alalia; height of the Etrusco–Punic alliance
	Stelae in the shape of thrones and Egyptian shrines in the topheth of Salammbo
c. 530–510	**Hasdrubal, son of Mago, king of Carthage**
	Male masks in the tombs at Carthage
524	First victory of Aristodemus of Cumae over the Etruscans
c. 520–510	Dorieus tries to settle first in Tripolitania and then at Eryx
	Carthaginian war against the Libyans
c. 510	Hasdrubal killed in Sardinia
509	The Etruscan kings expelled from Rome
508	First Romano–Punic treaty
504	Battle of Aricia
c. 500	Carthage comes to the rescue of Gades
	Mogador abandoned
	Foundation of Lixus
c. 510–490	**Hamilcar, grandson of Mago, king of Carthage**
c. 500–490	Darius sends an embassy to Carthage
493	Anaxilas, tyrant of Rhegium

6

DATE B.C.	EVENTS
Beginning of 5th century	Thefarie Veliunas, king of Caere, introduces the worship of Astarte at Pyrgi
	Male and female masks in the Carthaginian tombs
485	Gelon seizes Syracuse
480	Battle of Himera
480–440 (?)	**Hanno the navigator, king of Carthage**
480–460	Conquest of African territory
470	Voyage of Sataspes
c. 460	Expeditions of Hanno and Himilco along the Atlantic coast
	Stelae in the shape of thrones inscribed with the name of Ba'al alone, in the topheth
459–450	Sicilian revolt against the Greeks
453	War between Selinus and Segesta
440–406 (?)	**Hannibal, king of Carthage**
416	Athenian expedition to Sicily
413	Defeat of the Athenians at Syracuse
	Selinus attacks Segesta
410	Hannibal invades Sicily
Spring 409	Destruction of Selinus
End of 409	Destruction of Himera
	Carthaginian embassy to Athens
Spring 406	Death of Hannibal
406–396	**Himilco, king of Carthage**
December 406	Destruction of Agrigentum
405	Dionysius, tyrant of Syracuse
	Capture of Gela
	Siege of Syracuse
End of 405	First treaty between Dionysius and Carthage
398	Dionysius declares war on Carthage
397	Foundation of Lilybaeum
Winter 397–396	Siege of Syracuse
Spring 396	Second treaty between Dionysius and Carthage
	Repentance and suicide of Himilco
396–375	**Mago, king of Carthage**
	Revolt of the Libyans

7

DATE B.C.	EVENTS
396	Introduction of the cult of Demeter/Kore in Carthage; levelling of the topheth; first appearance of Tanit
	Council of the One Hundred and Four instituted (?)
393	Campaign of Mago in Sicily
	Third treaty with Dionysius
	Hegemony of Dionysius in Italy
386	Capture of Rome by the Gauls
382	The war with Sicily resumed
	Punic expeditionary force in Southern Italy
378	Restoration of Hipponion by the Carthaginians
375	Defeat of Cabala; death of Mago
	Defeat of Dionysius
	Fourth treaty between Dionysius and Carthage
c. 370	End of the Magonid Dynasty
	Epidemic in Carthage; Sardinian and Libyan revolt
	Hanno I, the Great, seizes power in Carthage
368	War with Sicily resumed
	Trial of Eshmuniaton
367	Death of Dionysius I
	Accession of Dionysius II
	Hanno's campaigns in Africa
	Tanit now definitely takes the ascendant over Ba'al Hammon
	First inscribed stelae in the topheth
	Punic domination asserts itself on the African and Spanish coasts
360 (?)	Fall of Hanno the Great; the aristocratic régime becomes firmly established in Carthage
357	Dion seizes power in Syracuse with the help of Carthage
354–350	Rome frees herself from Caerian domination

8

DATE B.C.	EVENTS
348	Second Romano–Punic treaty
	Artaxerxes III captures Sidon
347	Dionysius II restored to power
345	Civil war between Dionysius and Hiketas
	Hanno lands in Sicily
344	Timoleon in Syracuse
343	Mago's fleet in Syracuse; trial and suicide of Mago
	Rome unites with Capua
341	Hasdrubal and Hamilcar in Sicily
339	Battle of Crimisus; trial and death of Hasdrubal
	Gisco, son of Hanno the Great, king of Carthage
338	Peace between Timoleon and the Carthaginians
	Appearance of the first marble sarcophagi at Sainte Monique
334	Tyre captured by Alexander
328–303	Samnite wars
325	Pytheas' voyage
319	Hamilcar, king of Carthage
316	Hamilcar helps Agathocles to seize power in Syracuse
313	Hamilcar, son of Gisco, king of Carthage
	Treaty between Hamilcar and Agathocles
311	Breach of the alliance between the Etruscans and Carthage
	Rome conquers Northern Etruria
20 August 310	Agathocles lands on Cap Bon
End of 310	Agathocles in Tunis
309	Hamilcar, son of Gisco, put to death at Syracuse
	Bomilcar, king of Carthage
Summer 308	Ophellas joins Agathocles
October 308	Ophellas is assassinated
	Attempted *coup d'état* and death of Bomilcar
	End of the monarchy in Carthage

9

DATE B.C.	EVENTS
307	Agathocles enters Syracuse with Etruscan help
306	Romano–Punic alliance renewed
	The Diadochi take the title of king
306–284	Ptolemy I Soter, king of Egypt
	Important economic relations between Alexandria and Carthage
	Sarcophagi of Hellenistic type at Sainte Monique; stelae decorated with scroll-ornament in the topheth
289	Death of Agathocles
	The Mamertines seize Messina
288–280	Phintias, tyrant of Agrigentum, allied to Carthage
	Hiketas, tyrant of Syracuse
281	Pyrrhus lands in Italy
281	Battle of Asculum
Autumn 279	Mago's Carthaginian fleet before Ostia
	Fourth Romano–Punic alliance
Beginning of 278	Sosistratus and Thoenon divide Syracuse between them
	The Carthaginian fleet enters Syracuse harbour
Autumn of 278	Pyrrhus in Syracuse
277	Pyrrhus conquers the Punic epicracy in Sicily
276	Sicily revolts against Pyrrhus
Summer 276	The Carthaginian fleet destroys that of Pyrrhus
Autumn 276	Pyrrhus returns to Italy
264	Roman intervention at Messina
263	Alliance between Rome and Hieron II
262	Agrigentum occupied by the Romans
260	Battle of Mylae
259	The inhabitants of Eryx transferred to Drepanum
256	Battle of Ecnomus
256–255	Expedition of Regulus to Africa

DATE B.C.	EVENTS
217	Battle of Lake Trasimene
	Dictatorship of Q. Fabius Maximus
216	Battle of Cannae
	Defection of Capua
215	Defeat of Hasdrubal at Dertosa
	Death of Hieron II
	Alliance between Hannibal and Philip V of Macedon
	Appearance of the first society of Publicani
215–213 ? 212 ?	Rebellion of Syphax
214	Assassination of Hieronymus
	Saguntum captured by the Romans
213	Himilco and Bomilcar in Sicily
212	Alliance of the Romans with the Aetolians
211	Hannibal marches on Rome
	Syracuse and Capua captured by the Romans
	Death of the Scipios in Spain
210	The young Scipio appointed commander-in-chief in Spain
209	Cartagena captured by the Romans
208 (?)	Battle of Baecula
207	Battle of the Metaurus
207–206	Oesalces, king of the Massyli
206	Battle of Ilipa
	Gades refuses to open her gates to Mago
	Mago on Minorca
205	Consulship of Scipio
	Peace of Phoinike
	Alliances of Carthage with Syphax and of Rome with Masinissa
	Mago in Liguria; Hannibal in Croton
204	Scipio lands in Africa
203	Battle of the Campi Magni
	Recall of Hannibal and Mago
	Truce between the Carthaginians and the Romans
202	Battle of Zama

DATE B.C.	EVENTS
201	Peace concluded between Carthage and Rome
200	War between Rome and Philip V
196	Hannibal elected suffete
196	Hannibal leaves Carthage
193 (?)	Masinissa occupies the Emporia district
	Hannibal sends Aristo to Carthage
183 (?) or 182 (?)	Hannibal commits suicide
182	Punico–Numidian territorial conflict
172–171	Rome acts as arbitrator in the conflict between Carthage and Masinissa
157	New Roman arbitration
155	The 'democratic' party regains power in Carthage
153 (?)	Cato's embassy to Carthage
152	Scipio Nasica's embassy to Carthage
End of 151	Leaders of the pro-Numidian party exiled from Carthage
150	Siege of Oroscopa
	Masinissa annexes the Great Plains and the district of Thusca
	Hasdrubal and the other democrat leaders are condemned to death in Carthage
Beginning of 149	Negotiations between the Romans and the Carthaginians in Rome
	Utica goes over to Rome
April 149	The Roman Senate declares war on Carthage
	The consuls Manilius and Marcius Censorinus at Lilybaeum
	The consular armies land at the Castra Cornelia
	The consuls reveal to the Carthaginians the Senate's decision to destroy the city
	The Carthaginians break off relations and prepare to resist
June–July (?) 149	The Romans lay siege to Carthage
November 149	Manilius suffers a setback at Nepheris
	Death of Cato

DATE B.C.	EVENTS
Beginning of 148	Death of Masinissa
April (?) 148	Desertion of Himilco Phameas
May (?) 148	Piso and Mancinus take up the command of the Roman forces
Summer 148	Roman setbacks before Clupea and Bizerta
Winter 148–147	Assassination of Hasdrubal, grandson of Masinissa
	Democrat extremists seize power in Carthage
November 148	Scipio Aemilianus elected consul
Spring 147	Mancinus' unexpected attack on Megara
	Arrival of Scipio Aemilianus in Africa
Summer 147	Construction of a mole across the harbour-mouth of Carthage
	The Romans capture the harbour quay
	Polybius explores the Moroccan and Mauretanian coasts
Autumn 147	Negotiations between Hasdrubal and Gulussa
Winter 147–146	Destruction of the Punic army at Nepheris
March or April 146	Capture and destruction of Carthage

I

Carthage before the Magonids

1. TYRE AND TARSHISH: THE DISCOVERY OF THE WEST

CARTHAGE was a Phoenician colony established not far from present-day Tunis, at the point where the African coast turns from east to south, and the Mediterranean is divided into its two great basins. The Phoenicians were a small Asiatic people, settled on that part of the Syrian coast which is now known as the Lebanon. They spoke roughly the same language as the Hebrews and belonged to the same great Semitic race. In contrast with their Arab cousins who settled along the North African coast eighteen centuries later and who gave it its definitive language and culture, the Phoenicians did not come to Africa overland on horses or camels, conquering the native population. They came in small numbers by ship, not to make war but in order to trade.

The date and the circumstances of this event have been recorded by the Ancients in well-known texts which are reasonably accurate but whose absolute reliability is now open to criticism. Before we examine this problem, it is essential that we should situate it against its historical background. In fact, we must recall briefly the information we possess on Phoenician navigation and trade in the Western Mediterranean, round about the year 1000 B.C.

The most important authentic information furnished by the Bible is the prophecy of Ezekiel, who tells us that this trade was directed towards a mysterious country called Tarshish:

O Tyrus, thou hast said, I am of perfect beauty.
Thy borders are in the midst of the seas . . .

The ships of Tarshish did sing of thee in thy market: and thou

15

wast replenished, and made very glorious in the midst of the
seas.
Thy rowers have brought thee into great waters . . .

Tarshish was thy merchant because of the multitude of all
kinds of riches; with silver, iron, tin and lead they traded in
their fairs.

(Ezekiel xxvii. 3–4, 25–26, 12)

It is to trade with Tarshish that Carthage owes its birth and
its wealth. The name of Tarshish recurs several times in the Old
Testament and it has been the cause of confusion because it
certainly had several different meanings according to the context
or the period. Sometimes it is the name of a country, sometimes
a type of merchandise (just as Cashmere is today) and it is
impossible to say which was its original meaning.[1] A   discussion
of this problem would take us far from Tyre and her trade but
it is interesting to recall that in the Old Testament the word
'Tarshish' is used to describe a special type of ship, and a type
of cargo which was necessary on far-ranging expeditions and of
which the greatest amount possible was to be carried. It is 'ships
of Tarshish' which go to Ophir, on the Red Sea, to fetch the gold,
ivory, and precious stones which Hiram, king of Tyre, who is
connected with Solomon, bought with copper mined at Eilat – a
trade which brought riches to both the kings (1 Kings ix. 26–27
and x. 22). But Tarshish is also the name of Tarsus in Cilicia.[2]
Finally it is the name given to a far-distant, indeterminate
country, situated somewhere in the Mediterranean towards the
setting sun – a land where a man could make his fortune, a Land
of Plenty, an Eldorado. To understand the looseness with which
this expression is used, it is necessary to remember that at the
time when these events took place, sailors and merchants who
sailed away to make their fortune, took several years to complete
their voyages, they often never returned, and – most important –
they would shroud their route and trade in the greatest secrecy
so as to preserve their monopoly. Out of this, therefore, there
grew up the mystery and legends which accompanied any account
of their wanderings. Nevertheless, Ezekiel's list of cargo brought
back from Tarshish – tin, iron, and lead – enables us to situate

the Tarshish to which the prophet was referring, in the mineral regions of the western half of the Mediterranean and, more specifically, in the south of the Iberian Peninsula. Literary tradition has made this the goal of the Phoenician maritime expeditions from the end of the twelfth century B.C. onwards and the source of the fabulous riches of Tyre at the end of the second and beginning of the first millennium B.C.

At this period, favourable circumstances had, in fact, enabled the Phoenicians to become the purveyors of the Middle East. The Minoan and Mycenaean thalassocracies had collapsed; Egypt had been undermined by the terrible 'Sea Peoples' and could no longer dominate efficiently her Asiatic subjects; Mitanni and the Hittite Empire, which had been the counterweight to Egyptian power, had also collapsed and decayed and had given birth to many small, turbulent, independent kingdoms.

Tyre was one of these kingdoms. Thanks to enterprising and able rulers – of whom Hiram is the most noteworthy – Tyre managed to avoid exhausting, ruinous, and useless petty wars with her neighbours and turned the situation to profit by providing the industries of the East with their necessary raw materials, and by selling luxury articles to her neighbours and to the conquerors and future lords of the Near East, the Assyrians.

Bronze was then one of the most common materials and was used not only by the army but also by the navy and in architecture: Shalmaneser III had the gates of his palace at Balawat covered with bronze. Copper was obtainable near at hand from Cyprus and Edom; tin was less common and it is doubtless the search for this metal which sent the Phoenician explorers towards the West and made them take advantage of the fact that the Mediterranean was free for all since it had been deserted by the Mycenaeans.

Many Greek and Roman texts tell of, or make allusion to, this exploration of the Western Lands by the Phoenicians. They tell us, in greater detail than does Ezekiel, of the different stages on these journeys.

Sicily is the first landfall for sailors coming from the East. According to Thucydides (VI, 2), the Phoenicians had settled along its promontories and on its neighbouring islands before the Greeks, that is to say, before the eighth century B.C. We can deduce that they used these ports as bases from which expeditions into the Western Mediterranean were launched. Diodorus Siculus, quoting Timaeus, a Greek historian of the fourth century B.C., states that they reached Libya, Sardinia, and the Iberian Peninsula (V, 20). They would thus have taken the southern route and by-passed Italy and the Gulf of Lions for reasons which are only too obvious. At sea, sailors would have had to face the terrible storms of the Gulf; on land they would have come into conflict with relatively civilized peoples who exploited their raw materials themselves, and who were warlike.[3]

The African coast, however, was almost uninhabited, was wooded and well stocked with game, and the peoples the Phoenicians came across were autochthonous, extremely primitive – the majority were still at a Neolithic stage of development – and easy to take advantage of. The coast offered beaches and natural harbours which were close enough, one to another, for their sailors to cover the distance between them in one stage – that is, on an average, every twenty to thirty miles.

According to Strabo, who quotes Posidonius (I, 3, 2), the Tyrians reached the Pillars of Hercules (the Straits of Gibraltar) soon after the Trojan War, in fact towards the end of the thirteenth century B.C. and only a few decades after the founding of Tyre. It seems that they even went through the Straits and, to protect the approaches, founded Lixus and Gadir or Gades ('fortress' in Phoenician) on the Atlantic coast.

Lixus is the first harbour, sheltered both from the north wind and from the Atlantic swell, which sailors reach after passing through the Straits of Gibraltar and its currents. Today the town of Larache, on the old Spanish Moroccan frontier, stands near the site of the ancient city. Lixus was on an estuary. It rose on hills which were separated from the hinterland by a loop of the river Lucus and by a deep valley. It was therefore not only protected from attack from the interior but it also stood at the mouth of the Lucus valley which was the only route inland. This part of Morocco is thickly wooded and at the time of which we are speaking it provided elephants, slaves, and gold in abundance. It was held that the shrine of Melqart, head of the Tyrian pantheon and also titular god of Lixus, had been built here before that of Gades – in fact round about 1100 B.C.

Gades (now called Cadiz) lay to the north and formed a counterpart to Lixus. The site on which the city was built is reminiscent of that of Tyre. It was an island just off the coast and running parallel to it, and was separated from the mainland by a channel which was, so Strabo tells us, 'about a stadion wide'. It overlooked magnificent roads where the warships of the Spanish Navy now manoeuvre. To the south of the island – now called the Isla de León – was the shrine of Melqart, patron of this city also. It stood on the Isla de Sancti Petri which has broken away from the main island but still formed part of it in Phoenician times.

The roads of Cadiz are formed by the estuary of the Baetis – the present-day Guadalquivir – whose valley is extremely fertile and is bordered on the north-east by mountains which are rich in copper, lead, and silver ores. The Andalusian plain is also the natural meeting-point for sailors from the Mediterranean with those of the Atlantic seaboard. Although the great megalithic culture, which had flourished along all the ocean coasts of Europe, had sadly declined by the year 1000 B.C., there nevertheless subsisted a tradition of contacts between the various peoples who had once belonged to this culture. The natives of Andalusia, indeed, received tin from Portugal and Galicia, and exported it to the East. It follows that the plain of the Baetis was the seat of a prosperous kingdom where life was easy and metal incredibly cheap. Diodorus maintains that the Phoenicians grew rich by buying silver from the Iberians, who were ignorant of its value, for a very small quantity of merchandise. Legends indicate that the Tartessian kingdom, as it is called, was probably known in the East from Mycenaean times onwards. Hesiod tells the tale of the kings who came out of the Ocean, of Chrysaor and of his heir Geryon, the monster-adversary of Hercules. Gargaris, the inventor of Agriculture, belonged to another race.

Strabo, a contemporary of Augustus', maintained that the Tartessian annals went back 6,000 years. It is certain that the Tartessians developed early their own form of writing. The identification of Tartessus with the Biblical Tarshish was long accepted, but philologists now reject it. As has been shown, the Hebrew term was applied to many lands, but in Ezekiel, at least, the name referred to the Baetis plain.

The profits realized during trading expeditions must have been enormous to have covered the costs. Voyages to the Land of Ophir, on the Red Sea coast, took three years and it is probable that, as ships could only sail in the summer months and that a cargo of minerals would certainly delay them, the even longer journey from Tyre to Gades and back took at least four years.

Velleius Paterculus (I, 2, 3) attributes the founding of Gades to the Heraclides on their return from the Trojan War, towards the end of the twelfth century B.C. His evidence agrees with that of Strabo and he states, furthermore, that the same sailors subsequently founded Utica a few years later, round about the year 1100 B.C. A late compiler confirms this and both authors agree in making the Tyrians the founders. Thus, according to literary tradition, Utica is the oldest Phoenician colony in Africa, but we shall see later that this tradition has now been contested. Pliny the Elder, when he wrote, gave a precise date – that of the founding of the Temple of Apollo in Utica 1,178 years earlier, that is in 1101 B.C. (*Historia Naturalis*, XVI, 216). However, if we admit that the Phoenicians sailed the Spanish seas at the end of the second millennium B.C., we must presuppose the prior existence of at least one Phoenician outpost in Tunisia. The siting of Utica recalls that of Lixus: the city was built at the mouth of the Bagradas or Medjerda, at the confluence of the Cherchera, on a hill surrounded by a meander of this wadi. Today, alluvial deposits brought down by the Medjerda have silted up the harbour and gulf of Utica and the ancient city is about six miles from the sea. It was a fine watering-place as the river is not liable to flooding even in the rainy season, and the site is covered with rich pastures. The Medjerda valley is the granary of Tunisia.[4]

In the ninth century B.C., according to tradition, the successors of Hiram continued his work. Josephus tells us of the founding of Auza in Libya by Ithobaal (*Ant. Jud.*, VIII, 13, 2). Strabo states that before the time of Homer, the Phoenicians owned the better part of Iberia (I, 3, 2 and III, 5, 5). The foundation of Tyrian colonies other than Gades on the shores of the Alboran sea east of Gibraltar, has therefore been ascribed to the ninth century – Abdera, Málaga (which has kept its name till modern times), and Sexi.

This tradition is perfectly valid historically. Since the Hebrews had lost Eziongeber, the Phoenicians could no longer sail the Red Sea.[1] [5]

Eastwards Phoenician trade had been hampered by the Assyrian advance ever since Assurnasirpal had captured Carchemish and 'washed his weapons in the great sea of the Land of Amurru'. It was only by increasing western trade that the Tyrians could maintain their prosperity. If, as J. G. Février has suggested the invention of ribbed hulls is to be dated to this period, the stronger ships now built would greatly have facilitated long-range expeditions.[6]

The archaeological discoveries of the late nineteenth and early twentieth centuries A.D. did not reveal any Phoenician remains earlier than the ninth century B.C. either in Sicily, or in Spain, or in Africa. Auza has never, indeed, been identified. It was then that Beloch demonstrated how unreliable the literary tradition was.[7] Until recent years, Beloch's theory seemed to be supported by archaeological research which continued to be extremely disappointing, and most excavators were in agreement with the German historian. The Tyrians had used Sicily as a base from which to launch their westward offensive and the Phoenicians, according to Thucydides, withdrew here after the arrival of the Greeks, but neither on the west nor on the east coasts of the island had any traces of their occupation been found below the levels of the Greek colonies. As only the Semitic origin of such place-names as Thapsus seemed to endorse the Greek historian's statement, such an argument was considered too slight and the theory of the colonization of the island by the Phoenicians was refuted.

At the beginning of this century, Taramelli discovered a bronze candlestick of Cypriot origin in the Sardinian temple of Santa Vittoria de Serri. This he dated to the end of the ninth century B.C. but it now seems that it could belong to the next century. It was perhaps brought to Sardinia by Phoenician merchants.[8] A stele was then dug up at Nora. It bore a Phoenician inscription which was also dated to the ninth century.[9] Although Albright's identification of the name of Tarshish in the inscription was not taken up, the stele nevertheless proves, without the least doubt, the presence of the Phoenicians in the island at the date when the text was carved.[10] Rhys Carpenter, however, contests the early date proposed by epigraphists and suggests that it may even be as late as the last quarter of the eighth century. None of the other numerous relics of the Phoenician colonization of Sardinia is earlier than the seventh century B.C.

Taradell and Ponsich's patient and methodical work at Lixus has not brought to light anything earlier than the sixth century B.C. which is attributable to the Tyrians.

In Spain the tombs of Carmona were excavated by Bonsor but although they produced ivories, some of which are of the Oriental type of the ninth century, the majority of the tomb furniture was of the seventh century. Nowhere else had there been any earlier Phoenician finds. At Cadiz, the site of ancient Gadir, there is nothing earlier than the sixth and at Málaga than the fifth century B.C. Finally, no object from the ancient necropolis of Utica, which Cintas excavated, can be dated with certainty any earlier than the last years of the eighth century B.C.

Before this mass of supporting evidence, Rhys Carpenter proposed the end of the eighth century B.C. as the date for the beginning of Phoenician navigation in the Western Mediterranean.[11] But during the last few years several discoveries have been made which have rather altered our view of the problem. Just off Sciacca, a little port near Agrigentum, a Sicilian fisherman brought up in his nets a small bronze statuette only 38 cm. high. It represents a god and is of a type found all over Phoenicia (for example at Byblos and Ugarit) between the fifteenth and eleventh century B.C. and which Chiappissi, who published it, dates to the eleventh century.[12]

Bernabo Brea's work on material from Sicily dating to the beginning of the first millennium B.C. appears in two publications.[13] [14] Here the author pointed out that pottery from the eastern side of the island (that is, the part of the island which the Phoenicians settled before the Greeks, according to Thucydides) is closely related to contemporary Palestinian types, and that the fibulas from the Lipari Islands are also very similar to prototypes from Megiddo. Finally, twenty tombs were accidentally discovered at a place known as Laurita, at Cerro de San Cristobal in the Province of Grenada. Among the grave-goods were alabaster jars bearing the cartouches of the Pharaohs Osorkon II (870–847), Sheshonq II (847), and Takelot II (847–823), Phoenician pottery types which are dated from the eleventh to ninth century in Palestine, to the eighth century in Cyprus and which appear in about 700 B.C. at Utica and Carthage, and finally Greek Proto–Corinthian bowls made towards the end of the eighth century B.C. This remarkable discovery enabled Pellicer Catalan to identify the site as that of Sexi.[15] He dates the necropolis to the beginning of the seventh century B.C. because of the presence in it of Greek vases. It does seem, however, as though some of the tombs might be earlier and go back to the eighth, but not as far back as the ninth century – the date of the alabaster jars it contains. The problem, therefore, is whether these jars were brought to Spain in the ninth century when they were made or only in the eighth when they were interred.

However, even if we do not find any traces of permanent Tyrian settlements dateable to about 1000 B.C., we must bear in mind that even at a much more recent date remains are few. The important fact is that there are traces of the comings and goings of Lebanese sailors in the Western Mediterranean between the ninth and eighth centuries B.C. If these traces are not sufficient evidence for it to be possible to confirm with absolute certainty the dates recorded by literary tradition, they do, nevertheless, call for a revision of the date proposed by Rhys Carpenter. The problem is, indeed, far from solved.

All this can be explained by maritime trading conditions in early times. Sailors did not come as conquerors; they tried neither to lay claim to land, nor to build anything permanent. All they needed was a sandy shore in a friendly land where they might beach their ships, and a site where they might build a few huts in which to shelter during the winter months. It is always difficult to find any traces of such temporary constructions. Cities were founded, ramparts thrown up, and harbours built at a much later date, either to resist invaders or to welcome compatriots who had left their homeland with, as we shall see, no intention of returning. The transition from one phase to the next took place in different areas at very different times. At Hippone (now called Bône or Annaba in Algeria) the site was not permanently settled till after 200 B.C. and the harbour only dates to the first century B.C.

There are several examples to illustrate this. In the case of the Cypriot town of Kition which the Tyrians called, for a time, Kart

Hadasht, like their African city, and which was their principal settlement in the island, the Swedish excavators have proved that from the eleventh century until 850 B.C. the Tyrians lived there in mutual interdependence with the local population but only moved in with their families and built a town in the second half of the ninth century.[16]

At Sabratha, a colony situated at the end of the Grande Syrte near Lepcis Magna, the excavations which Haynes is undertaking at present and which are so far unpublished, have revealed, under the floor level of the fifth-century houses, the remains of huts of the eighth century built on sand, and sherds of contemporary pottery.[17] Other huts date from the sixth and the beginning of the fifth century. It can be seen that the site was intermittently inhabited until settlers built their houses during the fifth century. At Histria, on the Black Sea, the Greeks did likewise. Condurachi has found on the beach near the local town, the remains of the huts which sheltered the Greek merchants who came to trade before the founding of their colony. When texts speak of the 'founding of a colony' they are doubtless alluding to some such settlement. Taradell wishes to reassess the dating of the famous temples (that of Melqart at Lixus in particular), taking the traditional date of their foundation as being, not that of their construction, but rather that of the consecration of the enclosure or *maqom* for open-air sacrifice.[18]

Homer perfectly describes the life of these sailors and merchants who went to seek their fortune in distant lands.[19] A voyage had been planned and fifty-two young oarsmen had been picked:

> When they had reached the ship and come down to the beach, they dragged the black vessel into deep water, put the mast and sails on board, fixed the oars in their leather loops, all ship-shape, and hauled the white sail up. Then they moored her well out in the water . . .

Meanwhile, the women had been loading the ship. Telemachus speaks:

> 'Listen, nurse, will you draw me off some flagons of wine? And let it be good stuff, the best you have . . . Fill me twelve flagons and put their stoppers on. And pour me out some barley-meal

24

in strong leather bags – twenty measures, please, of mill-crushed grain . . .'

When he had embarked:

The hawsers were cast off and Telemachus shouted to the crew to lay hands on the tackle. They obeyed with a will, hauled up the fir mast, stept it in its hollow box, made it fast with stays, and hoisted the white sail with plaited leather ropes.

In like fashion:

[Menelaus] was cruising in those distant parts (off the coast of Egypt) where people talk a foreign tongue, amassing a fortune in goods and gold . . .

In fine weather, in friendly waters, they would sail day and night. Otherwise, at dusk, they would run their ships inland as Odysseus did:

'It was not till they were beached that we lowered the sail. We then jumped out on the shore, (and) fell asleep.'

When Odysseus and his companions reached a good watering place:

'We disembarked to draw water, and my crews quickly set to on their midday meal by the ships.'

In order to replenish supplies, whenever there was a chance of hunting:

'We fetched our curved bows and our long spears from the ships, separated into three parties, and let fly at the game; in a short time Providence had sent us a satisfactory bag. There were twelve ships in my squadron: nine goats fell to each . . . So the whole day long till the sun set we sat and enjoyed this rich supply of meat, which was washed down by mellow wine, since the ships had not yet run dry of our red vintage . . . The sun went down, night fell, and we slept on the sea-shore.'

In bad weather they would sleep on board – each man at the foot of his bench and their captain on a bed which had been placed before the mast, above the hold where the expedition 'treasure' lay hidden.

Finally, this is how Homer describes the arrival of Phoenicians, in the words of Eumaeus:

'One day the island was visited by a party of those notorious Phoenician sailors, greedy rogues, with a whole cargo of gew-gaws in their black ship. Now there happened to be a woman of their race in my father's house, a fine strapping creature and clever too with her hands. But the double-dealing Phoenicians soon turned her head. One of them began it by making love to her when she was washing clothes, and seducing her by the ship's hull . . .'

She promptly decided to return to her native land but wished to embark secretly:

' "Buy your homeward freight as fast as you can. When the ship is fully victualled quickly send word to me up at the house. For I shall bring away some gold with me – all I can lay hands on. And there's something else I should gladly give you in payment for my passage. I'm nurse there in the house to a nobleman's child . . . He'd fetch you a fortune in any foreign port where you might put him up for sale." The traders stayed with us for a whole year, during which they bought and took on board a vast store of goods. When their hold was full and their ship ready for sea, they sent a messenger to pass the word to the woman.'

And so she ran off with the Phoenician sailors, taking Eumaeus with her.

In all these scenes, sketched from life, the 'black ship' was at one and the same time an hotel, a shop, and a warehouse, and the Phoenicians who carried off Eumaeus lived for as much as a year on the beach. These pioneer encampments, which could accommodate at least 500 men, must have resembled those of the Boers or the Mormons with the ships playing the same part as the wagons. Drawn up on the beach, the ships would form a bulwark and protect those sleeping out in the open or in the huts, not only from wild animals, but also from the local inhabitants who cannot always have been peaceably inclined. The famous shipyards of Saint Malo are only three and a half centuries old but we have only to look at the rows of rotting stakes to understand how difficult it would be to find traces of the temporary settlements of Tyrian pioneers thirty centuries old.

When temporary anchorages became established ports of call, the 'black ships' were still used in this way but were moored further out in calm water. Even in Augustan times, when Strabo wrote, the inhabitants of Gades lived on ships. Had it not been so, Gades would have been, after Rome, the most densely populated city in the Roman Empire (III, 1, 8). Thus were solved, not only the problem of desiccation which the hulls would otherwise have undergone if the ships had been laid up for the winter, but also the problem of lodgings, which, in such places as the island of Sancti Petri where Gades stood, was probably a very pressing one. These Phoenician anchorages must have looked rather like Chinese harbours where sampans are used as houses in the same way. Old cargo-boats were probably stripped down and used as docks and warehouses, but how can we expect to find traces of them today? The only constructions on dry land were a wooden palisade with ditch and stakes, like the outer fortification at Carthage at the time of the Punic Wars. The sacred precinct consisted of shrines and altars built of unbaked brick, like the diminutive building on virgin soil discovered by Cintas at Salammbo. There would also have been a few huts built of wattle and daub.

This is theory, but it helps to explain the siting of some Phoenician trading stations, which might otherwise seem bewildering. Vuillemot has made a systematic survey of such stations along the coast round Oran and has found that security and the necessities of day-time sailing were not of paramount importance in the choice of a site. The traditional watering-places were at twenty-mile intervals (a good day's sailing), protected from sea winds and situated either on an island near the coast, or at the foot of a promontory which could serve as a look-out post. The Phoenicians, however, often preferred other sites. Lixus stood at the mouth of a river; Utica even stood by a *marigot* (the branch-channel of a river) in spite of the unhealthy surroundings; lagoons were chosen; and notwithstanding difficulties of access in time of storm, we find trading stations at such places as Les Andalouses and Mersah Madakh, west of Oran. The last two sites are very close to each other but some are separated by several days' sailing, and finally some are exposed to easterly and some to westerly winds. The harbour area is the only characteristic all have in common and, as we shall see, this is a rule which Carthage also obeys.[20]

2. THE FOUNDING OF CARTHAGE

Lixus, Gadir, and Utica had all been founded: it was now the turn of Carthage. At about six miles south of Utica by sea, a peninsula of sandstone hills once separated the gulf into which the Medjerda still flows, from what is now the Bay of Tunis. The alluvial deposits of the river had not yet silted up the estuary, and the promontory stretched out into the open sea. Two sandy causeways joined it to the mainland, enclosing the present-day Lake of Tunis, which is well stocked with fish. The southern shore of this promontory ran from north-east to south-west and offered perfect opportunities for conversion into anchorages and harbours. The shore was sheltered from dangerous northerly and westerly winds so that large ships, when they passed through, could be drawn up on to dry land, as could the small coasters and the host of tenders which ferried crew and merchandise and brought up fish supplies.

A small estuary, into which flowed the wadi from the heights of the Malga, welcomed such ships as were left riding at anchor; it has now silted up but was then fairly deep. Finally, a channel led from the Bay of Le Kram, itself sheltered from all sea winds, to the two lagoons of Douar Chott, which thus formed a perfect natural harbour. The access to these inland havens and to the future city, was protected on the north by the steep and forbidding cliffs of the present-day Cape Sidi Bou Said, and on the south by a seven-and-a-half-mile isthmus – open ground which was easily defended.

There is an abundant fresh-water supply on the peninsula, the water-table is high and easily accessible, and in winter and summer alike there is a spring at the foot of the north cliff. The air is healthy and even fairly bracing in the hills, and that unpleasant south-easterly wind, the Sirocco, freshens as it crosses the Gulf before reaching Carthage. Finally, there is enough arable land round the site of the city to support a growing community. Wheat and barley grow on the plateaux, the vine flourishes on the sunny, sheltered slopes. In fact, everything was there that was needed to make the future Carthage the ideal port which Homer describes as follows:

A luxuriant island covered with woods, which is the home of innumerable goats . . . by no means a poor country, but capable of yielding any crop in due season. Along the shore of the grey sea there are soft water-meadows where the vine would never wither; and there is plenty of land level enough for the plough, where they could count on cutting a deep crop at every harvest-time, for the soil below the surface is exceedingly rich. Also it has a safe harbour, in which there is no occasion to tie up at all. You need neither cast anchor nor make fast with hawsers: all your crew have to do is to beach their boat and wait till the spirit moves them and the right wind blows. Finally, at the head of the harbour there is a stream of fresh water running out of a cave in a grove of poplar trees . . . [It] could serve [as a harbour for ships] plying to foreign ports in the course of that overseas traffic which ships have established between nations.[21]

The first group of colonists doubtless settled on the beaches, by the lagoons of Douar Chott, and on the hill of Byrsa – the future acropolis – which overlooks the whole place like a lighthouse. Such a site is infinitely preferable to that of Utica, and Carthage rapidly took over from the older town and became the Phoenician metropolis of the West. Such was its wealth, that legends grew up concerning it and particularly in connection with its foundation. Myth and fact have become inextricably entwined and the founding of Carthage is one of the most difficult problems of history.

Two facts have been responsible for this confusion. First of all, Carthage has no chronology of its own, with 'year one' as the date of the founding of the city. Literary tradition remains silent in this connection, Punic coins bear no date, and the method of dating an inscription was to refer to the magistrates holding office in that particular year. 'City Chronologies' were, in fact, a Greek invention which the Romans, and later the whole civilized world, adopted. But when Carthage was born, her scribes had, perforce, to follow Oriental tradition, as used in the Metropolis, and record in the City Annals the names of its kings, the number of years they reigned, and the main events which took place during each reign. This was how the historical books of the Bible were compiled. Later, in the last centuries of the city, the scribes copied the Greeks and drew up a list of eponymous magistrates, named *suffetes*, who were elected annually and whose names were used to date an event. When Scipio ordered the burning of Carthage in 146 B.C., the City Archives, the Annals, and the scribal lists of *suffetes* were destroyed, and with them any documents which might have enabled us to find out how long Carthage had, indeed, existed. Given this shortage of Punic texts, modern historians have to rely on Greek and Roman versions of the story of the foundation of Carthage. These versions disagree, however, not only with each other, but also with archaeological data.

Three groups of texts give three different dates. The first group derives from the Greek historian Philistus of Syracuse, who lived in the fourth century B.C. He ascribes the foundation of the city to Zor and Carchedon. Appian, and later Eudoxus of Cyzicus, followed his lead, and the latter dates the event to the eight hundred and third year of the 'Abraham Era', that is 1213 B.C.[22] This is manifestly impossible and the names of the two heroes are clearly transcriptions of the names Tyre (or Ṣur in Phoenician) and Kart Hadasht or Carthage (Carchedon in Greek). As for the so-called 'Abraham Era', it is a late invention and has no reliable backing.

Another group of texts dates the foundation of Carthage to the years 814 or 813 B.C. Timaeus, the Greek historian of the fourth century B.C., records that Carthage was founded by Elissa, sister of King Pygmalion, after her husband had been killed on the king's orders. Some Tyrians are supposed to have accompanied the princess, and after many adventures and trials, they reached Libya and founded a city. The local inhabitants called Elissa 'Deido' when she became queen. These events are said to have taken place 38 years before the First Olympiad, that is in 814 or 813 B.C. (Timaeus, F. 23).

Subsequently Justin, who condensed the work of the Roman

historian Pompeius Trogus (who lived in the first century B.C.), records a similar story which is patently inspired by the same source as the preceding one. It is more developed, however, and legend and history are more closely interwoven (XVIII, 4–6). The events still take place during the reign of Pygmalion of Tyre, and his sister Elissa is still the heroine. Her husband Acerbas was high-priest of Melqart but was killed on the king's orders. The princess fled and went first to Cyprus, where a group of Tyrian senators joined her. They carried off some women, so as to ensure their posterity, and the high-priest of Juno also joined them, bringing with him the cult statue of the goddess. They all sailed for Africa and finally disembarked on the site of the future Carthage. They received permission to settle on land which was not to exceed in size an area which could be covered by an ox-hide. The queen then had the hide cut into a narrow thong and thus gained possession of the future acropolis hill, which was called Byrsa for this reason (βύρση is the Greek for ox-hide). The oracles then told them where the city was to be built.

One site was rejected after the skull of an ox had been found – a sign of hard times and hard work. A second site was chosen when a horse's skull was found – a symbol of power. Then follows the tale of the queen's sacrifice. Iarbas, a local chieftain and king of the Gaetulians, insisted on marrying Elissa and threatened to destroy the city if she would not comply. The queen had a pyre built beneath the windows of her palace near the city gates, under pretext of sacrificing to her husband's *manes*. She pretended to accept Iarbas, in order to protect the city, but threw herself on to the pyre so as to remain faithful to her nuptial vows to Acerbas. Justin dates these events in relation to the founding of Rome 72 years later. If we follow the Varronian chronology, 72 becomes 62 and we obtain a date of 814 B.C., which is plausible. Servius, in this connection, quotes the figure 70, and Velleius Paterculus puts it at 65, which, if we adopt Polybius' Roman Era, again gives us 814 B.C. as the date.

But unfortunately Justin's evidence does not stand up to close scrutiny. The most plausible part of the story is practically identical to Timaeus' version, and was certainly drawn from it as Pompeius Trogus knew the Greek historian's work and often quoted it. Any new facts which Justin produces are certainly invented, for in addition to their general lack of plausibility, they are stock-in-trade legends used to legitimize the founding of a city and the domination of a new sovereign. The abduction of the Cypriot women recalls the Rape of the Sabines by the companions of Romulus; the mention of oracles, and Iarbas' matrimonial intentions, also have their parallels; while the sacrifice has all the characteristics of an aetiological tale, used to justify an ancient ritual, the sense and meaning of which has been lost. The fact that Timaeus' dating from the First Olympiad, and Justin's from the Roman Era, agree, would be remarkable if it formed an integral part of the story, and were not tagged on at the end. Justin does not, therefore, produce any evidence which might confirm Timaeus' tale.

A third text seems to derive from another source than Timaeus' and, using another chronological system than the Greek, produces the date 826 B.C. instead of 814 for the founding of Carthage. As we have said, Phoenician cities possessed Annals. Those of Carthage are lost, but extracts from those of Tyre have come down to us in the works of Flavius Josephus,[23] a Jewish historian of the first century A.D., who wrote to defend the Bible against Greek anti-Semitic attack. Josephus, in fact, quotes a Hellenistic writer, Menander of Ephesus, who had consulted the Chronicles of the kings of Tyre. He tells us that in the seventh year of King Pygmalion, the latter's sister fled to Libya and founded Carthage. According to the Chronicles, this event took place 155 years and eight months after the accession of that Hiram, king of Tyre and ally of David and Solomon, who helped in the building of the Temple in Jerusalem. The seventh year of the reign of Pygmalion works out at 826 B.C. Josephus' date is therefore close to Timaeus' but is not identical to it. (This difference of 13 years can be explained as the result either of the imperfect systems of reckoning used by Eastern chroniclers, or of a copying error.)

This might, at first, seem to indicate the existence of a Phoenician source which Timaeus and Menander both consulted independently, and which placed the foundation of Carthage in the reign of Pygmalion. Unfortunately, we cannot be certain that Menander and Josephus give us a faithful rendering of the Tyrian chronicles. It is certain, in fact, that one or the other has introduced into the account, anecdotes which come from another source. It is possible, therefore, that the Flight of Elissa is precisely one of these additions, for the tale does not throw a very favourable light on King Pygmalion, and it seems doubtful that it was recorded by the official scribes. It is even possible that either Menander or Josephus had incorporated in his account some piece of information culled from Timaeus – an author whose works they both knew and quoted.

Timaeus' date was accepted by most of the authors of Antiquity and in particular by Cicero and Appian. Only Apion, Josephus' adversary, favoured a more recent date, namely 751 B.C. No modern critic has attached much importance to the opinion of this discredited writer.[24]

Until the last few years, criticism of information concerning the founding of Carthage had always been based on a comparison of the texts. Gsell reluctantly accepted Timaeus' date of 814. Beloch, on the other hand, rejected it.[25] Only recently, Forrer's date, one and a half centuries later, was based entirely on historical criticism.[26] He believed that ancient historians had confused two Phoenician colonies with identical names, and inscriptions do, in fact, prove that the Cypriot town known later as Kition, was first called Kart Hadasht. He maintained that it was this Cypriot Carthage which was founded in 814 by Elissa, Pygmalion's sister, while the African Carthage was founded only in 663 by Dido and Anna, daughters of the Tyrian king Baalu, who were escaping from Phoenicia so as not to have to join the harem of Assurbanipal of Assyria. Virgil, indeed, tells us that Dido's father was a certain King Belus, and this sounds very much like a Latinized form of Baalu. Unfortunately, Virgil was rather free in his treatment of history and he dates these events to the Trojan War, that is to the thirteenth century B.C. His Dido, as we have said, is the daughter of Baalu, but this does not prevent her from being Pygmalion's sister.

It is hardly surprising, therefore, that faced with such inconsistencies, modern scholars are forsaking the study of ancient texts and are turning to archaeological evidence. We shall see further on that the oldest remains so far discovered in Carthage, are those of a chapel in the lowest levels of the Salammbo sanctuary which is[8] known today as the topheth. This chapel contained a collection of votive Greek vases made between 750 and 725. This piece of evidence would support a date towards the middle of the eighth century, which is, in fact, the date suggested by Apion.

It can be argued that the exploration of the lower levels of Carthage has been inadequate. The chapel we have just mentioned was only discovered by Cintas in 1947 in a section of the topheth which was methodically excavated down to virgin soil. Until this find was made there was no archaeological evidence available to support a date earlier than 700 B.C. If it had been possible to excavate the remainder of the topheth, part of which is built over, other remains of the earliest colonization period might have been found, some of which could have been even older.

Those who oppose 814 as the date for the founding of Carthage point out that none of the pottery excavated in the tombs belongs either to the first half or even to the third quarter of the eighth century. This even applies to pots found at the very bottom of the topheth in hollows in the bed rock, at the same level as Cintas' chapel. This can hardly be ascribed to chance or incomplete exploration. On all other sites, even those which have been rather summarily excavated, ceramic evidence of the earliest period of occupation has always been forthcoming. It is scarcely credible that the Phoenicians could have lived for more than eighty years in Carthage without leaving the slightest trace of their existence.

We are not, so far, in a position to resolve the problem. Only one thing is certain, and that is that Carthage certainly existed in the second half of the eighth century. One point is worth making, however: the fact that we cannot use Timaeus' date of 814 or Josephus' of 826 as a chronological criterion for dating archaeological material found on virgin soil, need not necessarily invalidate literary tradition. It is quite possible that a band of Tyrian sailors moored their ships in the lagoons of Le Kram in the shelter of Cape Carthage. It is also possible that this expedition was led by a royal princess named Dido and that, owing to her presence there, the new trading station should, from the first, have been more important than other Phoenician outposts in the West. Like these it would have consisted of no more than an anchorage for sea-going vessels which called in or wintered there and formed the economic centre of the community. On shore there would probably only have been a few small huts and one or two shrines built of light materials. There may have been a look-out post on the hill of Byrsa for the protection of the station. Probably there was no permanent population other than a few guards who would complete their term of office in this distant land and then return to their homes and families in Phoenicia. As we shall see, it was a century before Carthage developed such urban characteristics as an economic, social, political, and religious structure.

3. CARTHAGE, GATE TO THE WEST

So far, the information we possess does not enable us to reconstruct the physical geography of the first Carthage, that of Dido and her companions. Nor can we form a very clear picture of its social, political, and economic activities. The city is only mentioned once in texts before the accession to power of the Magonid family in about 550 B.C., and this is in connection with its sending a band of colonists to the island of Ibiza towards 654. Archaeology is thus our only source of information, even though it is restricted to finds made in the city's necropolis and in one of the sanctuaries, the topheth of Salammbo, which was the sacred precinct where young children were burnt and where their ashes were subsequently scattered.

The dead were supposed to lead much the same sort of life in the grave as they had on earth, and their descendants would furnish the tomb-chamber with all that was required for the afterlife. Pottery, the remains of chests, jewellery, toilet articles, and amulets were all found grouped round the body and give us an idea of the artistic production and prosperity of the city. This first Carthage had no industries and all the manufactured goods were imported. We can thus reconstruct, to some extent, the commercial network of the city and its periods of activity or decline.

In the topheth of Salammbo were found some figurines and an imposing collection of pottery which forms a useful addition to the corpus of funerary wares. From about 600 B.C. onwards, the jars containing the ashes of the victims also contained small sculptured objects. These are miniatures of the chapels, thrones, and altars dedicated to the gods.

There are, however, vast gaps in our knowledge. The existence led by the dead was only a pale reflection of life on earth. Unlike

35

Egypt, for instance, there is nothing to indicate the framework in which the latter was lived or the pomp and circumstance surrounding the deceased during his lifetime. Very occasionally a simple tool such as a fish-hook or a spindle-whorl may give us a hint of what were the day-to-day occupations of its owner. Generally we are left in ignorance as to the profession of the deceased, whether he was a priest, a merchant, a soldier, or a sailor. All have the same tomb furniture and only the type of pottery and the richness of the jewellery indicate a difference in financial status between the dead. The clothes of the deceased certainly bore some relationship to his occupation and social status but they have long since rotted away in the damp soil. Each man carried a seal and these seals each bore a distinctive sign carved on them which would doubtless furnish invaluable information if we could decipher them. No study of the social life and institutions of Carthage can be undertaken from these remains alone.

Finally a whole range of archaeological information is entirely lacking: there are no surviving traces of either public or private buildings and we have no plans, no evidence for methods of construction, or for larger artifacts such as craftsmen's tools, farmers' implements, sailors' ships and tackle, or soldiers' weapons. The following pages contain a brief outline of Punic crafts and trade before 550 but at any moment some new discovery may change the whole picture.

4. THE FIRST CITY

We do not know the exact location of the first city of Carthage. The Phoenician custom of burying the dead immediately outside the city gates does, however, enable us to obtain a fairly accurate picture of the area covered by the town and of its gradual growth throughout its history. Now, the earliest tombs from Punic Carthage so far known, and dated to about 700 B.C., extend in an arc round the coastal plain which lies beyond the beaches of the Gulf of Tunis, at the foot of the hills which overlook the promontory. To the north, the line of graves extends from the foot of the plateau of Borj Jedid on the north-west bank of the estuary of the Malga, a seasonal wadi. The line then turns to the west, crosses the wadi, and heads for the Hill of Juno. It runs along at the foot of this hill from a place called Douimes, at about the level of the tramline which linked Tunis to the Marsa.

The circular lagoon of Douar Chott probably marked the southern limit of the city, for beyond the present-day shores of the lake, at Salammbo, were found the remains of the famous infant sacrifices. These sacrifices, as we shall see, were offered in commemoration of Dido's, at the spot where her pyre had stood, and this, according to Justin, had been erected beneath the windows of her palace, at the gates of the town. In fact, merely for practical reasons, such a sanctuary could hardly have stood in the centre of the city, for only the slightest breeze blowing in the wrong direction could have caused a fire. Furthermore, the minute chapel which Cintas found on bedrock, in the lowest level of the excavations, was probably part of the original royal necropolis. Cintas believes that the first settlers must have disembarked and camped here. However this may be, the chapel is dated by the Greek pottery it contained to about 725 B.C. and is not only the earliest evidence of settlement found by archaeologists, but also the only monument to survive from the first city. It is an extremely poor mud-brick building, covering only two square metres in area. The ground plan is fairly involved. It consists of a central, almost square, building with a corbelled vault under which was housed the pottery deposit. In front of this was a courtyard, surrounded by a wall, in which stood the altar, and to the south the wall formed a sort of labyrinth. It seems unlikely that the houses in the town were any better constructed, and wattle and daub were probably the main building materials for there is no quarry on the hill itself. The sandstone beds which were used by the Punic architects of the sixth century lie on the other side of the Gulf, on Cap Bon.

5. ARTS AND CRAFTS

At first Carthage was only a port of call on the metal route and it remained relatively unimportant for some time. If it is true that the city was founded in 814, and if archaeologists really have discovered the oldest cemetery, then a whole century must have elapsed between the establishment of the earliest Phoenician anchorage and the arrival of the first settlers with their families to build a city. The earliest graves date to round about 700 B.C., and the first groups of 'moloch' sacrifices are found around and above the Cintas chapel and must belong to this same period.[27]

Several decades more were to elapse before the city developed its own arts and crafts. In the early stages, indeed, the Tyrian sailors and merchants took with them in their ships everything they needed, witness the young Telemachus, who went ashore only for drinking water, wood, game, and fish. Analysis has shown that there is a difference in density between the clay used in the pottery from the earliest tombs and the lowest levels of the Salammbo sanctuary, and the clay used in later pottery. The change occurs towards the middle of the seventh century B.C. Cintas himself writes as follows:

> The new-comers created new demands and soon had to learn to satisfy them on the spot. Although it must have taken some time to find good clay-beds, to arrange transport, to build ovens and dig water channels, and to set up shops for the products, it is certain that the potters, at least, must have got themselves organized fairly rapidly so as to be able to satisfy the needs of the new city.[28]

In the daily life and economy of ancient cities, pottery played a part which we find it hard to visualize today. Clay was used for crockery such as dishes, plates, bowls, jugs, and mugs – glass was too expensive; it was used for kilns, for the storage of oil, wine, and perfumes; large jars were used instead of cupboards. It is scarcely surprising, therefore, to find that the potter's was the first craft to become organized in any new town. The fact that Punic pottery was not made before the second quarter of the seventh century B.C. is important as the birth of the city proper cannot have antedated it by much, and a date round about 700 B.C. would therefore correspond well with the establishment of a first urban nucleus. Cintas goes on to say:

> Naturally [the potters] began by making their pottery according to the techniques then current in their country of origin and therefore produced wheel-made pottery.

Furthermore, they copied the shapes and decorative motifs fashionable in Phoenicia so that it is difficult to tell at a glance whether a pot was made in Carthage or is an oriental prototype. Later potters became more selective and the bright, carefully burnished red wares gradually disappeared in Carthage though they continued to be imported by Phoenician colonies in the West.

Figured wares appear at about the same time and the most remarkable examples are the masks of demons which were placed in the tombs. These show that the Carthaginian potters were in no way inferior in craftsmanship to their Tyrian precursors, while the best among them could compare favourably with their Greek colleagues and, more particularly, with those of Sparta.

Although its position on the metal route was the original reason for the founding of Carthage, metal ore seems only to have been conveyed in transit. Metal finds consist of small objects of iron or bronze for everyday use and these are of such inferior workmanship that it seems likely that objects of quality were imported and that only cheap millwright work, such as handles for chests, fish-hooks, arrows, and small knives, was carried out in the local workshops. It is hard to say whether the gold and silver jewellery which was found in the graves and had once adorned the living, was made in Carthage from older Phoenician prototypes or was imported from Tyrian and Cypriot workshops. It is a fair assumption that textiles and woodwork were produced locally, but this cannot be proved. One thing seems certain, however: until the fifth century, as we shall see, Carthage relied on Tyre and on foreign trade for all luxury goods and most manufactured goods.

6. TRADE

The lack of home industries in Carthage until the fifth century is brought home to us when we realize that although we know several of the city's suppliers, we know of no purchasers. The Phoenician merchant was just what Homer described him – a pedlar – and his Punic descendant was no different. During the whole period under discussion, the Carthaginian trader followed the Tyrian trade-routes. It is difficult to know whether Carthage had its own merchant navy at this period or whether it used that of the metropolis. Certain facts seem to support the first hypothesis, for Carthage was in the ascendant whereas Tyre was on the decline, and even if the Carthaginian colony on Ibiza was not established as early as is stated by literary tradition (i.e. 654 B.C.), it was certainly thriving a century later.

The presence of Greek pottery in the Cintas chapel hoard and foundation deposit is evidence that, from the beginning, the African colony had commercial relations with Hellenistic centres in the Islands, probably with either Tyre or Cyprus acting as middle-man. Therefore, it is probably owing to poverty rather than to isolation that the only import in the earliest tombs, dated to round about 700 B.C., is a small Proto–Corinthian style perfume flask of the type known as *aryballos* and dateable to the eighth century B.C. During the second quarter of the seventh century, imported goods become more frequent and increase in number until the middle of the sixth century. (There are only three Greek vases from the first quarter of the seventh century: cf. *Karthago*, XII.) The first to appear are Memphis scarabs, in the tombs. Then come amulets (also from Memphis); little perfume flasks from Corinth, decorated with rosettes, palmettes, and rows of animals; dishes, bowls, and boxes, most of which are of Corinthian origin as well, but a few of which were bought in Attica, Laconia, and in the Islands. These also were grave goods. Trade with Etruria must have begun towards the middle of the seventh century and small jugs and dishes in the black incised ware known as *bucchero nero* were imported.

Ivory objects such as combs, figurines, mirror handles, and dagger hilts, and a few small bronzes found in the tombs, seem to have come from the East. As we have seen, it is difficult to establish where different types of jewellery came from. Wherever the Phoenicians travelled, we find the same necklaces of gold or carnelian beads, which are often heart-shaped; pendants in the shape of masks, palmettes, or little boxes, and frequently with milled edges; ear-rings in the shape of a maltese cross (a good-luck symbol); heavy ear-rings, nose-rings, and bracelets; rings consisting of an Egyptian scarab set in gold or silver; seal-stones; and signet rings with a swivelling bezel consisting of a scarab in a gold setting.

Small perfume vessels of opaque glass in superimposed, brightly coloured zig-zags were made in Phoenicia and Greece, and later in Egypt, and it is quite impossible, without analysing the glass paste, to know their exact provenance.

When the Greeks founded a colony at Naucratis in the Nile Delta, they found good customers among the Carthaginians for the scarabs, vases, and amulets in glazed faience which they started to manufacture there in the beginning of the sixth century. An active trade was carried on until Cambyses destroyed Naucratis in 525.

This list of trades and goods only helps to emphasize the decadence of Tyre. Of the gold and silver dishes ornamented with incised or repoussé motifs, of the figurines and ivory plaques which decorated thrones and couches, not one has been found in Carthage; yet it was these which made Phoenicia famous during the second millennium and the beginning of the first millennium B.C.

7. PHOENICIAN AND GREEK COLONIZATION IN THE WEST

The spectacular rise of Carthage, during the seventh and sixth centuries, is neither an isolated nor a spontaneous manifestation; it forms part of a pattern of historical events to which the Assyrian conquest of the Middle East and the westward expansion of the Greeks also belong.

During the reigns of Sargon II, Sennacherib, and Esarhaddon, the Assyrians went from victory to victory and laid waste the Tyrian mainland. As Forrer has shown, the years between 670 and 662 must have been particularly difficult, and Esarhaddon boasts of punishing the city when it dared to send ships to support the hard-pressed Egyptian Pharaoh. The closure of the eastern market contributed to this growing sense of insecurity, and the Tyrians were obliged to emigrate to Africa in great numbers – or so we are led to deduce from the sudden increase in the number of Carthaginian tombs during the second quarter of the seventh century, and from the development of trade. The centre of commercial activity had shifted westwards and it was Carthage which was reaping the benefits.

Across the Mediterranean there lay another danger which threatened the only source of income which was left to Tyre and which enabled her to meet the huge tribute imposed on her by the Assyrians. Greece was overpopulated and the Greeks were seeking commercial outlets for their growing industries, particulary their luxury ceramics, and with this end in view they had undertaken the colonization of Southern Italy and of Sicily. The fabulous wealth of 'Tarshish' could not fail to excite their envy and the Phoenician metal route was threatened. Tyre was in a weak position alone against the superior numbers of the Greeks of the homeland and of Ionia. The latter built towns, and settled there with their wives and children, bringing with them hard currency, pottery, and bronzes, whereas Tyre's only advantages were her harbours, her relations with the local populations, and the heavier tonnage of her cargo-ships compared with the faster but lighter ships of the Hellenes, which, specialists are agreed in thinking, were ill-adapted for long journeys and the Atlantic swell.[29] Tyre did not, therefore, seek to oppose Greek expansion in these quarters by any direct aggression, but sought rather to restrict and confine this expansion while maintaining a few key positions where she also established families of colonists. Although we cannot be sure as to whether there were Tyrian counterparts to the Greek cities, we know that fortresses were built, and in this connection the name of Gadir, 'The Enceinte', is significant. In this way the Tyrians obtained the control of the southern part, at least, of the Western Mediterranean basin, through which passed the most direct route for the Pillars of Hercules, protected on either side by the forts of Gades and Lixus.

The relevant dates and facts are as follows: in Sicily the Greeks founded Naxos in 757 and Syracuse in 735, while on the Italian mainland Cumae and Tarentum were founded in 725 and 708 respectively. It is probably to this period that we must ascribe the evacuation of Eastern Sicily by the Phoenicians, mentioned by Thucydides, and their withdrawal to their westward allies, the Elymians, within easy sailing distance of Utica and Carthage. These two African cities and Sexi in Southern Spain were all developed during this period – the end of the eighth century B.C. There can be no question of Phoenician imperialism either in the Iberian peninsula, as Schulten has suggested, or in any of the countries mentioned. It is only with the coming of the Barcids that we can talk of an empire. Temporary harbour installations which had previously been used only at certain times of the year were now put on a firmer footing, however, and families lived in what had only been ports of call for sailors.

During the seventh century Hellenic colonization increased and Greek colonies were founded at Gela in 688, and at Selinus in 650; the Rhodians began trading in the Gulf of Lions and prospected along the Catalonian coasts. They founded Rhode (present-day Rosas) at the foot of the Spanish Pyrenees, and came into contact with the Tartessians (the Iberians who have already been mentioned as living near Portugal and having the monopoly for tin which, previously, they had sold only to the Phoenicians).

Half-way through the seventh century the Phoenicians founded a settlement on the island of Rachgoun, which guards the mouth of the Wadi Tafna, west of Oran. The island was barren and inhospitable and the Phoenicians deserted it towards the middle of the fifth century and moved to the more fertile coastal plain. From this outpost they were able to control the southern route to the Alboran Sea and so to the settlements of Sexi, Abdera, and Málaga. This was a necessary precaution for in about 640, a Samian called Colaeus, who was on his way to Egypt, was driven by a storm to Libya and thence, by way of the Pillars of Hercules, he reached the court of Arganthonius, king of Tartessus, who welcomed him and showered him with gifts. The Samian accumulated a large fortune but, according to Herodotus, this expedition was without precedent or sequel, which seems to indicate that the Gades route was well guarded.

Iberian wealth was not the only attraction in this race westwards. Elephants and gold from the African continent south of Lixus must have tempted audacious sailors, for there are traces of another Phoenician settlement, dating from the middle of the seventh century B.C., on the Atlantic coast of Morocco at Mogador.

Finally, the settlement of Motya, on the western tip of Sicily, is also to be dated to the middle of the seventh century. The channel between Sicily and the African continent was guarded by Motya to the north, and Carthage and Utica to the south, while the main harbours of Southern Sardinia, annexed by the end of the century, protected its northern exit.

In 631 B.C., however, the Phoenician thalassocracy was again threatened: the Greeks founded Cyrene on the African coast between Egypt and Syrtica, not far from present-day Benghazi. Direct communications by sea between Carthage and Egypt were thus interrupted. There existed a land route, however, which ran along a depression parallel to the coast, from Paraetonium (Mersah Matruh), west of the Nile, to the end of the Grande Syrte. There is no proof that it existed at the end of the seventh century B.C., but caravans used it in Herodotus' time although it ran through 'a waterless and sandy desert without life of any kind' (II, 32, p. 114). Oases are strung out along the route, the most important being Siwah, home of the famous Oracle of Ammon – the ram god – which Hannibal consulted; and Augula, which is surrounded by salt mountains but which is extremely fertile thanks to the presence of fresh-water springs. On an average, it is a ten-day march from one oasis to the next, through sand-dunes and sand-storms (when the desert or south wind blows) in which men and beasts can lose themselves and get buried in the burning dust-devils. Cambyses lost his army on the road to Siwah, and Alexander was only saved *in extremis* by a 'miraculous' shower of rain. The chief source of income for the local inhabitants, the Nasamonians, however, was caravan trading. Aristotle tells us how we should train to bear thirst:

> A certain Andros Archonides used to eat a great number of salty things and spent his whole life without suffering from thirst. Similarly Mago of Carthage crossed the waterless land three times, eating only dried meal and drinking nothing.
>
> *Treatise on Drunkenness*

The trail led to the end of the Grande Syrte, not far from Lepcis Magna, in Garamantes country. The fact that the growth of this city, in the last years of the seventh century, coincides with the founding of Cyrene, leads one to suppose that caravans used the road at least from then on. Egyptian trumpery wares were perfect for such trade as they were small and light. But even so, most of the Egyptian imports must have reached Carthage by sea for they suddenly stop appearing in tombs after the defeat of Himera when the maritime route between Carthage and the Eastern Mediterranean and Egypt was cut.

In about 600 B.C., when the situation seemed to be stabilized, the Phocaean Greeks of Ionia founded Massalia (Marseilles) near the Rhône delta, and then settled in Catalonia at Ampurias (Emporiae). They thus controlled, from these two key positions, all the northern part of the Western Mediterranean basin, and the traffic on the Rhône. This latter consisted, among other things, of shipments of tin from Cornwall and amber from the Baltic, which were sent through Gaul partly by carrier and partly along the waterways. Thence some of the merchandise was sent across the Alps into Italy and Etruria, while the remainder was sent to the coast and became a main source of income for the Phocaean colony, thus rapidly making it a dangerous rival of Carthage.

It is difficult to say exactly how important Carthage was, or what her relations with Tyre were at the beginning of the sixth century B.C. It seems as though she was still dependent upon the metropolis, for manufactured goods at least, but had become the most important staging post on the metal route and had already begun to eclipse Utica. If the Carthaginians really did found a colony on Ibiza round about 654 B.C., this would indicate that they already enjoyed some form of autonomy and that they probably possessed their own fleet. Until the middle of the sixth century, however, Tyre was still the dominant power, and excavations at Sexi, Rachgoun, Motya, and Lepcis Magna have shown that Carthage was in no way responsible for the provisioning of Phoenician colonies in the West. The pottery excavated is either Greek, Egyptian, or Phoenician, but never Punic.

8. RELIGION

When the Tyrian emigrants settled in Carthage, they brought with them their national gods, whom they continued to worship as had been their wont. It is true that we have no records for these early times, but from the first extant texts in the fourth century until the fall of Carthage, the Tyrian gods were worshipped in the African metropolis, and it had most probably always been so. The character and attributes of the gods were altered slightly, however, as time went on. In Semitic religion El, the father of the gods, had gradually been shorn of his power by his sons and relegated to a remote part of his heavenly home; in Carthage, on the other hand, he became, once more, the head of the pantheon, under the enigmatic title of Ba'al Hammon. The etymology of the word *hammon* is, indeed, obscure. It might derive from the root *ḥmn* (to heat or burn), and the god's name has therefore been translated 'Lord of the incense-burners (*ḥmmn*)', or 'Lord of the Furnace' – the most recent interpretation by

Février.[30] On the other hand, ḤMN is also a place- name and there is a suburb of Tyre which bears this name where a shrine to Melqart has been found.

Asherat, a fertility goddess, and El's consort in Phoenicia, does not seem to have been worshipped in Carthage, or at least not under that name. As we shall see, the consort of Ba'al Hammon, El's heir, was known as Tanit or Tinnit and this was possibly one of Asherat's titles (see below, p. 152). The secondary gods were Ba'al Shamim, the Lord of the Heavens; Resheph, god of fertility and the Underworld; Melqart and his consort Astarte, the Dii Patrii of Tyre; and Eshmun, the god of vegetation who dies and is born again according to the seasons.

The Carthaginians used to sacrifice their children to Ba'al Hammon. The custom had died out in Phoenicia but was revived in the North African colony and horrified the Persians, Greeks, and Romans, as it does us. According to written tradition, 'MLKh' was the name given to these infant holocausts, which took place in times of great danger: 'Moreover the Phoenicians, in great calamities, either of war or excessive dryness, or pestilence, sacrificed one of their dearest (children), who was selected . . . for this purpose. The Phoenician history also is replete with instances of men being sacrificed, which history was written by Sanchoniatho in Phoenician, and was interpreted into the Greek in 8 books by Philo Byblius.'[31] Such sacrifices do, in fact, seem to have been very numerous and excavations have revealed the remains of moloch piled up in their thousands in the sacred precinct of the topheth of Salammbo, at the gates of the city near the inner harbours. Urns containing the cremated bones of very young children, small animals, and dogs – all burnt together – were found round and above the Cintas chapel. The earliest were covered individually by little cairns of stones, but later the urns were grouped together and surmounted by carved votive stelae. Descriptions by Isaiah, Plutarch, and especially by Diodorus Siculus, have enabled Février to reconstruct these sinister proceedings. The ceremony took place at night, by moonlight. In the precinct stood a bronze statue of the god and at his feet a pit was dug in which a fire or topheth was lit. Around the statue stood the assistants and the parents of the victims, the musicians, and the dancers. A priest would bring the child 'dedicated' to the god, already killed according to 'secret rites', and lay him in the statue's arms from which he would roll into the flames. Then flutes, tambourines, and lyres would drown the cries of the parents and lead the dancers into a wild dance. There was, in fact, a taboo which forbade the assistants to see, cry out, or listen, for the child was supposed to have been seized by supernatural flames which had been lit by the divine breath, and the attention of the 'terrible demons of vengeance' was not to be attracted. Terracotta masks, representing hideous, grimacing demons, have been found in the tombs, and as they had been dedicated to the god of the topheth, it seems likely that they were copies of the ones worn by the dancers during the moloch ceremonies.

The number of urns, and their arrangement in the topheth, indicate that the ceremonies were frequent. Diodorus Siculus states that it was customary for sons of the most important families to be offered regularly to Ba'al Hammon. In times of danger, a special moloch was offered, as was the case when Agathocles landed on Cap Bon and threatened the city itself.

Justin's mythical story of the death of Dido is an attempt at explanation and justification of the moloch ritual by historical fact. As we have seen, the queen had, herself, ordered her funeral pyre to be built near her palace, and burnt herself to death in order to protect her city and to remain faithful to her husband Acerbas, rather than marry the Libyan king Iarbas. She was deified as a result and her cult was honoured on the same spot until the capture of Carthage by the Romans. According to Justin (or rather, according to the tradition current at the time in which he lived), the institution of the moloch went back to the beginnings of the city, and was related to funerary rites paid to the early kings. The Cintas chapel is, as we have seen, the earliest shrine in the topheth area of Salammbo, and the present author has shown that it is closely related to the enclosures discovered in the royal necropolis at Ugarit by Claude Schaeffer. There is no doubt, therefore, that the chapel must have been a funerary complex, set up for the hero worship of a victim by his followers (cf. Appendix p. 50). Cintas has found evidence for *refrigerium* rites and for libation, which were poured into the earth through stone slabs with holes in them, and were supposed to help the dead in their after-life. Heshas also fonnd a topheth stele depicting a priestess who is pouring a libation on a sacred mound. Furthermore, until the sixth century, the precinct must have resembled a burial ground for the funerary urns, containing the remains of sacrificed children, were either placed under cairns of stones and covered with earth, or were even placed in a small sarcophagus. The same rites were accorded to these children 'dedicated' to the god, as had been to the Phoenician kings of Ugarit.

Justin also tells us of the effect of such sacrifices: the strength and prosperity of the city were guaranteed, as they were by Dido's sacrifice. Frazer has studied and defined the ritual (often found among primitive societies) which consisted in the king, representative of the vital strength of the community, being put to death when his powers began to fail him. In a more evolved society, a substitute was found to take the place of the king, and this victim was generally the latter's son, as being the closest to him, so that the sacrifice would not lose its validity.[32] The connection between the king's sacrifice and moloch is illustrated by a story recorded by Philo of Byblos according to which El-Kronos (the Ba'al Hammon of the Carthaginians) sacrificed his son to his father Uranus. We shall see that during the course of its history, many of the rulers of Carthage were sacrificed, which proves that the story of Dido was based, not upon historical fact, but upon royal ritual.

It is difficult to know what reasons may have led to the revival of such primitive practices. One might expect human sacrifice among savages but scarcely in a civilized colony whose mother-city had long since abolished them. Perhaps the founders of Carthage thought that they had incurred divine wrath, and had indeed escaped from the vengeance of a king, as recorded by Timaeus, Justin, and Josephus. The cult of the topheth of Salammbo did, in fact, develop during the last quarter of the eighth century, that is about 100 years after the date indicated by these authors for the founding of the city, when the funerary chapel, doubtless built near the tomb of a king, had already fallen into ruin. The contemporaries of these deified kings would have been dead by then, and enough time would have elapsed for a cult of heroes to have developed.

There was no funerary cult, as such, for the deceased in general, but although they were not venerated as the gods were, they were nevertheless supposed to enjoy an after-life in their tombs, which were considered as 'halls of eternity'. Everything was done to help the dead in this after-life. The earliest tombs, dating to round about 700 B.C., are poor and rudimentary; they are merely pits, and often at this date the dead were cremated, whereas in Phoenicia, and later in Carthage, they were always interred. It was not long before slabs were placed above the grave, and sarcophagi of stone and probably of wood also (copper handles have been found) were used to house the corpse. The tombs were dug deeper and deeper into the ground and access to them was gained by a vertical shaft which was blocked immediately after burial. From the sixth century onwards, the rich built themselves 'halls of eternity' in well-dressed stone without mortar. Often the tomb had a cedar-wood ceiling with a pitched roof, made of stone slabs, above it to carry the weight. The interior walls were plastered and sometimes there was a moulded cornice near the ceiling. The deceased would take with him into the next world an assortment of pottery which seems to have been ritual and, from the sixth century onwards, always consisted of the same pieces: a lamp on a saucer, two jugs, and an amphora. Sometimes a small altar on the sarcophagus indicated at which end the head was, and it was at this altar that the gifts were offered at the time of the burial. The deceased was also buried with such ornaments as would indicate his station in life and his wealth; his toilet articles were beside him – doubtless for some ritual purpose – and consisted of a mirror, a hatchet-shaped razor, and a make-up box. Innumerable phylacteries completed the tomb furniture and included scarabs, ostrich eggs, cowrie shells, the Egyptian 'ankh' for Life, terracotta masks, copper bells, cymbals, Egyptian amulets – all intended to protect the dead and drive away evil spirits. Many of the bodies showed traces of embalming, done rather summarily with resin; some were painted with red colouring matter according to Libyan custom. There seems to be no rule about the way the body and the grave goods were disposed, and it is probable that there were social divisions or clans each of which had its own ritual. We never find, at this period, either statues or paintings to enrich the tombs.

*   *   *

This early Carthage, as we have seen, was very closely linked to the metropolis: close economic dependence on Tyre also meant

strong political links between the two cities. But there is no doubt
whatsoever that Carthage had already achieved some measure of
autonomy when the Magonids seized power. It is tempting to
imagine the harbour, no longer as a small port of call, but rather
as a half-way house where ships from the East would unload their
merchandise and take on a cargo of minerals before heading off
east again, while Carthaginian cargo ships would sail to Tarshish
to trade the merchandise of the metropolis, of Greece, and of Egypt
for these self-same minerals. In other words, Carthage must have
played then the part which our marshalling yards play today.

APPENDIX I

*The 'Cintas Chapel' and the funerary character of the topheth rites
celebrated in honour of the ashes of the victims of moloch sacrifice.*
(See Plates 1 and 2.)

The small building which Cintas discovered on bed-rock in the
Salammbo topheth can, as we have seen, be divided into three
sections.

(a) A chamber, about two metres square, built of dry stone, and
roofed with a corbelled vault. The springing of the vault can
still be seen. The chamber was entered through a doorway
which is 60 cm. high. Here, in a hollow in the rock, deposits
had been made on two separate occasions, first a group of
Greek and Phoenician pottery, and later an amphora containing the ashes of moloch sacrifice and small finds, which had
been deposited at the end of the seventh century B.C.

(b) Courtyards and passages. A courtyard situated to the east of
the chamber served as a fore-court. Fragments of lamps littered
its pavement of flat stones. To the north, the chamber was
flanked by an enclosure which surrounded a low altar built
against the dividing wall. There was no trace of offerings and
it seems never to have been used. Passages on the north and on
the south led to the courtyard and to the enclosure. Foundation
deposits enable us to date the complex to the period of the first
pottery deposit in the chamber.

(c) In the northern corner of this complex, between the enclosure with the altar and the passage leading to it, are sections of three concentric curved walls, indicating a triple enclosure. Cintas is probably right in thinking that this is a miniature labyrinth.

A mound covered the ruins of the building and votive offerings were buried in it. Some were even placed in small niches which were dug into the fallen masonry.

Here is Cintas' interpretation of the evidence[33]:

1. Before there were any buildings, there was just a hollow in the rock.

2. This hollow was enlarged in order that it might receive the first deposit of pottery and this, he suggests, may have been used for a sacrifice by the first Tyrian pioneers who thus wished to hallow their claim to a foreign land. Still according to Cintas, the Greek pottery would date this event to the beginning of the ninth century B.C.

3. After the departure of these first arrivals, the monument was abandoned and fell into ruin.

4. The Phoenicians who finally settled permanently in Carthage chose the site of this old and venerated shrine for the establishment of their topheth. Here they brought their offerings. This fourth phase should be dated to the last years of the ninth century or to the very beginning of the eighth. As a result of Cintas' publication, Hellenistic scholars have shown that the earliest Greek pottery in the shrine, together with the foundation deposit which dates the building, cannot have been placed there before 740–725 B.C.[34] Cintas' attractive suggestion thus conflicts with their authoritative opinion. It seems clear, therefore, that the earliest votive offerings (Vessels No. 1 and 2 in the *Atlas de Céramique Punique*, amphora No. 47, and jug No. 90 in the same publication) were almost exactly contemporary with the pottery of the foundation deposit. If, however, this highly venerated shrine was built after the founding of Carthage in the centre of a sacred precinct which was the scene of

constant activity, how then are we to explain the fact that it was abandoned and allowed to fall into ruin?

The present author believes that all this can be explained. It is suggested[35] that an artificial mound, or tumulus, was heaped up above the building as soon as its precious pottery deposit had been placed in the hollow. The building was badly constructed and promptly collapsed under the weight of earth piled above it. From then on it became the custom to bury offerings in the mound which had become as sacred as the building it covered. A tumulus, however, presupposes a tomb, and the 'Cintas Chapel' shows all the characteristics of a funerary building. Its main feature is the corbel-vaulted chamber which is a faithful miniature rendering of the Cretan tombs of which Claude Schaeffer has found such remarkable examples at Ras Shamra on the Syrian coast, belonging to the middle of the second millennium B.C.[36] By the beginning of the first millennium B.C. this form of burial had disappeared in Phoenicia but it was still current in Cyprus, for instance at Xylotimbou, and here, as with the Punic chapel, the tombs were covered by a tumulus. The maze of courtyards and passages which surround this chamber reproduce, on a greatly reduced scale, the plan of an oriental shrine, as Cintas has noted. At Ugarit there were arrangements for the libation of the dead, alongside the tombs of Mycenaean date. There are several indications that this was also the practice in the topheth of Salammbo. A libation table with holes pierced through it has been published by the present author,[37] the bottom of a basin with channels in it was discovered in this area, a stele from the Bardo Museum (Cb 687 bis) shows a kneeling priestess pouring a libation by torchlight, and a stele from the Carthage Museum shows the jar alone with a stream of water springing from it. We are therefore justified in thinking that the altar built against the chamber with the deposit may well have received the water from libations. The funerary character of the building is thus explained, and so are the labyrinth and the tumulus. The whole complex is revealed as the tomb of a child who was burnt as a sacrifice, and who was considered to be immortal by those who worshipped him.

It should be added that the remains which surround the 'Cintas Chapel' have the same funerary character. The whole of the lower level of the topheth consists, in fact, of urns which contain the ashes of moloch sacrifice, and these were placed in cavities in the rock, protected by a cairn or a miniature dolmen covered with a tumulus. It seems that nothing differentiates this sanctuary from an Iron Age necropolis for cremation burial, unless it be the nature of the ashes in the urns which are not the remains of the cremated dead, but the remains of children offered as a burnt sacrifice. At Hama in Syria, for instance, Riis excavated one of these cemeteries[38] where the ashes in the urns were accompanied by small offerings and pottery comparable to what has been found in the lowest level of the Salammbo topheth, with a small tumulus built over them. Sometimes, as at Carthage, a large stone or a roughly shaped stele, or even a betyl was set up at the top of the mound.

The aetiological tale, which Justin records as an explanation for the institution of moloch sacrifice, alludes to the funerary practices which were common in the topheth, when it states that after Dido's death, the deified queen was worshipped on the very spot where she sacrificed herself, until the fall of Carthage.

If we accept this interpretation, the 'Cintas Chapel' can no longer be regarded as the oldest Phoenician building in Tunisia, going back to the Tyrians' first arrival on Carthaginian soil. This theory had, as we have seen, been the cause of many of the difficulties surrounding the question of the date of the founding of Carthage which had to be brought down to the eighth century, contrary to literary tradition. Timaeus' ninth-century date would be fully justified if we consider the chapel to be an exceptionally large votive monument of the eighth century, and as only a small part of the sanctuary has so far been explored, it is possible, even probable, that other and older monuments may one day be discovered.

Notes and References

1. Cf. U. Täckholm, 'Tarsis, Tartessos und die Säulen des Herakles', *Opuscula Romana*, V (1965), pp. 143–96.
2. G. Garbini, 'Tarsis e Gen. X·4', *Bibbia e Oriente*, Genoa 1965, pp. 13–19.
3. In the spring of 1965 a wreck was discovered off the French coast of the Languedoc. The ship had been carrying a cargo of metal objects belonging to the Halstadt culture (first half of the first millennium B.C.), which proves the existence of maritime trade organized by autochthonous peoples.

4. Flavius Josephus (*Contra Apionem*, I, 119) mentions an expedition which Hiram of Tyre directed against Utica. He obtained his information from Menander of Ephesus and it presumably comes from the Royal Chronicles of Tyre. It is, indeed, possible that once Utica had become a flourishing city, she had refused to pay tribute. But Josephus does not specify whether he is, in fact, referring to African Utica, and many people believe nowadays that the rebel city he mentions is another Utica, though the whereabouts of this town is the subject of many conjectures.

5. N. Glueck, *BASOR*, 75 (1939), p. 16 ff., and 79 (1940), p. 3 ff.

6. J. G. Février, 'La marine phénicienne', *La Nouvelle Clio*, III.

7. For a discussion of this problem see Rhys Carpenter, 'The Phoenicians in the West', *AJA*, LXII (1958), pp. 35–53.

8. G. Pesce, *Sardegna punica*, Cagliari 1961, pl. 88.

9. Ibid. pl. 23; see also the discussion of the problem by U. Täckholm, op. cit.

10. Albright, *BASOR*, 83 (1941), p. 17 ff.

11. Rhys Carpenter, op. cit.

12. S. Chiappisi, *Il 'Melqart di Sciacca' e la questione fenicie in Sicilia*, Rome 1961.

13. I. Bernabo Brea and M. Cavalier, 'Civiltà preistoriche delle isole Eloia e del territorio di Milazzo', *Boll. di Palen. Ital.*, n.s. X (1956), I, pp. 7–100.

14. I. Bernabo Brea, *La Sicilia prima dei Greci*, Milan 1958. English translation: *Sicily before the Greeks*, London 1957.

15. M. Pellicer Catalan, 'Excavaciones en la necropolis punica "Laurita" de Cerro de San Cristobal (Almuneçar, Granada)', *Excavaciones Arqueologia en España*, 17, Madrid 1964.

16. E. Gjerstadt, *SCE*, IV-2, p. 436.

17. Th. Howard Carter, 'Western Phoenicians and Lepcis Magna', *AJA*, 69 (1965), p. 2, n. 4.

18. The Temple Annals recorded events from a 'year one' – the date of the building of the Temple. See M. Taradell, *Maruecos punico*, Tetuan 1960.

19. Homer, *Odyssey*, viii, 124; ii, 44; xv, 245; iii, 56; ix, 143, 145–6; xv, 249–50.

20. G. Vuillemot, *Reconnaissance aux échelles puniques d'Oranie*, autumn 1965, pp. 45–54.

21. Homer, *Odyssey*, ix, 144–5.

22. Eusebius quoted by George the Syncellus, Bonn edition, I, p. 324.

23. Flavius Josephus, *Contra Apionem*, I, 125–6.

24. Timaeus dated not only the foundation of Carthage but also that of Rome to the year 814. It has generally been supposed that Apion wished to bring down the two dates in accordance with the chronology for Rome which was accepted in his day, while preserving their synchronism. On the other hand, Cicero, Velleius Paterculus, and many others, were prepared to admit that Carthage was older than Rome.

25. J. Beloch, *Griechische Geschichte*.

26. E. Forrer, *Festschrift Franz Dornseiff*.

27. Cf. C. Picard, 'Notes de Chronologie Punique: le Problème du Ve Siècle', *Karthago*, XII.

28. P. Cintas, *Céramique Punique*, Tunis 1950, p. 447–8.

29. Cf. U. Täckholm, op. cit.

30. J. G. Février, 'Essai de reconstitution du Sacrifice Molek,' *J.A.*, 1950, p.173.

31. Porphyry, *De Abstinentia*, II, 56.

32. Frazer, *The Golden Bough*.

33. Cf. 'Un sactuaire précarthaginois sur la grève de Salammbo'. In *Rev, Tunisienne*, 1948, pp. 16–31; and *Céramique Punique*, Paris 1950, p. 490 ff.
34. Cf. P. Demargne in *Rev. Archéologique*, XXXVIII (1951), pp. 44–52.
35. Cf. C. Picard in *Rev. de gli Studi Orientali*, 1967, pp. 189–99.
36. *Ugaritica*, III, Paris 1939, p. 77 ff.; *Syria*, 1934, p. 114 ff.; 1935, p. 147; 1936, p. 112; 1937, p. 135.
37. G. Ch. Picard, *CRAI*, 1945, p. 143 ff.
38. *Hama II*, 3, *Les cimetières à crémation*, Copenhagen 1948, p. 27 ff.

2

The Magonids
550–396 B.C.

CARTHAGE remains shrouded in mystery until a little before the middle of the sixth century B.C. From then on, the works of Greek historians give us regular information concerning relations – generally strained – between their own race and the Western Phoenicians. In some cases their writings are extant but more often they have come down to us through Pompeius Trogus or through an abridged version of his works by Justin. Scant epigraphic and archaeological evidence fills, to some extent, the gaps in the knowledge thus conveyed. At least, from now on we are dealing with actual people and events.

1. MALCHUS

The first head of the Carthaginian state whose name has come down to us after Dido's, is mentioned in Justin's manuscripts as Maleus, Maceus or Mazeus (XVIII, 7). Vossius has substituted for this the word Malchus and this hypothesis has won general acceptance. It is not certain, however, whether this is a proper name of Semitic origin or, as seems to us more likely, a title.[1]

According to Justin, Malchus was a general (*dux*) who had been a successful commander in Sicily but was then less fortunate in Sardinia. As a punishment for his defeat, he was condemned to exile together with his army. The exiles failed to obtain a pardon and besieged the city. Meanwhile Malchus' son, Carthalo, who was a priest of Melqart, had been sent to Tyre with a tithe of the Sicilian booty. As he was returning to Africa his father pressed him to join the rebels. Carthalo refused at first and went to fulfil his religious obligations, but having received the consent of the people, he returned to his father. The latter, however, accused him of coming to insult and mock the exiles, and had him crucified in full view of the city, dressed in his priestly robes. Shortly after, Carthage was captured but Malchus showed moderation as regards reprisals and only ten senators were executed. Some time later, however, he was himself accused of tyranny and put to death.

Justin is the only author to mention Malchus;[2] both Herodotus and Diodorus record the Graeco-Phoenician struggle for supremacy in Sicily, but neither mentions this Carthaginian general who is supposed to have conquered a large part of the island. Apart from the first four chapters, and apart from the last sentence concerning Mago (to which we shall return), Justin's Book XVIII consists entirely of the story of Dido and that of Malchus, with a short paragraph between the two which deals with human sacrifices intended to check epidemics (the end of Chapter VI). These three sections have in common the fact that they all deal with human sacrifice of one sort or another. The story of Dido explains, as we have seen elsewhere, the ritual suicide of the king.[3]

The story of Malchus is an attempt at justifying the sacrifice of the king's son and his crucifixion; we have no other parallel for this at Carthage, but the Bible, at any rate, produces one. The section between these two stories deals with the sacrifice of private individuals with no political significance attached to it. The complete contents of the book deal with the development of this religious theme. There is no mention of politics, whether internal or external, between the reigns of Dido and Malchus. The Carthaginian colonization of Ibiza is completely ignored, although we know from Diodorus that it must have occurred either towards the middle of the seventh or, more probably, at the beginning of the sixth century B.C.

We must conclude, therefore, that Pompeius Trogus drew his information for this part of his work from a treatise on Carthaginian human sacrifice rather than from some historical source. The author of this work would have attempted to explain these inhuman rites by some putative historical event centred on some important historical figure, just as Lucian in his work on the Syrian goddess or his tale of Kombabus in which he finds an explanation for the castration of the Galles. Semitic myths were transposed, rationalized, and sentimentally and rhetorically improved.

The name of Malchus – if we accept Vossius' amendment – is none other than the title MLK, the semitic equivalent of 'king'. It is very possible that we have here a 'king' *par excellence* rather than a specific historical character. The crucifixion of Carthalo in his priest's robes, has all the attributes of a sacrifice. As late as the third century A.D. the victims offered to Ba'al Hammon, or, in his Latinized form, Saturn, were attired in the dress of the *sacerdotes Saturni*. This garment symbolized the ownership of the god and his right to demand the victim's life. The crucifixion of Carthalo, the king's son, should thus be seen as one particular example of the 'sacrifice of the king' whose name is, indeed, identical with that of Malchus. In contrast, the victim of moloch – another form of royal sacrifice as practised by Dido and attested to by history and archaeology – is not crucified, but burnt in a topheth. The Bible has preserved for us an example of the sacrifice of a king's sons by hanging or crucifixion, in circumstances which were probably very similar to those in fact surrounding the Malchus story. In order to put an end to a three-year famine, David handed over to the Gideonites the seven sons of Saul, 'and they hanged them in the hill before the Lord: and they fell all seven together, and were put to death in the days of harvest, in the first days, in the beginning of barley harvest' (2 Samuel xxi. 7–9). Sacrifice by hanging is found among other races as well, for instance among the Germanic peoples.

If we accept this hypothesis, the historical part of Justin's account loses value. In fact, we believe it to have been the work of Pompeius Trogus, himself, who wished to transpose the treatise on 'religious sacrifice' which he was using, in terms of political history, particularly that of Carthage in the third and second centuries B.C. We thus see the *gerontes* – that is, the senate – banish a defeated general and his army; the people grant immunity to Carthalo, which recalls the *adeia* of Classical law; finally, Malchus unfolds his plans for government before an Assembly. These are, as Gsell has noted, the earliest mentions of a People's Assembly in Carthage, and it seems to have played, at this remote date, a part which it certainly no longer played even in the time of Aristotle and which it only achieved again under the Barcids.

Malchus' military exploits are also very much open to suspicion. In spite of the victories he is supposed to have won over the

Libyans, Carthage was still paying tribute to the latter three or four generations later. In Sicily the Phoenicians had withdrawn into the western part of the island and had made an alliance with the Elymians,[4] with whom, in about 580 B.C. they fought the Greek Pentathlus, who had attempted to found a colony on the Lilybaeum headland. It is indeed possible that Malchus could have taken part in this war but Diodorus gives us Timaeus' account of it and makes no mention of any Carthaginians, but ascribes Pentathlus' defeat to the combined forces of the Elymians and of the Phoenicians of Sicily alone. The latter were still entirely autonomous, as proved by the excavations at Motya where the archaeological material is totally different from that of Carthage until 550 B.C. at the earliest. There is evidence of Carthaginian intervention in the centre and west of the island only from the very end of the sixth century onwards.

The only historical conclusion which we can draw from the legend of Malchus, therefore, is that religious kingship continued to exist in Carthage in the first half of the sixth century.

2. THE MAGONIDS

In about 550 B.C. a certain Mago founded a new dynasty which was to rule for one and a half centuries. It seems that this event marked a break with the past and certainly it heralded a change in foreign policy.[5] Carthage, from now on, ceased to be a city of the Western Phoenicians among many others: she claimed leadership and imposed her military authority throughout the Western Mediterranean. Only on an economic level did she remain subordinate to Tyre.

Mago's son, Hasdrubal, succeeded him and we have some definite information concerning him in spite of the Roman terminology which Justin adopts. He was, apparently, eleven times 'dictator' and was accorded a 'triumph' four times. In the next generation we have Hamilcar who seems to have been a grandson of Mago's, the son of a certain Hanno, probably a younger brother of Hasdrubal's, and of a Syracusan lady. It is this Hamilcar who was killed in 480 at the Battle of Himera, but Maurin has shown that this defeat did not mark the end of the dynasty which flourished for almost a century more. Justin, in fact, mentions three sons of Hasdrubal's by name, Hannibal, Hasdrubal, and Sapho;

5

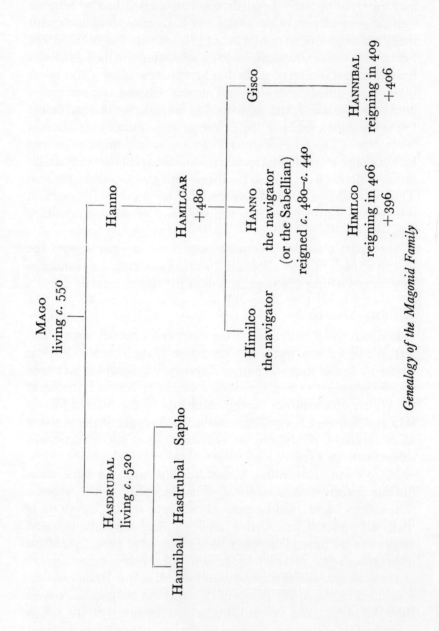

Genealogy of the Magonid Family

and three sons of Hamilcar's, Himilco, Hanno, and Gisco, all of whom were powerful in fifth-century Carthage. The only information we possess, however, concerns the last three. Gisco was exiled and withdrew to Selinus. His brother, Hanno, seems to have been the creator of the Carthaginian empire in Tunisia and is probably to be identified with the great navigator of that name, an account of whose voyage along the African coast has been preserved for us. The third brother, Himilco, was perhaps the explorer of the Northern Seas. In 410 the Carthaginian armies, under the command of the cousins Hannibal, son of Gisco, and Himilco, son of Hanno, resumed the campaign in Sicily, and their defeat brought about the downfall of the Magonid family, which is, henceforward, no longer mentioned.

3. ESTABLISHMENT OF THE EMPIRE

As we have seen, the defeat at Himera in 480 divides the Magonid era into distinct phases. During the earlier phase, there was active military expansion – a new phenomenon in the history of Carthage. To quote Justin: 'Mago, the general of the Carthaginians, (was) . . . the first, by regulating their military discipline, to lay the foundations of Punic power and . . . establish . . . the strength of the state, not less by his skill in the art of war than by his prowess.' This text contradicts the same author's statements concerning Malchus and his conquests, but is probably closer to historical fact. For once, literary and archaeological evidence agree in acknowledging Carthaginian supremacy along all the Western Mediterranean coastline in the second half of the sixth and first decade of the fifth century B.C. Owing to the vague and imprecise nature of the texts, especially those concerning Spain and Sardinia, the archaeological evidence is especially important. Under the Magonids, Carthage developed a culture of its own so that, from now on, it is possible to distinguish the remains of Punic occupation from those of other Western Phoenicians, and to date these remains.

We shall be studying the products of this home industry in the section dealing with Civilization, but it is necessary here to note the hall-marks of this culture and its distribution.

In contrast with the Greeks, the Carthaginians never manufactured luxury wares. Their pottery was coarse, with no value as

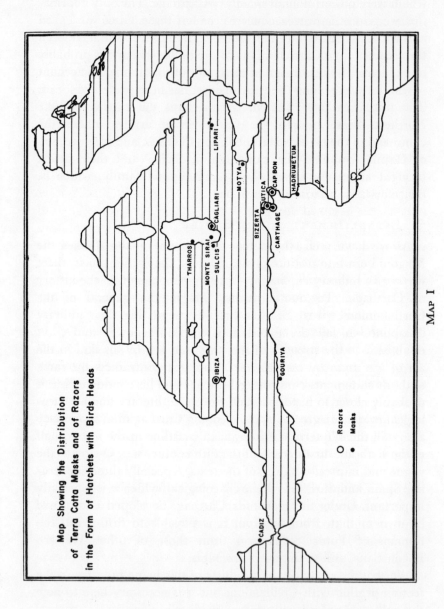

Map Showing the Distribution
of Terra Cotta Masks and of Razors
in the Form of Hatchets with Birds Heads

○ Razors
● Masks

MAP I

a trading commodity, but it is easily identifiable and is an indisputable proof, when found on a site (such as at Motya, for example, from 500 B.C. onwards), of their presence there. On the other hand, as early as about 600 B.C., the Carthaginians stopped manufacturing the red-burnished Cypro-Phoenician wares which the Western Phoenicians of Spain and Morocco continued to make until a very late date and which indicate their autonomy with relation to Carthage, as Taradell and Cintas have proved.[6]

Among other typical Punic artifacts of the sixth and fifth centuries, the terracotta masks, which we shall be discussing later, also deserve a mention. Similar or even identical objects are, in fact, found in Palestine, in Cyprus, and especially at Sparta in the sanctuary of Artemis Orthia. They are found in the Western Mediterranean, however, only in places where Carthaginians lived and a map of their distribution (page 62) is, at the same time, a map of the Magonid Empire, and includes – in addition to Africa – Motya, Sardinia, and Ibiza, but not Spain, Morocco, or the coast round Oran. This again indicates the autonomy of the Western Mediterranean lands which the distribution of the red-burnished wares has already suggested.

In the levels of the topheth of Carthage which can be dated to the seventh and the beginning of the sixth centuries B.C., we find terracotta figurines which look extremely primitive, with bell-shaped bodies, and prominent male or female sexual organs. Almost identical figurines have been found on Ibiza and Motya, and in Sardinia at Bithia and Tharros, and in these last three sites they continued in use during the fourth and even the third centuries B.C. In Carthage, however, they disappear in about 550.

The sanctuaries where the victims of human sacrifice were buried, known as topheths, are found, in Africa, at Carthage and Hadrumetum, and are numerous inland in those parts of Tunisia under Carthaginian rule (for instance at Mactar, Thignica, and in the neighbourhood of Thysdrus), and even in the Numidian kingdom (for example at El Hofra, at the gates of Cirta or Constantine). The topheths in the interior are of late date, however, and the earliest (among them, that of El Hofra) do not go back beyond the third century. Furthermore, we can be certain that there was no topheth at Utica or in the cities of Tripolitania.

At Motya, on the other hand, there was a topheth in use from about 550. Italian archaeologists have found topheths in Sardinia at Sulcis, Nora, and recently at Monte Sirai. The latter is late and dates to the third and second centuries.[7] The stelae found at Nora and Sulcis are not much earlier but clearly derive from a fifth-century Carthaginian prototype (in the shape of a little Egyptian-style temple) and have nothing whatsoever in common with the obelisk-stelae which we find in fourth-century Carthage.[8] The introduction of the cult can thus be dated to the beginning of the fifth century B.C.

From about 650 B.C., we find copper razors shaped like hatchet blades in the Carthaginian tombs, in Sardinia, and on Ibiza. These are not found on the Spanish mainland, however.

Painted ostrich eggs have a wider distribution and are found not only at Carthage, but also at Motya, on Ibiza, in Sardinia, and at Djidjelli and Gouraya on the Algerian coast. They are also found in a Spanish necropolis at Villaricos, but neither razors nor masks have been found here, and the eggs are decorated with rich and original designs[9] which are of completely different inspiration from the female faces painted on those from Carthage and Ibiza from 550 onwards. We cannot call the Villaricos necropolis Punic, merely because painted ostrich eggs have been found there, although it is generally classified as such.

These facts bear witness to the existence of actual Punic colonies from about 550 B.C. which were culturally dependent on Carthage. These colonies were situated at Motya, in various parts of Sardinia, and on Ibiza. The same facts also indicate that other Western Phoenician cities were culturally, and therefore politically, less closely controlled by the Magonids, for instance, those of Syrtica, Utica, Palermo, and probably Soluntum[10] in Sicily, Gades and other Spanish harbour-towns, Lixus, and the ports of call along the Moroccan coast and in the neighbourhood of Oran.

These archaeological deductions can now be compared with the evidence of the texts, in an attempt to define the extent and history of the 'Magonid Empire'.

It seems worth noting to begin with that, strange though it may seem, the Magonids did not succeed in improving the precarious situation of Carthage in Africa. At the beginning of his reign (probably towards 530 B.C.), Hasdrubal certainly tried to free his city from the humiliating tribute which she was forced to pay to the neighbouring Libyan tribes. He was defeated, however, and payment was resumed for another half-century. Even the nearest Phoenician cities refused to recognize – officially at least – the supremacy of Carthage. Utica is not mentioned in the treaty with Rome in 509, but she must have lost her diplomatic independence between then and 348, when her name occurs in the renewal of the alliance. The topheth at Hadrumetum was first used as late as about 600 B.C.,[11] but the city declared herself to be a Tyrian colony and was not, therefore, founded under Carthaginian auspices. The same applies to Lepcis and Sabratha in Syrtica. which were colonized a little earlier, around 650 B.C.[12] These towns were obliged to appeal for Carthaginian assistance in 520 or 510, however, when an exiled Spartan prince named Dorieus tried to settle a base 10 miles to the east of Lepcis. The Carthaginians were unable to intervene themselves, and were obliged to rely on a tribe of the neighbourhood, the Makes, for the expulsion of the Greeks.

On the other hand, the intervention of the Carthaginian fleets in Spain, in the harbours of Morocco and Western Algeria, and along the seaboard of Southern Gaul, was aggressive. Here the Phoenician colonies were obliged to accept Carthaginian domination and the Greeks were either expelled or were driven to taking up a defensive attitude. The Phoenician colonies in Sardinia were also compelled to toe the line, not only politically but also culturally, especially with regard to religious questions; Tyre maintained her supremacy only in the economic field. Mighty Carthaginian armies conquered the whole of Eastern Sardinia, while in Sicily they captured Panormus, Soluntum, and Motya and even settled this last with African colonists in about 550 B.C. Carthage intervened actively in the rivalries of the Greek cities and the internal politics of the island. She formed an alliance with Anaxilas, the tyrant of Rhegium and Zankle (Messina), who controlled the Straits. In Italy, an alliance with the Etruscans favoured the Carthaginians, and together they chased the Phocaeans out of Corsica. By 500, the Carthaginians had settled in, and were all but lords of the harbour town of Pyrgi, and the Tyrrhenian prince of Caere probably owed them his throne. When Etruscan domination of Campania and of the Latium began to weaken, the Carthaginians had no scruples in coming to terms with

65

the new power and as early as 509 B.C. they had formed a treaty of alliance with the Roman Republic.

The details of this expansion seem to be as follows. Diodorus (V, 16) tells us that in Spain the Carthaginians established a colony on Ibiza, the most southern island of the Balearic group, 160 years after the foundation of their own city. It is generally admitted that Diodorus, who drew a great deal of his information from Timaeus, dated the latter event at 814 B.C. Ibiza would therefore have been colonized in 654 B.C. In the wealth of archaeological material belonging to the Punic occupation of the island there is nothing, however, which can be dated earlier than 600 B.C. This discrepancy between recorded history and archaeology would not occur if we supposed Diodorus to have adopted the same date as Apion for the foundation of Carthage, that is 751 B.C. Ibiza would then have been colonized in 591 B.C. Whatever the date of its colonization, however, the island was certainly the first Punic base in that area and, until the Barcid conquest, it remained the only direct Carthaginian dependency.

At some unspecified date, generally thought to be about 500 B.C., the Magonids intervened in the Iberian peninsula in order to protect the Phoenician colonies there, especially Gades, from attack by the native population. Schulten and many others see in this intervention the first step in the founding of a Punic empire in Spain, which they suppose to have lasted until the end of the fourth century. The Carthaginian armies would have destroyed Tartessus and subjugated the ancient kingdom of Arganthonius. This, however, is not borne out by archaeology. In fact, the site of Tartessus has not been found and this famous city may never have existed. The name might well be that of a region comprising the Baetis valley, the present-day Guadalquivir. What seems more probable is that Punic intervention broke up the Tartessian kingdom which, by the third century, had been divided between the Turdetani of Andalusia and the Bastetani of the Granada region. Some of the latter, known to the Romans as 'Bastulo-Punic', and living on the coast between Gibraltar and Málaga, adopted Phoenician speech and culture. Furthermore, the old Tyrian cities of Gades, Sexi, Abdera, and Málaga had to sign a treaty of alliance with Carthage which, although it restricted their political freedom, preserved their internal autonomy and cultural traditions. Archaeological material from Phoenician Spain includes, therefore, very few typically Punic artifacts.

In their relations with the native population of the peninsula, the Carthaginians had to be content with treaties allowing them to recruit mercenaries. In this connection the Iberians first fought in Hamilcar's army at the Battle of Himera in 480. Furthermore, these treaties seem to have guaranteed Carthage very favourable terms and the best of the output of the Sierra mines. It is only in the fourth century that Carthage began to monopolize Iberian trade; whereas the treaty with Rome in 509 does not mention Spain as one of the zones to which Italian merchants were forbidden access, that of 348 specifically does.

On the other hand, the Magonids do not seem to have neglected a single opportunity of driving the Greeks from this area, especially as these were represented by the Phocaeans who were always the sworn enemies of Carthage. A Hellenic colony had been founded very·close to Málaga, at Mainake, and was probably destroyed around 500 B.C. Then followed a desperate struggle for control of the coast to the north of the Cabo de la Náo, of which we know only of the last episode, unfortunately. This was the Battle of Artemision, which took place at about the same time as that of Himera and which was fatal to Punic aspirations. Previously, the Carthaginians had been able to ignore the Greek efforts at Ampurias and Rhode, and had been able to sail the coasts of the Levant, of Catalonia, and of the Rousillon with impunity. In fact, mercenaries from this last region fought in Hamilcar's army at Himera.[13]

By acquiring supremacy over Southern Spain, the Carthaginians also found themselves in charge of other western lands: the Oran region, Morocco, and Portugal. This is reflected in changes in the types of archaeological finds, from levels which can be dated to about 500 B.C. onwards, at sites from Les Andalouses near Oran[14] to Mogador in the very south of Morocco. Here, although Punic influence is manifest, nevertheless it remains discreet and the most typical Carthaginian artifacts (masks, razors, etc. . . .) do not seem to have been imported.

In Sicily, the Magonids were content, at first, to maintain the territory they had acquired, by relying on a triple alliance consisting of the two Phoenician cities of Panormus and Soluntum, and of the Elymians. From 550 onwards, however, they were also the Lords of Motya and consecrated a topheth there. This city they used as their base in the struggle against the Spartan Dorieus, in which they played a decisive part. In about 510, after his failure to settle in Libya, Dorieus endeavoured to seize Eryx, but he was killed in the attempt. His followers, however, tried to found the city of Heraclea, but the whole of Western Sicily united to exterminate them.

It is worth noting that the Dorieus episode took place at about the same time as the signing of the Romano-Punic alliance, which marked the weakening and, shortly afterwards, the rejection of the Etrusco-Punic alliance. From now on, the Etruscans were to follow an aggressive policy, on their own account, along the coasts of Southern Italy, in the region of the Straits of Messina and into Sicily itself. It is probably this turn of events which governed the decision of Hamilcar (who came to power at about this time) to intervene actively in the eastern half of the island, where the Phoenicians had renounced any claims for several centuries.

There was another reason for this change in orientation, based on the internal development of the Greek cities in Western Sicily. Most of these had been governed, since their foundation, by oligarchies of big landowners who had maintained a relatively peaceful foreign policy. (Those of Syracuse were known by the significant name of Gamores.) At the time of which we are speaking, however, the cities were tending to pass into the hands of tyrants who declared themselves champions of the people against the oligarchs, but soon sought to extend their personal power whilst appealing to the nationalist feelings of their subjects so as to detract their attention from their loss of freedom. The Magonids certainly had no ideological reason for opposing a way of government which was not so different from their own; but they did, naturally enough, attempt to curb the imperialist tendencies of the more powerful tyrants.

Agrigentum had hardly been founded when she fell under the sway of the cruel Phalaris (570–554). The latter does not seem to have had any disputes with Carthage during the sixteen years of his reign, a fact which supports our view of a Punic policy of non-interference at this period in Sicily. The peace lasted during the reigns of Phalaris' successors until 480 when Theron, who was largely responsible for the collapse of the Magonid political structure, came to the throne.

At Syracuse, on the other hand, the Gamores aristocracy managed to keep in power for some considerable time, in spite of the claims of the middle and lower classes, and of the rival ambitions of the tyrants of the small neighbouring town of Gela. They were ably supported by the Magonids, and Hanno married a Syracusan girl to mark the agreement. This alliance with Syracuse opened up the road to the Greek world, to Phoenicia, and to Persian Asia. It was a catastrophic event for Carthage when, in 485 B.C., Gelon, tyrant of Gela, finally succeeded in capturing Syracuse and drove out the Gamores. There was simultaneously, however, an important diplomatic success which compensated for this set-back. Since 493 the tyrant Anaxilas had been ruling in Rhegium, now called Reggio di Calabria. He had his eye on the city of Zankle – the site of present-day Messina – on the other side of the Straits. The inhabitants of Zankle were driven out of their city by a group of Samians, after which Anaxilas managed to seize it and settled it with Messenians who are supposed to have fled from Lacedaemon oppression in the Peloponnesus, thus giving the city its new name. Furthermore, Anaxilas was married to the daughter of Terillus, tyrant of Himera on the north coast of Sicily, and the latter was bound by ties of hospitality to the Magonid, Hamilcar. Through this ally, therefore, Carthage gained control of the Straits.[15] We shall see, further on, the momentous consequences arising from this situation.

Control of the Straits of Messina was all the more important to the Magonids as they had particular interests in Sardinia. First Mago, and later Hasdrubal, had undertaken a systematic conquest of that island. The latter was victorious for many years before finally meeting his end there, probably around 510 B.C. Simultaneously with the founding of Carthage, the Tyrians, with Cypriot assistance, were settling along the Sardinian coast, their oldest colony probably being that of Nora, half-way along the south coast, opposite Africa. This city, together with neighbouring Caralis (Cagliari) which was later to become the capital, Tharros on the west coast, and Olbia on a northern headland, were forced to recognize Carthaginian supremacy. There is nowhere else, in

Western Phoenicia, where archaeology has revealed clearer proof of direct Carthaginian influence. The topheths of Nora and Sulcis contain stelae which are almost identical to those of Salammbo, while the masks and funerary figurines from Tharros, Sulcis, and Caralis prove not only the existence of a thriving cultural community, but also, from the end of the sixth century onwards, the presence of numerous Carthaginians who had come from Africa. The Phoenician colonists in Sardinia received from the Magonids, in exchange for their liberty, efficient protection against the native population. Before the Phoenicians, there had been a flourishing autochthonous civilization in Sardinia, which has left us not only the *nuraghi*, but also some remarkable bronze figurines. Sardinian objects from the Etruscan tombs at Vetulonia prove that it was still thriving in the eighth and seventh centuries B.C., but it then declined so rapidly that this cannot be due solely to military events. Hasdrubal and his successors were able, therefore, to establish themselves firmly throughout the western half of the island, so that the Phoenicians of Sardinia enjoyed a freedom of movement which the Carthaginians did not yet possess in Africa.

In Corsica, on the other hand, Mago had not been able to prevent the Phocaeans, who had been chased from Anatolia by the Persian conquest, from making use of the maritime superiority which was still theirs, and from settling on the east coast at Aleria. The active piracy which they immediately undertook, was as harmful to the Carthaginians as it was to their allies, the Etruscans. The two nations united to expel these intruders, who, though victorious, had suffered such losses that they were obliged to seek a new haven elsewhere in about 535 B.C.

4. THE ETRUSCAN ALLIANCE

The Magonid political structure would not, in fact, have been complete without a close alliance with the other great Western Mediterranean power of the period: the Tyrrhenian Empire or, to be more accurate, Confederation, which comprised Tuscany, the Latium, and Campania. Though not so strong a naval power as it had been a century before, it was, nevertheless, at this period, engaged in the conquest of the Po valley from Felsina (Bologna) to Spina, key to the Adriatic.

The Etrusco-Punic alliance is one of the best documented events of this obscure period. Herodotus, who wrote less than a century later, mentions it in connection with the Phocaean episode (I, 166). The problem is to decide whether this was a temporary coalition or a lasting *entente*. It is an important question and one that has been much discussed, and has been strikingly elucidated by a most important archaeological discovery.

The Italian Etruscologist, Pallotino, was directing excavations in the summer of 1964 at Pyrgi, the harbour-town of Caere, one of the most southern Etruscan cities, and therefore one of the nearest to Rome, and an alley-way between two temples was being cleared, when three folded sheets of gold were found in a context which can be dated with certainty to around the year 500 B.C. When the sheets were unrolled, they were each found to bear an inscription of the greatest interest. Two of them are inscribed in Etruscan and the third is in Phoenician. They were all three written at the same time, refer to the same events, and are in the name of Thefarie Veliunas, the ruler of Caere and Pyrgi. The latter is dedicating an ex-voto to the Phoenician goddess Astarte, who was assimilated to the Etruscan Uni, the Roman Juno. Everyone is agreed on this point but opinions differ on the interpretation of the three inscriptions, and the Phoenician one is just as problematic as the two Etruscan ones.

From these documents we learn of the existence of an important Phoenician colony at Pyrgi at the end of the sixth century. This would explain the fact that the next port-of-call to the north is shown as Punicum on Roman maps. We do not know, however, whether these Phoenicians came from Carthage or not. Levi della Vida and Dupont Sommer think that they were Cypriots, and the latter suggests that they may have come to Italy via Sardinia; Garbini does not agree with this. In fact, historically speaking, the question is of purely academic interest, as there were Cypriots among the population of Carthage itself, and in any case in the year 500 B.C. the Phoenicians of Sardinia acknowledged Carthaginian supremacy.

The Phoenician colony at Pyrgi played an important part in the political and cultural life of Caere and of its port. It formed a counterbalance to the Greek colony which seems to have been fairly active. In fact, the name of the city itself is Hellenic (it means 'the towers'), and the goddess who was worshipped there as Uni, and

71

is identified by Veliunas with Astarte, was known to the Greeks by the name of Leucothea.

Caere is not the only Etruscan state to have been in close contact with the Carthaginians at this period. An ivory plaque was found at Carthage which bears a Tyrrhenian inscription and seems to have been written at Vulci; while pottery from the same city has been found in African cemeteries.

5. The End of the Etrusco-Punic Alliance

The victory of Alalia threw open to the Etruscan and Punic allies a whole range of attractive possibilities; in the last years of the sixth century they even seem to have contemplated the complete expulsion of the Greeks from the Tyrrhenian Sea by closing the Straits of Messina to them. The first thing they had to do, however, was to seize the Hellenistic colonies in Campania, for once they had control of these, the Etruscans could easily go south to join up with the Carthaginians in Sicily. In 524, therefore, a formidable Etruscan army attacked Cumae.[16] They were heavily defeated by the inhabitants of this ancient Chalcidian colony, led by a certain Aristodemus. The latter followed up his victory by making himself tyrant and used the power thus acquired to further some rather odd fantasies. He made the young men dress up as girls and vice-versa, and earned himself the nick-name of 'soft'.

The victory of Aristodemus was to have disastrous consequences for the southern provinces of the Etruscan Empire. It was certainly the direct cause of the revolution of 509 which drove the Tarquin dynasty from Rome. For the last century the Tarquins had governed the Latin tribes in the name of the Tyrrhenian federation. The leader of this federation, Lars Porsena of Clusium, immediately intervened against the rebels and probably succeeded in reconquering Rome for a short space. The Latins appealed to Aristodemus of Cumae and in 504 the latter obtained a decisive victory over the Etruscan army beneath the walls of Aricia.

Now the year 509, which marked the expulsion of the Tarquins from Rome, is also the date which Polybius gives for the first treaty with that city. Here is the text of the treaty.

There shall be friendship between the Romans and their allies, and the Carthaginians and their allies, on these conditions:

Neither the Romans nor their allies are to sail beyond the Fair Promontory, unless driven by stress of weather or the fear of enemies. If any one of them be driven ashore he shall not buy or take aught for himself save what is needful for the repair of his ship and the service of the gods, and he shall depart within five days.

Men landing for traffic shall strike no bargain save in the presence of a herald or town-clerk. Whatever is sold in the presence of these, let the price be secured to the seller on the credit of the state – that is to say, if such sale be in Libya or Sardinia.

If any Roman come to the Carthaginian province in Sicily he shall enjoy all rights enjoyed by others. The Carthaginians shall do no injury to the people of Ardea, Antium, Laurentium, Circeii, Tarracina, nor any other people of the Latins that are subject to Rome.

From these townships even which are not subject to Rome they shall hold their hands; and if they take one, shall deliver it unharmed to the Romans. They shall build no fort in Latium; if they enter the district in arms, they shall not stay a night therein.

A great deal has been, and still is being written about this document. Nowadays opinions seem to be divided into two groups, one of which accepts Polybius' date while the other would place the treaty in the fourth century with all the others which succeeded it. Let us first summarize the arguments presented in favour of a later date by its most able defender, Andreas Alföldi.[17]

1. Polybius dates the treaty with reference to the consulship of M. Horatius and Junius Brutus. Now the list of consuls for the first two centuries of the Republic was only drawn up in 304 B.C. There are many reasons for believing these consuls to be imaginary.
2. Antium and Terracina are situated on the frontiers of Campania and of Latium and could not have belonged to Rome in 509–508. The territory which belonged, at that time, to the future metropolis of the world, did not yet extend to the sea and Rome did not possess a navy of its own.

73

3. As shown by Aymard, [18] the second treaty quoted by Polybius is, in fact, an adaptation of the first. This would imply that the two documents were written within a few years of each other, but we know for certain that the second treaty was concluded soon after the middle of the fourth century. The date of the first treaty would, therefore, have been falsified by Fabius Pictor, who wished to carry the origins of Roman power back into the past, and thus misled Polybius.

Alföldi's chronological arguments have, to some extent, been refuted by Robert Werner.[19] The latter has pointed out that the treaty itself contained no mention of any consul or of any other form of dating. The same applies to the treaty between Philip V of Macedon and Hannibal, and to numerous other Greek ones. Cato is probably responsible for the date of 509, to which Polybius added a reference to Xerxes' expedition for the benefit of his Greek readers. As we depend, in either case, on the accuracy of the authors and of their sources of information, it is perhaps safer to attempt to date the treaty according to its historical content. Werner has tried to prove that this corresponds neither to the political situation of the sixth century, nor to that of the fourth, but to that of the fifth. Thus the Carthaginians could hardly have forbidden trade with Libya[20] before they had conquered the Tunisian hinterland. He argues that the Phoenician cities of Sicily remained autonomous allies of Carthage until the Battle of Himera. After this defeat they were forced to depend more closely on Carthage. He further states that the situation in Latium is that which prevailed before the conquest of the Volsci in about 460 B.C. The treaty could therefore be dated to about 470 B.C. Etruscan kings would have continued to reign in Rome till then,[21] so that Cato and Polybius would have been right in placing the treaty at the very origins of the Republic.

Toynbee[22] and Cassola both accept the Polybian date. The former has analysed what we know of Roman and Punic history from the last years of the sixth to the middle of the fourth century, and has shown that there were only two instances when Rome and Carthage could have made such an agreement. These are either at the end of the sixth and in the first years of the fifth century, or in the last quarter of the fifth and the first decade of the fourth, when Carthage was resuming the Sicilian offensive and the Romans were showing evidence of their power by overcoming the Volsci and conquering Veii. We believe, however, that Professor Toynbee's most valuable contribution to the problem, is his rejection of Aymard's statement that the second treaty consisted, in fact, in a series of amendments to the first. In this he was following Taubler[23] and Schachermeyer.[24] The lay-out of the two documents is, in fact, completely different. The first consists of two parts, each of which applies to one of the two contracting parties. The second is divided into three chapters, each of which deals with one particular subject. Schachermeyer has shown that this arrangement is in keeping with Greek diplomatic style, which the Carthaginians would have adopted in the fourth century. Furthermore, Polybius notes, concerning the first but not the second treaty, that it was drawn up in a very archaic form of Latin which even the best antiquarians, when he wrote, had difficulty in understanding.

Thus, it seems to us that those who defend the Polybian date are in a far stronger position than their opponents. Certainly there is nothing to authenticate the first Republican consuls, but their names do not appear in the text of the treaty. We do not, therefore, know in what relationship it stood to the Capitoline era, which is known definitely thanks to the custom of driving a nail into the temple wall annually. As has already been said, the Tarquins ruled not only in Rome, but also throughout Latium; the same applied under Lars Porsena's occupation of the city. Thus a treaty concluded either before or after the fall of the Tarquins would naturally have related to the whole Latin territory. On the other hand, although the Republican government ruled only in Rome, it doubtless considered itself heir to the Tarquinian lands in their entirety – hence the continual wars between Rome and the other peoples of Latium until 348. In this case, a treaty concluded with Republican Rome would certainly have had to recognize these claims, even though they would have borne no relation to reality. As far as Antium and Terracina are concerned, these cities were, in any case, cut off from the rest of Latium by the advance of the Volsci, a mountain people who descended to the plains after the fall of the Tarquins.

Werner's arguments in favour of a date as late as 475 do not, in

our opinion, stand up to close scrutiny. As has already been said –
and here we disagree with Professor Toynbee as well – the
restricted area in Africa could not have been the coast east of Cape
Porto Farina where Punic interests were minimal.[25] It is more
probable, as Polybius wrote, that the forbidden zone referred to
Byzacenia, Syrtica, and Tripolitania. It was not necessary for the
Carthaginians to be masters of the hinterland in order to forbid
trade, and in any case it seems most unlikely that they were able
to conquer the whole of Western Tunisia in the ten years which
followed the Battle of Himera, as suggested by Werner. This
scholar further proposes that the forbidden zone was Northern
Tunisia and the Algerian coast, but this is completely unacceptable
for the Carthaginians never succeeded in controlling the Tellians
of the Algerian Atlas, or in disciplining the wild Kroumirian
tribes. Thus, the Romano-Punic treaty could have been concluded
at any time after Carthage had obtained control of the ports of
Byzacenia and Tripolitania. Excavation at Hadrumetum, Lepcis,
and Sabratha, has shown that this took place gradually during the
sixth century and that by the fifth they were Punic trading
stations – all of which agrees well with what we know of Punic
intervention against Dorieus in about 520.

In connection with Sardinia, Werner's statement that Hasdrubal
was unable to gain control of the island, is in flat contradiction of
both textual[26] and archaeological evidence. Finally, in connection
with Sicily, it is paradoxical to talk of a closer dependence of
Soluntum, Panormus, and of the Elymians on Carthage after
Himera than before. Everything, on the contrary, seems to prove
that after Hamilcar's defeat, the Carthaginians lost interest in the
island, and were content with the occupation of Motya, which, in
any case, shows a marked decline.[27]

Finally, there remains the impossibility of there being a Romano-
Punic treaty so soon after Himera: from 480 to about 450, Carthage
lived in complete autarchy and received no imports whatsoever.
In the second half of the fifth century some contact with Egypt was
renewed, but nothing was imported from either Italy or Greece
until 400 B.C. Whatever the reasons for this break in trade relations,
whether it was voluntary or the result of circumstance, it nevertheless rules out any possibility of a detailed agreement allowing
the Romans to trade in Carthage, being drawn up at this time.

The Pyrgi discovery had not been made when Alföldi, Werner, and Toynbee wrote, and it is, of course, a very convincing argument in favour of the Polybian date. Thanks to it we know that, in about 500 B.C., a large Punic colony, which was politically most active, was settled some 38 miles from Rome. Caere, through the intermediary of her king, Thefarie Veliunas, was to all intents and purposes under Punic control; and Caere was also the Etruscan city which enjoyed the closest and most friendly relations with Rome. Even Alföldi himself admits that after the fall of the Tarquins, Caere (which was remarkably independent of the Tyrrhenian federation, politically) became Rome's chief ally and served as her intermediary with Greece and, of course, with Carthage. As Miss Sordi has shown[28] the Romano-Caerian agreement resulted, by the beginning of the fourth century, in what was, in fact, a federation.

If we admit the authenticity of the treaty and the accuracy of Polybius' dating, we are, nevertheless, left with one very important historical problem, namely: who was governing Rome in 509 B.C.? Was it Tarquin, Lars Porsena, or the Latin Republicans? No one seems to be able to tell, although the general consensus of opinion seems to favour the Etruscans who had either remained the masters or recovered mastery of the city. In this case the treaty belongs to the Etrusco-Punic series. There are some facts, however, which indicate that Carthage may well have come to an agreement with the Republican government, so as not to be on the wrong side of the revolution. The Etrusco-Punic *entente*, indeed, shows signs of weakening considerably around 500 B.C. There were no Etruscan troops fighting with Hamilcar at the Battle of Himera. Furthermore, Anaxilas of Rhegium, the Carthaginians' principal Greek ally, was on such bad terms with the Etruscans that he undertook the task of building a rampart across the isthmus of Skyllaion in order to prevent their attacking him.[29] On the other hand, the Etruscans were alone when, in the first years of the fifth century, they led a series of unsuccessful attacks on the Lipari Islands. A Latin inscription from Tarquinia even seems to indicate that a magistrate from this city led an expedition to Sicily.[30] It is also remarkable that the same magistrate had, at an earlier date, fought against Caere, the ally of Rome and Carthage. Finally, from the end of the sixth century, there is a sudden drop in the number of Etruscan imports in Carthage. All this cannot be explained as the result of the economic restrictions which followed upon Himera, since they antedate the battle by twenty years.

It would seem, therefore, that Aristodemus' victories and the defection of Latium had the most serious consequences both with regards to the unity of the Etruscan confederation, and to the Etrusco-Punic alliance. The realistic approach which characterized the Magonids, is found throughout Punic history. Over and over again, Carthage abandoned her friends when they were in difficulties and allied herself with the victors. The Carthaginians' excuse, in this case, was that the Etruscans did not present a united front, while their closest allies, the people of Caere, had themselves broken away from the federation and formed an *entente* with Rome. On the other hand, the Tyrrhenian federation was active on her own behalf in Sicily, regardless of Carthaginian interests there.[31]

It is possible that the hope of Persian help had something to do with the Carthaginians' casual disregard for the Etruscan alliance. The great Achaemenid kings considered themselves to be the overlords of all Phoenicians and backed those of Asia and Cyprus in their rivalry with the Greeks. Cambyses had, indeed, planned to overcome Carthage by force, but his successors were content with moral, and perhaps even political, superiority. According to Justin, Darius had sent Carthage an edict in which he forbade human sacrifice and recommended cremation of the dead in preference to inhumation (this last is most implausible). The Carthaginians received these injunctions respectfully but did not, for all that, comply with them. Ephorus and Diodorus state that Xerxes sent an embassy, consisting of important Phoenicians and Persians, to the Carthaginians and invited them to cause a diversion in Sicily while he led his expedition against Greece. As a result, an alliance was, apparently, concluded. Whatever the truth of this statement, Xerxes certainly showed interest in the extreme West, as is witnessed by his sending Sataspes on a voyage of exploration beyond the Straits of Gibraltar.

This, then was the situation at the beginning of the year 480 B.C., during which the fate of the Mediterranean world was to be decided. At first glance it would seem that a vast Triple Alliance had been formed, consisting of Asia, Africa, and of a large part of

Europe, which was preparing to crush the Greeks. When we look at it more closely, however, we realize that the alliance totally lacked the cohesion of modern coalitions. The Etruscans and Carthaginians were politically independent of each other and, whereas the former probably had no contact with the Great King, the latter had considerable difficulty in co-ordinating their troops with his. Furthermore, all Greeks were not enemies and each of the three powers had friends among them, whom they sought to protect. Nevertheless, the war which was about to break out stirred up the religious and ethnic hatred which had gradually arisen out of political and economic rivalry. The Hellenes, from Asia Minor to Gaul, united against the Barbarians, while the latter, consisting of Iranians and Semites, began to feel an ideological hatred for Hellenism.

6. THE GREEK VICTORIES

Simultaneously with Xerxes' arrival in Greece, Hamilcar set sail from Carthage with a formidable armada. Diodorus tells us that, to the Greeks, it seemed like an army of 300,000 enemy soldiers. In any case, it was certainly the greatest army ever to have landed in Sicily, and consisted of a Carthaginian minority, of Sardinians, of Corsicans, of Iberians from Spain, the Rousillon, and Liguria, and naturally of Libyans, while a Latin author, Frontinus, assures us that it even included Negroes. The cavalry was backed by chariots; and it had taken three years to gather together, and provide for the expedition.

The excuse for the expedition was a small incident in Sicilian politics: Theron of Agrigentum had just seized the throne of Terillus of Himera, the father-in-law of Anaxilas who had been Hamilcar's host. As Theron was the ally of Gelon, this action united the principal forces of Hellenistic Sicily.

The campaign had an inauspicious beginning when a storm deprived the Carthaginians of their horses and chariots The remaining troops were more than sufficient, however, to blockade Theron in Himera. Gelon came to the rescue of his ally. He had been able to recruit only 50,000 hoplites, but his superiority over Hamilcar lay in his 5,000 cavalry.

We do not know the course of the battle which took place, according to some, on the same day as that of Salamina and, according to others, on the same day as Thermopylae. Much to the surprise of the Greeks, Hamilcar did not fight even though he was renowned for his valour; he had to stay behind in the camp to fulfil his religious duties. The Greek cavalry proved to be the decisive element in the battle. They carried the Carthaginian camp by storm and Hamilcar committed ritual suicide. They then set fire to the ships which had been used to fortify the camp. The leaderless infantry broke rank and fled, and were either massacred or reduced to slavery. Gelon dedicated a tithe of the loot at Delphi, as is still testified by inscribed pedestals.

It was doubtless at about this time that the Massilians and other Phocaeans of the West began to turn their attention towards Spain Under the leadership of an Ionian exile, Heraclides of Mylasa, they won a brilliant naval victory at the foot of the sanctuary to Artemis which stood on the Cabo de la Náo.[32]

Five years later, the Etruscans must have regretted not having come to the assistance of the Carthaginians. Gelon did not long survive his victory, but his successor, Hieron, sent his fleet to the support of Cumae, which was again being besieged, and crushed the Tyrrhenian navy once and for all. The Persians had just been defeated in the East, and Hellenism was thus also victorious in the West.

Himera was the turning-point in Punic history. The Carthaginians did not allow themselves to be discouraged by the defeat; on the contrary it hardened their tenacious resolve. Contrarily to what was previously thought, it does not seem that the political régime altered. In fact, as we shall see, the aristocracy was not yet powerful enough to overthrow the monarchy. The new generation of Magonids abandoned the expansionist politics of their predecessors, and Carthage turned away from the outside world and retired within itself, thus becoming increasingly nationalist.

7. THE TYPE OF POWER WIELDED BY THE MAGONIDS

In all the Greek texts, Mago and his successors are given the title βασιλεύς. It is very probable that this is the translation of the Punic MLK (king), and not ŠFT (judge) as Gsell, and most modern writers, seem to think. We shall see, further on, that the suffetes were originally petty magistrates, and only became Punic heads-of-state at a much later date, and even then their power was civil and never military, however close or pressing might be the danger. Now the Magonids were, above all, military leaders. The Pyrgi discovery gives indirect confirmation of this translation which had already been suggested by Beloch. In the Phoenician version, Thefarie Veliunas is given the title MLK ʿL KSRY which can be rendered as 'reigning in Caere'. Further on we find the words L MLKY in a context which is not very clear, unfortunately, but in which Thefarie Veliunas gives the reasons for his gratitude to Astarte. There is a difference between the expression for 'reigning in' and that for 'king of' which normally describes legitimate rulers. In fact, Etruscologists agree in thinking that Veliunas was probably not a real king, or *lauchume* in Etruscan (Latinized to *lucumo*). He was, more likely, the sort of dictator whom the Greeks called 'tyrant' and the Etruscans themselves *zilch* or *zilath*. Indeed, at Pyrgi the word *zilacal* is found in the Etruscan inscriptions, in a place which corresponds to that of L MLKY in the Phoenician.

If the Carthaginians had been in the habit, at this period, of using the term ŠFT to describe their paramount leaders it is probable that they would have used it to translate *zilch*. As they did not, in fact, do this, and as they used an expression in which the root MLK is included, it would seem that this best conveyed to them the idea of supreme sovereignty.

The Greeks translated MLK by βασιλεύς rather than by τύραννος because the Magonids were appointed by established legal procedure; they were 'kings by right of law' as Diodorus says (XIII, 43, 5 and XIV, 34, 5). Herodotus (VII, 166) says that Hamilcar had been chosen as king because of his valour. We need not conclude from this that the kings were elected by the Assembly of the People or by the Gerontion from among the mass of citizens, but merely that the monarchy was not automatically transferred from father to son, and that the personal qualities of the possible candidates were taken into account. It seems, in fact, that Hamilcar himself belonged to the cadet branch of the dynasty even though the senior branch, descended from Hasdrubal, was represented by three heirs. The choice was always made within the dynasty, however.

Who, then, chose the king, and what was the power conferred upon him? Until recently it was generally thought that the electors were a political body such as the Assembly of the People or the Council of Elders. But it seems that the earlier custom prevailed and that the power of the monarchy was still religious rather than political. Contrary to what was to happen in the next century, the rulers were drawn from the same family – and this fact alone indicates that the family was believed to possess some supernatural qualities. The stories of Hamilcar and of Himilco are confirmation that the power they wielded was religious. Thanks to Herodotus' contemporary account, the first story is well known. During the battle of Himera, Hamilcar had remained in the camp in order to offer burnt sacrifices, rather than lead his army. He was a brave man, and would hardly have followed this rather inglorious line of conduct, if his religious duties had not been more important than his military ones. When he learnt of the defeat, the king threw himself into the flames. After Hamilcar's suicide, the Carthaginians consecrated a cult to him, and put up monuments to his memory in the capital and in each of the colonies. We have here another example of royal self-sacrifice, followed by hero-worship, which recalls exactly the story of Dido.

The Himilco episode has been recorded by Diodorus and explained by Maurin.[33] During the course of his campaigns, the Carthaginian king committed sacrilege after sacrilege: he destroyed the tomb of Theron at Agrigentum, and that of Gelon near Syracuse. His soldiers sacked a great many Greek temples and dragged from them those who had sought sanctuary there. Himilco, himself, set up his headquarters in the Temple of Zeus at Syracuse, thus desecrating it; and in addition, he allowed the Temple of Demeter and Kore in the suburb of Achradina to be pillaged. It does seem, however, that these outrages were caused neither by impiety, nor by excessive leniency of a leader with regard to his followers. They seem to have been caused, indeed, by conscious fanaticism and the desecration of the tombs of Gelon and Theron, seen in this light, is a just revenge against Hamilcar's principal opponents in 480, and the logical conclusion of a ritual which Himilco celebrated in memory of his exalted grandfather, and in which human sacrifice played a large part. Only a section of the Punic aristocracy accepted the possibility of syncretism in religion, hence the defiling of the Greek shrines. Himilco's behaviour, therefore, is that of an intolerant and fanatical high priest, who seeks to impose a dynastic religion so that his family may benefit from it.

This behaviour brought shattering retribution: an epidemic decimated the Carthaginian army, and the fleet which was besieging Syracuse was destroyed by fire. Himilco lost his head and, after negotiating in haste for shameful peace terms, he fled to Africa leaving his Iberian and Libyan mercenaries to the mercy of the Greeks. In Carthage, Himilco made public penance: he went round the city temples dressed in a slave's tunic, filthy and unkempt, and finally returned to his house where he committed suicide.

As we have seen, Justin tells us that Hasdrubal was appointed 'dictator' eleven times. The present author believes that this means that he was only in office for a certain period of time and once this had expired he had to be re-elected. There are examples of power being temporarily and periodically bestowed in other Mediterranean monarchies. In Egypt, the renewal of power took place during the Sed Festival. In Minoan Crete the ruler had to visit the sacred cave on Mount Ida every nine years, both to give an account of his actions and for reinvestiture. What is surprising, in Carthage, is the fact that the term of office should have been so short that it had to be renewed eleven times in one reign. No doubt the aristocracy took advantage of this to control and weaken royal power.

The Magonids were not only priest kings: they were also military commanders, and celebrated their victories with 'triumphs'. Hasdrubal was honoured in this way four times. It is probable that the ritual of this ceremony was derived from Egypt; in the only fragmentary description of it which has come down to us, the victor (in this case a fourth-century king) places his foot on the necks of the prisoners just as Pharaoh did.[34]

Generally speaking, it is probable that many of the characteristics of the Carthaginian monarchy were modelled on the Egyptian. The Pharaoh, taking part in some ceremony or other, is frequently represented on Punic engraved razors of the third century, and on carved stones. These are not mere copies of Egyptian objects: the royal ritual which they illustrate had been accepted and assimilated by the Carthaginians.

Even though the Punic monarchy was still theocratic to some

83

extent, in the sixth and fifth centuries B.C., it did not have anything remotely approaching the absolute authority of the Pharoahs of Egypt or the Great Kings of Persia. Diodorus calls the Magonids and their successors 'constitutional monarchs' (βασιλεῖς κατὰ νόμους). Contemporary sources confirm that they were not alone in representing the political community, and state that they were subject to legal jurisdiction. The contracting parties as listed in the Romano-Punic treaty of 509 are Carthaginians and Romans but there is nothing to indicate whether they are kings or magistrates. On the other hand, the treaty of 216 was concluded between Hannibal and his council on one hand and King Philip of Macedon on the other. The introduction to the Voyage of Hanno states that he undertook the journey at the request of the Carthaginians.

In much the same way, the king could not undertake a military campaign without the permission of the assemblies.[35]

The Magonid kings were the true heads of state, invested with full military, religious, and doubtless civil power. They could only use this power, however, with the permission of consultative assemblies, to which they had to report on the political situation. The most important of these assemblies was probably the Council of Elders, the first mention of which occurs towards the end of the fifth century (Diodorus XIV, 47, 1); the other was the People's Assembly.

It is quite impossible to say whether these were instituted at the time of the foundation of the city, or whether they were of more recent date. The legends of both Dido and of Malchus have been corrupted to such an extent, as we have seen, that we are unable to draw any conclusions from such political information as they contain. There is no Carthaginian equivalent for the Latin *senatus* or the Greek *gerousia, syncletos, synedrion, boule* etc. . . . Even in Roman times, the senate of Lepcis Magna was referred to by the circumlocution *addire 'lepqi*, 'the Great Ones of Lepcis'. There are, however, names for the various religious groupings, so that the present author believes that the political assembly was a fairly late development among the Phoenicians. It is probable that it evolved in Carthage owing to Greek and Etruscan influence, and as a result of economic and social growth. At the beginning of the first millennium, maritime trade was a royal monopoly and Hiram controlled that of Tyre in the same way that Solomon controlled that of Israel. By the fifth century, however, King Hanno could only set sail after a vote and decree of authorization.

The change must have taken place gradually. Pygmalion no longer enjoyed such a complete monopoly as Hiram. Then Carthage was founded and settled by various groups of immigrants from Tyre and elsewhere. Each group arrived with its own fleet and certainly did not put it at the local king's disposal without reserving the right to a share of the proceeds. From the seventh century onwards, therefore, the king had to take into account the wishes of a certain number of important shipowners before organizing an expedition. There were times, of course, when there was disagreement between the various parties, and the crews were called in to arbitrate in much the same way as in Homeric times, the people indicated, probably by acclamation, where their preference lay, although they did not have the right to make decisions.[36] This procedure still existed in Aristotle's time but obviously dated back to the days when the king's authority was only beginning to be contested.

The conditions of maritime trade in Antiquity were so uncertain as to preclude the establishment of a stable aristocracy in a city whose *raison d'être* was the sea. A series of shipwrecks could reduce even the largest fortune to nothing and only the community as a whole had sufficient reserves to fall back on in such an eventuality. It was from his position as administrator of these reserves that the king derived most of his power. The king's authority was further increased by Mago's military reforms, for the latter gave the army the shape it was to keep till the wars with Rome. It was almost entirely composed of barbarian mercenaries[37] but the framework of the army and the young noblemen who made up the contingent for the 'sacred battallion' must have felt personal esteem and affection for the king. The 'sacred battallion' was probably his personal bodyguard, like that of the kings of Sparta, and although we have no evidence for it before the fourth century (Diodorus XVI, 80, 4), it must have existed earlier.

Thus, although it was weakened by the encroaching power of the aristocracy, the Punic monarchy was still strong enough politically, at the beginning of the sixth century, to survive the crisis of 480. The monarchy only finally collapsed when, as a result of territorial conquest, the aristocracy had acquired the stability which landownership bestows.

8. Hanno the Navigator: the Conquest of the African Dominions

The defeat at Himera resulted in the complete political re-orientation of Carthage. She withdrew into herself and closed her markets to all imports wherever they might come from. In Sicily and Sardinia she maintained the *status quo* but with no attempt to extend her dominions. The garrison of Motya mouldered away on its island, where the buildings collapsed owing to lack of mainten-ance. The old allies of Carthage, the Elymians, were free to submit to Greek influence, and their coinage, which appears immediately after Himera, is evidence of their economic and cultural integra-tion into the Hellenistic world.[38] This is further attested by the Doric temple which they began building in their capital, probably around 430 B.C., and which was never completed owing to the Atheno-Syracusan war. In 456, Segesta sought to escape Syracusan hegemony by joining the Athenian alliance and Carthage did not exercise her veto even though Athens was planning to conquer Carthage once she had subjugated Syracuse. Here again we have evidence of the complete lack of interest which the Carthaginian rulers now felt concerning the affairs of the island which they had once coveted. The faithful vassal-city of Selinus showed a complete reversal of loyalties, accepted Syracusan hegemony, and began to follow an aggressive policy with regard to the Elymians. In the centre and western part of Sicily, from 461 onwards, an energetic leader named Ducetius encouraged the native Sicilians to revolt against the Hellenes. By 453 he had succeeded in uniting all the townships and forming a league of which he was the supreme civil and military commander; Syracuse and Agrigentum joined forces against him and were soundly beaten at Motyon. If a Cartha-ginian army had landed then, the Greeks could have been driven from the island; but Carthage did not stir. The Syracusans got their second wind and by 451 Ducetius had been so hounded and betrayed that he had no alternative but to cry for mercy at the altar of the agora of Syracuse.

This renunciation by the Magonids was to have extremely serious consequences as regards the cultural life of the Phoenicians in Sicily; for three-quarters of a century the Carthaginians did nothing and, as Hellenism was a vital and aggressive force, Phoenician civilization in the west of the island could not survive. When the Carthaginians returned to the island in 409, they came as destroyers and brought nothing constructive or positive.

The same stagnation must have affected Sardinia but we lack evidence here. Later monuments follow the traditions which the Carthaginians had brought at the end of the sixth and beginning of the fifth centuries, which seems to point to a break in relations.

In Carthage itself, the fifth-century tombs are so poor and insignificant that it was thought for a long time that they had not yet been discovered. Indeed, if we were to rely on the above evidence, we might well be forgiven for thinking that the 'Tyre of the West' had suffered a severe reversal which had sapped its vital strength.

Thucydides, however, states that in 415 Carthage had large amounts of gold and silver at her disposal (VI, 34). At one time Gsell considered that the fall of the Magonids from power was the immediate result of the Battle of Himera, and also the reason for Carthaginian withdrawal. We now know, thanks to Maurin's work, that the dynasty remained securely in power until 396. It would seem, therefore, that the new political situation was the result of the deliberate policy of one of the Magonids who can be identified with that Hanno, son of Hamilcar, to whose name Pompeius Trogus attached the curious epithet 'Sabellius', probably a corrupted version of the original title. It was doubtless this Hanno who was responsible for the two great Punic ventures from 480 onwards. One was the conquest of the African dominions; the other was the exploration of the Atlantic coast.

This complete reorientation must have caused disagreement within the dynastic family itself. Hanno's brother Gisco was exiled and withdrew to Selinus where he died. It was Gisco's son Hannibal, however, who was chosen as king, probably after Hanno's death, and who returned, in 410, to the aggressive policy of his grandfather Hamilcar.

Hanno's first task, probably begun immediately after Himera, was the conquest of further African territory. Pompeius Trogus wrote of it but unfortunately Justin did not consider that it merited

87

more than a line, doubtless because it did not afford enough scope
for rhetoric:

> War was waged against the Moors; they fought against the
> Numidians, and the Africans were forced to renounce their claim
> to the tribute they had been receiving for the foundation of
> Carthage.

Other than this brief sentence, all literary tradition can offer us
in the way of evidence is one line from the orator Dio Chrysostom,
who lived at the end of the first century A.D.:

> (Hanno) transformed the Carthaginians from Tyrians into
> Africans; thanks to him they lived in Africa rather than in
> Phoenicia, became very wealthy, acquired many markets, ports,
> and ships, and ruled on land and sea.

From this we can see that, in their concise reports, the two authors
have summarized the activities of Hanno on land and sea. Justin
gives the word 'Moors' its usual meaning, and his first words must
refer to the expedition along the Atlantic coast.

It is extremely difficult, not to say impossible, to establish the
extent of Hanno's conquests in present-day Tunisia. As we shall
see, the country was divided into districts ('RṢT; Latin, *pagi*;
Greek, χώραι) in the fourth century, of which we know fairly
exactly (see Map II, p. 179) the extent of the following:[39]

1. Pagus Muxsi lay to the north of the Medjerda valley, in the
   hinterland of Utica, and probably extended as far as the
   Algero-Tunisian frontier.
2. Great Plains comprised the middle Medjerda valley together
   with its northern tributaries, with Vaga (present-day Béja) as
   its capital.
3. Pagus Zeugei (the Zeugitania of the Imperial era) probably lay
   south-west of Carthage, between the Medjerda and Wadi
   Miliana, and included Mont Zaghouan, which may have
   derived its name from that of the *pagus*.
4. Pagus Gunzuzi, south of the preceding *pagus*, probably lay in
   the valley of Oued el Kebir.

5. Cap Bon was probably directly dependent on Carthage, but we do not know its Punic name.
6. Byzacenia lay to the south of the autonomous region of Hadrumetum, which was fairly extensive. It was circular in shape and had a circumference of 2000 *stadia* (Polybius, XII). This means a radius of 35 miles. It probably had Thysdrus (present-day El Jem) as its centre.
7. Pagus Thuscae, the land of Maktar, which was east of Hadrumetum and south of Pagus Gunzuzi, and which, in the middle of the second century, included no less than fifty towns.

At the time of the Punic Wars, these lands were defended by a ditch on their eastward side, and beyond them lay forts which were also under Carthaginian control: Sicca Veneria (now called Le Kef) was settled by Elymian colonists, and Theveste or Hecatompyle (present-day Tebessa) also came under this category. It is extremely doubtful whether they formed part of the Punic territory itself. For instance, between Sicca and Maktar lay all the lands of the Massyli Numidians, with Zama as their capital, which always seem to have been independent. On the other hand, between Sicca and Theveste there lived the powerful tribe of the Musulames, whom the Romans had great trouble in subjugating in the reign of Tiberius. Appian, in fact, tells us that the Carthaginians occupied isolated townships, beyond the frontier ditch, whence they took hostages (*Libyca*, 54).

Two at least of the *pagi* mentioned above seem to have been conquered at a later date than the others, for Masinissa was to claim the Great Plains and Thusca as having belonged to his ancestors. The earliest Punic remains to have been found at Maktar do not, in fact, antedate the second century B.C. at the earliest.

Magonid conquests, therefore, seem to have included only the northern part of the Tell to the east of the Mogod chain (the hinterland of Bizerta and Utica), the lower valleys of the Medjerda and Wadi Miliana as far as the Dorsale, the key position of the Zaghouan, Cap Bon, and the Sahelian coast in the direction of Sfax. Even then, the greater part of this last region had to be given over to the inhabitants of the Phoenician free cities – especially those of Hadrumetum – which had certainly contributed to a large extent towards the success of the conquest.

Although this territory, which can be included in its entirety within a line drawn between Bizerta and Sfax, may seem rather small to us, it includes, nevertheless, the greater part of the Tunisian fertile belt. Thanks to it, Carthage controlled a larger province than any other city on the Mediterranean seaboard.

We know nothing of the conditions under which the war was fought, or of its length. We may deduce that it was waged simultaneously from the many Carthaginian and allied strongholds along the coast, such as the quarry of El Haouaria on the northern tip of Cap Bon which the Carthaginians controlled from the end of the sixth century. The people of Hadrumetum poured oil upon the troubled waters around their city, so to speak, which explains why they were allowed to keep a large proportion of the territory they had pacified. In the present state of our knowledge, it is impossible to tell whether the other Phoenician cities of Byzacenia, Thapsus (which certainly existed by the middle of the fourth century), Lepcis Minor, Sullectum, or Acholla had been founded before the conquest. In the case of Acholla, the city seems to have been founded by Maltese colonists, doubtless called in by the Carthaginians. The origins of Tunis, which already existed in the fourth century, are shrouded in mystery. Further north it would seem that Bizerta as well as Utica had already been founded before the Magonid conquest; indeed, since Morel's excavations have shown how late was the development of Bône, the Hippo which Sallust mentions as being a Phoenician colony can only be identified with Bizerta. We do not know exactly where Theudalis stood, but it must have been situated in the hinterland not far from Bizerta, and may also have been a Phoenician colony.

These cities enjoyed an independence which was limited and defined by a treaty of alliance with Carthage. In addition to these, the Carthaginians founded several towns in their own territory which were granted a certain municipal autonomy against payment of a heavy tribute, at a late – but indeterminate – date. The greater part of the plain was divided up into the great properties which belonged to members of the aristocracy. In the immediate neighbourhood of Carthage and of Cap Bon, the natural resources of the land were exploited and we find tree plantations, vine-growing, and cattle-rearing especially. The effects of this agrarian transformation are immediately reflected in the archaeological material, for from now on storage jars for oil and wine are found, bearing the name of the owner on the shoulder.[40] The earliest of these jars belong to the fifth century B.C. They prove that the newly conquered lands were exploited immediately. The fields of the Medjerda and of the Wadi Miliana, and those of Byzacenia, were turned over primarily to the cultivation of wheat. The farming seems to have been undertaken by Libyan peasants, who had to hand over a third of the harvest at least, and quite often more. These peasants must, indeed, have lived under conditions which approached serfdom. At the beginning of the fourth century the first of a long series of revolts took place. These were to succeed one another until the fall of Carthage and were always crushed with great severity.

9. THE ATLANTIC EXPEDITIONS

Once his conquests on land had been completed, Hanno turned his attention to the second part of his programme. He aimed to obtain for Carthage the monopoly of all the resources which the West had to offer and which had been exploited by the Phoenicians as long as Tyre had remained powerful enough to direct operations.

In the fifth century B.C. the Mediterranean world turned its interest towards the Sahara and even towards West Africa.[41] Already at the end of the seventh century, the Pharaoh Necho had hired Phoenician crews who had circumnavigated the African continent in what was, without doubt, the most extraordinary maritime expedition before the great discoveries of the sixteenth century of our era.

Towards 470, Xerxes had given orders that the same feat should be performed in the opposite direction, beginning with the Pillars of Hercules. Although he knew that he would be impaled if he failed, Sataspes was becalmed in equatorial waters and had to turn back. At the same time, expeditions took place on land across the Sahara, which was not as dry as it is today, and which could be crossed with horses carrying water supplies. In Cyrenaica, Herodotus collected information concerning the desert and he seems to refer to the Hoggar mountains. He tells the tale of the Nasamonian youths (the native inhabitants of Southern Cyrenaica, around the oasis of Aujila) who reached Lake Chad or the Niger. In Fezzan was the famous kingdom of the Garamantes, the ancestors of the Tuareg, who survived throughout Antiquity and who greatly facilitated such expeditions. The Phoenicians of Tripolitania controlled the most important of the trans-Saharan routes and it was not long, doubtless, before they began to explore them themselves. They were probably followed by the Carthaginians as early as the end of the sixth century.

Those Phoenicians who had settled beyond the Pillars of Hercules, and those of Gades in particular, soon undertook expeditions along the Moroccan coast. From natives they had learnt of the existence of gold mines far off to the south, those of Guinea. The Negroes who exploited the mines brought the gold across the Mauretanian Sahara to the coast which was later to be called the Rio de Oro. Mediterranean merchants found here the basis for a profitable trade which was, in fact, flourishing in Herodotus' time. The historian describes the ritual which attended this trade. The sailors spread out their wares on the beach and returned to their ships. The Negroes then approached, laid their gold on the beach, and withdrew. The traders then returned and if they found a sufficient quantity of gold, they took it. If not they went back to their ships, and in this case the Negroes added more gold until they were satisfied. By the time that Herodotus was writing, the trade was already under the control of Carthaginians, who must have taken it over from the merchants of Gades.[42]

Apart from Lixus, the only other Phoenician site so far discovered along the Atlantic coast of Morocco is Mogador. Even though it lies 450 miles from the Straits of Gibraltar, the site was settled extremely early, by the middle of the seventh century, by Western Phoenicians probably from Gades. These settlers brought with them Attic amphorae, and a quantity of their own characteristic red-burnished wares. This first phase of occupation lasted until 500 B.C., after which the island was deserted. It was visited from time to time by passing ships – probably Carthaginian – and was finally permanently resettled at the very beginning of our era in the reign of Juba II. After a further period of desertion, the Romans moved in and even built a house with mosaics there in the fourth century A.D., when their holdings in Morocco had been reduced to the peninsula of Ceuta and the trading station of

Sala. In the present author's view, this whole extraordinary state of affairs can only be explained by the fact that the island was probably, throughout Antiquity, an outpost for the gold trade with Guinea.

As Carcopino has shown, it is this trade which is the explanation for the expedition which the Carthaginian king, Hanno, undertook along the Atlantic coast of Africa, and of which the account has come down to us.[43]

King Hanno was certainly a Magonid for, as we have seen, this family alone supplied Carthage with her kings at the period of the Voyage (sixth or fifth century). We know of two Hannos within the family: the father of the Hamilcar who was defeated at Himera, and the latter's son. It seems, although we cannot be categorical about this, that the first Hanno did not reign. Pliny (*Nat. Hist.*, V, 8) tells us that the Voyage took place at a time when the power of Carthage was at its height. Both Villard[44] and Harden[45] have concluded from this that it took place before the Battle of Himera. As we have seen, however, Carthage recovered extremely rapidly from the defeat, so that this argument is without foundation. On the contrary, Carthage would have been most unlikely to have sent her fleet beyond the Pillars of Hercules at a time when her navy was engaged not only in Sicilian, but also in Tyrrhenian and Spanish waters. The colonists whom Hanno settled on the Moroccan coast were, for the most part, Libyo-Phoenicians, that is Libyan subjects of Carthage. They could not have been recruited before the conquest of the African lands.

Pliny (II, 169) also tells us that Hanno's Voyage took place at almost the same time as that of Himilco northwards along the Atlantic coast. It happens that the son of the Hamilcar who was defeated at Himera, was called Himilco.

In his account of Hanno's reign, Justin tells us, as we have seen, of war against the Moors; this may well allude to an expedition beyond the pillars of Hercules. For his part, Dio Chrysostom, who is probably writing about the same king, mentions his naval victories.

Herodotus knew of the journey of Sataspes, which must have taken place around 470 B.C., but makes no mention of those of Hanno or Himilco. He was not very well informed as regards Carthaginian affairs, it is true, but he shows a lively interest in anything to do with exploration, particularly in connection with the African continent. This is one reason for dating the Voyage after 470, but it cannot be dated much later than 460: Hanno must have been at least 20 when he succeeded his father in 480 and he could only have accomplished such an exhausting journey when in his prime.

The evacuation of Mogador around 500 B.C. seems, to the present author, to be a *terminus post quem* for the Voyage. Indeed, if Mogador is to be equated with the island of Cerne, mentioned in the account of the Voyage, and which Hanno found to be deserted, then he must have sailed after it was abandoned by the Phoenicians of the West. As we shall see, however, it seems more probable that Cerne was situated farther south, on the Rio de Oro coast. If Mogador had been inhabited by Phoenicians, Hanno would doubtless have stopped off there and used it as a base. Whatever the identification for Cerne, therefore, the Voyage must have taken place after the island had been deserted.

That part of the account of the Voyage which deals with the Lixitae (see p. 96) would seem to provide us with a *terminus ante quem*. Carcopino has shown, in a most convincing manner, that the Lixitae were inhabitants of the valley of the Lucus, as it is still called, which flows into the sea at Larache in Southern Morocco. The conclusions drawn by Germain and by the present author (in connection with § VII) confirm this identification, as we shall see further on (see Appendix II, pp. 115–9 below). It is, in fact, obvious that the Negroes and Troglodytes already mentioned above did not live in the Larache area; we are dealing here, as we shall see, with a sentence borrowed from Herodotus which has, therefore, no possible historical value. The Lixitae have no town; the Lixus which Taradell's excavations have revealed, did not exist as yet. Nevertheless, the Carthaginians were warmly welcomed by the Lixitae, who are obviously Libyans. They certainly spoke the same language as they provided the Carthaginians with interpreters; they must also have been sailors as they knew the inhabitants of what is now Mauretania, and spoke their language.

This may seem somewhat disconcerting, but in fact it agrees fairly well with the results of Taradell's excavations. These have shown that, although traditionally older than Gades, Lixus was not built before the sixth century B.C. Villard has demonstrated that the Lixus pottery sequence follows on from that of Mogador, and that the former city was founded when the latter was abandoned.[46]

We can therefore agree with Taradell's suggestion that the Lixitae were not Phoenicians, but Phoenicianized Libyans. For centuries they welcomed the Phoenicians, accepted their religion, and learnt their language, but they clung to their pastoral economy and nomadic way of life, and finally decided to build a city only in the fifth century.

We can conclude, therefore, that Hanno's Voyage probably took place after the evacuation of Mogador and before the founding of Lixus, that is, in the first half of the fifth century. We might even go so far as to see some relationship between these events.

What, then, was the reason which led the Phoenicians to abandon Mogador, which they had occupied for a century and a half? If we accept the suggestion that the Lixitae were not Phoenicians, then the only big city which could have founded the Mogador trading station, is Gades. We have already seen, however, that in about 500 B.C. Gades was attacked by her autochthonous neighbours and had to ask for Carthaginian assistance. It was probably this crisis which resulted in Mogador being abandoned. The Carthaginians made the most of the situation and seized control of the profitable gold trade. Once they had settled their more pressing problems – such as the Sicilian Wars and the conquest of their hinterland – they set about converting a temporary holding into a permanent possession.

The Carthaginians found no difficulty in recruiting colonists in their newly acquired Tunisian lands. To these they may well have added emigrants from Asia Minor who had fled from their country when the Greeks reconquered it after the Median Wars.[47] Hanno had been commissioned to found a line of colonies so that they might be in complete control of the Atlantic coast. His first task was to establish friendly relations with the Lixitae, who had already been partly Phoenicianized as a result of the long years during which they had been in touch with Gades. He may or may not have left colonists there, but he certainly encouraged the Lixitae to build a town, and must have left architects and plans.

The account of the Voyage which has come down to us, has been preserved in a short Greek treatise and purports to be the

Greek translation of an inscription which was dedicated by Hanno himself in the Temple of Kronos at Carthage, by which the topheth is probably meant.

In answer to a Carthaginian decree, Hanno set sail with sixty ships, each manned by fifty oarsmen, and carrying altogether 30,000 men and women.[48] Their aim was to found colonies beyond the Pillars of Hercules, on the Atlantic coast of Morocco. In the first six paragraphs we have an account of how this mission was fulfilled. Six colonies were founded: Thymiaterion, Karikon Teichos (the Carian Wall), Gytte, Akra, Melitta, and Arambys. There have been innumerable suggestions as to their location, but none has so far been found. Furthermore, Hanno founded a shrine on Cape Soloeis (probably Cap Cantin) which he dedicated to the Phoenician god of the sea. This is still mentioned in the fourth century in the Greek sailing instructions which have come down to us under the title of the *Periplus* of Pseudo-Scylax.

It was then, after the founding of the colonies, that they reached the land of the Lixitae. Carcopino has shown that this entailed returning to the north, in order to prepare a second expedition in a land inhabited by their friends.

This second expedition is described in §§ VIII–XI. After sailing south along the desert coastline for two days, the Carthaginians reached an island called Cerne where they founded a settlement. Cerne was the same distance from the Pillars of Hercules as Carthage, and it should therefore lie in the Cap Juby area, but there is no island there. Polybius visited Cerne and situated it opposite the Anti Atlas range, in fact just about where Mogador stands. The name may well have been applied to several different outlandish places, however, just as Thule was in Antiquity, and the Indies (East and West) were in more recent times, depending on the date and the traveller. There are good reasons for placing Hanno's Cerne in the Rio de Oro, as Carcopino has suggested most convincingly. Not only is there an island just off the coast called Hern Island but, even more important, this part of the Saharan coast was the centre for the gold trade throughout the Middle Ages and until the discovery of South America. It was, after all, gold which the Carthaginians were seeking, and after them the Romans of late imperial times also sailed these difficult waters for the same reason.

From Cerne the Carthaginians sailed up a big river called the Chretes. This led to a lake in which were three islands. The mountains surrounding the lake were inhabited by savages who prevented them from disembarking. They carried out a reconnaissance of yet another river which was teeming with crocodiles and hippopotami, and then returned to Cerne.

The third expedition led the Carthaginians even farther afield. Hanno sailed along a coast which was inhabited by Negroes who fled at the sight of the ships. After twelve days they finally anchored at the foot of high mountains clad with trees whose wood was sweet-smelling and coloured. Further on lay an immense gulf and beyond this they reached a great bay, known as the Western Horn, which contained islands. It was surrounded by forests from which came strange music and it was lit by many fires at night. The Carthaginians then came to a volcano called the Chariot of the Gods and sailed past a plain covered with flowing lava. In yet another bay, the Southern Horn, lay an island inhabited by hairy creatures similar to men. The Carthaginians captured three females but had to kill them as they proved vicious. They brought their skins back to Carthage, however, where they were hung up in the temple of Tanit until the fall of the city, so Pliny tells us.

It would be useless, here, to embark on the endless discussion regarding the identification of the places visited by Hanno. It seems undeniable that the Carthaginian fleet sailed a long way in the direction of the Equator, despite the theory that the ships of ancient and of mediaeval times were not capable of sailing beyond Cap Juby. The present author has already argued against this theory, and it would seem that his arguments have been generally accepted.[49]

It is undeniable that the Carthaginians and the Romans visited the Canary Islands, which the Arabs were never able to reach, and this fact alone proves that their pilots were capable of overcoming the difficulties which daunted mediaeval sailors. The Carthaginians used oared galleys which enabled them to turn back northwards, after having entered equatorial waters, and sail along the Saharan coastline in spite of the trade-winds and the Canary Island currents. The Sahara generally was not nearly as dry as it is now and there was a sufficient fresh-water supply along the Mauretanian coast to render such a feat possible.

There are no Punic remains south of Mogador so that we have no material evidence in support of our case, but the very absence of such remains does not conflict with Hanno's account of his Voyage, for he expressly states that he only stopped off fairly briefly at Cerne, and it was only here that he made contact with the local population. Furthermore, archaeological investigation in the Sahara and in Mauretania has barely been undertaken. Finally, so far no trace of Punic remains has been found between Lixus and Mogador although they must exist here. Indeed, it is impossible to imagine the Carthaginians covering this distance of some 375 miles along a difficult coast without putting in to land. These ports of call have disappeared without leaving a trace, it is true, and this makes the oft-repeated discussions as to the whereabouts of Hanno's colonies, a complete waste of time. We cannot hope, therefore, to be more fortunate in this respect as regards the coast south of Mogador even if we do eventually succeed in discovering the exact whereabouts of Hanno's Cerne.

Although there can be no doubt that Hanno's Voyage did actually take place, we must not exaggerate the importance of its results. It was certainly a remarkable feat and was probably never repeated, but its practical contribution was limited. From the fact that no colonies of Hanno's have been found, we must deduce that they were soon swept away by the native population. It is also most improbable that another Carthaginian captain should have followed in Hanno's wake along the dangerous coast of West Africa. Cerne continued to be visited, however; the so-called *Periplus* of Pseudo-Scylax is a Greek work of the middle of the fourth century and mentions the island as the centre of an important trade with the 'Ethiopians'. There was no permanent settlement on the island, it seems, and the traders lived in tents. Scylax's Cerne was twelve days' sail from Gibraltar (approximately 750 miles) and must therefore have been to the south of Mogador, which lay only some 450 miles from the Straits. Scylax adds that navigation south of Cerne was impossible owing to shallow waters and seaweed. It was probably here that Carthage obtained the greater part of her gold supply, and this was certainly abundant at the end of the fifth century if we are to believe Thucydides.

Himilco's voyage in Northern Atlantic waters took place, as we have seen, at about the same time as Hanno's. The log-book was preserved and extracts from it survive in the *Ora Maritima* of Festus Avienus, a Roman nobleman of the fourth century A.D. This is a collection of the earliest records of maritime voyages which the author could find. It seems that the voyage in question lasted some four months and that Himilco reached the Oestrymnian islands. The ships were becalmed and encountered such perils as shallow waters, seaweed, fog, and sea monsters.

There are fairly numerous Punic remains in Portugal.[50] There is a funeral stele of the Imperial period in the Vigo Museum (Galicia), which contains the sign of Tanit combined with the crescent and sun – all of which are most certainly Punic and betray the influence of Carthaginian culture along the coast of Galicia. It is surprising, however, that these stelae are the most typically Carthaginian objects yet to be found throughout the whole peninsula. There must, therefore, have been a full-scale colonization of this area before the Barcids, who are mainly responsible for the exploitation of Eastern and Central Spain. It would seem that Himilco also founded colonies during the course of his voyage, but that his, as opposed to Hanno's Moroccan colonies, survived.

On the other hand, no Carthaginian or Phoenician remains have been found on the west coast of France, in Brittany, or in the British Isles.[51]

A mysterious sacred stone from Ireland is far too slender evidence for the visit of oriental traders. All Carthaginian coins from France have been found inland and bear witness, as we shall see, to Hannibal's contacts with the Gauls.

In the present state of our knowledge, therefore, it seems justifiable to identify the Oestrymnian islands with the islands or peninsulas of Galicia, which is a tin-producing area, while the Oestrymnian peninsula can be equated with the Spanish Finisterre. The view that the Phoenicians sailed the Cantabrian waters and ventured into the Bay of Biscay and even that they reached Northern Europe is widely held but, to our way of thinking, barely tenable. Cornish tin must have been carried to Gades along the famous western 'tin route' by local ships plying their trade from one harbour to the next.

The expeditions of Hanno and Himilco at any rate served to

affirm Carthaginian supremacy over the remainder of the Western Phoenicians. In principle the Straits of Gibraltar were closed to all foreign shipping and especially to the Greeks and Etruscans. The fleets of Antiquity were not in a position to enforce an effective blockade, it is true, but ships which did run this gauntlet knew that they could expect no mercy if they were caught. If, in addition, the Carthaginians controlled the ports of call immediately to the north and south on the western side of the Straits, such a violation of the blockade would have been impossible.

10. REVENGE IN SICILY

The gold of Guinea, the silver of Spain, and the tin of Galicia enabled the Carthaginians to develop a flourishing bronze industry around 400 B.C., and made it possible for the Magonids to fill their war coffers and prepare to avenge Himera.

It seems that the Sicilian come-back could have taken place earlier, in the third quarter of the fifth century. Why then was it delayed until 409 B.C.? This period in Carthaginian history is another which is most obscure. Hanno the Navigator was born in about 500 and it is unlikely that he lived much after 430. It does seem that his life and his reign continued for some time after his Voyage, however, if we are right in equating him with the Hanno mentioned in certain anecdotes which Pliny, Plutarch, and Aelianus recorded. This Hanno was supposed to have parrots and a tame lion, and his success as an animal-tamer no less than the propaganda value he drew from it, caused his compatriots to banish him. Gsell dismissed these tales as ridiculous, but although they may be childish, they are no more so than similar stories concerning other potentates such as Demetrius Poliorcetes or Antony the triumvir, for example. It is very easy to picture the old sea-dog taking a stroll through the main square of Carthage, with a parrot on his shoulder and his pet lion following at his heels.

In 410 the king of Carthage was Hannibal, grandson of the Hamilcar who was defeated at Himera, and son of the Gisco who had been exiled and had settled in Selinus. He was already an elderly man and we do not know how long he had already been reigning. The aggressive policy which he embarked upon in Sicily from 409 onwards was perfectly in keeping with his character.

Diodorus tells us that he felt an instinctive hatred for the Greeks. This is, however, in marked contrast to the policy which Carthage had hitherto followed.

It is worth recalling, in fact, that the political situation in Sicily between the years 460 and 410 had presented Carthage with innumerable opportunities for intervention had she been so disposed. All these opportunities had been allowed to pass. Between 459 and 450, the Siculi, led by Ducetius, had been in revolt; from 453 Carthage lost two of her allies who quarrelled and joined rival factions: the Elymians of Segesta were drawn into alliance with Athens, while the Greeks of Selinus joined the Syracusans, and in this way the conflict between Athens and Sparta had its repercussions on the very frontiers of the Greek World. Carthage remained impassive and only began to show signs of interest again in 416 when the quarrel between Segesta and Selinus had come to such a pitch that Athens tried to profit from the situation and annex Sicily to her empire. The Carthaginians cannot have ignored the fact that Alcibiades and his friends spoke freely and rashly of invading their city once they had completed the conquest of Sicily. Some of the Athenians, it is true, were more realistic in their approach. After Alcibiades' recall, an Athenian trireme sailed into the harbour of Carthage bearing an offer of alliance which was rejected. The Athenians also tried to form an alliance with the Etruscans. It would seem, therefore, that, in spite of his age, Hannibal was probably not on the throne between 415 and 409, but succeeded a king whose political outlook was as pacific as Hanno's. This ruler may well have been a descendant of the senior branch of the family, which was still extremely powerful, so Justin tells us, Hanno's contemporaries being another Hannibal, Hasdrubal, and Sapho. This hypothesis is all the more plausible when we consider that Hannibal, the son of an exile, can only have come to power as the result of a political upheaval. On the other hand, Diodorus tells us that in 409 public opinion in Carthage was very much divided and the king was only able to get his aggressive policy accepted after a long series of discussions, and even then he was obliged to concede a great many points to those who were not in favour of intervention.

It is possible, of course, that, in spite of his hatred of the Greeks, Hannibal was afraid of suffering the fate of his forebear. Syracuse had revealed how powerful she was, when she destroyed the Athenian armada. Prior to the successes of 410 and 409, it was possible to doubt Carthaginian superiority. The king may well have altered his outlook and let impetuosity get the better of caution.

In 410 the inhabitants of Segesta had no other course open to them but to appeal once more for Carthaginian assistance. The Athenian army had been annihilated in 413, Syracuse was all-powerful, and the inhabitants of Selinus were conducting a vigorous offensive against their rivals. The pacifist faction in Carthage was still strong enough to oblige the government to attempt to solve differences by diplomacy. Peace overtures were rejected by both Syracuse and Selinus, and Hannibal therefore led the few men he could call to arms at a moment's notice into Sicily. His main force consisted of 5,000 Libyans, to which he added some Oscan mercenaries who had previously served in the Athenian army. With this small force he was able to drive the inhabitants of Selinus from Elymian territory. The next year (409) his army was swelled by the arrival of mercenaries who had been recruited in Spain, and more Libyans. The king now commanded some 50,000 men and had powerful siege-engines as well. Selinus was besieged and fell in nine days. The population was brutally massacred and the town never recovered fully from this disaster. The huge temples, which had been the city's pride, were reduced to ruins, and when the few inhabitants who had been able to escape to Agrigentum, were granted permission to return, they merely built huts from the debris of destroyed buildings.

The Siculi had not forgotten Ducetius, and flocked to join the victor. Hannibal was able, then, to organize what amounted, in fact, to a Holy War against the Greeks. He marched on Himera in order to avenge his forebear. The Syracusans had been caught short by the attack on Selinus, but they now made an attempt to save the little city. A large part of their fleet was away in Greece, however, fighting for the Lacedaemonians. The only thing which Diocles, the leader of the relief force, was able to do, in the circumstances, was evacuate part of the population. Three thousand prisoners were tortured and slaughtered in a vast human sacrifice offered to the *manes* of Hamilcar.

The king returned in triumph to Carthage but during his

absence the commander of the Syracusan expeditionary force to Greece, Hermocrates, returned to Sicily and briefly reoccupied Himera and Selinus. Hannibal made this the excuse for rallying all the Carthaginians, at last, in a fight to the death. They sent an embassy to conclude the alliance with Athens which they had rejected a few years earlier (407).[52] If the Carthaginians had taken this step in 410 when, thanks to Alcibiades and Thrasybulus, the fortunes of war were smiling upon Athens, then it might have been of the first importance. In 407, however, Lysander had just taken command of the Spartan fleet and Athens was in the throes of civil war. Even the final recall of the Syracusan army could not change the course of the Peloponnesian War. The treaty did, however, have one result: two Ionian colonies in Sicily, Naxos and Catania, refused to join the anti-Punic coalition out of sympathy with Athens.

It is worth noting that, whereas Carthage was concluding an alliance with Athens, the Great King was giving his full support to the Spartans. The Phoenicians of Africa were no longer subject, even nominally, to Persian overlordship.

This new expedition was also entrusted to the leadership of Hannibal but, owing to his advanced age, he was assisted by his cousin Himilco, son of Hanno the Navigator.[53] This is the first time that military power was divided and we must deduce from this that the king was no longer in a fit state to assume the entire responsibility. The power remained within the dynasty, however, for Himilco was one of his closest relations. The army which was put at the disposal of the two commanders was of a considerable size; Diodorus writes of 120,000 men, which is obviously an exaggeration. In 409 the Carthaginians had been severely hampered by the superiority of the Syracusan navy, and to counteract this disadvantage they gathered together a fleet of 120 triremes.

After the fall of Selinus and Himera, Agrigentum was the most westerly of the Greek cities. Hannibal called upon her to join the Carthaginian alliance or at least to remain neutral. When she refused, he laid siege to the city.

The Greeks had become accustomed, by now, to the Carthaginian siege-engines, and when the latter brought towers up to the walls, they wrecked them. The Carthaginian army set about destroying the monumental mausolea which stood outside the walls, but this was done not only because of strategic necessity but also out of religious fanaticism. The monument to Theron, the tyrant who had fought at Himera in 480, fared particularly badly, but while it was in the course of destruction, the tomb was struck by lightning. Superstitious fear spread through the army and the priests saw in this incident the mark of divine disapproval, while the terrified sentinels thought they saw the ghost of the dead tyrant roaming at night and crying for vengeance.

An epidemic which broke out among the Carthaginians at this time was also ascribed to divine fury. King Hannibal was one of the first victims. Himilco immediately seized the supreme command, but without having the title of king. Diodorus only tells us that he was proclaimed king in 396; it is probable that the king could only be crowned in Carthage and that the ceremony had to be postponed until Himilco returned from Sicily. He did, however, celebrate certain purification rites: he cut a child's throat in honour of Ba'al Hammon and a quantity of animals were drowned and dedicated to the sea-god. These were expiation sacrifices which were supposed to put an end to the epidemic and must not be confused with the moloch.

Meanwhile, a strong relief force had left Syracuse, was successful in its first engagement with the Carthaginians, and managed to blockade them within their camp. Himilco would have been reduced to desperate straits had not his fleet succeeded in capturing a Greek supply convoy.

The Greeks were undisciplined and poorly led, and in this lay the salvation of the Punic army. The *stratēgoi* who had been elected to defend Agrigentum, had great difficulty in getting the mercenaries to obey them. These latter consisted mainly of Campanians, and since the Athenian expedition they had no scruples about changing sides. Many of the Agrigentine generals were accused of inefficiency and were massacred by the people. The mercenaries went over to the enemy or returned to their homes. The Agrigentines lost heart and decided to evacuate the city so that Himilco entered a dead town. Since he could take no prisoners, he had to be content with plundering the city, but his hatred of the Greeks did not prevent him from carefully collecting together a mass of works of art which were sent to Carthage.

Among these was the famous brazen bull in which Phalaris had roasted his enemies. Himilco then ordered his army to march on Gela where the Agrigentine refugees had gathered.

The Greeks were faced with complete destruction but they now made a successful move. A young Syracusan officer named Dionysius was elected *stratēgos* and vested with complete power. This, in fact, amounted to dictatorship, and was soon to become tyranny. The Dionysius régime has sinister connotations, largely due to Plato, who attempted to make the tyrant see his failings and whose trustfulness nearly cost him his freedom. From then on, Dionysius was held up as an example of the worst type of despot. There is no doubt that he was totally without moral scruples, but he was the most able of military commanders and statesmen and he was destined to save Western Hellenism.

Dionysius was unable, however, to prevent Himilco from capturing Gela and Camarina. The inhabitants of these cities fled in terror at the approach of the enemy and barely offered resistance. Both the Greek and the Punic commander had reason to be unsure of their armies and avoided a pitched battle. Nevertheless it would have been logical had Himilco followed up his successes by attacking Syracuse where confidence in Dionysius was on the ebb. The aristocratic party was openly accusing the latter of treason, in fact. Instead, the Carthaginian general stopped in his tracks and concluded peace. Diodorus tells us that this was because the epidemic still raged in spite of the sacrifices before Agrigentum, and the Carthaginian army was reduced to half its original number. We have no reason to reject this hypothesis but it is possible that politics also played a part in the decision. Warmington points out that the Peloponnesian War had just come to an end and Sparta was now mistress of Hellas and was in a position to undertake a crusade against the Barbarians of the West, who controlled the waters she had more than once attempted to sail. It is probable that politics at home also influenced Himilco's decision and he must have been anxious to return to Carthage and be officially installed as king. In any case, peace was concluded, whatever may have been the reason, and Carthage was granted sovereignty over the greater part of the island. In addition to the three original Phoenician cities of Motya, Panormus, and Soluntum, and the Elymian territory, the Carthaginians annexed the lands of the Sicani and the Greek city-states they had conquered. This annexation, though official, was nominal rather than actual. The Agrigentine and Selinuntine survivors were given permission to return to their cities but were made to pay tribute and were forbidden to build fortifications.

Himilco had every right to be proud of his success. Carthage now had an empire which was bigger than any she had possessed before, even in the glorious days of Hasdrubal and Hamilcar. It would seem that serious steps were taken to organize the administration of these lands: a governor must have been appointed and colonists from Africa settled in several places near Himera, one of which was Cephaloedium, which became known as Cape Melqart.[54] Coins bearing Punic inscriptions have been found in other cities such as Panormus, and indicate an attempt at revitalizing Punic culture.[55] The cult of Tanit was soon introduced in Panormus, the capital of the province. Nevertheless there was no attempt to uproot Hellenistic culture as is proved by the fact that the Agrigentines and Selinuntines were allowed to return to their cities. In fact, these new Carthaginian colonies were instrumental in introducing Hellenism in Africa, where it developed extremely rapidly.

Dionysius had also been obliged to recognize the freedom of the Greek cities outside the Punic *territorium*. He chose to disregard this part of the agreement and set about the systematic destruction of the ancient cities of Naxos, Catania, and Leontini, carrying their inhabitants off to Syracuse. Some of the Siculian cities were also obliged to acknowledge his suzerainty. A huge fortress was built in Syracuse itself, on the island of Ortygia, to ensure protection both against the citizens and against enemy attack. A second fort was built above the city at the Epipolès. Work in the boatyards went on apace and ships with four banks of oars – a new invention – were soon added to the triremes. Dionysius was also the first to use catapults and Syracuse became the most important military power in the Mediterranean.

These preparations lasted seven years, but Carthage took no steps to oppose them. The victorious army had brought home the plague from Sicily and the Carthaginian population was decimated. In 398 a Syracusan herald came to present them with an ultimatum. He demanded the liberation of Greek subjects under

Punic domination and read his message before the Council of Elders and then before the People's Assembly.

As soon as this formality had been completed, Dionysius marched westwards with an army of 80,000 men. He rapidly went through the Carthaginian provinces where the Greeks flocked to him, and where he massacred any of the Phoenicians whom he could lay hands on. His aim was Motya, the ancient stronghold which had been in Carthaginian hands since the beginning of the fifth century. The city was on an island and was easily defended. The population had rapidly fortified it and had used blocks from a ruined temple to build the enceinte. This proves that the attack was not unforeseen. Motya was besieged by land and sea for a vast Greek fleet, consisting of 200 galleys and 500 transport ships, had sailed up along the south coast of Sicily. Himilco came to the rescue, but his fleet was smaller and he was unable to land. Motya was taken by storm and razed to the ground.

By now Himilco had got together a large enough force and he landed at Panormus while Dionysius was laying waste the countryside. There then took place one of those complete reversals of situation which seem to be so frequent in Sicilian history. The Syracusan tyrant was obliged to relinquish all his conquests and fall back upon his capital, followed by Himilco, who stopped only to destroy Messina. The Greek fleet had been heavily defeated and the Siculi had flocked to join the Carthaginians. The fortifications of Syracuse were too massive for Himilco to take by storm, however, and he was always reluctant to stake everything on a throw. It was now that he committed the sacrilege which was generally believed to be the cause of his defeat. He set up his headquarters in the Temple of Zeus, ordered the tombs to be destroyed – among them the tomb of Gelon – and, especially, he allowed the Temple of Demeter and Persephone in the suburb of Achradina to be pillaged. These agrarian goddesses had been assimilated to ancient indigenous deities and were extremely popular not only with the Greeks, but also with the Siculi, and already among some of the Carthaginians. This desecration of the shrines must have troubled quite a proportion of the Carthaginian army, and when disasters followed rapidly upon it, they were naturally interpreted by all as divine punishment. The epidemic spread like wildfire, which is hardly surprising if we consider that the Carthaginian camp was situated in a marshy plain and that it was midsummer. Dionysius seized the opportunity to launch an attack simultaneously by land and sea. The camp withstood the attack but the fleet was largely destroyed. Himilco lost heart, opened secret negotiations, and fled with the Carthaginian citizens, leaving the Libyans and the mercenaries to the mercy of the Greeks (summer 396).

This was the disaster which caused the downfall of the Magonid dynasty. Maurin has shown that, according to public opinion, Himilco had forfeited the divine right of kingship which he had inherited. As we have already seen, the king himself believed this and sought to purge his sins by doing public penance before committing suicide.

It is certain that Himilco was lacking in the qualities necessary to make a military commander. He was prudent and over-cautious and on more than one occasion when he could have crushed a rash enemy once and for all, he allowed the opportunity to pass. It was, however, in the successes of his predecessors more than in his personal failure that the seed of the collapse of the regime lay. Monarchy by divine right in Carthage was a survival from the city's oriental heritage. The break in relations as a result of Himera, and the subsequent reorientation of policy, had transformed Carthage into a Western Mediterranean city with much more in common with her rivals, the neighbouring Greek cities, than with the Lebanese centres, which, from now on, began to decline. This reorientation of policy could not be confined to one field alone. There had to be a political, economic, social, and religious reorganization. The conquest of a state on the African mainland, the control of the extreme West, victories in Sicily – all these formed the basis for this new impetus. It is natural, therefore, that the end of the fifth century should witness a fundamental change, the first phase of which was marked by the disappearance of sacred kingship, for this institution is always incompatible with city organization.

II. Cultural and Economic Life

Carthage gained her political independence in the second half of the sixth century, thanks to the Magonids. Economic independence only came later as a result of the defeat at Himera on the one hand and of the collapse of Tyre on the other. This latter event followed upon the Persian reversal at Salamina. In the cultural field, however, the Magonids proved incapable of leading the necessary revolution and making the African city the centre of an autonomous civilization.

The period under discussion can be divided into three phases. The first comprises the years immediately before Himera; the second, those after the defeat during which the régime was one of national self-sufficiency and the whole economy of the country was reorientated; during the third phase the Carthaginians began to reap the benefits of this reorientation.

Archaeology is still our sole source of information: funerary goods and ex-votos from the topheth of Salammbo. There is no change here during the second half of the sixth century and the first twenty years of the fifth. Pottery is still the only local product which has survived to this day and it is poor in comparison with that from Greece: the Carthaginians seem to have been well aware of this, for they never sought to sell their wares on foreign markets. We find Punic pottery, therefore, only on sites which were inhabited by Carthaginians. In Tripolitania and Tunisia we find it in small quantities in the trading stations under immediate Carthaginian control, such as Lepcis Magna and Sabratha, from the end of the sixth century onwards; from the fifth century it appears at Motya, the Punic garrison town of Sicily, and in Sardinia. This pottery has not been found in Andalusia, in Morocco, or even in Algeria, while the wares excavated at Ibiza have not been sufficiently studied so far for it to be possible to decide whether they are sixth- and fifth-century vessels of local, of Phoenician, or of Punic manufacture.

The sole aim of the potters seems to have been improvement of production methods to keep pace with the demands of the increasing population. Better techniques were evolved and firing at higher temperatures produced stronger wares so that the shapes became less squat and heavy, but also, it must be admitted, less aesthetic. The decoration on the pot became simplified and consisted of purplish-brown bands of paint round the body.

Representative ceramic art was now at the height of its development but, since it was not exported, its popularity was due entirely to religious reasons. The Magonid period marks the zenith in the manufacture of pottery masks. These masks were used in religious ceremonies and represented grimacing demon faces which can be compared with those worn by the cult dancers of Artemis Orthia at Sparta, whose wrinkles and warts were derived from the half-human monsters of Assyria. They are in contrast to the peaceful protomae which are representations of human figures, half mask, half low-relief, at the end of a long neck. We have examples of bearded men with nose-rings, and especially of smiling women. The Egyptian prototype, which is to be found, wearing the klaft head-dress, on all Nilotic mummy-cases, is replaced, during the second half of the sixth century, by the elongated smiling face of contemporary Greek figurines. There are certain changes in style, following Greek fashion: the hair and the fillet that holds it in place, are covered with a veil, and later, on the eve of the Median Wars, the lips become pinched and the expression sullen, like that of the famous *core* of Antenor. These pottery masks and protomae are reproductions of *sacra* dedicated to the topheth deities: Ba'al Hammon and his consort who, from the fourth century onwards, was to become the head of the pantheon under the name of Tanit Pene Ba'al. These models spread from Carthage to all the satellite cities which had a topheth. At Motya, Italian excavators have just discovered a group consisting of female protomae in the Egyptian-izing style, and a superb wrinkled and grimacing mask, which had been placed above the urns containing the ashes of the victims of moloch sacrifice. This ceremony was supposed to regenerate the vital energy of the nation, as we have seen, and the masks must certainly have been placed beside the dead to keep life within the tomb. The demon-heads were doubtless copies of the masks for ritual dances which accompanied sacrifices, like those at Sparta. The protomae may well have been dedicated to Tanit, just as those of Delos were offered to her counterpart Hera during religious ceremonies which were intended to call down divine protection on young couples and make their marriage fruitful. This protection would be just as necessary in life after death which was believed to be a second life bestowed by Tanit.

The rise to power of the Magonids did not produce any change in the arrangement or in the type of grave goods in the topheth of Salammbo. There are still stelae, carved in El Haouaria sand-stone, above the urns. The stelae are better cut, however, and the decoration is more carefully executed and consists, in moulded cornices, of the representation of little chapels with a circle to mark the centre, and multiple doors to give an impression of depth. Two are shaped like thrones and inscribed with a dedication to Ba'al (that is, Ba'al Hammon) and, for the only time in the topheth, the name of the sacrifice: 'MLK' on one and 'MLKT' (feminine) on the other. Unfortunately, the composite sandstone on which these inscriptions were carved is not suitable for the purpose and these are the only examples.

During the first phase of Magonid power, manufactured goods from the tombs of Carthage still came mainly from the East via Etruria. Any change in the type of grave goods is due to political events and not to a change in the trading network. Corinth was on the decline and Athenian pottery was taking the place of Corinthian wares on the world market. Attic pottery still does not appear among the Greek wares in Carthage, however, and the latter continued to come from Corinth though in smaller quantities, even though they are now of poorer quality. Etruscan pottery is also rarer in proportion to the decline in relations between Carthage and Etruria. In fact, even as early as the last quarter of the century, there is not a single Italian pot or object in the tombs. Boucher Colozier dated this break in Etruscan imports to about 550 B.C., but a detailed study of the dating of the tombs would seem to indicate a date at the end of the century.[56]

The lack of luxury wares is counterbalanced by the appearance of terracotta figurines made in the ceramic workshops of the Greek islands. Enthroned ladies wearing the high *polos* head-dress come from Rhodes, the figures of *cores* standing to attention and holding a turtle-dove against the heart are Samian, and from Cyprus we have seated pregnant Mother-goddesses, wearing clinging robes and a curious head-dress consisting of a veil draped over horn-shapes which adorn their ears, and holding a dulcimer or a fan. Each of these, in its own way, is a fertility symbol, representing life and dedicated to such fertility goddesses as Athena at Rhodes, Hera at Samos, and probably Astarte in Cyprus. These figurines were supposed to help the dead to survive in the tomb.

To this list we must add Egyptian amulets, scarabs, and glazed unguent flasks shaped like monkeys or men wearing feathered head-dresses, and made at Naucratis until that city was sacked by Cambyses and the workshops were destroyed. Figurines of gods were made in Memphis, while perfume phials of variegated glass as well as chased jewellery probably came from Cyprus. It is worth noting, however, that gold and precious stones are found less and less during the course of the sixth century.

This consistency in the type of imports is an indication of the continuing dependence of Carthage on Tyre for manufactured goods, and the lack of home industries. Although Tyre had allowed or, more likely, had been compelled to allow Carthage to become politically independent, and had even entrusted her with some of her military obligations, nevertheless, the mother-city had preserved her commercial monopoly. In this way, the African city was, economically at least, part of the Persian Empire, and was excluded from the trading network of Athens and the West.

As we have seen, there was a break in relations between Carthage and the Eastern Mediterranean as a result of the defeats at Himera and Salamina. Tyrian fortunes were on the ebb and Carthage had to supply to her own needs. She took action in two different ways in order to avoid the decline in power which other Western Phoenician cities suffered at this time. The hinterland of Carthage was conquered and exploited and from now on produced the necessary food supplies for the city. A metalworking industry was organized to deal with the copper, tin, and silver from Spain and Portugal, and the gold from Guinea. The great voyages took place only around 460 and 450, however, and the grave goods in the tombs dating to the period immediately after Himera are incredibly poor. Only six ritual types of pottery are to be found with the dead, and a meagre selection of toilet articles made from a very poor alloy of copper which contained only an extremely small proportion of tin. Sometimes a mask or a female protome is to be found. This poverty seems to be universal and we must deduce from this that all available sources were being used in the struggle against the Libyans.

This period of poverty seems to have been fairly short, however, judging from the fact that there are only ninety tombs of this type. These were succeeded by a group of tombs which was formerly ascribed to the sixth century but which the present author has now shown to belong to the second half of the fifth century.[57] This group consists of tombs containing a large amount of local pottery, small toilet articles and bronze charms, Egyptian amulets, rather shoddy silver rings and a very few gold ones, and masks and protomae of terracotta. In fact, there is nothing in the general shape of the vessels, nor is there any foreign import which can be used as a criterion for the dating of this group. The only dating evidence we have is the context of the group within the cemetery (which is of doubtful validity), a few examples of figured pottery decoration, the shape and ornamentation of the little axe-like razors and the type of alloy used in their manufacture – all of which point to the later date. It is sad to think that, when Carthage cut herself off from the outside world, and more particularly the Greek world, she was unable to create a valid art form of her own. There was no change in either the shape or the decoration of the coarse wares; the masks and protomae became stereotyped, with wooden expressions, while the female portraits were reduced to caricatures. The only progress seems to be in the field of bronze casting. From now on there is a far great proportion of tin to copper and the alloy is less brittle. The razors can now be made much thinner and larger, and are decorated with patterns of dots forming stripes, zig-zags, and chevrons. During the last few years of the fifth century, the shape changes: one end becomes crescent-shaped while the tang or handle is now shaped like a bird's neck and head with a long, half-open beak.

This discouraging monotony in fifth-century grave goods is only relieved by one object: a superb jug or oenochoe of gilded bronze found by Père Delattre in a built tomb on the hill of Byrsa.[58] It stands $12\frac{1}{2}$ inches high, and has a pear-shaped body resting on a ring-base, a high flaring neck, and a trefoil rim. It has a strap handle consisting of three tubes laid side by side and soldered to two attachments which are fastened by rivets to the rim and body of the pot. The upper one is in the shape of the cow's head of Hathor with the solar disc flanked by two uraei, while the lower one is a Cypro-Phoenician palmette. The shape of the oenochoe is an ancient Greek one, however, which, together with Egyptian and Phoenician decoration and Rhodian technique, forms a composite whole which can only have been conceived by a Phoenician. There remains the problem of deciding whether he was a Phoenician from Tyre, from Cyprus, or from Carthage. No bronze vessel of this type or period has so far been found in the East, but there are several oenochoe with handles decorated with attachments in Egyptianizing style, from fourth-century Punic tombs, and it is likely that the Byrsa vessel is one of the first products of the new workshops founded in the fifth century by the Magonids, to enable Carthage to meet the demands which Tyre was no longer able to meet. The technique used and the masterful treatment of the decoration which was never equalled, may indicate that the craftsman who made the vessel came from the East; he may have come to Carthage in order to teach the Carthaginians his craft.

Another new industry was born in Magonid Carthage at this time for, with the conquest of Sardinia, green jasper became available. This stone is easy to work and carve and from now on Carthage manufactured the scarabs it had previously bought in Egypt. Both the shape and the decoration of the Egyptian scarabs were carefully and faithfully reproduced.

There is no important change during this period in the type of votive stelae in the topheth of Salammbo: chapels in the Egyptian style and thrones bearing representations of betyls are still being carved from the El Haouaria sandstone. The technique has improved, however, the decoration is executed with greater care, and the memorials are more imposing. Some new shapes make their appearance towards the end of the century, and anticipate the renaissance of the fourth century: the carved niches are now filled with geometric representations of idols or offerings, shaped like spindles or lozenges. Some of the stelae are shaped like horned or stepped altars on a high podium decorated with mouldings, with representations of funerary urns standing on them.

These memorials are, in effect, models of buildings, and give us some idea of what Carthage may have looked like architecturally at this period. Excavations have so far revealed only one important building from Magonid times. This is the temple of Motya, which has already been mentioned on several occasions. According to the plan, there was a large rectangular cella, divided into a central nave and two aisles just as a Christian church is. This resemblance is further emphasized by the fact that there is a sort of narthex built out into the rectangular sacred court, which may have been surrounded by a colonnade. The courtyard probably had several other buildings in it. One of the most remarkable architectural features of the elevation was the cornice decorated with moulding in Egyptian style. One rectangular capital has also been found; it had originally capped one of the piers in the entrance. To one side of the temple stood a pedestal which may once have supported three betyls. The British expedition led by Isserlin has discovered proof that, in its primitive state, the temple was first built in about 600. It is therefore Western Phoenician rather than Punic, since the Carthaginians only obtained control of Motya in about 550. They showed very little interest in the building, which was falling into ruin in 396 when parts of it were reused in the construction of the ramparts.[59]

The archaeological evidence confirms the historical analysis: the defeat in Sicily and the Punic Wars made it imperative for Carthage to change from a colonial to an autarchic system of administration. This reorganization is reflected in an initial lowering of the standard of living. It was only towards the end of the fifth century that conditions began to improve, almost certainly as a result of conquests in the extreme West which gave Carthage access to mineral deposits. Evidence of this improvement is to be found in the appearance of the bronze industry, the manufacture of small luxury goods, and the better quality of the ex-votos in the topheth. At this period the greater part of the income went into the war coffers, but quite a considerable proportion of it was transformed into coinage, which was first struck only in Sicily and used for the payment of mercenaries.[60] The Carthaginian community was still subject, therefore, in all spheres of activity, to rigid control. Public welfare was put before that of the individual, and the individual was soon to react against this state of affairs.

APPENDIX II

Concerning the authenticity of Hanno's Voyage.

The account of Hanno's Voyage is not only by far the most important source of information which has come down to us for the Magonid period, but it is also a document of the first importance for Carthaginian history in general. Germain, a classical scholar who has lived for some time in Morocco, has recently written an article dealing with the subject, the title of which is an indication of its length: 'Qu'est-ce que le Périple d'Hannon? Document, amplification littéraire ou faux intégral?' Before we can use this account, we must discuss in detail the arguments put forward in this article, which does not, so far, seem to have been studied in any detail.[61]

On philological grounds alone, Germain has been able to reach certain positive conclusions. The first seven paragraphs are written in normal Attic, whereas the remainder differ in that poetic expressions are used, and there are several words which are given different meanings from those they usually have, or are used ambiguously. Many of the terms used have meanings which they only acquired during the Hellenistic period. All this leads Germain to conclude that the text was either a wholesale invention of the so-called translator, or had, at least, been to a large extent corrupted by translation. This conclusion does seem to be very much open to discussion and the present author finds it especially hard to accept Germain's statement that several parts of the account are plagiarized from Herodotus. There seems to be only one sentence which might justify such a conclusion: in paragraph VII, Ethiopians and Troglodytes are said to live in the neighbourhood of Lixus. Before having read Germain's article, the present author had already suggested that this must be a later insertion.[62] All other similarities between Hanno's Voyage and Herodotus are those which it has in common with all accounts of journeys in the tropics: savages wearing animal-skins and speaking some unknown language, inpenetrable forests, etc. . . . Far more remarkable are the basic differences between Hanno's Voyage and Herodotus. Sataspes (Herodotus IV, 43) and the Nasamonians (II, 32) reached the steppes south of the Sahara which were then inhabited by Pygmies. Hanno, on the other hand, explored a land of jungles where he found Negroes or 'gorillas' who have frequently been identified with Negrillos. The behaviour of these creatures, as described by Hanno, is in complete contradiction of Herodotus' account of the Pygmies, who were supposed to be reasonably civilized, lived in villages, spoke some form of human language, wore clothes, and treated their prisoners decently. On the other hand, the more characteristic and the more remarkable details of the Voyage – forests from which music rises at night, flaming mountains, and rivers of fire etc. – are not to be found in Herodotus.

Germain's argument is based mainly on the language. The points he raises can easily be given another explanation, however. Like all Semites, the Carthaginians favoured a flowery style and an extensive use of imagery which it is always difficult for the European mind to understand, let alone translate. A recent example of this has been the mention of stars at the end of the dedicatory inscription in Phoenician from Pyrgi, the exact meaning of which still eludes the linguists of today. There is nothing surprising, therefore, in that the translator of the Voyage should have used poetical terms, should have varied the meanings of some words, and should, here and there, have inserted an expression from everyday speech which had not yet been accepted in Greek literature.

It is a pity that Germain has not investigated the interesting possibility that certain turns of phrase in the account of the Voyage might represent Semitic expressions. In this context it is worth raising one point at least: In his article (p. 226), Germain has remarked upon the fact that, although the name 'Hanno' was extremely common, and the one who took part in the Voyage was a member of a leading family, nevertheless, no details are vouchsafed as to his lineage and descent, and 'the forger's carelessness betrays him here'. It is unfortunate that, when he was studying Punic inscriptions, Germain examined only epitaphs or dedications. He failed to refer to official inscriptions. The patronymic of the first suffete has been omitted both in the dedicatory inscription in the Temple of Astarte and Tanit in the Lebanon (*R.E.S.*, I, 17), and in the Neo-Punic inscription, drawn up according to Carthaginian traditions, in the Temple of Thinissut (*C.R.A.I.*, 1908, p. 362). In the treaty of 216 between Hannibal and Philip of Macedon, whereas the Greek gave the name of his father, neither Hannibal, nor any of his Carthaginian co-signatories, gave any indication as to their descent. The so-called anomaly which Germain has picked upon is, therefore, an added proof of authenticity, contrary to what he supposed.

Germain has set out to prove that the account of the Voyage is a forgery or, failing this, that the Carthaginian original is barely recognizable in the work of an unconscientious adaptor. Yet the most convincing arguments in favour of its authenticity are drawn from literary history and, as he is a specialist in Greek literature, these ought to have led him to reach completely different conclusions.

Several Greek writers of fiction have described imaginary journeys to distant and more or less mythical lands. Hecataeus of Abdera and Euhemerus are the best-known authors in this class, and while Diodorus accepted their tales as gospel truth, Lucian wrote a parody of the genre in his *True History*. This class of literature has certain characteristics which are easy to recognize: mythological anecdotes are inserted within the framework of the story wherever possible (although even the most serious historians have no scruples in doing this), and descriptions of Barbarians are used as a pretext for philosophical or moral digressions (in this case following Plato's august example). There is absolutely no trace of mythological or religious parentheses in the account of Hanno's Voyage, even though the subject matter was perfectly adapted to such insertions. In paragraph XIV, for instance, fires and music in the forests at night are attributed by the Carthaginians to some supernatural agency and their sooth-sayers bid them leave the island. A Greek – and by this we do not necessarily mean a writer of fiction, but anyone with Herodotus' turn of mind – would have sought some explanation for this within the realms of mythology, and would have expounded at length on the subject. Hanno's silence betrays a completely different frame of mind. Germain suggests that the burning rivers of paragraph XVII are inspired by the streams of hell-fire which Plato mentions at the end of *Phaedo*. This is one of the many superficial comparisons which his article contains; but in any case, had he been a Greek, would not the author of the Voyage have seized this opportunity of invoking the gods of Hades?

There certainly are comparisons to be made between the *Sacred History* of Euhemerus and the account of the Voyage, though Germain has ignored these.[64] Euhemerus was careful to situate the fictitious inscription on which his theories are based, in a place where no epigraphist was likely to go and check his reading of it. There was nothing to prevent the postulated forger of the Voyage from doing likewise; he would then, doubtless, have begun his tale as follows: 'Having sailed beyond the Pillars of Hercules, we came upon a ruined temple in which we found the inscription which Hanno, king of the Carthaginians had set up on his return from his voyage'. In this way, the forger could have made himself known for, according to Germain's theory, he must have been, at one and the same time, the most untruthful and the most modest of Greeks.

In addition, the forger must have had supernatural powers for he invented a tale in which all the main points are borne out by the geography of tropical Africa. Germain suggests a date in the fourth century for the greater part of the 'forgery'.[65] If Hanno had not made his Voyage, then no one in the Mediterranean basin could have had first-hand knowledge of the tropical forests of Africa at this period. It was only towards the beginning of our era that men sent by King Juba brought back some confused accounts of the great rivers and forests of this part of the world.[66] As we have seen, neither Sataspes nor the Nasamonian explorers went further than the savannah of the southern Sahara. The account of the journey undertaken by Necho's Phoenicians appeared in an incredibly dry Greek version which contained no descriptions of the coasts they had sailed along at all. The forger would have had to rely entirely on his own imagination, and it would be remarkable indeed if he had succeeded, as he has, in avoiding any mistake.

Notes and References

1. The word MLK means 'king' in Semitic languages. It can be applied to gods but in Hebrew it is also a proper name (1 Chronicles viii. 35). There is one example of its being used in this way at Carthage but epigraphists think that it is then an abbreviation of a longer name such as MLKḤLṢ which means the 'king (i.e. the god) has succoured'. Cf. G. Halff, 'L'onomastique punique de Carthage', Karthago, XII (1965), p. 121.

2. Paulus Orosius, a fifth-century writer, also mentions him and makes him a contemporary of Cyrus'. He has obviously, however, culled the information from Pompeius Trogus.

3. Gilbert Charles Picard, Les Religions de l'Afrique Antique, Paris 1954, p. 47.

4. The Elymians probably came from Asia in the second millennium B.C. and had established their capital at Segesta.

5. Justin's information concerning Mago is divided into two sentences – the last of Bk. XVIII and the first of Bk. XIX. In his Struttura e metodo dell'Epitome di Giustino, pp. 82–4, L. Ferrero suggests that Pompeius Trogus told the story of Mago in the part of his work which corresponded with Justin's Bk. XVIII. The present author holds a different view, in opposition to that held by Ferrero and Maurin ('Himilcon le Magonide, crises et mutations à Carthage au début IVᵉ siecle av. J. C.', Semitica, XII, 1962 Bibliography, p. 39).
He believes that Justin's two sentences are not equivalent: in Bk. XVIII Mago extends the empire built up by Malchus, while in

Bk. XIX he is the creator (*primus omnium*) of the army and empire of Carthage. The present author believes that Pompeius Trogus had brought together all the legends on the origins of Carthage in his equivalent to Bk. XVIII. The purely historical section begins with Bk. XIX and the history of the Magonids. The last sentence of Bk. XVIII would have been inserted by the compiler, who was unaware that he would be contradicting it in the next sentence, as a link with Bk. XIX.

6. M. Taradell, *Marruecos Punicos*, pp. 197–208, including a bibliography; and P. Cintas, *Expansion Carthaginoise au Maroc*, p. 45 ff.

7. See G. Garbini, in Bibliography.

8. There is only one stele of this type which is clearly an import; see G. Pesce, *Sardegna Punica*, fig. 83.

9. M. Astruc, 'Traditions funéraires de Carthage', *Cahiers de Byrsa*, VI (1957), pp. 29–58.

10. Concerning Soluntum, see V. Tusa, 'La questione di Solunto e la dea feminile seduta', *Karthago*, XII (1965), pp. 3–14. Only the Hellenistic city of Soluntum, rebuilt from the fourth century onwards, has so far been discovered. The statue of a seated goddess is evidence for the existence of an earlier Phoenician settlement which might have been on a site known as 'Cannita', where anthropomorphic sarcophagi, of a type unknown in Carthage, have been found.

11. P. Cintas, 'Le sanctuaire punique de Sousse', *Revue Africaine*, 1947, pp. 1–82; and L. Foucher, *Hadrumetum*, 1964, p. 34 ff.

12. *AJA*, 69 (1965).

13. Thucydides (I, 13) and Pausanias (X, 8, 6–7 and 18, 7) allude to a naval victory which the Greeks of Massalia won over the Carthaginians. Their dating of this event is most involved and, in one case, manifestly wrong (the linking of this victory with the founding of Marseilles). They were perhaps referring to the Battle of Artemision, which we shall be discussing further on.

14. G. Vuillemot, *Reconnaissance aux échelles puniques d'Oranie*, autumn 1965.

15. G. Vallet, *Rhegion et Zancle*, p. 356 ff.

16. A. Alföldi, *Rome and the Early Latins*, pp. 56–84.

17. *Rome and the Early Latins*, 1965, pp. 345–55; and see also the exhaustive bibliography on the subject collected by F. Cassola, *I gruppi politici romani nel III secolo*, 1962, p. 14 ff.

18. A. Aymard, *Revue des Etudes Anciennes*, 59 (1957), p. 277 ff.

19. *Der Beginn des Romischen Republik*, 1963, pp. 300–40.

20. Werner identifies the 'Fair Promontory' with Cape Porto Farina, which did, indeed, bear the name of Promontorium Pulchri in Antiquity. He suggests that the forbidden zone extended to the east of this Cape. This opinion, which conflicts with that of Polybius, is not new (cf. S. Gsell, *H.A.A.N.*, I, p. 458) but does not seem, to us, to be tenable. The Carthaginians never possessed anything other than small ports-of-call along the Tunisian, Constantinian, and Algerian coasts, whose contribution to trade was minimal.

21. This opinion is now shared by a great many historians of the early years of Rome. Cf. R. Bloch, 'Rome de 509 à 475 environ', in *REL*, XXXVII (1959), pp. 118–31.

22. A. J. Toynbee, *Hannibal's Legacy*, I, 1965, p. 526 ff.

23. *Imperium Romanum*, I, *Die Staatsvertrage und verträgenhältnisse*, 1913, pp. 262–3.

24. 'Die romisch-punischen verträge', *Rheinisches Museum*, 79 (1930), pp. 350–70.

25. J. P. Morel gave an account of his recent excavations at Hippo to the Comité des Travaux Historiques on 20 December 1965. He showed then that Hippo Regius (Bône or Annaba) remained unimportant until the establishment of the Numidian kingdom in the second century B.C. On the other hand, Vuillemot (op. cit. p. 318 ff.) has shown that the Carthaginians sailed to the Western Algerian and Moroccan coasts by way of Spain and the Balearic Islands, as there was a strong current which made westerly navigation along the Algerian coasts difficult.

26. Werner bases his argument on a sentence of Justin's which follows the account of Hasdrubal's death: *hostibus quoque creuere animi, ueluti cum duce uires Poenorum decidissent*. But the continuation of the text shows that this applies to the Sicilian Greeks and not to the Sardinians.

27. The great temple fell into ruin during the fifth century and the stones were re-used in the building of the fortifications in about 400 B.C. (V. Tusa, *Mozia*, I, p. 39). The meagre offerings in the topheth also reflect the poverty of the garrison.

28. M. Sordi, *I Rapporti Romano-Ceriti*, Rome 1960.

29. Strabo, VI, I, 15; Dunbabin, *Western Greeks*, p. 395; G. Vallet, *Rhegion* p. 368. The latter thinks the episode took place after Himera, when Anaxilas was obliged to bring himself into line, politically, with Hieron. He believes, wrongly however, that the Etrusco-Punic alliance lasted until 480.

30. J. Heurgon, *Mélanges de l'Ecole Française de Rome*, LXIII (1951), p. 129 ff.

31. It may well be at this time that Etruria and Carthage found themselves rivals for the possession of a mysterious island in the Atlantic Ocean – perhaps Madeira? Diodorus tells us of the incident (V, 19, 20). Cf. S. Gsell, *H.A.A.N.*, I, p. 520.

32. The date of this event is uncertain. The question is discussed by F. Villard, *La céramique grecque de Marseille*, p. 85 ff. The Battle of Artemision certainly took place after 495, as Heraclides of Mylasa was still fighting in Ionia then. We disagree with Villard's opinion that it took place before Himera: the Carthaginians would not have been able to levy troops for that battle from the Rousillon and Liguria if they had just been defeated by the Marseillais. The opposite must be true and the news of Himera and the resultant weakening of the Punic navy probably encouraged the latter to take up arms. They may even have entered into some sort of an agreement with Gelon and Hieron.

33. L. Maurin, op. cit. p. 25 ff.

34. Polyaenus' *Stratēgēmata*, V, 11.

35. This is probably how Diodorus XIII, 43, 5 ought to be interpreted, for although Hannibal is already king, he is elected *stratēgos* in 410 so as to be able to lead the Sicilian expedition. For a further discussion of this problem cf. Maurin, op. cit. pp. 16–17.

36. In an article which only appeared after this section had been written, W. Seston in *Revue Historique*, 1967, p. 277 ff. has maintained that popular assemblies, similar to those in Greek and Italian cities, never took place in Carthage. The people merely expressed their opinions in gatherings by the city gates. Seston finds evidence of an analogous situation in the Bible

and believes that such gatherings are characteristic of Semitic society. We are not of this opinion as regards the Barcid period when, as we shall see, Carthage really did have a democratic government, with an Assembly which met in the agora. Under the Magonids the situation may well have been similar to that described by Seston. We believe, nevertheless, that even at this period the sailors exercised a certain amount of power in the city, and this would explain why the place of assembly should have been near the harbour, as it was in most maritime cities.

37. S. Gsell, *H.A.A.N.*, II, p. 344. Gsell thinks that the army had previously consisted of Carthaginian citizens. This he deduces from the story of Malchus, but it is as inadmissible as all the other 'historical' information which Justin gives us in this connection. At the beginning of the sixth century, Carthage was far less densely populated than it was to become later. Furthermore, it was necessary to garrison the city, which was constantly threatened by Libyan attack.

38. B. V. Head, *Historia Numorum*, pp. 164–66.

39. G. Ch. Picard, 'L'administration territoriale de Carthage', *Mélanges A. Piganiol* Paris 1966 – see below. One of the main difficulties in trying to establish the probable line of the Punico-Numidian frontier was the identification of the Pagus Thuscae with the Maktar area (see also *C.R.A.I.* 1963, pp. 121–130). Gsell thought this area lay round Thugga and Camps placed it in the Kroumirian region but in either case this would mean extending Carthaginian territory to somewhere near the Algero-Tunisian frontier. The lands of the Massyli would thus be completely surrounded by Punic dominions in a way which is quite incomprehensible. We can now affirm that, at the time of its maximum expansion, and if we exclude isolated outposts beyond the frontier, the Carthaginian territory consisted of the Roman republican province of Africa with the addition of only the two *pagi* of the Great Plains and of Thusca.

40. C. Picard, *Karthago*, XII (1965), pp. 21–2

41. The problem of the relations between Carthage and black Africa will only be solved by archaeological discoveries south of the Sahara. Since 1944 Bernard Fagg has discovered the Nok culture in Northern Nigeria, the manifestations of a Negro race which knew metallurgy and terracotta sculpture. The dates proposed for the appearance of this culture vary, according to the author, from 900 B.C. to 250 B.C.; it is generally admitted that it may have gone on until the end of the first century A.D. and perhaps even until the end of the second century. It is thus contemporary with Carthage. Even though specialists are loath to admit that the Nok culture came under the influence of the Western Mediterranean, it must be admitted that it is strange that the difficult and rare technique of terracotta sculpture should have flourished simultaneously both north and south of the Sahara, and should then have disappeared from both areas, without there existing some link between them. Furthermore, the Ife culture, which is also Nigerian, and which William Fagg believes to be derived from the Nok culture, used the *cire-perdue* process of bronze casting. According to Elsy Leuzinger (*Africa: the Art of the Negro People*, Art of the World Series. London 1960, p. 42) this technique would have reached Nigeria by two routes: on the one hand from the Upper Nile through the Sudan, and on the other hand across the Sahara. The existence of this second route would be proved, according to the same author, by the presence, in the art of the

Ife culture, of Sardinian and Etruscan motifs. If this is so, then Carthage was certainly an intermediary.

See also Eliot Elisofon and William Fagg, *The Sculpture of Africa*, London 1958, p. 58; William Fagg and Margaret Plass, *African Sculpture*, London 1964, p. 9; and J. Maquet, *Les Civilisations Noires*, 1962, pp. 194–6.

42. We do not agree with the following views, expressed by J. Villard in *Bull. d'Arch. Marocaine*, IV (1960), p. 20:
   (a) that this trade took place in Morocco (Herodotus only says 'beyond the Pillars of Hercules');
   (b) that we have here an echo of what things were like before the cities were founded;
   (c) that the traders were Western Phoenicians and not Carthaginians' Herodotus obtained his information from the Cyrenians, who had themselves obtained it from the Carthaginians.

43. J. Carcopino, *Maroc Antique*, p. 108.

44. J. Villard, op. cit., p. 23, n. 2.

45. D. B. Harden, *Antiquity*, XXII (1948), p. 142.

46. Op. cit., p. 15.

47. The name of one of the colonies founded by Hanno suggests this. It was called Karikon Teichos, 'the Wall of the Carians', and may have been intended for refugees who had had to leave Caria after the Athenian victory at Eurymedon in 468. The Carians had been in the habit of fighting in Phoenician armies for some considerable time: Athaliah had Carian mercenaries (2 Kings xi. 4: mistranslated 'captains' in A.V.; cf. Ecole Biblique translation).

48. M. Euzennat, 'Héritage punique et influences gréco-romaines au Maroc'. *Le Rayonnement des Civilisations Grecques et Romaines* (Actes du VIIIe Congrès International d'Archéologie Classique, Paris 1963), p. 261 ff.
   Here the problem of Hanno's colonies is discussed. Paradoxically, whereas no Punic remains have been found on the Moroccan coast, sites in the interior have produced traces of Punic civilization going back to the third century at least, and probably as early as the fifth. Volubilis, for example, had suffetes from the third century and must have followed Carthage in its constitutional evolution, just as Gades did. Banasa is another example, cf. A. Luquet, *Bull. Arch. Maroc.*, V (1964), p. 116 ff. Perhaps Hanno's colonists were carried off into the interior by the Moors.

49. *Vie Quotidienne à Carthage*, 2nd edition, pp. 230–1; and *Daily Life in Carthage*, London 1961, p. 228 ff.

50. A record of these has been drawn up in an unpublished monograph at the University of Coïmbra, under the direction of Professor Bairrão Oleiro.

51. A gold stater from Cyrene was found, a few years ago, on the coast of Brittany. It has been published by J. Bousquet in *Gallia*, XIX, 2 (1961), pp. 351–2. He believes that it was brought there by a merchant from Marseilles, but it could just as easily have been brought by a Carthaginian ship.

52. D. D. Meritt, *Athens and Carthage*. Harvard Studies in Classical Philology, Suppl. Vol. I (1940), pp. 247–53. A decree of the *boulē* of Athens mentions Hannibal and Himilco.

53. L. Maurin, op. cit., p. 13, n. 2, does not think that Himilco can have been the son of Hanno the Navigator (or the Sabellian) because of the difference between his age and Hannibal's. There is nothing extraordinary, however,

in that there should be an age difference of twenty years and more between first cousins. Hanno the Navigator was in his prime in 450 and his son may well have been born then.

54. Coins inscribed with RŠ MLQRT are generally ascribed to this town; cf. B. V. Head, *Historia Numorum*, 2nd ed. Oxford 1911, p. 136.

55. B. V. Head, op. cit., p. 161 ff.

56. Cf. *Karthago*, XII (1965), pp. 24 and 25.

57. Cf. *Karthago*, XII, pp. 17–27.

58. C. Picard, 'Les oenochoes de bronze de Carthage', *Rev. Arch.*, 1959, pp. 29–32.

59. J. I. S. Whitaker, *Motya*, pp. 131 and 202 ff.; J. Isserlin, and others, *Motya 1955*, p. 12 ff.; and V. Tusa, *Mozia*, I, pp. 21–60.

60. S. Gsell, *H.A.A.N.*, II, pp. 324–5.

61. *Hesperis*, 1957/2, pp. 205–48. Although Germain's article has had few repercussions outside France, both Maurin (op. cit., p. 21, n. 3) and Villard ('Céramique Grecque du Maroc' in *B.A.M.*, LV (1960), p. 23, n. 2) have referred to it in favourable terms.

62. *Vie Quotidienne à Carthage*, p. 234; and *Daily Life in Carthage*, London 1961, p. 232.

63. S. Gsell thinks that the Carthaginians, who had come across monkeys in North Africa, would have recognized the anthropoids for what they were. This does not necessarily follow, however, and there is a world of difference between a Barbary ape and a gorilla.

64. These comparisons are so striking that they suggest the possibility that Euhemerus got the idea for his book from reading the Voyage.

65. The account is first mentioned in the *De mirabilibus auscultationibus* which was wrongly attributed to Aristotle but which was written by a contemporary of Agathocles of Syracuse.

66. The present author still holds this opinion in spite of the arguments against it by J. Desanges, *Catalogue des Tribus Africaines de l'Antiquité Classique*, Dakar 1960.

3

Carthage Under the Oligarchy
396–263 B.C.

B Y THE end of the fourth century, Carthage appears as we
normally like to imagine her: she has become a sort of Venice
of the Ancients, an aristocratic republic, reserved and well-
ordered, in which the individual is subject to laws administered by
the well disciplined and austere rich. Aristotle described this state
of affairs in about 340, and it met with his approval. From his
description it is evident that this period was in marked contrast not
only to that which preceded it but also to that which followed upon
it, and it is extremely difficult for the modern historian, once he
has grasped this fact, to understand how it can have come about.

1. TRANSITION AND REVOLUTION: 396–373

Upheavals and changes have made the first quarter of the fourth
century extremely confused. By summarizing the events which
took place at this time, however, it may be possible to draw some
conclusions.

Upon the death of Himilco, the Carthaginians chose a new king
called Mago. This king's first task was the quelling of a violent
revolt of the Libyans. Thousands of rebels streamed down from
the mountains and invaded Punic territory, carrying the serfs of
the countryside along with them. The Carthaginians were obliged
to withdraw within their walls and were besieged. Tunis was
occupied by the enemy and refugees thronged into Carthage. An
epidemic broke out in the crowded city and laid it waste. The
Libyans, however, lacked cohesion. Diodorus tells us that there
were 200,000 of them and they soon began to suffer from famine,
some of their leaders were bribed off, and they gradually broke up
and returned to their homes.

Mago was finally free to think of revenge in Sicily. Dionysius was already finding the island too small to contain his ambition and was attempting to get control of the straits prior to moving across into Italy. The Siculi of Etna and the inhabitants of Rhegium on the very tip of Calabria offered strong resistance. In 393 Agrigentum and Messina rose simultaneously against the tyrant and Mago made the most of the opportunity. Unlike his predecessor Hannibal in 409, he came as a champion of liberty and not as a destructive conqueror. He marched on Messina and called upon the Greeks and the Siculi to rally to him.

Although he did not win a military victory, Mago succeeded in an important diplomatic manoeuvre. Dionysius had had no scruples in forming an alliance with the Lucani (a southern branch of the Osco-Umbrian peoples of the Appenines) against the Greeks of Italy, and the latter formed a confederation and allied themselves with the Carthaginians in order to withstand him. Furthermore, the Etruscans and, more especially, the people of Caere were anxiously watching the spread of Syracusan imperialism, and were only too happy to be able to produce from their archives the pacts which had been concluded by Thefarie Veliunas. Caere was an important city once more thanks to union with Rome, which amounted to federation, and she had built up her navy again and patrolled the seas between Italy, Corsica, and Sardinia. Rome had recently conquered Veii, thereby doubling her territory.

Dionysius was surrounded by a mighty coalition, and had no scruples in calling in the most formidable of auxiliary troops, the Gauls. The latter had overrun Etruria Padana, which had only been conquered a century earlier; they were masters of Felsina, which they had renamed Bologna; they were overflowing into the north-eastern part of the peninsula and had occupied Emilia and the Marche as far as Rimini. Their hordes were beginning to cross the Appennines and they offered their services to the tyrant of Syracuse. The latter was not put off by the wild appearance of these unexpected allies, and their capture of Rome in 386 came as a timely indication of their worth.

Thus, just as in the beginning of the fifth century, the whole of the Central Mediterranean was about to be involved in war. Dionysius attacked from the west and was successful at first. He at last managed to capture Rhegium (387) and his fleet occupied systematically, one after another, the islands and naval bases of the Ionian sea, in the direction of Greece. His ambassadors were booed whenever they appeared at religious Pan-Hellenic festivals.

Mago did not hesitate, and for the first time in Carthaginian history troops landed in Southern Italy (383). He succeeded in resettling in their homes the inhabitants of the small Greek city of Hipponium (Vibona) in the Bruttium, who had been deported by Dionysius (379). Unfortunately, however, Mago's military gifts once more fell short of his diplomatic qualities. A major confrontation of the two opposing armies had been avoided in the previous campaign, but when the Carthaginian and Syracusan armies now met at Cabala, Mago fell on the field of battle together with a large number of his followers. His son took command and avenged him in a striking way: the Syracusan army was defeated at Cronion with a loss of 14,000 souls, among them Dionysius' brother and most able commander, Leptines. In Carthage, however, there was a recurrence both of the Libyan revolt, and of that terrible plague which seems to have raged almost without interruption for thirty years. The Council of Elders decided to discuss terms for an honourable and advantageous peace. Carthage was naturally allowed to keep the whole western part of Sicily with Selinus and the country of the Elymians; she was obliged to renounce her claims to Agrigentum, although she retained part of its *territorium* on the west bank of the Halycus river; while Dionysius admitted defeat when he agreed to pay a war indemnity of 1000 talents.

We know of these events from bad, one-sided Greek accounts of them: Carthage is the perpetual enemy, but is not otherwise worthy of any interest, and appears in much the same light as Germany does in the history books in French primary schools. It is scarcely surprising, therefore, that we, today, should have some difficulty in reconstructing from this fragmentary evidence the internal political evolution at this very important period in her history.

The first point which calls for our attention is this: did the defeat of Himilco result in a basic change of régime? This is the view[1] held by Maurin, who, as we have seen, has brilliantly interpreted the history of internal affairs under the Magonid Dynasty. He believes that Himilco was the last of his family, which was cursed after his suicide and from then on barred from the throne. According to him, the aristocracy seized power in 396 and instituted the political tribunal of the One Hundred and Four, as a safeguard against personal power.

The present author does not find this view convincing. Diodorus tells us that a certain Mago commanded the fleet of Himilco in 398–396 (XIV, 59–60). It is extremely likely that this general was also[8] the successor of the defeated king. At this time all the important military posts were still the prerogative of members of the ruling dynasty, and it is more than probable that Mago, who bore the name of the founder of that dynasty, should have been a member of it. Beloch and Warmington are also of this opinion.

Mago seems to have exercised the same power as his predecessors: he was a king first and then a general, and he remained king until his death. He was buried with great pomp, which indicates his sacred character, and he was succeeded by his son. Maurin has attempted to show that he was more dependent upon the Council of Elders than his predecessors in the fifth century. He is bound to admit, however, that the only occasion on which we have evidence of the Council's intervention, was after the Battle of Cronion, in fact after the death of Mago, when the throne was vacant. Just as in the case of Himilco in 406, the heir to the throne could only be crowned in Carthage, and until then his powers were limited. Mago's son had, therefore, to send back to Carthage the peace terms which had been proposed by Dionysius. Even in the fifth century, however, the Magonid rulers had to submit any important diplomatic decisions to the Elders and the People. There is perfect co-ordination between military action and diplomatic moves in the years 391–383, and this seems to indicate that control of the foreign policy of Carthage lay in the hands of one man only at this time.

On the other hand, there is no sign of any activity of the Tribunal of the One Hundred and Four during the first few years of the fourth century. During the campaigns of 393–391, Mago suffered nothing but set-backs. Yet there is no indication that sanctions were taken or that his authority was in any way diminished. The first big political trial in Carthage which we know of, is that of Eshmuniaton (Suniaton) in 368, and we do not know by what court he was tried. We do know, however, that the accused was a leader of the party which most strongly opposed the

Magonids. The first evidence we have for legal action against a member of the Imperialist party, is when Hanno the Great was put to death in 360, and even then we have no means of knowing whether he was tried before his execution.

All authorities agree that the oligarchic régime was established by the land-owning aristocracy. In 396, however, the Libyan revolt which overran Punic lands in Africa had certainly brought temporary ruin to any farming projects, and reduced Carthage to the state she had been in before the conquests of Hanno. It is unlikely that the landowners were able to exercise any political power before they had rebuilt their fortunes.

Maurin's main reason for dating the aristocratic revolution to 396 B.C. is the synchronism he sees between this event and the establishment of the cult of Demeter and Kore in the same year. There is no doubt that this innovation marks a decisive step in the Hellenization of Carthage, nor can we contest the fact that the oligarchic and peace-loving faction was philhellenic. Eshmuniaton (Suniaton) who was leader of this party in 368 was imbued with Greek culture. Furthermore, where the Carthaginian landlords were the richest – that is, on the Cap Bon peninsula – the new cult became the most firmly established. This fact is all the more remarkable when we consider that 'Cereres' goddesses, as the Romans called them, are first and foremost corn goddesses, whereas the Cap Bon climate is unsuitable for the growing of cereals and, then as now, it was arboriculture, viticulture, and the raising of cattle which were the main sources of income for its inhabitants. Demeter and her daughter, therefore, were not called upon to fulfil their usual functions. It is worth adding that Cap Bon is the part of Punic territory which is richest in Greek imports, and that only the Greek name of several of its cities has survived (Neapolis is known today as Nabeul, and Aspis became Clupea and then Kelibia). It is more than probable that Greeks from Sicily were settled as colonists in this area, which then became one of the strongholds of oligarchy and philhellenism.

The development of the cult of Demeter is not an isolated phenomenon, however, nor does it betoken a violent break with the past. The oligarchic revolution went hand in hand with yet another religious reform which is all the more important because it concerns the principal cult of Carthage, namely that of Tanit, who became increasingly important and finally usurped the position previously occupied by Ba'al Hammon. As we shall see towards the end of this chapter, the process was a gradual one which went on throughout the period under discussion.

Everything seems to indicate, therefore, that the political and religious revolutions were the result of progressive transition rather than brutal upheaval. The same is true in the field of economics where the policy of self-sufficiency imposed after Himera gave way to an economy based on unlimited trade. The first stage in this transition can be dated to the end of the fifth century B.C. when a few foreign traders began to be allowed into Carthage and the first steps were taken towards establishing an export trade. Imports begin appearing regularly in the tombs only towards the middle of the century, but Diodorus tells us, nevertheless, that from 398 onwards Punic merchants were trading from Syracuse and that Carthaginian ships were mooring in the city's harbour.

A further important development was the establishment of a Carthaginian mint. As we have already seen, the Magonids began striking coins in Sicily towards the end of the fifth century, but these were exclusively used for the payment of mercenaries. At some time during the first half of the fourth century, a mint was set up on Byrsa. Even before this, however, Sicilian coinage had been put into general circulation, and a hoard which was presumably buried during the Libyan revolt in 396, and which was found near Bizerta in 1907, contained only Greek coins which had been struck, mostly in Sicily, in the fifth century.[1] This was doubtless the booty of a soldier in the army of Hannibal or of Himilco, but he had certainly not brought home this money as a souvenir. Coins minted in Carthage begin to appear in the tombs on the lower slopes of the Ard el Morali, which are most likely to belong to the third quarter of the fourth century.[2] It seems that the state had, by now, put some of the precious metal which it had previously used only for political ends, at the disposal of the individual. Naturally enough, this favoured the development of an economy based on trade, and enabled the merchants to import objects which had, until then, been either forbidden or severely restricted.

All these facts lead us to adopt a date round about 373 for the final downfall of Magonid rule, and to see this downfall as the result, not of a coup, but of a slow evolution. It seems, indeed, as though Mago's son – who was called Himilco, according to Beloch – never reigned. It is strange that he should not have come to the throne when he had just given proof, at Cronion, of military leadership far superior to that of his father. Perhaps the reason for this was his untimely death, a victim to the plague which had so weakened Carthage from 406 onwards? We do not know, but one thing is certain, the aristocracy must have been delighted to be able to put an end to a tradition of government which thwarted its interests. The two figures who now dominate the political scene are Hanno the Great and Eshmuniaton (Suniaton). Both owed their position to their riches and to the importance of their followers. According to such information as we have, it does not seem as though either of them was given the title 'king'. This title did not, however, disappear, but those who bore it did not wield the same authority under the same conditions of stability as did the Magonids.

2. HANNO THE GREAT

The peace of 373 did not last any longer than the others had. Our two sources of information, both of them poor, disagree as to where the responsibility lay for a breach of the peace: according to Diodorus we are to blame Dionysius, and according to Justin, the Carthaginians. This latter statement is the more acceptable, as it seems that one Punic party violently opposed the war – a thing they would scarcely have been in a position to do had the Syracusan tyrant been the aggressor.

Thus, for the first time we see Carthage divided into two rival factions of approximately equal strength, engaged in a fight to the death. The group which we shall call 'imperialist' was led by Hanno the Great, whose riches, according to Justin, were almost equal to the state's. The same author gives Hanno the title of *princeps Carthaginiensium*. Are we to assume from this, that this title described a specific office which can be none other than kingship? If Justin is quoting Pompeius Trogus in this instance, then the word *princeps* probably has the same meaning as it has when used by Cicero and by Caesar, namely superiority in fact, rather than legally defined pre-eminence, exemplified by that of Pompey in Rome in about 60 B.C. If, on the other hand, the term is Justin's own, then it must have the meaning it had at the time when he was writing – that is, in the second century A.D. – when *princeps* was used to describe the Emperor as well as a civilian head of state.

Justin calls Hanno's rival Suniaton, which is probably a corruption of Eshmuniaton, 'Gift of Eshmun', one of the most common of Carthaginian names. In 368 Eshmuniaton was, again according to Justin, *potentissimus Poenorum*. The Abbé Paul, who translated the text in 1774, interprets the expression as 'he who was most esteemed in Carthage' which is fairly close to the Latin. Eshmuniaton would therefore have been, not a magistrate, but the leader of the majority in the Council of the Elders. We must probably visualize him as the head of the faction which comprised all the great landowners who had finally succeeded in gaining control of the political scene in Carthage. Aristotle's analysis of the constitution shows us that this party had established a collegiate form of government, in which the authority was wielded by a series of committees which were as anonymous as possible. Thus Eshmuniaton was able to be 'most esteemed in Carthage' without, for all that, holding any particularly striking appointment. He must have achieved this position during the crisis which seems to have taken place after Mago's death, and which resulted in his son's expulsion. Since the royal title could no longer be applied to a Magonid, it must have been passed on to some inoffensive puppet, while the real power was in the hands of the private committees of the Elders.

The appointment of Hanno the Great as commander-in-chief seems to have been the result of a reversal of the political situation. Popular nationalist feeling may have constrained the Elders to accept him. Aristotle, as we shall see, emphasized the part played in the political life of Carthage by the societies which he called *sissytia*, and which were, in fact, banquet-brotherhoods or clubs. The philosopher is doubtless Hellenizing one of the oldest and most long-lasting Phoenician institutions, the *mizrah*, which we shall be studying further on. The account of the fall of Hanno indicates that he relied for support on the *mizrah*, and these seem to have existed in spite of strong opposition from a number of members of the Assembly.

Hanno was thus appointed general. Previously the post had been filled by a royal nominee who was replaced if he was not capable.

From now on the office of military commander was autonomous and was the result of the fragmentation of royal power.

Soon after, Eshmuniaton was accused of high treason, was tried, condemned, and presumably executed, although Justin neglects to inform us on whose authority the death sentence was imposed. It is probable that the tribunal of the One Hundred and Four was already in existence, but the greater part of this aristocratic gathering must have sympathized with the accused. It may well be that public opinion obliged them to condemn him against their will. It would seem that Carthage, at this period, was the prey to a wave of nationalist xenophobia, just as it had been in 409. The Elders are even supposed to have published a decree forbidding the teaching of Greek! This measure is so absurd and so obviously impossible to put into practice that our information in this case must be correct, as forgers invent only credible stories. Letters written in Greek, and purporting to be those from Eshmuniaton to Dionysius, were produced as evidence. They informed the tyrant of the plans of the Punic high command, and insisted strongly on the defects in Hanno's character, stressing in particular his indolence. It is extremely tempting to believe that these letters were forged by Hanno in order to put the opposition into disrepute and get rid of its leader. He knew that the majority of the Elders were hostile to him, and he therefore set out to terrorize them.

This war was as indecisive as the preceding ones. Dionysius attempted to repeat the manoeuvre which he had found so successful in 398, and set out to capture the principal Punic naval base before the enemy had time to disembark. He therefore crossed the whole of the island, without meeting with any oppostiion, and launched an attack on Lilybaeum, present-day Marsala, which had replaced Motya. The fact that he was able to conduct this raid with such ease is a proof that the Carthaginians maintained only a small standing army in their province. In fact, at the beginning of every campaign, they had to wait until they had recruited their mercenaries before they were able to get under way. Lilybaeum put up a strong resistance, however, and the tyrant was forced to retreat. Disaster then overcame Carthage when a fire broke out in the arsenal. When Dionysius heard the news he decided that he need no longer fear a naval attack, and thereupon sent the greater part of his fleet back to Syracuse. One Greek naval division remained at anchor in the lee of Mount Eryx, however, and this was surprised and captured by a Carthaginian squadron of 200 ships which had escaped the fire. Hanno then landed with his army but did not press home his advantage; winter was approaching and a truce was concluded. Dionysius died in the spring of 367, before it came to an end.

The disappearance of their principal opponent was an un-expected piece of good luck for the Carthaginians. Dionysius the Younger, who succeeded his father, was certainly not cast in the same mould. Furthermore, before he did anything else, he had to establish his authority, surrounded as he was by innumerable enemies, not the least of whom were members of his own family. The peace was therefore renewed under the same terms as that of 376 B.C.

Hanno's restraint is surprising, and he was soon to regret it. A new factor had arisen, however, to compensate for the death of Dionysius, and although it did not directly affect Carthage, it nevertheless rendered impracticable the policy of besieging Syracuse, which Mago had first instituted. Simultaneously with the old tyrant's death, Archytas seized power in Tarentum and soon transformed the old Spartan colony into the capital of the Magna Graecia confederacy. Even the Italic tribes of Apulia and Lucania had to accept Greek hegemony. Syracuse and Tarentum – both Dorian settlements – had always been on friendly terms with each other, and this friendship was now sealed by a formal treaty between Archytas and Dionysius II. This meant that the cities of the straits now lost all hope of independence, and the Cartha-ginians all possibility of action in this area.

To compensate for this, there is no doubt that the Carthaginians strengthened their ties with Etruria. A famous passage from Aristotle, which has been the subject of many commentaries, bears witness to the close relations between the two peoples (*Pol.*, III, 5, 9 = 1280 a). Its precise meaning has been established by Brunel.[3] He shows that the philosopher was attempting to prove by *reductio ad absurdum* that whatever the relation between individuals or groupings, this in itself does not constitute a city. If a political agreement, whatever its nature, is all that is needed to unite the contracting parties into a single city, then this would be so in the case of the Etruscans and Carthaginians, for instance. By this, of course, Aristotle does not mean that Etruria and Carthage had amalgamated to form one State – as many have interpreted it. In fact, he immediately adds that they have no federal institutions or constitutional principles in common and 'it is certain that the two peoples are united by agreements concerning imports, by pacts forbidding each to cause injury to the other, and by military treaties'.

By the third quarter of the fourth century B.C., therefore, a series of diplomatic documents had been drawn up uniting Carthage to various Etruscan cities and, doubtless, to their confederacy. Some of these agreements concerned trade and brought assurances of mutual protection of nationals. They corresponded to points dealt with in the Romano-Punic treaties of 508 and 348, which must certainly have been drawn up on the Etrusco-Punic model. Other clauses had wider implications and concerned the establishment of a military alliance between Carthage and some of the Etruscan cities. These clauses can have related to only a few towns such as Caere, for, in spite of federal institutions, the Tyrrhenian peoples never succeeded in presenting a united front, and far less in the fourth century than at any other time.

Modern historians have discussed the possibility that the treaties mentioned by Aristotle were not drawn up while he was writing, but had been ratified in the past, and went back to the sixth century. We have seen, in this connection, that the agreements which had united the two peoples at the time of the Battle of Alalia had since been relaxed. The example of the Romano-Punic alliance shows that, even when not actively put into practice, a treaty could remain valid in theory over a long period of time, but that it had to be confirmed and amended when times of stress made closer relations necessary. This is probably what took place between the Carthaginian and Tyrrhenian peoples at the time of the united struggle against Dionysius: political and economic conditions had altered too greatly during the past two centuries for the old agreements still to be fully applicable.

As a result of these pacts, a number of Etruscans came to settle in Carthage. Traces of their presence have been found: an ivory plaque from a tomb from Sainte Monique bears an Etruscan inscription giving the name of a man described as being Carthaginian, who must have been a Tyrrhenian who lived in Africa. He probably had the same status as the metics of Athens, who had rights as citizens but who remained faithful to their mother-tongue.[4] Two paterae of the Genucilia type must have come from Caere towards the middle of the fourth century.[5] The most important material witness to these relations, however, is the presence of the famous sarcophagi with statues from the same necropolis, which are paralleled at Tarquinia. These tombs give rise to a number of problems which we shall be investigating further on. It is worth pointing out here, however, that they belonged to members of the Punic aristocracy and illustrate their close relations with Etruria.

Caere was the leading Etruscan city during the first half of the fourth century. Until about 354 B.C. – according to Signorina Sordi – there were close links with Rome, but the same author has shown that Caere was also on friendly terms with Marseilles. Thanks, most probably, to the city's intervention, relations seem to have temporarily improved between Phocaean and Phoenician colonists, and the reconciliation can be presumed to have lasted long enough for Pytheas to have obtained permission, soon after 330, to sail beyond the Pillars of Hercules.

This did not prevent the Carthaginians from following an extremely active and aggressive policy in Southern Spain. It seems that their armies destroyed a number of Iberian townships in the Alicante hinterland and on the peninsula of the Cabo de la Náo towards the middle of the fourth century.

We can be certain that further military operations took place in Africa. With the repression of the Libyan revolt, it is probable that new territories were annexed. It is perhaps at this stage that the land of Thusca and the Great Plains of the Medjerda were conquered. Hanno led these campaigns and allied himself with a 'Moorish 'chief whom he was later to attempt to capture in order that he might seize his lands. It is difficult to believe that this 'Moor' could have lived in what was later to be called Mauretania and then Morocco, as he would have been too far away to inter-vene at all usefully on behalf of Carthage.

In spite of these few wars which we can dimly guess at, the quarter of a century immediately after Dionysius' death seems to have been one of the quietest in the whole history of Carthage. We thus find it difficult to agree with most modern historians that the city was under the rule of Hanno the Great – whose nationalist and imperialist tendencies had been evident from the very beginning of his career – during most of this period, and that he was replaced by a pacific and philhellenic oligarchy at the very moment when war was due to break out once more.

Justin gives very vague information concerning the date of the fall of Hanno, yet he is our main source. The first three chapters of Book XXI of his History are devoted to the tyranny of Dionysius the Younger, of his overthrow by Dion in 357–355 (told in an extremely sketchy manner), and of his (Dionysius') governorship of Rhegium and Locri, where he had sought refuge during his ten-year exile. Chapter 4 tells of the fall of Hanno which is supposed to be contemporary with the preceding events, and Chapter 5 deals with Dionysius' second Syracusan tyranny (346–344). The fall of Hanno must certainly have taken place before 346, therefore, although several modern historians would date it to 344. It can have taken place, however, at any time during the years 367 to 346, as Justin uses the expression *dum haec in Sicilia geruntur* covering not only Chapter 4, which deals with Dionysius II in Rhegium, but also the three preceding chapters, which tell of events in Sicily. Information given by Aristotle does not disagree with this conclusion. At the time when he was engaged in the preparation of Book II of his *Politics* (one of the earliest in the series) he does not seem to have heard of Hanno. He mentions him, however, in Book V, which must be dated at the earliest to 336 as it also mentions the assassination of Philip II of Macedon.[6] We cannot deduce from this, however, that Hanno's attempted *coup d'état* took place just before 336. During the interval between the writing of Books II and V, Aristotle extended his knowledge of Carthage and learnt, for instance, of the existence of the Magonid monarchy, which he described as a tyranny (V, 12).

On the other hand, the picture which Aristotle gives us of Carthage in Book II, shows us a ruling aristocracy with democratic or oligarchic sympathies which is certainly not what we might imagine a society dominated by the *princeps* Hanno to be like.

Hanno must certainly have remained in power for several years after 368; Pompeius Trogus devoted a whole book to him and dealt, among other things, with his deeds in Africa. As we have seen, however, he cannot have done more than repress the Libyans once and for all after their revolt of 379 (there were to be no more Libyan risings until 241 B.C.), annex certain territories in Northern and Central Tunisia, and carry out a few raids for some distance into unsubdued lands in order to discourage the independent tribes from lending support to their conquered neighbours. Even if we are in favour of adding to this list the wars in Spain and the dispatch of an expeditionary force along the coast of the Maghreb, all this activity need not have taken more than a decade.

The present author believes, therefore, that Hanno must have disappeared from the political scene by 357 B.C., when Dion, brother-in-law of Dionysius the Elder, set out to overthrow his nephew. The expedition sailed from Athens but, owing to contrary winds, it made its landfall at Heraclea Minoa in the Carthaginian province. Dion was well received by the town's commander, who was named Synalus. The Punic government, on the other hand, had done nothing to encourage or hinder the little fleet when it had sailed past the Kerkenna Islands in the Gulf of Gabès, nor did it depart from an amiable neutrality, and it took no part in the overthrow of Dionysius in 355. It is interesting to note that Synalus was a Greek, and we can deduce from this that Carthage was governed at the time by pacific philhellenes who allowed a great deal of autonomy to their Sicilian subjects. It would seem that Eshmuniaton's old supporters were in power.

Hanno fell in about 360, therefore. We have Justin's colourful and dramatic account of the conspiracy, which nevertheless gives us some valuable historical information:

While this affair occurred in Sicily, Hanno, a leading man among the Carthaginians, in Africa, employed his power, which surpassed that of the government, to secure the sovereignty for himself, and endeavoured to establish himself as king by killing the Elders. For the execution of this atrocity he fixed on the day of his daughter's marriage, in order that his nefarious plot might be the better concealed in the pomp of religious ceremonies. He accordingly prepared a banquet for the common people in the public porticos, and another for the Elders in his own house, so that, by poisoning the cups, he might take off the Elders privately and without witnesses, and then more easily seize the government, when none were left to prevent him. The plot being disclosed to the magistrates by the agents, his destructive intentions were frustrated, but not punished, lest the matter, if publicly known, should occasion more trouble, in the case of so powerful a man, than the mere design of it had caused. Satisfied, therefore, with putting a stop to it, they merely set bounds by a decree to the expenses of marriage entertainments, and ordered the decree to be obeyed, not by him alone, but universally, that nothing seem to be intended. Prevented by this measure, he, for a second attempt, raised the slaves and appointed another day for the massacre of the Elders, but finding himself again betrayed, he threw himself, for fear of being brought to trial, into a strong fortress with a body of twenty thousand armed slaves. Here, while he was soliciting the Africans and the king of the Moors to join him, he was captured, and after being scourged, having his eyes put out, and his arms and legs broken, as if atonement was to be exacted from every limb, he was put to death in the sight of the people, and his body, mangled with stripes, was nailed to a cross. All his children and relations, too, though guiltless, were delivered to the executioner, that no member of so nefarious a family might survive either to imitate his villainy, or to revenge his death.

Although it contains a mass of political, social, and economic information concerning Carthage, which is clearly apparent in spite of its author's rhetoric, this text has never been properly analysed.

Let us first consider Hanno himself. As Gsell has already noted, he is very different from the normal run of Greek tyrant. The latter generally relied on the lower classes or on the army for support when seizing power. Hanno did neither, for although he was a general, he did not have any troops at his command – which shows, incidentally, that the war in Africa was ended by then. The people played no part in the plot. Certainly, during the second part of the story, Hanno was in a position to arm 20,000 slaves, but we are not told that he incited the proletariat to revolt; in fact, such a move was still unfashionable in the fourth century. Nor are we told that he employed slaves other than his own; these were probably the serfs from his lands, and the fortress to which he withdrew was doubtless his country seat. From there he incited

10

the 'Africans' to rebellion – that is, the Libyan subjects of Carthage. He also enlisted the support of a mighty caïd. His actions are far more those of a Berber prince than of a political agitator of the Classical world. Throughout the history of the Maghreb, political unrest has always been caused by the sudden expansion of a tribe under the leadership of a dynamic chief and of his clan.

This 'African' side of Hanno's character, however, is only revealed in his second bid for power. During his first attempt, he made use of specifically Punic institutions. We must bear in mind that the Carthaginian wedding banquet, accompanied by religious ceremonies, was not a family affair rendered remarkable by the particularly numerous guests. Brotherhoods centred on the Temples were also involved. It is most unlikely that, at this period in Carthage, there were 'public porticos' other than those surrounding the temple courtyards.[7] On the contrary, we know that Punic temples normally contained a hall reserved for sacred banquets. It was here that the various brotherhoods (*mizrah, marzeah, sapah*) were accustomed to meet, and from here that their political influence (described by Aristotle) extended. These were the brotherhoods which Hanno invited, and, by doing so, he was grouping together an *élite* of citizens which was far larger that that from which the Elders were drawn, and which was in a strong enough position to oppose the latter. It is probable that these brotherhoods had already forced the issue in the case of Hanno's victory over Eshmuniaton in 368. This time they refused to support him, for his plans were too ambitious, and oligarchic propaganda did its best to emphasize this. It is probable, also, that the extraordinary plan for mass assassination of the members of the Council was also dreamed up by this propaganda.

In opposition to Hanno, and siding with the Elders, we have a group of magistrates. We do not know what title they bore, nor are their functions clearly defined, but they controlled sumptuary matters and doubtless employed a police force. Those who revealed the conspiracy are called *ministri* by Justin and were probably the agents of these magistrates rather than those of the plotters.[8]

The story of Hanno gives us a side-light on the social organization, which seems surprisingly unsophisticated in comparison with that of contemporary Greek cities. It is the organization of a city where wealth is still unevenly distributed, and where 'clans' or brotherhoods are not yet fused into a civic unity. In order to find the equivalent situation in Greece, we must go back to the sixth or even seventh century B.C. Aristotle was right in comparing the Carthaginian Republic to some of the most archaic Greek cities of Lacedaemon and Crete.

3. THE ARISTOTELIAN CONSTITUTION

The information which Aristotle has preserved for us concerning the constitution of Carthage, is by far our most valuable source for Punic common law. It was collected soon after the middle of the fourth century. Weil has most ably shown the various stages in Aristotle's attitude with regard to the great African city.[9] His initial attitude is revealed in certain passages in Book VII of his *Politics* in which the Carthaginians appear as Barbarians on the same plane as the Persians, the Celts, and even the Macedonians. The philosopher's interest seems to have been purely ethnographic. Later he realized that their constitution was comparable to those of Lacedaemon and Crete. Thus, in spite of its 'deviations', it was close to his ideal of a *politeia*. In this frame of mind he wrote Chapter II of Book II, which is not an analysis of the Punic constitution, on the same basis as his treatise on the *Constitution of Athens*; but it is an attempt at defining its principal characteristics in relation to the Greek methods of government which he had already examined. In this way he sought to fit it into the framework of his Sociological Categories. Finally, in the last months of his life, Aristotle collected new information on Punic history and laws: he learnt of the Magonid monarchy and of Hanno's *coup d'état*. Either his point of view had altered, or recent events had caused him to change his mind, but he now included Carthage among the democracies. If we take all this into account, it explains some of the difficulties which confront us if we wish to interpret Aristotle's views on Carthaginian government. We should point out that modern historians have delighted in adding to these difficulties, for instead of accepting the text as it stands, they have almost always attempted to find agreement between it and any other information we may have concerning the Punic constitution, irrespective of date, presupposing, doubtless, that the latter had remained unaltered throughout the ages. In so doing, they have raised non-existent problems.

We plan to follow the text step by step, on the basic assumption that it reflects the state of affairs during the second half of the fourth century. We should be wrong to seek here a description of the Magonid monarchy, or an account of the democracy in the time of Hannibal. Chapter II of Book II begins with an encomium of the Punic constitution, which is compared to those of Lacedaemon and Crete, already discussed in the preceding chapters. The inhabitants are subject to laws, but there has been neither tyranny, nor revolution. This optimism was tempered when Aristotle discovered later about the Magonid monarchy; this he classifies as a tyranny. He also learnt of Hanno's revolutionary attempts. The philosopher then pointed out parallels with Lacedaemonian institutions: the 'Syssitia' he equates with the Spartan 'Phiditia'. These, as we have already shown, are the 'clans' and 'thiasoi' (*mizrah, shapah, marzeah*), the old pagan or religious groupings which formed the framework of civic life, and whose meetings often took the form of banquets. Although Aristotle's equation is understandable, yet it is hardly justifiable. There is nothing in common between the 'phiditia', or clubs of comrades-in-arms, of the Lacedaemonians, and the Semitic religious brotherhoods.

Aristotle then goes on to equate the Tribunal of the One Hundred and Four with the Ephors, and this comparison is less superficial. Although these two institutions were very differently organized, yet they were both intended to protect an aristocratic régime. In this connection Aristotle tells us that the One Hundred and Four were chosen on merit (ἀριστίνδην): in fact, they were co-opted by the pentarchies, as we shall see further on. He considered this system preferable to election by the Apella, which was the method of recruiting the Ephors. This remark is sufficient proof that the kings of Carthage, who then come under discussion and who are equated with the *basileis* of Sparta, cannot be the same as the suffetes, who were elected for a year by the Assembly and whom we come across in the time of Hannibal. If this were otherwise, then Aristotle would have had to withdraw the encomium he had bestowed upon the Carthaginians in connection with the choice of the One Hundred and Four, and he would have pointed out that they nevertheless relied on the people for the election of their chief magistrates. In fact, Aristotle goes on to describe the system of choosing a king, but the terms he uses are not clear. He tells us that they are not hereditary in one family, nor are they chosen by lot, and further on he tells us (§ 5) that both kings and generals were selected on merit and because of their wealth. Candidates for such posts probably had to qualify by expending some vast sum in favour of the community. This presumably involved giving feasts and banquets – as Hanno the Great did when making his bid for supreme power – and constructing monuments and public buildings, equipping armies and fleets, etc. . . . . This was the practice in Roman Africa where public benefactors were officially awarded honorary titles such as Friend of the Citizens, or Adorner of the Nation, etc. . . . . Aristotle expressly mentions that the election of the kings followed the same routine as that of the generals, and that the same jury had to choose from among the candidates applying for one or other post In this connection Diodorus informs us that in 310 it was the Gerousia which entrusted Hanno and Bomilcar with the conduct of the war against Agathocles.

It is certain that in the fourth century, both kings and generals stayed in power for several years at a stretch. Hanno the Great exercised authority over a long period and so did his son Gisco, his grandson King Hamilcar – the Hamilcar who gave Agathocles initial backing – and Bomilcar, who resisted the latter's invasion. It is both senseless and inconceivable to suppose that they were elected for a year and then regularly re-elected. In fact, in the second century, the annual suffetes could not stand for re-election (cf. below, p. 210).

Hamilcar, the grandson of Hanno the Great, bore the title of *melek* or king (Diodorus XX, 33, 2). His father Gisco probably bore it as well, if we are to judge by the 'triumph' he celebrated over his enemies (Polyaenus: *Stratēgēmata*, V, 11), which seems to have been a royal ritual of Pharaonic origin. Beloch was right in speaking of a Hannonian dynasty. In the following generation, however, the royal title passed to a rival family and was borne, in 309, by Bomilcar, whose uncle, Hamilcar, had been the predecessor in Sicily, and the rival of that other Hamilcar, the king, and son of Gisco (Justin XXII, 7, 7). There was some procedure, therefore, whereby the royal title could be transferred from one family to another. Furthermore, the function of military general, which had been closely linked with and subordinated to the monarchy in Magonid times, was now independent of it. The Elders often arranged matters in such a way that a king would find himself up against a general who belonged to an opposing faction. In this way, the command in Italy was divided, from 318–314, between the two Hamilcars. In 309, in spite of the presence in Africa of Agathocles, King Hamilcar had as his counterpart the general Hanno, who nourished an hereditary hatred against him. (Can this Hanno be yet another descendant of Hanno the Great?).

Bomilcar's attempted *coup d'état* in 309 or 308 finally caused the aristocracy to abolish the monarchy. From now on there are no more kings at the head of the army, but only generals. The title *melek* does not disappear but it is no more than an empty, honorific survival.

Both kings and generals had to submit equally to the control of the political Tribunal of the One Hundred or the One Hundred and Four. Aristotle mentions this institution twice: in § 2 he compares it to the board of Ephors in Sparta, and in § 4 he tells us that the judges were elected by the pentarchies.

Aristotle describes the latter as follows:

> The committees of five, the Pentarchies, which have control over many important matters, not only fill up vacancies on their own by co-option, but appoint members of the Hundred, the highest constitutional authority. Moreover, they enjoy a longer tenure of office than the rest; they begin to exercise authority before they become members of the committee and continue to do so after they have ceased to be members. On the other hand we must allow as aristocratic the fact that they receive no pay and are not chosen by lot. . . .

No other document concerning Carthage mentions these committees of five members, and Aristotle, in fact, remains silent on their number and exact function. It would seem that these are executive committees, equivalent to the *probouloi*, who, in some Greek cities, held powerful office within the framework of the council.[10]

In the third century, neither Polybius, nor Livy make any

mention of pentarchies. In fact, they write of only one restricted privy council within the framework of the Council of Elders, and this Aristotle ignores.[11] It is possible, though by no means certain, that this privy-council was formed by the amalgamation of several pentarchies.

Aristotle mentions only the two principal magisterial authorities of monarchy and generalship, but he implies the existence of lesser posts (in § 6, monarchy and generalship are described as μενίσται τῶν ἀρχῶν).

Of these posts, at least two, at this period, were filled by the suffetes. In the third century, suffetes were, above all, judges, and this function corresponds exactly to the Semitic meaning of the word. According to Aristotle, all lawsuits were tried by the same magistrates, and there were no specialized courts as in Sparta. At first glance, it might seem as though this meant that all legal power was in the hands of the One Hundred and Four. It seems, however, as though the philosopher considers these as political magistrates rather than judges. It is probable, therefore, that the suffetes gave judgement in both civil and criminal cases.

The powers of the Assembly of the People are clearly defined in § 3:

> When the kings and the Elders agree that certain matters are to be referred to the people, that is done; but it is also done when they do not agree! Moreover when a matter agreed upon by the kings and Elders is referred to them, they have the right not merely to listen to the decisions of the higher bodies but to give independent judgement; and it is open to all and sundry to oppose and speak against the proposals that have been laid before them. This right does not exist in the other two constitutions (i.e. in Crete or Lacedaemonia).

This right of arbitration between king and aristocratic council, seems to be very ancient. Thus, until the monarchy definitely weakened towards the end of the fourth century, the people had important privileges.

The picture of Punic institutions painted by Aristotle can therefore be summarized as follows. The aristocracy was still not all-powerful within the state, but had already been able to weaken the monarchy considerably by breaking its dynastic continuity and by transferring to others a large part of its authority. The direction of military campaigns was more and more entrusted to generals, while civil magistrates – and especially the suffetes – took over the conduct of internal affairs. The nobility was in close control of everything thanks to two organizations: the Tribunal of the One Hundred and Four, which was always ready to condemn most forcefully any errors or attempts at rebellion against the established order, and the pentarchies, each of which specialized in the conduct of a certain type of business, and co-ordinated and duplicated the work of the magistrates. In this well-organized system there was little outlet for the theoretically important authority of the Assembly of the People.

4. RELIGIOUS REFORM

The royal cult of Ba'al Hammon was a guarantee of the power of the sovereign, who was, to some extent, the god's representative on earth. It too was to decline at the beginning of the fourth century in the same way as had the monarchy. Just as the kings remained in office and were merely divested of some of their authority, so the god remained in the Carthaginian pantheon but was ousted from first place. Historical events in conjunction with spiritual evolution among the Carthaginians were responsible for the disfavour under which this antiquated and truly horrifying religion fell. The god had, in fact, proved incapable of preventing Himilco's defeat, or of stopping the plague which raged through the town. One of the principal benefits which the moloch sacrifice was supposed to bestow, however, was the prevention of such calamities. Furthermore, the more cultured Carthaginians were increasingly repelled at having to sacrifice their own children and were ashamed at being branded as inhuman in the eyes of the Greeks, who, though their rivals on the economic and political plane, were their betters as far as civilization was concerned. When Diodorus (XX, 14) describes the panic which Agathocles' advance caused in Carthage, he remarks that Ba'al Hammon had been neglected for some length of time by the Carthaginians, and that they only sacrificed the sons of slaves, whom they bought and fed in secret. This, he tells us, is what had irritated the god, and the Carthaginians hastened to atone for their neglect of him. This text proves that the divine patron of the Magonids had fallen into disrepute and was no longer head of the pantheon. What, then, was the reason for this?

The first blow at the structure of the national and ancestral religion was struck in 396, when the cult of Demeter and Kore was officially introduced into the city. This was the doing of members of the land-owning aristocracy who were also preparing to seize power. The introduction of this new cult was thus the reaction of a wealthy and cultured upper class against the primitive and antiquated aspects of the Canaanite religion, and also a political move intended to break the power of a monarchy which ruled by divine authority.

There are neither descriptions nor remains to enable us to reconstruct the appearance of the new sanctuary. It probably resembled Greek temples from Sicily, however, and, like most of these, it must have belonged to the Doric order, which the Carthaginians had not previously used but which, from now on, was to become a feature of religious and domestic architecture.

This new religion was a symbol of the power of an extremely small proportion of the Carthaginian population which was isolated and differentiated from the remainder of the nation by its culture and ambitions. The new cult, as we shall see, remained foreign with no appeal to the working classes, the sailors, merchants, and artisans of the city: it did not answer their needs and, in addition, it must have run counter to the national feelings of those Semites who still felt strongly attached to Tyre. That this was so is proved by the wave of xenophobia which engulfed Carthage in 310 B.C.

A study of the votive deposits in the topheth of Salammbo at this period shows that, in spite of the decline in popularity of Ba'al Hammon, the number of sacrifices of the moloch type went on increasing. There is some change in the way in which these are disposed, however, and a reformation was obviously in progress which finally achieved its aims towards the middle of the fourth century. The first point worth noting is that, during the first few years of the fourth century, the sacred enclosure was filled in and levelled off so that earlier ex-votos were buried beneath the new level of the soil. This was not only done in order that there should be more room for new offerings, but also seems to indicate a break with the past, which was literally buried. The date of this levelling can be determined with absolute accuracy: all the buried stelae and pottery types have exact parallels at Motya, but among those from the new level, several are completely unknown on the Sicilian site. The reorganization of the topheth must therefore be contemporary with the destruction of Motya by Dionysius I in 397.

During the next thirty or forty years, the topheth gives an impression of great confusion. We find monuments of the old type (Egyptianizing chapels and stepped altars) side by side with Ionic cellae, pillars, and miniature obelisks, which are no longer carved in El Haouaria sandstone but for which a new material is used – an oolitic limestone quarried near Zaghouan – and there is even a circular stele carved in imported Vulci marble! The decoration of these monuments is as varied as the materials from which they are cut. Some are carved in very low relief and some are engraved, but they are too numerous for it to be possible to describe them all. Side by side with the old geometric betyls, we have human representations of both sexes, very highly stylized, and in a variety of different positions. Especially important are the two new symbols which now make their appearance and which soon become more popular than the old. One of these is known as the 'sign of Tanit' and consists of a triangle with a horizontal bar, the ends of which are curved upwards, and a circle, both resting on its apex.

The symbol looks rather like a human silhouette with out-stretched arms bent upwards at the elbow, like the 'bell-shaped' Minoan idols. It is difficult, since we cannot base ourselves on textual evidence, to define the exact meaning of this sign. Many suggestions have been put forward. It has been compared to the Egyptian *ankh* sign for life; it has been proposed that it was an ideogram indicating the union of the terrestial and celestial worlds with the triangle representing the earth, and the circle standing for the sun-disc; or that it was an idol derived from Cretan figurines with both arms raised. Since it seems evident that the sign originated in the stylization of a human figure, it would appear that this figure once epitomized worship and prayer addressed to Tanit, and perhaps, more specifically, the dedication which linked the worshipper to the goddess, together with the benefits which might result from such a link. A raised hand is shown on many Punic stelae and must represent in the same way either a prayer addressed to the deity, or divine blessing, or both in many cases. It seems equally certain that the meaning of the sign of Tanit varied from one period to another. It is probable that in the last years of the fourth century B.C., under the influence of the Pythagorean theories which were then fashionable, certain initiates considered the sign to be a cosmograph reflecting the union of the worshipper with his goddess. In the Barcid period, however, the sign of Tanit was certainly a phylactery which called down divine benediction, and it is found as an amulet, or as decoration for the floors of houses. After the fall of Carthage the sign reverted to its original form and became semi-anthropomorphic. It was no longer associated directly with the supreme goddess, but served as an intermediary between heaven and earth, between the goddess and mankind. It was through the power of this sign that the human race received divine benefits, as can be seen on the stelae of La Ghorfa.

The 'bottle sign' looks like a flask with a pear-shaped body and a high, wide neck, and in this case it recalls the Aegean fiddle-shaped idols. In many cases, this symbol is carved with a face, breasts, and braces, but since it looks like a sacred vessel, the sculptors have emphasized this resemblance and have thereby given the symbol a double meaning. A stele in Carthage Museum shows that the bottle sign is, in fact, a combination of two objects: the vessel which contained the ashes of the sacrificed child, and a schematic rendering of this child's silhouette. It therefore symbolizes the offerings made to Tanit and Ba'al during moloch sacrifices. In fact, the sign disappears from the sacred repertoire at the end of the third century, when infant sacrifices became mere fictions, and a lamb was offered in a child's stead. In its place there appears the representation of a lamb, which decorated ex-votos from then on.

The Caduceus is very often 'brandished' by the sign of Tanit and, more rarely, by the bottle sign. It is also found on its own, or on the top of a staff, or fixed on an altar. There is no doubt that we are here dealing with Hermes' Wand. We know, furthermore, that the Greek god had given his name to one of the promontories, and was worshipped in Carthage. It is extremely probable that he was assimilated to the Canaanite god Sakon who appears in the name Gersakon or Gisco which was so common in Carthage. Homer, in fact, mentions a Hermes Saka and this dual appellation cannot be explained in any other way. Sakon was a Pillar-god as was his Greek counterpart, and this was doubtless the deified funerary pillar.[12] It would therefore be to this god that the betyls and pillar-shaped stelae, which were set up on mounds of the topheth in the seventh and sixth centuries B.C., were dedicated. G. Picard and Cintas had thought that these ex-votos were aniconic representations of the lords of the sanctuary. The discovery of a similar betyl in the cremation cemetery of Hama in Syria invalidates this theory. Originally, when the tumuli only covered one votive deposit, the betyls were isolated, and stood in a niche or on a throne. When collective burials were introduced, and the mounds covered two, three, or four deposits, betyls were often set up in groups of two, three, or even four. Their differing sizes may, in some way, be connected with the relative importance of the dedicator or of the offering. Then, at the time when Hellenism was gaining in importance, and symbolism was becoming fashionable, the Greek and Punic Pillar-gods became fused, the old betyls disappeared, and the Caduceus grew to be associated with the emblems of the Punic gods. On a Hellenistic stele there is even a representation of the god's head wearing his petasus hat. He is also shown on a Neo-Punic stele from La Ghorfa instead of the sign of Tanit, and acts as minister of the supreme goddess Coelestis who has by then taken the place of the Lady of Carthage.

Another innovation in the period we are discussing lies in the fact that, whereas the sandstone stelae were practically never inscribed, the limestone obelisks almost all bear a dedication which varies very little in its form:

> TO THE LADY TANIT, FACE OF BA'AL, AND TO
> THE LORD BA'AL HAMMON, SO-AND-SO, SON OF
> SO-AND-SO, HAS DEDICATED THIS.[13]

The few previous stelae inscriptions had always mentioned Ba'al alone. There must therefore have been a fundamental change which consigned the god to second place in the pantheon, and promoted the goddess, who must formerly have been his subordinate, as the epithet attached to her, 'Face of Ba'al', implies. This revolution must certainly be connected with the other phenomena which we have just discussed: the levelling of the topheth, the change in the type of funerary monuments, and especially the appearance of the Tanit and bottle symbols. In spite of anything which may have been said to the contrary, these latter must symbolize the triumphant goddess, since their appearance coincides with that of the inscriptions in which, for the first time, she takes pride of place.

This revolution occurred in 397. It is therefore connected with the political and moral upheaval which followed upon Himilco's defeat, and is a parallel development to the introduction of the cult of Demeter. Just as the Magonid Dynasty was not immediately abolished, however, so the Tanit cult did not obtain immediate acceptance by the whole Carthaginian population. Hence arose a religious confusion which is reflected in the variety of ex-votos over quite a long period of time. When the aristocratic régime finally gained the upper hand, in about 360, the opposition of the 'old believers' disappeared, and from then onwards there was to be only one type of ex-voto in the topheth. This was a limestone stele, shaped like an obelisk, bearing a dedication to Tanit and Ba'al, and decorated with the Tanit and bottle signs in conjunction with a crescent inverted over a disc.

We must now discuss the problem of the origin of Tanit, which can be approached from the philological or the archaeological angle. Of the Tanit examples so far found in the Lebanon, none antedates those from the topheth. The only bottle symbol so far found in the East was discovered recently by the Italian Expedition at Tell Akziv in Palestine. It is carved on a sandstone stele which bears the representation of a niche in Egyptianizing style, within which it stands. This stele was found in fill and cannot therefore be dated with absolute certainty, but it does seem to be con-temporary with the Carthaginian stelae of the beginning of the fourth century B.C. The Italian archaeologist who discovered it, Sabatino Moscati, believes that this unique ex-voto is the Phoenician ancestor of the Punic bottle symbols. It might just as plausibly be a Phoenician copy of a Punic prototype. Owing to lack of evidence, we are unable to decide for the moment.

The name TNT is also problematic. Some epigraphists believe that it is connected with the root NTN – to give. Thus the goddess would be 'the one who gives'. Others believe that she is a Libyan divinity who was adopted by the Carthaginians after the conquest of African territory. Their argument lies in the fact that the initial T form is common in Africa; but this seems an unlikely hypothesis in view of the backward and menial state in which the autochthonous subjects of the Republic lived. A new hypothesis has been suggested by Sznycer, Cross, and Garbini.[14] In text No. 347 of the Proto-Canaanite inscriptions of Sinai, we find the name TNT (tinnit) used as an epithet to qualify Asherat, 'the Lady of the Sea Monster or Dragon'. Thus TNT would be the feminine of TN, a name which is found in its plural form TNM in Ugaritic texts. The Lady of Carthage would indeed be Asherat, as Dussaud had suggested. In support of this theory we can quote the union of Tanit with Ba'al Hammon which is reflected in her appearance as Pene Ba'al, and which corresponds to that of Asherat with El in Phoenicia. Further proofs are afforded by the fact that her astral emblems are found at an earlier date in the Tyrian sphere, and by the dedication to 'Tanit of Lebanon'. Like her Phoenician counterpart, Tanit is a sea goddess and boats were offered to her as ex-votos. Some philologists believe the name of Tanit to be a means of distinguishing the Astarte of Carthage from those worshipped at Tyre or at Paphos. The Lady of Carthage is, in fact, closely related to the oriental goddess. Both are funerary and fertility goddesses, as we shall see, and sometimes they even share the same shrines in Carthage itself, and in Malta. The two deities seem to have distinct identies, however, for the dedication of the Temple in Carthage was to 'Tanit of the Lebanon *and* to Astarte,' while stelae from Salammbo are inscribed by 'servants of Astarte' to Tanit Pene Ba'al. Even their emblems are not the same: Tanit is represented by the crescent moon, and Astarte by the planet Venus. Furthermore, none of the offerings ascribed to Tanit shows her as anything but chaste, she is always represented clothed, and religious prostitution, which was an important feature of Astarte's cult, was not practised in Carthage. Finally, the Greeks and the Romans assimilated the consort of Ba'al-Saturn to Artemis and to Hera-Juno, but never to Aphrodite or Venus.

It is possible, however, that Astarte may have been worshipped in the topheth of Salammbo, before the reformation, together with Tanit. Ba'al Hammon was, in fact, assisted by one or more fertility goddesses to whom feminine idols were offered. Some of these latter were made of coarse clay with the sexual parts emphasized, while others showed women holding their breasts. They were probably dedicated to the oriental goddess. These figurines disappeared from the topheth, however, as soon as Tanit gained predominance, and it would seem that the Tyrian goddess was ousted by her African rival.

There are a great many carvings on the stelae of Salammbo, from the third century onwards, which illustrate Tanit's attributes: palm-trees weighed down with dates, ripe pomegranates ready to burst, lotus or lilies coming into flower, fish, doves, frogs, etc. . . . She is the dispenser to mankind of the vital energy which is Ba'al Hammon's. She acts in his name as a sort of minister. In the inscriptions, the worshipper specifies that he 'has dedicated' the ex-voto because the goddess 'has blessed him, has heard his voice'.

The moloch had changed its character and, from being a national ceremony celebrated by the government representative or representatives, it had become a private family festival. The *devotio* of small children was no longer regarded as tribute imposed by an inexorable god, but as thanksgiving and the voluntary repayment of a personal debt towards the gods, incurred by the faithful when some favour was granted. As Février has shown, the requests of the worshipper were no longer centred on the well-being and prosperity of the State, but on his own, and consisted, particularly, in demands that his house might be blessed by the birth of a child; Tanit would then be described as 'Mother'. Personal success was also considered one of the benefits of moloch sacrifice, and many tools and forms of equipment are depicted on the stelae – ploughs, boats, mason's tools, etc. . . . Finally, when we come to examine the ashes contained in the topheth urns from the beginning of the fourth century, it is clear immediately that the rules governing the sacrifice have been considerably relaxed. There are relatively few human remains, and the majority of the ashes are those of animals – lambs have been substituted for babies, and have been dedicated to Tanit. Only a few fanatics continued to consign their children to the flames, and they were to go on doing so until the destruction of the city.

Another result of the reformation was to extend the circle of the faithful who offered moloch sacrifices. Previously, so Diodorus tells us, this was restricted to suffetes, the *rab* or 'great ones', and priests, etc. . . . It was now open to artisans, freed-men, and even slaves, women of all stations, and finally to strangers, who were encouraged to make their offerings.

Benefits bestowed by Tanit did not cease with death. She was the source of life and caused the dead to live again for eternity. She is therefore carved on the sarcophagi of Sainte Monique. A stele in the topheth shows a priestess who is prostrating herself and pouring a libation on a mound which is like that of the tomb. According to Latin authors, Dido's funerary cult went on being celebrated in the topheth until the fall of Carthage. It is probable that it was closely associated with that of the goddess.

Tanit appears, therefore, as another manifestation of those great Mother Goddesses whose worship was often extremely ancient, and whose popularity suddenly increased during the Hellenistic period. It is true that she always remained 'The Lady of Carthage' and was never elevated to the position of an Isis or a Cybele, although she resembled these goddesses closely. She was not an international goddess at this time, and had to wait till the Romans adopted her cult and renamed her Coelestis, or until the Africans came to the Imperial throne in the third century A.D. The ease with which she could be assimilated to foreign deities, however, meant that she could exert her influence on their worshippers. The popularization of her worship certainly contributed to some extent in breaking through the wall of isolation which had surrounded Carthage.

5. THE HOUSE OF HANNO RESTORED TO POWER: 345–339.

By the middle of the fourth century the leaders in Carthage were able to survey the political situation, both within the Republic and outside it, with complacency.

The fall of Hanno the Great had meant that the aristocratic régime had become firmly established: kings and generals quailed before the power of the One Hundred and Four and the People had lost the right of intervention which had been theirs in the days of conflicts between the two rival powers, and could only ratify the decisions imposed upon them by the government.

In Sicily, the death of Dionysius had shaken the foundations of the Greek Empire of the West, which that great tyrant had sought to establish with a perseverance that was only surpassed by a complete lack of scruples. Anarchy reigned in Syracuse, punctuated by constant *coups d'état*. Adventurers of all nationalities seized the other Sicilian towns, and almost all these princelings sought to counter a possible re-establishment of the Syracusan Empire or revolt of their own subjects by entering into an alliance with Carthage. Among these princelings were those of Agrigentum, Gela, Camarina and, especially, the tyrant Hiketas of Leontini.

The Oscans represented the only power in the island other than Carthage. From the end of the fifth century they had been infiltrating as mercenaries but now no longer made any secret of their intention to conquer the island for their own profit. It made little difference to them whether a city was free, such as Catania (which Mamercus had just seized), or a Carthaginian vassal, such as Entella.

This Oscan expansion into Sicily was all the more disquieting in that it represented the second wave of a great political movement with its centre in the heart of the Italian peninsula. During the whole of the fifth century, other Oscans had come down from the Apennines and conquered Campania, leaving only Naples and Ischia to the Greeks. These constituted the first wave, had become firmly established, had mixed with Hellenes and Etruscans, and had soon lost their uncouthness. They were subject to constant pressure from the rear, however, from those of their tribe who had remained in the mountains but were eager, in their turn, to descend to the plain and enjoy its riches and proximity to the sea. Thus, though they came from the same ethnic and linguistic stock, the Samnites and the Campanians had conflicting interests. While they were fighting over it, however, the land was seized by a third party.

As we have already seen, Dionysius' political moves had had repercussions as far afield as Latium and Etruria. Rome had been destroyed in 386 by the Syracusan's Celtic allies and had then to submit to being, in effect, a protectorate of Caere, the ally of Carthage. Rome had lost her control over the Latin League, which continued to act as an independent power. This situation, which was very much to the advantage of Carthage, was completely reversed in the decade between 360 and 350 B.C. The conflict between the Patricians and Plebeians had been resolved, and from

11

366 onwards the Roman Republic was in the hands of a new political party. With the decline of Syracusan power, Etruscan protection was no longer as necessary and the Romans waged what amounted to a war of liberation against Caere and Tarquinia (354–350). As a result of this war, Latin unity was re-established (in 354) in an agreement which favoured Rome. She seems to have drawn full advantage from the situation for she colonized the Pontine plain, thus gaining control of the road into Campania. The founding of Ostia was soon to bear witness to the growth of Roman maritime ambitions.

The Punic leaders followed these events closely as they bore a direct relation to their own political moves. The collapse of the Romano-Caerite union weakened their chief northern ally considerably. In 508 the Magonids had had no scruples in backing the newly established Roman Republic at the expense of their Tyrrhenian allies. Their successors were equally realistic in their approach and in 348 the old alliance was renewed in terms which naturally enough reflected the evolution in the political situation. Carthage obtained recognition of her hegemony over Utica and the coasts of Southern Spain. Even Tyre was included in this agreement, and this indicates a surprising political development in the East which we shall be examining. On the other hand, those clauses which concerned the relations between Carthaginians and Latins were altered in favour of Rome: should Punic pirates seize a Latin city which was not subject to Rome, they could keep the male prisoners and the booty but had to hand over the city together with the women and children to the Romans. This threat weighed heavily on any Latins who sought to defend their liberty.

In Greece the political situation was similar to that in Sicily. Continual discord between the Hellenic cities made them the prey of foreigners, and Philip of Macedon made the most of the Sacred Wars to build up his hegemony over the remains of the Athenian, Spartan, and Theban Empires. For the time being, it would seem, no one in Hellas had much time to think about what was happening in the West.

In the East, the political situation offered interesting possibilities to the Carthaginians. During the reign of Artaxerxes II (404–358 B.C.), the Persian Empire had been subjected to harem conspiracies and it was breaking up. The countries where the Phoenician civilization had first flourished seemed ready to regain the independence they had lost 500 years before. Egypt was the first to cast off the Persian yoke in 399, and had established a national dynasty which was to last for more than half a century. The satraps of Asia Minor were in permanent revolt and were engaged in carving out kingdoms for themselves. Evagoras united Cyprus and liberated it. The Phoenician kings, at the centre of all this activity, naturally sought to regain their independence, and the Egyptian Pharaoh was only too willing to help them. From 380 onwards, the Tyrian fleet was at the disposal of Evagoras. When, after the death of Artaxerxes II, his successor Artaxerxes III Ochus, set out to re-establish imperial unity, Tabnit, king of Sidon, led a national resistance movement which the Great King had the utmost difficulty in quelling, and which he punished by putting the leaders to death with great cruelty. This took place in 348 – the very year in which Tyre became a signatory to the Romano-Punic treaty. This fact alone is sufficient indication that Carthage was aware of her mother-city's troubles. Close ties bound Carthage and Egypt, and the Punic leaders could not but endorse an attempt at the restoration of national independence initiated by the Pharaohs.

All this must be taken into account if we are to explain the large-scale Carthaginian military undertaking in Sicily in 345. A general named Hanno was put at the head of an expedition of some size which consisted of 150 warships, 50,000 infantry, a large body of cavalry, 300 war-chariots, and a whole battery of siege-engines.[15] This weight of arms recalls the Magonid wars of the end of the fifth century, but the political framework was very different now. It was no longer a question of crushing Hellenism. Diodorus (XVI, 67, 1) gives us Timaeus' version of these events (the latter's father was lord of Taormina at the time) and insists on the friendly liberalism (*philanthropia*) with which the Carthaginians treated their Greek allies. Military action was backed by a far-reaching diplomatic campaign. It was necessary to persuade the Greeks that Punic protection would bring with it complete security both at home and abroad. The two adversaries whom it was necessary to overthrow were the Campanians of Entella, who had just renounced the Punic alliance, and Dionysius the Younger, who had returned to Syracuse where he had inititated a reign of terror. Sicily would then be rid both of Barbarians and of Tyrants. Peace in Sicily looked all the more certain as the Romans seemed to be controlling the Oscan threat at its source. They were about to form an alliance with the Capuans and engage in a fight to the death against the Samnites. If Carthage managed to control the Western Mediterranean in this way, she would then be free to throw in her lot decisively on the side of Tyre and Egypt against the Persian Empire, regenerated under Artaxerxes III.

Unfortunately for Carthage, events turned out rather differently and almost all her hopes were dashed. The principal reason for this failure was the fact that Hellenism was by no means as dead as it had seemed. On the contrary, its temporary weakness was due to a revival crisis from which Hellenism was to emerge full of a new energy and terrible aggressiveness, capable of jeopardizing the very existence of all the other Mediterranean civilizations. Far from being in a position to reign peacefully over the West, Carthage was obliged to fear and fight for her very existence as never before. Furthermore, her trials abroad were soon to unsettle the balance which had finally been attained at home, for the aristocratic régime proved itself ill-suited to the conduct of war.

The Syracusan patriots who wanted neither Dionysius nor Carthaginian domination, had turned in desperation to their mother-city, Corinth. By some miracle, though powerless herself and incapable or providing effective assistance, Corinth was able to find for these patriots exactly the man they needed: the virtuous Timoleon. The latter seems to have been born for the express purpose of serving as a model for Plutarch, who did not fail to write his biography. He had acquired a great reputation by killing his own brother, who had sought to establish a tyranny in their home-town, Corinth. During the course of the century, the republican institutions of the cities had proved incapable of adapting themselves to the new historical conditions, but Timoleon dreamt of their regeneration. He was superstitious but, although his ideas were Utopian, he was an able general, as the Carthaginians were soon to learn to their cost.

The Punic fleet endeavoured to intercept the Corinthian before he had a chance to land. It failed, and Mago, who had succeeded Hanno as commander, marched on Syracuse. The general situation in that city was strangely confused: Dionysius II held the fort which his father had built on the island of Ortygia, Hiketas occupied one quarter of the town, Timoleon another, while the Punic armada controlled the harbour. Timoleon finally gained the upper hand, thanks mainly to the timely and efficient aid supplied by Mamercus of Catania. Dionysius also played into his hands since he preferred to retire peacefully to Corinth and handed over his stronghold. Mago then deemed it wise to withdraw, thus abandoning Hiketas, who made temporary peace with Timoleon. The latter immediately attacked the Carthaginians and the tyrants who were their allies. Unfortunately, in the cause of liberty, he had no scruples in using the Oscan mercenaries of whom the Carthaginians had been trying to rid Sicily. The Campanians of Entella followed Mamercus' example and rallied to Timoleon's side. The city of which he was in command is situated in the midst of the mountains of Eastern Sicily, overlooking the inland depression which leads from Palermo and Soluntum to Selinus. Timoleon controlled the very heart of the Carthaginian province, therefore, and was in a position to make all movement there impossible.

The Punic government had little reason to be proud. Mago was called before the One Hundred and Four but preferred suicide to crucifixion. This is the first time that we have certain evidence of a general's falling victim of this formidable body, not because of treachery but because of negligence or ill fortune. Two new leaders were chosen: Hasdrubal and Hamilcar, and important military measures were called for. The élite of the army was a 'Sacred Battalion' composed of three thousand young noblemen, and it set sail for Sicily accompanied by a large body of citizens who had been mobilized, and by Libyan auxiliaries. They were joined by Iberian, Celtic, and Ligurian mercenaries. The outcome of the campaign was decided in the mountains and valleys which separate Entella and Segesta. The Carthaginians were surprised as they were crossing the river Crimisus and were defeated in a battle during the course of which the 'Sacred Battalion' was annihilated. It was the most severe Carthaginian defeat since the Battle of Himera in 480 B.C.

This disaster naturally had its repercussions on politics at home. One of the generals, Hasdrubal, was condemned to death and executed. Public feeling turned against the whole party in power, and the Elders were obliged to recall from exile Gisco, son of Hanno the Great. This event is recorded not only by Diodorus, but also by Polyaenus in his *Stratēgēmata*, and the latter tells us that Gisco had a brother called Hamilcar who, after having been a brilliant commander throughout several campaigns, had been condemned to death on the suspicion that his ambitions were directed to the establishment of a tyranny. Perhaps this is supposed to be Hanno the Great, and Polyaenus not only confused the names but also the relationship with Gisco. This section of the *Stratēgēmata* (V, 11), which we have already alluded to several times, is doubly interesting. It gives us the only description we have of a Punic 'triumph', which was obviously inspired by an Egyptian ritual, for the Carthaginian king trod his prostrate enemies underfoot just as the Pharaoh did. This text also gives us an insight into the strength of the reaction there now was against the aristocratic régime.

The nobles who were responsible for the overthrow of Hanno the Great and were now opposed to Gisco, were treated as public enemies. Gisco had the wisdom to pardon them, after a humiliating ceremony during which they were dishonoured. It is certain that he was, himself, invested with full military and royal powers. At the same time it was decided that the army should be reorganized. The Carthaginians were still suffering from the shock which the destruction of the Sacred Battalion had caused, and they therefore resolved that citizens should no longer be engaged in wars overseas, with the exception, naturally, of officers. This measure did much to increase Gisco's popularity, while at the same time strengthening his authority, for mercenaries found it easier to obey the orders of the commanders they were accustomed to, rather than those of civil authorities.

The king did not try to benefit from the situation by seeking to avenge the Sicilian defeat. He did, however, sail to Lilybaeum with a fleet of 70 ships and an army which included a large number of Greek mercenaries – a unique occurrence in Carthaginian military history. These troops were not really called upon to give battle. It is surprising that Timoleon should not have sought to hold the admirable site of Entella or come to the relief of Selinus. He realized, however, that Hellenism in Sicily could only survive if it was concentrated. He therefore abandoned the western part of the island as far as the Halycus and the Himeras to the Carthaginians, with the sole condition that any Greek who so wished might come and settle in the eastern part of the island. Timoleon set about uniting this region into a federation of cities under a moderate oligarchical régime, which was not so different, in fact, from that of Carthage itself.

Gsell has suggested that the Carthaginians were all the more ready to come to terms, because they were eager to rid themselves of Gisco, but there is nothing to indicate that the latter fell from power once peace had been concluded. Those kings of Carthage whom we know, at the end of the fourth century B.C., either certainly or most probably belonged to his family. From 339 to 309 there do not seem to have been any more condemnations of generals, though party struggles continued, and the descendants of Hanno the Great had several enemies among the aristocracy. Probably Hamilcar, and certainly Bomilcar, were not satisfied with purely constitutional power, and it is probable that they each contemplated a *coup d'état* to give themselves absolute power. During this period, however, that balance seems to have been maintained between the three powers which Aristotle considered to be the basis and chief virtue of the Punic constitution.

6. THE DEVELOPMENT OF A NEW WORLD ORDER

The treaty they had signed with Timoleon resulted in a great improvement in the Carthaginians' economic and cultural life. During the twenty-five years of peace which followed, the Punic standard of living went up, and a luxury industry and foreign relations were both developed. This progress can be studied thanks to the graves of Ard el Morali, Ard el Kheraib, and the earliest tomb-chambers of Sainte Monique – all of which belong to this period.

Luxury wares were imported from Italy, and among them the 'plate of Genucilia' from the workshops of Caere, which is one of the finest known examples of this type of pottery and is decorated with a female head. Quantities of decorated saucers came from the same place, and there were also cups, bowls, and dishes of highly burnished black Pre-Campanian ware decorated with incised lines and palmettes. Finally, from Attica came flat, circular, saucer-lamps with one burner. The bronze industry developed and the better quality alloy made possible the production of luxury objects such as vases and razors. Jugs reproduced fifth-century Etruscan models with their characteristic trefoil mouth and elongated pouring lip, short neck, and body in the shape of a truncated cone with the handle decorated with an anchor-shaped palmette. The hatchet-shaped razors ending in the neck and head of a bird became more refined in execution and shape. The blade became sharper, the bird's neck longer, and it curved over in a half-moon. These razors were now carved with designs executed with a graver – a technique which seems to have come from Etruria. Although the first attempts were clumsy, we can recognize lotus blossom, fish, boats, etc. . . .

Terracotta figurines were imported from Sicily and we find representations of small grotesque figures, flute-players, Europa and the bull, Hermes carrying a ram, etc. The island had, in fact, also made the most of Timoleon's peace and had rebuilt her ruined buildings and re-opened her ceramic workshops. Wars had prevented her from following the new fashions which had appeared meanwhile in Greece, and work was resumed according to the old routines and methods, using the old moulds as they stood. This renaissance is therefore characterized by a late survival of classicism, and the statuettes of the second half of the fourth century still have column-shaped bodies and severe features, and are completely smothered in the heavy folds of their clothing.

Punic potters were strongly influenced by the wares from Ionian Sicily, and copied the round-bellied, high-necked jars, decorated with bands of dark red or purple paint on a cream slip. They also began, at about this time, to produce small unguent flasks with no handles, a low neck, and a spherical body.

It is to this period that we must ascribe the only Punic objects which are really worthy of being called works of art. These are the sacrophagi of the aristocracy which were discovered by Père Delattre in the tomb-chambers of Sainte Monique, and ten of which are so far known. They are carved in Sicilian marble and must have been produced between the peace of Timoleon and the conquest of the island by the Romans (339–260). They can be divided into two groups according to their shape: temple-shaped sarcophagi, and sarcophagi with statues. Furthermore, in both groups there are examples of the later severe style which is characteristic of the Timoleonian Renaissance, while others are influenced by Hellenistic art and must belong to the last years of the fourth and the first decades of the third century B.C.

The temple-shaped sarcophagi reproduce exactly the Greek naos with its pitched roof represented by the lid. The Carthaginians have done away with the corner-columns and capitals which are to be found on Sicilian prototypes. The mouldings of the base and cornice have been preserved, however, with egg- and dart-shaped decoration. These mouldings were painted in bright colours – mainly scarlet and blue – as were the acroteria and the slopes of the pediment. The prototypes of these sarcophagi appear in Sicily as early as the sixth century and were still made in Gela in about 340 B.C.

In the second series, the roof of the temple has been flattened and a statue has been carved with a cushion beneath its head. Most of these statues represent an elderly, bearded man, either bare-headed with short curling hair, or wearing a skull-cap held in place by a turban. The heavy, columnar body is clad in a short-sleeved, ankle-length tunic decorated on the left shoulder with a fringed 'epitoga'. The figure is shod with thonged sandals or closed shoes. The right leg, which is pushed forward slightly, is alone discernible beneath the heavy material of the robe. The open right hand is raised to shoulder level in a gesture of greeting, prayer, or benediction, which frequently occurs in representations both of men and of gods on Punic monuments.[16] He holds his left hand against his chest and grasps a cup or box. His features are regular and placid but lifeless. This almost complete stiffness and idealization is paralleled in the 'Timoleonian' sculptures of Sicily (339–310).

One tomb-chamber in Sainte Monique contained, in addition to a sarcophagus with the statue of a man, one with the statue of a woman. She is young and, like the protomae of the fifth century, she wears a veil from which escapes a row of curls round the forehead and along the shoulders. She is also wearing ear-rings in the shape of an inverted cone below which hangs a bead. The upper part of her body is wrapped in a peplos which is ornamented round the neck by bands and two claw-like attachments. The really surprising feature in this representation, however, is the huge bird of prey on which she lies, whose head hoods hers, and whose folded wings cover her hips and her legs. At Thinissut in the

Cap Bon district, terracotta statues have been found in a sanctuary of the first century B.C. and these represent a lion-headed goddess whose legs are likewise wrapped in a wing 'skirt'. These are probably all representations of Tanit.

The statue of Sainte Monique holds a dove head-downwards in one hand and ears of corn in the other. The archaic head-dress of this Tanit, and her regular and placid features, are indications that she belongs to the late severe style, prior to the advent in Carthage of the first Hellenistic influences in about 305. This dating is confirmed by the ear-rings, for identical ones are represented on the Genucilia plates, painted at Caere by the 'Princeton Painter'.[17]

Only one sarcophagus of the statue type is known outside Carthage. It was found at Tarquinia and is doubtless an Etruscan copy of an African prototype. Here again we have an indication of the close links which existed between the two civilizations. In spite of what has been said to the contrary, these sarcophagi have nothing in common with the Phoenician 'anthropoid' sarcophagi which are to be found from Sidon to Soluntum and Cadiz. These latter are copies of the Egyptian mummy-coffins, which follow the shape of the body. The Carthaginian examples, on the other hand, combine, most illogically, the representation of a temple with the statue of a live person lying on the roof. In the fourth century, the Etruscans of Caere, Vulci, and Chiusi frequently represented the dead stretched out as though in sleep, on a couch raised on a high base with pediments at each end. It was this which probably first gave the Carthaginians the idea of combining the temple-sarcophagus of the Sicilians with the Tyrrhenian couch-sarcophagus.

Several experts, among them Carcopino, have ascribed the workmanship of the Sainte Monique sarcophagi to Greeks living in Carthage. It is certain that the Carthaginians were not used to working marble, and even the smallest details of these tomb monuments are executed with a skill which is in marked contrast to the usual carelessness of Punic craftsmen. The heads present none of the customary oriental features such as hooked noses, huge almond-shaped eyes, and fleshy lips, which the Phoenicians reproduced for generations as characteristic of their race. We have seen, furthermore, that there is a close stylistic affinity between the Carthaginian sarcophagi and contemporary Sicilian monuments of the time of Timoleon. It would seem likely, therefore, that the

Punic examples were executed by Siceliot craftsmen working, however, under the close supervision of Carthaginians, for only the latter could have conceived such hybrid compositions, so alien to the Hellenistic concept.

Carcopino suggested that the sarcophagi had been ordered by Hellenized Carthaginians, followers of 'salvation' cults, particularly that of Demeter. In fact, he failed to find any emblem, either of Demeter or of Dionysius, and these would certainly not have been lacking in the tombs of initiates. The appearance of a representation of Tanit would indicate, rather, that the occupants of the tomb-chambers had remained faithful to the religion of their fathers. Apart from a few very special cases – such as the victims of the moloch – this religion does not seem to have admitted the possibility of the worship of heroes after death before the Barcid period. We do not, therefore, hold the view that the statues represent the deified dead. On the contrary, an idea which was equally as current among the Egyptians as among the Phoenicians, was that the gods protected the dead man, resurrected him, and enabled him to live again in his tomb. This is doubtless the part played by the Sainte Monique Tanit. The most likely suggestion is that we have here portraits of the dead men as found on Etruscan tombs. The type is very close to that found in innumerable statues and stelae which were made to be erected on the tombs. In the 'epitoga' which adorns the shoulder of the Sainte Monique statues, it is tempting to see the insignia of some high dignitary or magistrate. Furthermore, the epitaphs indicate that the whole area was reserved for the burial of important personnages. It must be admitted, however, that there is nothing to prove that this interpretation is any more correct than that which sees in the austere figures, gods watching over the sleep of the dead.

7. THE END OF THE PUNIC MONARCHY

The peace which followed the war with Timoleon was still in force in about 325. It was at this time that the navigator from Marseilles, Pytheas, obtained permission to sail through the Straits of Gibraltar on an expedition along the western and northern coasts of Europe. As we have already seen, relations between Carthage and Marseilles had improved, thanks to the intervention of Caere some forty years earlier. This relaxing of the veto normally imposed on all foreign sailors would be inexplicable in the light of the views at present held concerning Carthaginian trade (and which the present author subscribed to for a long time), namely, that the Carthaginians held the monopoly of the tin trade with Cornwall by the sea route via the ports of Gascony, Poitou, and Brittany. The Romano-Punic treaty of 348 had re-enforced the prohibitions in this respect, which had first been formulated in 509. The Romans were, for example, completely forbidden to trade in Sardinia and Libya (except with Carthage), and also in Spain. The complete absence of any Punic object along the coasts of France and in the British Isles has already been discussed in connection with the voyage of Himilco, and constrains us to admit that Carthage never controlled the Atlantic sea-board north of Galicia and the Cape Finisterre in Spain, though her presence is well attested here. On the other hand, the Marseillais had long had access to tin from the Scilly Isles by way of the rivers of Gaul. Thus, the voyage of Pytheas did not affect any essential Phoenician interest, and the sailor was only seeking to reach, by a new route, a region which was already part of his city's economic sphere. This fact does nothing to detract from the exceptional quality of this friendly Carthaginian move in allowing Pytheas access to the Alboran sea, passage through the Pillars of Hercules, and use, naturally, of the Phoenician ports and facilities along the Portuguese coast. We must admit, in the light of this evidence, that the Phocaeans and Carthaginians seem to have been able, for a time at least, to sink their differences in the pursuit of common interests.

It has been suggested that better relations between Carthage and Marseilles had been inspired by fear of Alexander. Indeed, if the Carthaginians had ever entertained the hope of seeing their metropolis independent and the East free, this hope had been rapidly and cruelly shattered. First of all, Artaxerxes III Ochus had followed up his brutal repression of the Phoenician revolt by subduing Egypt once again in 345. Twelve years later, as a result of the battle of Issus, Alexander forced his way into Syria. The Sidonians were still suffering from the after-effects of their war and welcomed their new master enthusiastically. Tyre had succeeded in not getting herself involved in the war against Ochus, and believed that the time had come for her to turn the situation to her own advantage. Under pretext of helping the Persians repel the invasion, she had equipped a considerable fleet, part of which was in the Aegean, and the Tyrian king, Azmilk, had made the most of these operations and had entered into relations with Sparta and Athens. He hoped that the collapse of the Persian Empire and the weakness of the Macedonian navy would enable him, at last, to gain his independence. It was the time of the great sacrifice for the Rebirth of Melqart – a sacrifice which had been instituted by Hiram. Carthage sent a delegation to attend it. Alexander intimated that he would come himself to officiate and this would have established him as overlord of the Phoenicians. Azmilk answered that the gates of the city would be closed to him.

The Punic ambassadors probably approved of this determined stand. When Tyre was blockaded, however, and when the other Phoenician cities had gone over to the Macedonians, the government of Carthage thought it unwise to commit itself further. Azmilk was told that he could expect no help from the Carthaginians though any non-combatants who had fled before the harbours were closed were given refuge. The members of the Carthaginian delegation remained within the town to the very end and took refuge with the king in the Temple of Melqart when the city fell. They were given their freedom, but Alexander bade them beware: he would soon carry the war into their homeland. The Macedonian's untimely end did not enable him to carry out his threat. The thirst for conquest which his example had produced among the Greeks, could only be satisfied, however, at the expense of the African metropolis.

Timoleon's constitution did not last long in Syracuse. After a period of unrest which began in 330, the head of the democratic party – a potter's son named Agathocles – seized power in 316. He had been helped by the Carthaginian general who was in command in Sicily at that time, and who was called Hamilcar. This same Hamilcar concluded a treaty with the tyrant three years later, according to which the latter was recognized as ruler of all the Greeks who were not under Carthaginian domination, and especially over Agrigentum, which had, until then, vigorously defended her liberty. There is good reason to agree with Beloch's view that this Hamilcar was another member of the family of Hanno the Great.[18] He may have been a nephew of Gisco, whose son was also called Hamilcar. In any case, the one we are dealing with was suspected of treason because of his agreement with Agathocles, while some even went as far as to suggest that he intended to use the Syracusans to help him become tyrant of Carthage. He was fined (Justin maintains that he was secretly condemned to death), and on his death he was succeeded as commander in Sicily by Gisco's son. The latter was probably invested with royal powers at the same time (these may also have belonged to his namesake) for he was certainly king at a later date. This choice, like that of Bomilcar later on, is an indication that the influence of the dynasty was still strongly felt and that the Elders, although they mistrusted it, could not get rid of it. The son of Gisco obtained important concessions for, in spite of the decisions which had been made after the battle of Crimisus, an élite battalion was recruited for him, which consisted of 2000 noblemen. In addition, 10,000 Libyans, 1000 Etruscan mercenaries, 200 chariot-drivers of the same nationality, and 1000 Iberian sling-men were enlisted, and 130 galleys were equipped. This armada suffered from the effects of a storm, but Hamilcar assembled yet more troops in Sicily. In the summer of 311 he met Agathocles at Ecnomus and defeated him. This success gave the Carthaginians control of almost the whole island apart from Syracuse, where Agathocles was preparing to sustain a siege.

It was then that the tyrant completely reversed the course of the war by a move of such temerity that only a contemporary of Alexander's could have conceived it. He left Syracuse to defend herself and carried the war into Africa. This enterprise could only succeed if surprise were complete, and not the least of Agathocles' achievements was his ability to equip a fleet and an army without the Carthaginians being aware of his intentions. He also succeeded in baffling the Punic fleet which was blockading the harbour of Syracuse and, on 20 August 310 B.C., he just managed to escape pursuit and landed on the tip of Cap Bon, near the famous quarries of El Haouaria.

The Carthaginian leaders had never even contemplated the possibility of such an undertaking and no measures had been taken to counter it. There were, doubtless, troops on the Libyan frontier, but in the neighbourhood of Carthage and in the city itself there was not one soldier or one magistrate with any experience in the calling up of troops and their command. Only the king could have done this, but he was in Sicily. Agathocles was able to lay waste Cap Bon at his leisure for several days, for this was where the rich Carthaginians had their finest properties and the peninsula was covered with flourishing townships. He began by 'burning his boats' (the proverbial expression derives from this episode), and then seized and destroyed two towns: Megalopolis and White Tunis, the exact whereabouts are not known. (It is certain the last-mentioned city cannot be identified with present-day Tunis, where Agathocles later settled.)

The news of these events reached Carthage in an extremely confused form which bore little relation to actual events, and it naturally caused consternation and panic. When things had calmed down slightly, the Elders formally and severely blamed the commanders of the fleet for negligence, and appointed two generals, Hanno and Bomilcar, who belonged, according to Diodorus, to rival families. Bomilcar was the nephew of Hamilcar, Agathocles' first ally, and probably belonged, therefore, to the house of Hanno the Great, as did King Hamilcar, the son of Gisco, whose title he was soon to acquire.

Members of the dynastic faction had been obliged to have recourse to that traditional usage whereby generalship which a king was unable to exercise in person became the prerogative of a member of his family. Bomilcar was unpopular among the nobility, however, and belonged to a hard core of monarchists who dreamt of imposing an authoritarian régime on Carthage. Hanno was therefore associated with him to keep an eye on him. All citizens capable of bearing arms were mobilized, and Hanno and Bomilcar were thus able to assemble 45,000 men – almost three times the number that Agathocles commanded. The Syracusan managed to offer battle on a site where he had the advantage, since the Carthaginians could not deploy their forces and their generals were unable to co-ordinate their actions. Hanno soon fell at the head of his phalanx and Bomilcar (through treachery, so Diodorus tells us) ordered a retreat which soon became a rout.

This unexpected defeat, following, as it did, on a seemingly unbelievable attack, resulted in a fanatical reaction among the Carthaginians generally. The Phoenicians believed, like the Hebrews, that political defeat was a punishment inflicted by their national gods on an unfaithful people. It was held that the leaders who were responsible had to do penance and offer themselves or, at least some substitute victim, in atonement. In the present case, public indignation must have been exceptionally strong, for many people must have found the religious innovations which had been introduced since the beginning of the century, extremely hard to accept. As we have seen, however, these new cults had been favoured mainly by the aristocracy, and it was the nobles who had opened the door to foreign influences. The anger of the people turned against them, doubtless much to Bomilcar's relief, as his suspect, or at any rate inefficient, conduct was thus forgotten. The victims were 300 unfortunate children of noble birth whose parents had managed to avoid sacrificing them by providing young slaves as substitutes. These children were already several years old, and they were offered to the terrible brazen statue whose hands moved downwards and dropped them into the flaming topheth.

Agathocles could not, however, attack Carthage itself as the city was probably well fortified by now. He fell back upon Tunis, beneath the walls of which he established his camp, thus cutting Carthage off from the mainland. He then carried out raids for booty into the countryside, and sought to draw the Libyans away from their allegiance. During his first raid he swept through Byzacenia and seized Hadrumetum.

Meanwhile King Hamilcar had sent some relief troops to Africa and was carrying on with the siege of Syracuse. During the summer of 309 he again tried to take the city by storm, but was captured and tortured to death. His head was sent to Agathocles, who, according to Diodorus, came himself to exhibit it to the Carthaginians, who fell prostrate before these remains, thus bearing witness to the religious veneration which the monarchy still inspired. Bomilcar was proclaimed *melek* with sole power on all fronts.

Agathocles, however, had to contend with the lack of discipline of his troops, who had become conscious of the fact that it was now impossible to gain a decisive victory over the enemy. He managed to quell a first mutiny and to defeat an army which the Carthaginians had succeeded in getting out of the town. He then turned his attention to plotting, in order to obtain the necessary troops to complete the war. One of Alexander's companions, Ophellas, had succeeded in carving out a princedom for himself in Cyrenaica. Agathocles promised to surrender Carthage to him, if he first helped him seize the city. When Ophellas arrived after a trying march across the desert of Syrtica, the Syracusan assassinated him and took his troops under his own command.[19]

Meanwhile, another dramatic event was taking place in Carthage. Bomilcar had barely acceded to the royal office when he made an attempt to seize absolute power. To that end he had sent most of the officers of the nobility to fight away from home, and had assembled in one of the suburbs the troops on whom he could depend, consisting mainly of mercenaries. He marched on the centre of the city, but the people, who had previously supported him against the aristocracy, did not want a tyrant. The young men ran to arms, and from the high buildings overlooking the agora they rained weapons on to the dissident troops who were driven from the centre of the city and were obliged to capitulate and abandon the king to the revenge of the nobles. who were finally in a position to make Bomilcar pay, and all the pent-up hatred against him and against his forebears was let loose, and the fear which he had caused them to live under and the horrible slaughter of their unfortunate offspring had to be atoned for. The king was scientifically tortured before being crucified on the main square. Before he finally died, however, he had enough strength left, according to Justin, to shriek his hatred of his tormentors, and shout of the execution of Hanno the Great, the exile of Gisco, and the intrigues against Hamilcar. Punic monarchy was, indeed, dying on this cross. Although it was not abolished, its titularies no longer exercised either political or military authority, and only held purely honorary function. They left no mark in history and only the name of one of them has come down to us. (This was Bomilcar II, who was a son-in-law of Hamilcar Barca. See below p. 207.)

*

8. CARTHAGE – QUEEN OF THE WESTERN MEDITERRANEAN: 307–264

The end of Punic monarchy is, in fact, the most important result, even though unintentional, of Agathocles' campaign. We do not know how the various political institutions were modified since we have no information whatsoever concerning Carthaginian affairs at home from the death of Bomilcar until the outbreak of the war against Rome. Perhaps it was now that an Inner Committee of thirty members, within the Council of the Elders, was instituted which henceforward constituted the real government of the Republic. In any case, the Elders certainly undertook a complete re-organization of the army, and three generals, named Hanno, Himilco, and Hasdrubal, were appointed to conduct the war in Africa. These generals were not called upon to confront Agathocles immediately. The latter was as versatile as he was imaginative and audacious and, just at the moment when the advent of the troops of Ophellas seemed to make a direct attack on Carthage possible, he changed his plans. He found it preferable to conquer Utica and Bizerta, with the intention of surrounding Carthage with a series of Greek bases. For this reason he also founded, on the tip of Cap Bon, a city which he named Aspis (the shield), rendered into Latin as Clupea. This still survives, almost unchanged, as Kelibia. Agathocles then re-embarked for Sicily and began fighting in the Punic province. He left his army in Africa under the command of his sons, and sent an expeditionary force along the African coast to the west, under the orders of Eumachus. It seems that the latter reached the region round Constantine. The Greeks were soon confronted simultaneously by three Carthaginian armies, however, and were severely defeated on several occasions. Agathocles returned for some time to Africa, but he also was defeated. He then fled in secret to Syracuse, abandoning his sons, who were massacred by their troops since the latter were eager to make peace with Carthage.

Agathocles' expedition had shown how strong was the hold of Carthage over her African territory. Whereas, at the beginning of the century, the Libyans had been in constant revolt, at the time with which we are dealing the Syracusan had been able to rally only one chief of any importance to his side. This chief was Ailymas, and since he had soon after gone over to the other side, the Greeks had been obliged to get rid of him. The loyalty of the Phoenician towns had not stood so firm. It would seem that Utica, a particularly privileged city, had at first opened her gates to the invader, but she then had second thoughts and so was destroyed. She was to follow the same line of conduct in the Mercenary War and in the Third War against Rome.

On his return to Syracuse, Agathocles settled down to a new career. He was unexpectedly successful in ridding himself of the Republican faction, which had always been opposed to him, and he then proclaimed himself king and was recognized as such not only in Syracuse but also throughout that part of Sicily which was independent of Carthage.

During the last quarter-century of his life, he followed a policy which was very close to what Dionysius' had been. He sought to gather under his rule Western Hellenism in its entirety, he made contact with the Graeco-Macedonian kingdoms which were left over from Alexander's Empire, and he even occupied the island of Corfu.

It might well seem as though this change of orientation were yet another aspect of Agathocles' versatility. In fact, the tyrant's war against Carthage cannot be disassociated from the great conflict which, at this time, held the whole of the Italian peninsula in its throes. This was the Romano-Samnite War for possession of Campania, into which all the Italian states were gradually being drawn. Two facts indicate this: in 307 Agathocles was only able to remain in Syracuse thanks to an Etruscan fleet which helped him to raise the Punic blockade, and in 306 Rome and Carthage renewed their alliance. According to Philinus, a Greek historian from Sicily in Hannibal's entourage, the two powers agreed that Sicily should belong to Carthage and Italy to Rome. Polybius has bitterly accused Philinus of inventing this treaty, but most modern historians agree that in this case, as in many others, the Achaean was misled by pro-Roman propaganda.[20]

From this information we can deduce that in 307-306 an Etrusco-Syracusan coalition was in opposition to a Romano-Punic coalition, and that from then on Rome and Carthage were agreed to do away with Western Hellenism and to share the spoils. In view of the events of the preceding years, such a state of affairs is easily understandable. At the beginning of the Romano-Samnite wars, the Etruscans remained neutral. When they did finally decide to intervene in 311, it was too late. While they remained inactive, and probably thanks to this same inactivity, the fate of Italy was being decided, round about 320 B.C., at the time when the legions had just been crushed at the Caudine Forks. This neutrality may have been partly dictated by Carthage, who did her utmost to maintain the peace between her old and new allies. In 311 the Etruscans finally saw where this ill-omened neutrality was leading them. They broke off relations with both Rome and Carthage and made an alliance with Agathocles. For their part, the Roman leaders rapidly grasped the fact that they could not hope to conquer Campania and the Southern Apennines without getting involved in Greek affairs. Naples was their ally at first, but changed sides in 327 at the instigation of Tarentum, under the leadership of Agathocles. Throughout the course of the Samnite war, Tarentum constantly opposed Roman policy, more or less openly, and her diplomacy was frequently responsible for the formation of Italic coalitions.[21] Although the Hellenes, the Italiots, and the Siceliots were incapable of sinking their secular differences, they nevertheless realized that only by uniting and seeking help from Greece could they hope to preserve their liberty. This was the policy which Agathocles pursued during the second half of his life and which even led him to occupy Naples for a short time. He did not, however, lose sight of the Carthaginian threat, and at the time of his death in 289 he was engaged in building a fleet to back a new landing in Africa.

His disappearance from the scene was the signal for the reappearance of anarchy in Greek Sicily. Tyrants seized power once more in each city as they had after the death of Dionysius I. The most powerful was Phintias of Agrigentum but his sole policy was opposition to Hiketas in Syracuse. To this end he even, unwillingly, accepted Punic overlordship. Finally, Hiketas was driven from Syracuse and the city was divided between Theonon, who held the fort of Ortygia, and Sosistratus, who held the city, while the Carthaginians sailed into the harbour under the pretext of settling the dispute. Meanwhile, a band of Oscans who had served under Agathocles, seized Messina, massacred the male population, and kept the women-folk and the loot. These brigands took the name of Mamertini, or sons of Mars, and robbed with impartiality all the inhabitants of the north-eastern part of the island for more than twenty years. Carthage made the most of the chaotic situation and occupied all the key positions, such as the Lipari Islands. Nor were Greek affairs any better on the Italian mainland. In 302 Rome had promised Tarentum that she would not send her fleet beyond Cape Lacinium. Once Agathocles was dead, however, the legionaries were called in, first by the Greeks of Thurii and then by other Italiots, to protect them from the Lucanians. Tarentum was once again directly threatened.

Tarentum had already sent to Greek leaders several times appealing for help against the Barbarians. In 281 she appealed to the king of Illyria, Pyrrhus, who dreamt of a Western Empire and glory equal to that of Alexander. He had married several princesses, one of whom was a daughter of Agathocles. This 'New Achilles' determined to continue the work of his father-in-law and of Dionysius, and save Western Hellenism. He almost succeeded in driving the Romans back into Latium, and in a lightning campaign he wrested the whole of Sicily from Carthage, except for Lilybaeum. Once again, however, the Greeks of the West showed themselves incapable of accepting the discipline which would have saved them. Pyrrhus finally abandoned the West to Rome and Carthage, and was killed in Argos.

Thus, without expending much effort, the Punic government obtained absolute control of the channel between the two halves of the Mediterranean: the Carthaginians were lords of Sicily, Malta, and Sardinia, and had an important fleet in this area and could boast, with reason, of controlling all contacts between East and West.

The importance of this result was increased when viewed in relation to the current Graeco-Asiatic situation, which also seemed to favour Carthaginian politics. There was no longer any hope, after Ipsus (301), of re-establishing the unity of Alexander's empire. Ptolemy I, Soter, had ruled Egypt since the death of Alexander and assumed the title of king in 305. He then added Coele Syria to his lands (that is, Palestine and Phoenicia) and his fleet gave him control of the whole of the eastern part of the Mediterranean. The two other great Hellenistic monarchies did not become properly established before 280 B.C., but in this Egypto-Phoenician state we have much the same grouping as had been conceived during the first half of the century. This political grouping could not fail to attract Carthage, especially as the Lagids sought to convert Alexander's military imperialism into an economic imperialism, which was far less intimidating. Ptolemy I showed real interest in Phoenician affairs and soon substituted their talent for the Attic talent which Alexander had adopted. This further strengthened the relations between Carthage, Alexandria, and Alexandria's allies – among them Tarentum, the most active of the cities of Magna Graecia. Indeed, products from the Egyptian capital and from Italy are to be found in Punic tombs at this time. A black ware with metallic highlights is characteristic of the Alexandrine cemetery of Sciatbi, and we also find Nilotic trumpery wares, vases from Gnathia, and soon, Campanian A pottery.

The terracotta figurines, whether imported or manufactured on the spot, have lost their stiffness. Their heads are bent, and the weight of the body rests on one leg, while the dress clings to the body. A ribbed hair-style and new, fashionable ear-rings have been adopted. Glass-makers manufactured pin-heads on which are represented a double female head with curly hair-style, or multi-coloured masks wearing a hooped bun.

There do not seem to be any more bronze vessels in the Etruscan style, but Attic prototypes were imitated, with their trefoil lip and high S-shaped handles decorated with attachments in the likeness of a woman's head, a helmeted warrior, and, especially, masks of Satyrs, or promotae of Isis wearing the disc and horns of Hathor or the atef crown.

The raids of Agathocles and his army did not break up all the great fortunes, and nobles continued to have themselves interred in marble sarcophagi. These still belong to the same two types, but their style has evolved. The figure is draped in his tunic with its 'epitoga', like his predecessors, but the body beneath it has some shape, and the garment clings to it. The figure of a lady removing her veil has been justly compared by Père Delattre to a fourth-century Attic funerary statue. We cannot tell whether she is supposed to represent Demeter welcoming a worshipper, or one of these same worshippers imploring the goddess's protection.

The temple sarcophagi which are not adorned with statues, have also evolved, and now bear fresco decoration on the pediments: a winged Scylla is depicted according to a Tarentine model. This monster was supposed to guard the Straits of Messina and was well-known both in Etruria and in Magna Graecia. On another sarcophagus, two Persian griffons face each other in an heraldic pose, while their tails are prolonged by a scroll-pattern of leaves. The fashion for hybrid figures was now beginning to spread throughout the Hellenistic world. The most curious of these sarcophagi is an exact reproduction of the wooden coffins which have been found at Abousir in Egypt. The sculptor has even indicated the gap between the planks. One of the panels is decorated with busts emerging from bushes of acanthus which end in scrolls; the motif, line, and colour are all faithfully copied from Graeco-Egyptian originals.

Bronze engraving and stone-carving reached their zenith. The razors are made of excellent bronze and are very elegantly shaped. The designs are restrained and executed with great assurance. On the stelae of the topheth, the divine emblems are often represented within a chapel. This chapel either imitates those for funerary rites depicted on Tarentine vessels of the end of the fourth century, or they come under Alexandrine influence and fantastic decoration is added in which the scroll plays an important part. The sacred vase is now represented as a pistil framed by plant volutes escaping from bunches of acanthus. One stele bearing this type of decoration was, indeed, dedicated by a Greek, Arcestus, son of Protarchus. The style is, however, rather dry and abstract, which shows that the Carthaginians were not really at home with these themes from the repertoire of Hellenistic fantasy.

A series of particularly interesting stelae can be dated to this period. They show priests exercising their office. The most famous actually depicts the 'cohen' holding the child which is going to be sacrificed. This stele must have been dedicated by a member of the traditional school of thought who did not approve of relaxing the rules attached to this horrible practice. There is no doubt, however, that this is a monument from the end of the fourth century for the priest wears a cylindrical cap and transparent Egyptian robe, which recall exactly those on Baaliaton's stele, found near Tyre and preserved in the Ny Carlsberg Museum in Copenhagen. Owing to the style in which his features have been rendered, Baaliaton cannot have lived before 300 B.C. at the earliest. The decoration of the Carthaginian stele is obviously Hellenistic in inspiration with its friezes of ovolo and scroll motifs, its rose framed by dolphins, symbolizing the sun, and the palmette on its pediment. Another stele shows a priest with a shaven head, and wearing an Egyptian robe which is ornamented with the sign of Tanit, praying before an altar. The Louvre possesses a third representation of a priest who, in this case, is bearded, whose head is veiled, and who is pouring a libation.

Tanit and Ba'al Hammon are the only gods mentioned in the dedicatory inscriptions, but two minor gods, subordinate to the 'Lady' and the 'Lord', were also honoured in the topheth. Sakon was assimilated to Hermes and, towards the end of the third century, another 'minister-god' began to gain the ascendant. This was Shed, an old Canaanite deity who had long been assimilated to Horus and who was, first and foremost, a god of healing. His name developed into Shadrapa, which means 'Shed heals'. Shadrapa's rise in favour was mainly due to the fact that he was assimilated to Dionysus and that, under his aegis, it was possible to develop Bacchic rites in Carthage. Thus, from the end of the fourth century onwards, Dionysiac emblems make their appearance and we not infrequently find the wine-cup and ivy-leaf. In the second century a bunch of grapes is carved beside the sign for Tanit, and one stele even bears the representation of a dancing Satyr. Shadrapa himself is depicted on the ex-votos either as the falcon Horus (also to be found on razors), or as a squatting child subduing a scorpion or a serpent (Shed's protection was mainly invoked against snake-bites). It seems that the children who were sacrificed were assimilated to him.

In spite of the popularity of Tanit, the topheth was not the only focus for Carthaginian religious activity. Tyrian refugees fleeing from Alexander must have brought back the cult of Melqart, though it is mainly in the Barcid period that we witness that god's spectacular rise in favour as the patron of the illustrious family of Hamilcar. Even then he was venerated as the protector of the dead, and as a saviour. The Barcids' deeds also brought into favour a warrior-god who was assimilated to Mars and Ares, but whose Phoenician name is not known with any certainty. He may have been Hadad, who was generally worshipped as Ba'al Saphon. A large inscription of the third century, known as the 'Tariff of Marseilles' because at some unknown date it was brought to that city, gives the regulations for the sacrifices to be offered in his temple. The Temple of Eshmun was built on the slopes of a hill overlooking the northern part of the town, where the Romans later excavated their theatre. He was worshipped by the Greeks as Asclepius. Yet another sanctuary was the sumptuous one of Reshef

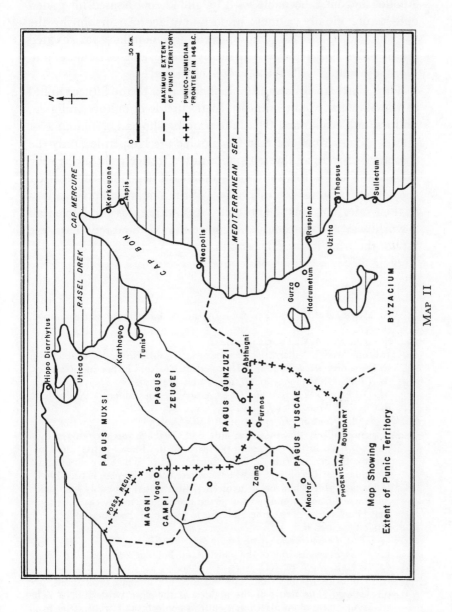

Map Showing
Extent of Punic Territory

MAP II

between the harbours and the agora. The god was represented as Apollo, and his tabernacle with its gilded roof housed his gilded cult-statue. Finally, a most important place of worship for the Carthaginians, which became increasingly popular, was situated on the hill of Borj Jedid, where the Syracusan rites of Demeter and Kore, associated with Pluto, were celebrated.

Thus Carthage followed her inclination to be the future capital of the Western Mediterranean, in the fields of culture, religion, politics, and economics. Of all the peoples who had, at one time or another, come from the East to colonize the Hesperides, only the Phoenicians were still able to offer any effective resistance to the advance of the autochthonous peoples. All depended on whether they could rally the representatives of the threatened civilizations to their side. This was the problem; its solution was going to entail a world war and determine, for more than a thousand years, the fate of the Mediterranean peoples.

Notes and References

1. A. Merlin, *B.A.C.*, 1907, p. CCXL; and A. Blanchet, *Rev. Num.*, 1907, p. 533.
2. S. Gsell, *H.A.A.N.*, IV, p. 459, n. 1.
3. J. Brunel and J. Villard, *La céramique grecque de Marseille*, pp. 85–86, n. 5.
4. E. Benveniste, *Studi Etruschi*, VII (1933), p. 245; and E. Boucher-Colozier, *M.E.F.R.*, LXV (1953), p. 66, n. 3 (bibliography).
5. M. Del Chiaro, *The Genucilia Group*, University of California Publications in Classical Archaeology, 3, 4 (1957), pp. 255–6.
6. R. Weil, *Aristote et l'Histoire*, pp. 181, 253–4, 323.
7. It seems unlikely that the main square in Carthage was surrounded by a portico. Even in Greece, agora porticos, on the Ionian pattern, did not become the general rule until the fourth century. There are none round the squares at Lepcis and at Mactar where the Punic plan is preserved.
8. If Hanno's slaves had been involved, Justin would probably have been more specific and would have used the word *ipsius*; in any case, we know that Hanno's slaves remained faithful to him until the bitter end.
9. Op. cit., p. 228 ff.
10. G. Glotz, *La cité grecque*, p. 102–3.
11. Livy's *Consilium Senectius* of the Thirty, and Polibius' γέρουσια.
12. Cf. G. Half, *Karthago*, XII (1963–4), p. 70.
13. All Punic inscriptions, and this includes the topheth dedications, are unvocalized. The name of the goddess is therefore written TNT. The traditional form of vocalization is entirely conjectural. Certain stelae from El Hofra near Constantine are inscribed in Greek characters and give us the forms Thinith and Theneith. The name was probably pronounced Tinit.

14. Cf. F. Cross, *Eretz Israel*, 1967, p. 12 and n. 27.

15. Some consider that this is none other than Hanno I, the Great (cf. S. Gsell, *H.A.A.N.*, II, p. 246, n. 2 who suggests this hypothesis but does not necessarily subscribe to it). We have already considered the reasons against bringing forward the date of the fall of Hanno I, the Great, as far as this. In any case, Hanno is the most common of all Punic personal names.

16. Cf. R. Brilliant, *Gesture and Rank in Roman Art*, pp. 23–25; and cf. various stelae such as that of Ba'al from Sousse where both the god and the worshipper make the same gesture. There are also votive and funerary statues and figurines. This gesture is found among other Semitic peoples.

17. The face of the Tanit of Saint Monique has certain similarities with the 'Dama de Elche' whose heavy headdress emphasizes classically regular features. The 'Dama de Elche' is Iberian but is closely influenced by Punic civilization. She can be dated to the fourth century.
Cf. A. Blanco, *Museo del Prado: Cat. de la Escultura*, pp. 130–3.

18. J. Beloch, *Klio*, VII (1907), p. 27. According to Justin (XXII, 7), this same Hamilcar was the paternal uncle of King Bomilcar who was crucified in 307. In the speech which the latter made before his death, he reproached the Carthaginians for their conduct as regards Hanno the Great and Gisco and it is most unlikely that he should have taken the side of the enemies of his family.

19. The chronology of these events is uncertain since Diodorus' evidence conflicts with that of the Paros inscription; cf. Gsell, *H.A.A.N.*, III, p. 44 n. 3 and p. 60, n. 3. The death of Hamilcar, son of Gisco, certainly occurred towards the beginning of summer 309. The deaths of Ophellas and Bomilcar were contemporary and are dated by Gsell and Beloch to October 309, whereas Diodorus would place them a year later. The present author would adopt the chronology of Diodorus for the following reasons:

   (a) Bomilcar was proclaimed king on the death of Hamilcar. He cannot have been so proclaimed without the assent of the Elders and he was at that time, as we have seen, popular with the people. His fall from power was the result of a violent disagreement with both the Elders and the people. It is likely, therefore, that some time elapsed between his accession to power and his attempted *coup d'état*, and during this period the political situation deteriorated.

   (b) All sources and experts agree in dating the reorganization of the Punic army and the appointment of Himilco, Hanno, and Hasdrubal to the generalship in 307 (cf. Gsell, op. cit., p. 60, n. 3). It is unlikely that the Elders would have allowed more than a year to elapse after the death of Bomilcar before reorganizing the conduct of the war.

20. Cf. F. Cassola, *Gruppi politici romani nel III° secolo*, p. 37.
21. P. Wuilleumier, *Tarente*, pp. 89–98.

4

The First War Against Rome
(264–241 B.C.)

THE history of this period was written by the Romans or their allies. The conflicts between Rome and Carthage are thus known as the Punic Wars, but it would be paradoxical to use this term in a work on Carthage. We shall therefore call these the First and Second Wars against Rome.

1. THE CAUSES OF THE WAR

Before 264 B.C. nothing seemed to foreshadow or justify a death-struggle between the two powers which controlled the Western Mediterranean. During the last two-thirds of the fourth century and the first three decades of the third, Rome had gradually brought under her military domination the whole of the Italian peninsula. Her own *territorium* was divided into 35 'tribes', corresponding roughly to the region which in modern times belonged to the Roman Church, and stretching diagonally across the peninsula from the Tyrrhenian coast to the Adriatic. It included Latium, Northern Campania and Southern Etruria, the mountainous part of the Apennines where the Sabines and other Sabellian tribes lived, and finally, on the Adriatic side, Picenum with its Illyrian and Gallic population. To this core of the Republic we can add what is rather inaccurately called the Italian Confederation. This was a mass of Etruscan, Umbrian, Sabellian, and Greek cities and tribes, each united to Rome by its own individual treaty which defined its status. In its structure, the Roman Republic was, in fact, not unlike its Punic counterpart in Africa, where the *territorium* was divided into 'departments', each of which contained allied and more or less autonomous towns. The difference lay in that Carthage also ruled a 'colonial empire' with, first and foremost, the Sicilian province, which consisted of more than two-thirds of the island from its most western point. In addition to Sicily, there were also the Sardinian coasts with their many Phoenician towns, the Balearic Islands, and a certain number of federated trading posts and cities along the African coast, along the Mediterranean and Atlantic sea-boards of Morocco, and in Southern Spain and Portugal.

Though the two powers were not dissimilar politically, they were very different economically. Rome lagged far behind and still relied mainly on a traditionalist agriculture based on the family unit, and producing only enough to satisfy her own immediate needs. Apart from the yield of the land, Rome had no income other than tribute and booty. She allowed her Campanian allies to reorganize, for their own profit, the industry and trade of the peninsula, she had no navy worth speaking of, and was only just beginning to establish diplomatic relations with a few of the Greek cities and kingdoms of the Eastern Mediterranean. Carthage, on the other hand, although she relied for a quite a proportion of her income on the revenue from her holdings on the mainland, still derived the greater part of her profits from maritime enterprise, while most of her agricultural produce was exported.

It was in the interests both of the Carthaginians and of the Romans that Western Hellenism should not revive, for both had built their fortunes on its ruins. In 270 Hieron had skilfully re-established Agathocles' Syracusan monarchy, and there was still a possibility that he might seek to carry out some of his predecessor's grandiose projects. The Pyrrhus episode had ended in failure only, in fact, because that ambitious king of Epirus had not had sufficiently strong bases across the Adriatic. It would be quite another state of affairs if the campaign were resumed by, for instance, the Antigonid monarchy of Macedonia, which, thanks to its able king Gonatas, succeeded in re-establishing its supremacy over Greece in 263–262 B.C.

In spite of the different temperaments exhibited by the two peoples, there was a long tradition of friendship uniting Rome and Carthage. It went back to the time when the Latin city had first broken away from Etruscan domination and become independent. At that time (that is at the end of the sixth century B.C.) the Carthaginians, as we have already seen, had what amounted to a trading concession in the Etruscan city of Caere, and in its port of Pyrgi – both only a short distance north-west of Rome. The Punic merchants were doubtless fairly numerous there and were under the protection of Thefarie Veliunas, the Etruscan prince who worshipped Astarte. These traders probably spread from here into the neighbouring cities, first among them being those of the valley of the Tiber, which was governed by the Tarquins. The Carthaginians were realistic enough, and sufficiently free from prejudice, to be able to profit immediately from the results of the revolution of 510, which expelled the Tyrrhenian dynasty and substituted for it a Latin patriciate. We are convinced, therefore, that Polybius was not mistaken when he ascribed the first Romano-Punic treaty to the first year of the Consular Republic, that is 509 B.C. It would seem to be, in fact, a renewal of some agreement between the Carthaginians and Tarquins, made at a time when the latter held the mandate for the whole Etruscan Confederation, and exercised a supremacy over Latium that was, at the very least, honorific.

When they heard of the Roman revolution, the Punic leaders sought to turn this rather unsatisfactory state of affairs to their advantage in order that it might not compromise too greatly the system of diplomatic interdependence which had been built up against Greek imperialism in the West. They therefore suggested to the Consuls that the treaty be renewed, and, since they were eager not to offend their new partners, they accepted that the terms of the old agreement be preserved even though they no longer corresponded in the least to the present extent of the new Republic. When she freed herself, Rome had been unable to keep for herself the supremacy which her Etruscan masters had once exercised over all the Latin states. Yet, like all newly established régimes, she was loath to renounce any part of her inheritance from the previous government, however tenuous might be her claims. Thus the treaty of 509 B.C. ascribed to Rome a territorial domination which was hers, in fact, only one and a half centuries later. It is a misunderstanding of this fact which has misled a considerable number of historians and even of specialists in the field of early Roman history, into lowering the date of this first treaty considerably. Polybius, however, tells us that it was written in archaic Latin which very few people still understood at the time when he was writing! This alone excludes all possibility of its having been written as late as the fourth century.

Furthermore, since it no longer corresponded to an actual state of affairs, this treaty must have remained a dead letter for some considerable time. Rome was fully occupied in struggles with her immediate neighbours, and no longer had the means of indulging in the luxury of politics on a grand scale. On the other hand, the Greek victories had broken up the 'great alliance' between the Persians, the Phoenicians and the Etruscans, and Carthage, for her part, had withdrawn into her African homeland between 480 and 409 and then thrown her full weight into the war against Dionysius of Syracuse. It was during the course of this conflict that the old Punico-Etruscan grouping reappeared stronger than ever. If we are to accept Miss Sordi's recent suggestion, Rome formed part of this coalition with Caere as intermediary. Thus the treaty of 509 once more became effective, and in 348 it even became necessary to renew it and readapt it to suit the new state of affairs. As Aymard has shown, the 'second treaty' mentioned by Polybius is nothing other than an amendment of the first. Its principal innovation consists in a clause whereby Punic pirates were to assist Rome against such Latin states as had maintained their independence. When they had seized one of their cities, the Carthaginians were to hand over to the Romans anything which they could not carry away, together with the women and children: they could keep all movable property and the male prisoners. Such a city would then be ready to receive Roman colonists, who would find wives and servants awaiting them. It does not seem that such a realistic clause was, in fact, ever applied. For their part, the Romans agreed not to sail along coasts controlled by the Carthaginians (North Africa and Spain), and accepted a tight check on their dealings with Sicily and Sardinia. The Roman navy was too small, however, for such restrictions to have been inconvenient. The treaty was, therefore, mainly to Rome's advantage.

This advantage was to be increased almost immediately. While Timoleon was defeating the Carthaginians in Sicily (341), the Romans were uniting with Capua to form a sort of federal union, and this gave them the maritime and industrial power which Latium lacked (343 B.C.). In this way, they also outflanked the

Latin league, which was obliged to capitulate in 335. This diplomatic success marks the first step in the growth of Roman imperialism, but had the immediate result of involving Rome in a war against the Samnites, who had grown accustomed to consider Campania as a natural adjunct to their mountains and an essential outlet for their numerous and war-like population. This struggle took up the last three decades of the fourth century and decided the fate of the whole of Italy, whose various inhabitants were obliged to admit that their independence would not survive that of the Samnites. The Etruscans especially were threatened, but it was only later in 311 – and by then it was too late – that they finally decided to come to the assistance of the Samnites, only to be crushed with them. It is probable that Carthage was partly responsible for this Etruscan neutrality and she must have used all means diplomatically available to her in order to avert a conflict between two peoples who were her allies. This hypothesis is rendered all the more plausible by the fact that as soon as battle between the Romans and Etruscans was joined, the Punico-Tyrrhenian alliance was broken off. In 307 the Etruscan fleet came to the assistance of Syracuse, which was being besieged by the Carthaginians. Thus, there must have been a complete reversal of loyalties, for which Carthage was doubtless responsible, faced as she was with the choice beteeen two allies whom she had not been able to keep on friendly terms. With her habitual realism, she chose the stronger of the two parties involved, in spite of the close cultural and political ties which, to quote Aristotle, had made Tyrrhenians and Phoenicians as the citizens of one nation.

At the same time, the Romans indicated their wish to become a maritime power by instituting *duumviri navales*, or officials to equip a fleet. Under these conditions it is understandable that a new, revised Romano-Punic treaty had to be drawn up in the year 306 according to Livy. Since they had sacrificed their old Etruscan friends, the Carthaginians were anxious to obtain effective Roman assistance against the Greeks, who, led by Agathocles, were attacking them for the first time on African soil. The legions were already on the march, however, and were crossing devastated Samnium in order to probe into the land of the Italiot Hellenes. The latter were fully aware of the danger, and the champion they chose, Pyrrhus of Epirus, fought in Italy against the Romans, who he tried to contain within central Italy with its peasant mediocrity, and fought in Sicily against the Carthaginians. An alliance which had been four times amended should have proved efficient but, on the contrary, its two co-signatories were most dilatory in applying it. When Pyrrhus threatened Rome, Carthage was content with a demonstration of naval strength which could not in any way hinder the Epirot. When the latter turned his attention to Sicily, the Romans were delighted to see the scourge removed and certainly did nothing to prevent his departure. Furthermore, the Carthaginians soon signed a separate peace treaty – this had been categorically forbidden in their agreements with Rome – and even provided Pyrrhus with the ships he needed to cross the straits of Messina and return to Italy.

Both partners had proved themselves equally perfidious, and this would seem to indicate basically divergent interests. This discord did not escape Pyrrhus, who is supposed to have declared, as he left Sicily: 'What a fine battle-field we leave for the Carthaginians and the Romans!'

It is doubtful whether the Romans were already contemplating the conquest of Sicily, two-thirds of which still belonged to Carthage. Heluss, who wrote a lengthy study of the first Punic War and the beginnings of Roman imperialism, denied that the senators had any conscious desire to seize the island, that the conflict started almost by chance, for insignificant reasons, and only developed into a full-scale war when the Romans realized that they were surrounded by the naval bases of their enemies and that these proved a constant threat.

According to another school of thought, however, the conquest of Sicily was the logical consequence of the Romano-Campanian union of 343 B.C. Contrary to all the other treaties between Rome and the various Italian states, that between Rome and Campania had proved really fair, and advantageous to both parties. The former might, indeed, reserve for herself political pre-eminence, but Capua obtained more lasting benefits and her merchants and craftsmen profited by the wars which were ruining all the other chief commercial and industrial centres of Italy. As late as 289 the Romans began striking their own coinage – a heavy bronze currency which looks extraordinarily archaic. The Campanians, on the other hand, were minting fine silver coins of the Greek type in the name of the confederacy. Their black polished wares were already beginning to replace the vessels of Apulia and Tarentum, and were spreading throughout the Western Mediterranean, on all the routes followed by their shrewd businessmen, who were flooding the markets with their oil and wines. Some of these Campanians even got themselves admitted into the Roman *curia*, which was then fairly accessible to the allied nobility. Among these newcomers were the Decii, whom a later tradition transformed into heroic patriots; they were soon to be followed by the Atilii, from whom Regulus was descended. Other Capuans remained at home but married Roman girls: Appius Claudius the Blind, who dominated the end of the third century, gave his daughter in marriage to a Capuan aristocrat. These marriages reflect common interests: the Roman families involved were breaking away from patriarchal traditions and were adopting new and less restrictive practices; they began to modernize the farming of their lands and even considered increasing their income by trade and industry.

Very naturally, these Romanized Campanians and Campanianized Romans were already contemplating harnessing the power of the legions to serve their own interests, which stretched far beyond the coasts of the Italian peninsula. Appius Claudius Caecus was the first great champion of this renewed imperialism. He was extremely broad-minded and his enemies maintained that the gods had blinded him as a punishment for his 'modernizing' the cult of Hercules, of which he was a patron. This great man, whose reactions were sometimes those of a demagogue, strengthened the Romano-Campanian alliance by building the Appian Way, which led the legions southwards. Towards the end of his life he strongly opposed the proposals of Cineas, the ambassador of Pyrrhus, who offered the Romans peace on condition that they withdraw into Central Italy. As we shall see, a close relation of Appius Claudius Caecus – traditionally supposed to have been his younger brother – played a decisive part in launching the Sicilian campaign.

For a century, the large island had been a tempting prey for the avid Oscan tribes of the southern Apennines. Plato spent the years 368 to 366 in Syracuse, and already predicted that the Phoenicians and the Oscans would one day smother Sicilian Hellenism. The Greeks themselves had been rash enough to summon bands of Italian mercenaries across the straits. Like the *condottieri* of the Middle Ages, these adventurers seized the first opportunity that presented itself and massacred all the inhabitants of a town which then became their stronghold. This had already happened several times during the first half of the fourth century. It was repeated more spectacularly in 289 when a band of Sabellians in the service of Agathocles, the Mamertines (men of Mars), upon the latter's death seized the city of Messina, where they founded a brigand state, and from which they laid waste the north-eastern part of the island.

Strong ties still survived between these brigands from the mountains and their more civilized relations settled in the rich Campanian plain. The bands of pillaging brigands were soon followed by Capuan merchants, who drew along with them their Roman confederates. Thus there was a group in the Senate, led by the Claudii, whose interests were very much involved in the island, but which had played its part in Roman affairs by sending corn to the starving plebeians during times of famine.

Those who believed that the future of Rome lay in the south, however, were opposed in the Senate by formidable adversaries. Many of the Fathers considered that Roman expansion should be northwards to include Etruria, whose political decadence and still considerable riches spelt an easy and fruitful victory. First among these were the Fabii, whose ancestral lands stretched along the right bank of the Tiber and whose forebears had at one time been engaged in epic struggles against the people of Veii and Caere. The Fabii were probably the most illustrious of the patrician families, and their political authority was considerable. During the whole course of the Punic Wars, they were to advocate a moderate policy as regards the African Republic, and were to be sympathetic towards the great Punic landowners. But precisely at this moment, in 265, an accident occurred which caused them to disappear for a generation from the political scene. The chief of the clan, Fabius Gurges, was then consul. In this capacity he was responsible for the intervention of Roman troops, which he led against the serfs who had headed a social revolution in the

Etruscan city of Volsinii. This military operation was perfectly in keeping with the political and social views held by the family. It was successful, but it cost Gurges his life. He was mortally wounded by one of the besieged. For some unknown reason, his son (whose name has not even come down to us) played no part in politics. It was only eighteen years later that the Fabii were once more to lead Rome, and they only regained their former prestige during the next generation under Gurges' grandson, who was surnamed Cunctator. This eclipse in the power of the Fabii enabled the Claudii to obtain support for their policy, and led to war with Carthage.

Carthage was in no way responsible, therefore, for the war that was to prove fatal to her. Not one of her nobles, not even among the minority of belligerents, had any idea of intervening in Italy. They could find far more fruitful and certain ways of satisfying their ambitions elsewhere. Throughout the long war they maintained a purely defensive attitude. The Carthaginian pirates did indeed carry out successful but limited raids against the Italian coast, but these served only to irritate the Romans, who detailed a few of their troops to deal with a menace which affected the towns of their allies rather than their own. This apathy was certainly one of the main causes for the defeat of Carthage.

2. The Course of War up till the Expedition of Regulus: (264–256)

We only have very brief accounts of the first war between Rome and Carthage, and these baffle the modern historian by their obscure treatment of many essential points. In particular, it is extremely difficult to establish the chronology with any certainty, owing to the inaccuracy of the Roman calendar, which often failed to correspond to the astronomical calendar. Thus, according to the calculations of the German historian Beloch, the Consuls for the year 264, Fulvius and Claudius Caudex, only took up their appointments in the month of June, while the second-named did not intervene in Sicily till the spring of 263. This theory meets with a great many objections, however, and has been rejected by G. de Sanctis.

It was owing to two minor peoples that Rome and Carthage finally came into conflict. The Mamertines, as we have seen, were those Oscan mercenaries of Agathocles' who became masters of Messina and plundered the Greeks for a quarter of a century. In 270, the Syracusans finally found an energetic leader, Hieron. He led an offensive against the Mamertines, and was so successful that he managed to blockade the latter in Messina. The Mamertines were afraid that at last they were to be called to account, and they appealed to the Punic fleet, stationed in the Lipari Islands. Led by their admiral Hanno, the Carthaginians occupied the citadel without being asked. The Mamertines soon began to resent this occupation and, remembering their Italic origins, and doubtless using some of their Campanian cousins who were in the service of Rome, as emissaries, they sought the assistance of the Roman garrison on the other side of the Straits, at Rhegium. By some coincidence, which cannot have been entirely fortuitous, the officer in command was related to the Consul Claudius. He was lucky enough to capture one of the forts of Messina together with Hanno, who bought his liberty with the total evacuation of the city. On his return to Carthage, the latter was condemned for high treason by the Council of the One Hundred and Four, and was crucified – the first of a whole series of generals to be put to death.

The Consul Claudius now undertook to regularize the initiative which his subordinate and relation had taken. He was loyal to the family tradition, and had already so frequently suggested that Rome should build up a fleet worthy of the name, that he had been given the nickname 'Caudex', which is roughly equivalent to a dinghy. In fact, he had a great deal of trouble in getting his views accepted: the Senate were doubtless still under the influence of the Fabii, and maintained their reserve. Finally, by more or less legal means, the motion was put before the people, who finally admitted the Mamertines to the Roman alliance, and authorized the legions to cross over into Sicily in order to protect them.

In principle, the Romans were sent against the only real enemy of the Mamertines, Hieron. The latter, who had just assumed the kingship of Syracuse, was clever enough to realize the impossibility of defeating Rome. After a year's fighting, he came to terms with Rome. He had to abandon quite a considerable part of his kingdom, but managed to preserve enough of it to enable him to live off its revenues for fifty peaceful years, in a sumptuous palace, a patron of arts and letters (263 B.C.).

The Romans had no more scope for their imperialism on this side of the island, and they now turned their attention to the Punic half. Segesta was the chief city of the Elymians, who claimed to be descended from Asiatic settlers, related to the Romans' Trojan ancestors. The Segestans now also sought to join the Roman alliance. The Mamertines were of Italian extraction and had never been subject to Carthage, but Segesta was situated near Palermo in the very centre of Punic territory, and her defection resulted in the collapse of the Punic province, while the fact that the Romans accepted her proves that they had no particular intention of sparing the Carthaginians and sharing the island with them.

The Carthaginians now finally understood to what a pass their apathy had brought them. They had certainly believed that Hieron would hold out against the Romans, and counted on each of the opponents wearing the other out so that she might reap the benefits. The separate peace which the Syracusan signed, shattered their hopes. Reluctantly the Elders agreed on the necessity of waging war, and a general called Hannibal, son of Gisco, who was strongly supported by the aristocratic faction, was put at the head of mercenaries from Spain, Gaul, and Liguria. These forces were gathered together in Agrigentium, whch was, after Syracuse, the second largest city in Sicily, and which had belonged to the Punic alliance for some considerable time. Meanwhile the Romans brought over to Sicily all their available forces under the command of two consuls (summer 262). Agrigentum was besieged for seven months. Finally, after repelling the attacks of a relief force, the Romans succeeded in capturing the city, though Hannibal, son of Gisco, was able to withdraw with most of his troops.

This defeat brought many other Sicilian cities flocking to the Romans' side, and proved to the Carthaginians that they could not defeat the former in open battle. They decided, therefore, to use tactics which were better adapted to the means at their disposal, and to this end, they shut up their land forces in a few heavily fortified strongholds. The Carthaginians were tenacious, and had good engineers who had learnt from the Greeks and had several secret techniques of their own; they were, in fact, past masters in the art of siege-warfare, which had advanced considerably since the time of Alexander, and were certain of their superiority in this respect. Thus, while the Romans were wearing themselves out against the walls of these fortresses, the Punic pirates were to carry out raids along the Italian coast, and light commandos were to attack isolated groups of soldiers and convoys of food supplies, and were to punish any of their subjects who had gone over to the enemy.

On the whole, these plans proved successful. Thanks to them, the *status quo* was maintained in Sicily during the next five years (261–256). Cities such as Enna and Camarina which had called in the Romans, returned to the Punic alliance. The Carthaginian generals were experienced and remained several years running at the head of their troops, while the Roman consuls were renewed each spring and, in their inexperience, often committed fatal mistakes. The Italian allies who fought alongside the legionaries, had their own reasons for fighting, and were often undisciplined. A general named Hamilcar, whom the Ancients confused with Hamilcar Barca, made the most of this discord and won a victory near Paropus, in 259, in which 3000 Italians were killed. During the course of the same year, Hamilcar also transferred the inhabitants of Eryx to Drepanum, thus organizing a stronghold which the Romans would never succeed in capturing by mere force of arms.

At this point, however, Carthage suffered a set-back which brought all her efforts to nought. The Romans were exasperated by the pirate raids and were anxious about supplying their troops. They finally decided, in 260 B.C., to build the navy which they had been discussing for fifty years. Claudius Caudex is not mentioned after his consulship, but the representatives of other noble families also held his views. In 260 and 259 two brothers held the consulship in succession – Cnaeus and Lucius Cornelius Scipio. They belonged to a branch of a Patrician *gens* which was almost as illustrious as that of the Fabii, and their father, Scipio Barbatus, had distinguished himself in the Samnite Wars. Lucius and Cnaeus began that association of their family with maritime imperialism which was to carry their descendants to the heights of glory. Lucius' epitaph was found in the family vault in the eighteenth century, and it recalls proudly his victories in Corsica and the conquest of the city of Aleria, which is now being excavated by M. Jehasse. Nevertheless, it would seem that the two brothers were poor tacticians: the elder, Cnaeus, was captured together with seventeen ships and had to pay ransom before he was freed. The Roman people gave him the nickname of 'donkey'. Luckily his colleague, the Consul Gaius Duilius – a man of humble origin – saved the honour and interests of Rome by crushing the Punic fleet, under the command of Hannibal, son of Gisco, off Mylae. The Carthaginians lost 50 galleys and their flag-ship – a vast 'dreadnought' with seven banks of oars, which the Carthaginians had captured from Pyrrhus. Hannibal, who had previously been defeated at Agrigentum, had sufficiently powerful friends among the oligarchs, to avoid condemnation by the One Hundred and Four. Some time later, however, while he was fighting in Sardinia, his own mercenaries, who were tired of his incompetence, finally crucified him.

The victory of Mylae brought great honour to Duilius. His statue was set up on top of a column which was adorned with the prows of the ships he had captured – the original *rostrum*. His merits were recorded in an inscription which has come down to us, and Rome was already becoming accustomed to the leadership cult which was to change its destiny. It seems that the Carthaginian ships were immobilized by boarding-bridges into which had been fixed grappling irons, thus enabling them to be stormed by the legionaries. It is surprising that the Carthaginians were caught out by such a simple trick. Legends have grown up round the birth of Rome's fleet, but they mainly serve to hide those really responsible for the success, namely the Greeks of Southern Italy who built the ships, manned them, and piloted them. Those legends which tell us that the Romans were so ignorant of naval matters that they had to copy the hulls of wrecks, and exercise their oarsmen on the sand, ignore the skilful Greeks. The Senate's chief merit, and that, especially, of its Romano-Campanian businessmen, who had the most to gain, was that it put huge sums of money at the disposal of the Tarentine shipyards, and thus enabled Rome to launch, in one go, a fleet which was larger than those of even the mightiest of Alexander's heirs. Scipio and Duilius had at their command 100 quinqueremes and 20 triremes, and all were new.

The victory of Mylae did not have any immediately decisive consequences, however. Carthage still had sufficient resources to fall back on to make up her losses, and the war in Sicily got bogged down in a series of sieges and skirmishes.

3. THE EXPEDITION OF REGULUS

Among the Campanian families which had been admitted to the Roman Senate, the foremost was, at that time, that of the Atilii. It consisted of numerous branches: the Calatini, the Serrani, the Reguli, etc., and a member of one or other of these was consul almost every year. They thus equalled the most favoured of the Patrician *gentes*, such as the Cornelii and the Valerii, and naturally enough they represented that section of Rome's southern allies which was most interested in the conquest of Sicily and the destruction of the Carthaginian navy, since it was mainly the southern harbours which were being raided.

One of the members of this clan, M. Atilius Regulus, consul in 256, suggested an audacious plan in order to put an end to the war. He wished to follow Agathocles' example, carry the war into Africa, and capture Carthage, or, at least, force her to capitulate by fear. This project was in complete opposition to the customary Roman prudence and was strongly countered. Nevertheless, Regulus was allowed to assemble a large concentration of troops at Ecnomus in the south of Sicily, east of Agrigentum – some 40,000 men and 330 ships. The Carthaginians sent an equally formidable fleet against this armada, under the command of two generals, one named Hanno, a member of the aristocratic party (the same Hanno who, in 262, had vainly sought to save Agrigentum), and the other Hamilcar, who belonged to a less conservative party, it seems, and who had the victory of Paropus to his credit.

Hamilcar attempted a skilful manoeuvre which foreshadows that of Hannibal at Cannae: he withdrew the centre of his battle-line and tried to entice the Roman fleet into the gap thus left, when it would be surrounded. Unfortunately, the Punic fleet was unable to keep in formation and, after a day's hard fighting, the Romans succeeded in capturing or destroying more than one hundred enemy galleys (early spring 256). There was nothing, now, to stop an invasion of Africa. In spite of Agathocles' war, the Carthaginians had taken no precautions against a possible renewal of such an attack nor any serious steps to defend the rich countryside which surrounded the city. There was only a simple police force, and the city magistrates were totally incompetent and inexperienced as far as military matters were concerned. Regulus and his colleague, Manlius Vulso, were thus able to land on Cap Bon just as the king of Syracuse had done previously. They first seized the citadel of Clupea (now Kelibia) and then struck north-east without meeting any serious resistance. On their way, they laid waste the rich lands from which Carthage drew most of her supplies of meat, oil, and wine. About six miles north of Kelibia lay a small town which now bears the name of Dar es Safi, and which is in the course of excavation. It was captured and burnt, as were many others. Innumerable prisoners and valuable booty soon enriched the consular army.

These events took place during the summer of 256. At the beginning of the winter, the Senate recalled Manlius Vulso and the greater part of the fleet, doubtless fearing that it might be destroyed by storms on that dangerous and unsheltered coast. It is probable, however, that continued jealousy within the Senate towards Regulus also played a part in this decision, which, in any case, had catastrophic results.

Meanwhile, the Carthaginians were organizing their resistance. They recalled their best general from Sicily – Hamilcar, the victor of Paropus – and appointed with him Hasdrubal, son of Hanno, and Bostar. Nevertheless, although he had only 15,000 legionaries and 500 cavalry left to him, Regulus won an important victory at the beginning of 255, beneath the walls of Adys (later called Uthina, and today known as Oudna) in a hilly region some 40 miles south-east of Carthage. This victory enabled him to occupy Tunis and so cut the communications between the peninsula of Carthage and the interior. The Libyan peasantry began to revolt in the country, and the unsubdued Numidians ravaged the regions which had so far escaped Roman plunder. A mass of refugees had come to seek asylum beneath the walls of the capital, bearing terrifying tales with them. Food was running short and there was the threat of disease. Regulus thought the time had come to offer terms, for he knew that the defences of the entrenched camp would hold his forces in check. Such was the level of discouragement in the city that his overtures were accepted. The consul received the delegation with disdain, however, and his demands were outrageous. He requested the evacuation not only of the whole of Sicily, but also of Corsica and Sardinia, the disarmament of almost the whole fleet of war, and a political agreement which made Carthage a vassal of Rome. The negotiations were broken off.

Meanwhile, Punic agents had gone to Greece to recruit mercenaries. Normally they avoided applying to the Hellenic *condottieri*, who were expensive and had dangerous ambitions. These were not normal times, however, and the Carthaginians had to find soldiers capable of withstanding the legions. In the recruiting market of Cape Tenare, the agents found an officer of fortune named Xanthippus, a Lacedaemonian who had received excellent training in his country's war-schools. They engaged the Spartan as technical adviser. He soon reorganized the forces and explained their mistakes to the generals, the chief of these being their opposing the enemy on rough ground where the flexible legions had the advantage over the heavy phalanx of the Hoplites. If, on the other hand, the Carthaginians could meet the Romans in the plain, the former would be able to draw full benefit from their superiority in cavalry and from their elephants, who played the same part, in those times, as tanks do nowadays.

Regulus had become over-confident as a result of his victories, and made the mistake of accepting battle on ground chosen by Xanthippus, probably in the Plain of Tunis. In order to resist the attack of the elephants, he grouped his men in close formation, thus restricting the movement of their maniples. The result was catastrophic. The legionaries were surrounded by the phalanx and the cavalry, and crushed by the elephants; all but two thousand of them were either killed or captured, together with their consul. The remainder of Regulus' life is legendary and Polybius tells us nothing about it. All we know is that he died in captivity. Terrible accounts have been handed down to us by the Romans, who had every excuse for doing so, but although the Carthaginians are perfectly capable of having tortured Regulus, we cannot rely solely on Roman evidence.

In spite of its disastrous end, the Roman invasion had been a heavy blow for Carthage. The internal security of the mainland dependencies had been severely undermined, and the spirit of revolt had spread to the Libyan peasantry, while the unsubdued tribes had been encouraged in their lawlessness. From the economic point of view, the losses had been catastrophic, and the Punic government's first task was the reorganization of affairs in

Africa. The best Carthaginian general, Hamilcar of Paropus, ended his career as military governor of the Libyan territory, where he treated the rebels with the utmost severity. The great land-owners did not think him severe enough, however, and from now on the Elders among them formed a group which had interests in common and which soon imposed its views on the Assembly in general. In about 250, this group found a leader in the person of Hanno II, the Great, who was – or so we believe – a descendant of his fourth-century namesake, whose tragic story we have already recounted. Hanno succeeded Hamilcar of Paropus as supreme governor of the African territories, and did all within his power to discourage Carthage from military and other undertakings over-seas. The war was therefore fought with far less vigour, and the more enthusiastic combatants were left very much to themselves.

The failure of Regulus had been compensated, for the Romans, by a great victory in Sicily. In 256, the consuls Atilius Calatinus, who belonged to the same family as Regulus, and Scipio the Donkey, who had regained his popularity, succeeded in seizing Palermo, the only large city of the island which had a majority of Carthaginians in its population, and which was therefore the capital of the Punic province. The Carthaginians now held only the fortresses in the extreme west of the island – Lilybaeum which was under the command of an energetic leader called Himilco, and Drepanum where the fleet was stationed. Lilybaeum was closely besieged but resisted heroically, buoyed up by the exploits of Hannibal, called the 'Rhodian', whose light and swift ship defied Roman pursuit. A counter-offensive in the direction of Palermo in 251 was a lamentable failure, however. In 249, the Comitia appointed as consul P. Appius Claudius Pulcher (the Handsome), who was either the son or the grandson of Appius Claudius Caecus. This proud and presumptuous man determined to end with one blow the war which his family had started, by destroying the fleet at Drepanum. The Punic ships were far more manoeuvrable than the Roman, and their admiral, Adherbal, was an excellent tactician; the Carthaginians were victorious and 96 Roman galleys, with their crews, were either captured or destroyed.

This was the most severe defeat that the Romans had suffered so far during the course of the war, and the imperialist party fell out of favour. For several years now, the Fabii had been rebuilding their network of political alliances and directing public opinion. The Claudii were discredited in a strong propaganda campaign. It was said that the defeat was the result of their gross lack of piety, which was already well known. Was it not true that Pulcher had drowned the sacred chickens which had provided him with unfavourable omens? In 247 Fabius Buteo was elected consul, and he was succeeded, for the next two years, by members of his family: this was a fine revenge for the house which had been kept away from the highest political office since 265!

Meanwhile, in Carthage the great landowners were getting rid of those who were in favour of war to the death. In that same year 247, the two worthiest generals, Himilco the defender of Lilybaeum, and Adherbal the victor of Drepanum, were relieved of their command. They were replaced by a young officer, Hamilcar Barca, who was, indeed, full of enthusiasm, but who had very limited means at his disposal. On the other hand, Hanno the Great, who had replaced Hamilcar of Paropus (thus obtaining the removal of another advocate of the war), organized a large expedition against the tribes of the Sahara and captured, in that same year of 247, the city of Theveste, present-day Tebessa.

Logically, peace ought to have been concluded, but the negotiations which were opened, also in 247, only resulted in an exchange of prisoners. Since they could not reach an agreement, the two governments concerned allowed the war to stagnate, each side being represented by confederate troops. The Roman consuls no longer went to Sicily, but resumed the colonization of Southern Etruria – the traditional aim of the Fabii – and Alsium and Fregena were founded in 247 and 245 respectively. On both sides, those responsible for finances refused to subscribe to the shipyards. In Carthage, indeed, the treasury was empty – probably since the time of Regulus' invasion. Ptolemy II Philadelphus (who died in 246) had refused an application for a loan. This able ruler had had close business relations with the Phoenicians and, from 270 onwards, with the Romans. He excused himself from aiding one or other of his friends during the conflict.

The monotony of the years 247–241 is only relieved by the deeds of Hamilcar Barca, who first carried out naval raids along the Italian coast until either lack of funds or orders from the Elders constrained him to abandon them. Finally, since the enemy were pressing in on Lilybaeum and Drepanum, Hamilcar established himself on the acropolis of Eryx, which was dedicated to an oriental goddess whom the Phoenicians worshipped as Astarte and the Romans as Venus. From this crow's-nest he carried out skilful raids in the defence of the two fortresses without costing his country a penny, for he fed his mercenaries on produce from the country-side and paid them with booty.

The Romano-Campanian capitalists decided to make one last attempt to oust the Carthaginians. Neither the Senate nor the Roman people had any confidence left in them, so that they had to appeal for permission to build a fleet, at their own expense, which would only be reimbursed in the event of victory. Two hundred quinquaremes were built and entrusted to Lutatius Catulus, who was a newcomer just as Duilius had been. At the head of this fleet, the consul succeeded in intercepting a large convoy which was attempting to supply Lilybaeum. The Punic warships were hampered by the heavy merchantmen which they were escorting, and their pilots were no longer those of yore. Twenty years of war had taken a heavy toll of officers and sailors and these could no longer be replaced. The admiral Hanno could not avoid defeat, but he paid for it on the cross. Carthage, without its fleet, could only come to terms.

Fortunately for her, it would seem that Lutatius Catulus belonged to the pro-Fabian party. He made demands which were moderate in comparison with those of Regulus. The evacuation of Sicily was taken for granted. Hamilcar Barca had the sad task of representing his government during the armistice discussions, but he succeeded in obtaining freedom and the honours of war for his men and for Gisco, the commander of Lilybaeum. Carthage was allowed to keep her other territorial possessions, and maintained her political independence on condition that she join the Roman alliance and promise not to attack Hieron in any way. No limits were imposed on her land or her sea forces, but for 20 years she had to pay an indemnity of 2,200 Euboean talents – the equivalent of £540,000.

Thus, amid a general feeling of lassitude, the war came to an end. It had cost more in materials and supplies and had lasted longer than all the wars of Alexander and his successors. Rome owed her victory not only to her better army, but even more so to the economic strength of the Italian Confederation, which had never been seriously threatened by her enemies' blows. Her leaders had not proved particularly capable either in the political or in the military field. Carthage, on the other hand, had always been served by good generals, especially in the latter part of the war. Their ability and courage had been cancelled out by the selfishness, inertia, and cruelty of the oligarchical leaders. The latter had followed the events without participating in them. They had ignored any openings for diplomatic action – Rome's chief enemies, the Gauls and the Ligurians of the Po valley had remained inactive during the war, in marked contrast to their usual turbulence. It is true that Carthage sent them agents to recruit mercenaries, but she did not send them a single ambassador capable of showing them that their interest lay in attacking the legions from the rear. Neither had she been able to obtain any advantage from her relations with Greek rulers, which were far closer than those of Rome. In the conduct of operations, she had first proved herself unable to mobilize her troops in time at the outbreak of the war, and then had failed to follow up her defeats of the enemy, in 256 and 247 especially, by any attempt at reversing the situation in her favour. She had supported inefficient generals while inflicting appalling punishment on others who were unlucky rather than guilty. Finally, on the economic plane, the government of Carthage had shown itself to be quite unable to mobilize such resources as it commanded; failure in this field was due, most probably, to the weakness of Punic organization, which was almost entirely dependent on distant maritime contacts, but was doubtless also due to the excessive complacence with which those in authority treated private interests.

The oligarchical régime had thus shown itself to be neither efficient nor disinterested, in spite of the severe discipline which it imposed on its citizens. Patriotism had remained very much alive, however, and had even been increased by the anxieties, sufferings, and set-backs of the war. It was inevitable, therefore, that the defeat should be followed by a revolution, from which Carthage was to emerge completely transformed.

5

The Barcid Revolution
241–219 B.C.

THE Barcid revolution, which broke out immediately after the
peace of Lutatius was concluded, can be divided into three
phases. During the first of these, Carthage was threatened by
an extremely serious social crisis which seemed likely to annihilate
not only the ruling class and the profiteers of the régime, but also
the whole colonial society of the Western Phoenicians. Faced with
this menace, the 'conservatives' and 'progressives' managed, in spite
of difficulties, to achieve some sort of unity. Once the peril was
past, the nationalists, backed by popular feeling, though not by the
proletariat, gained the upper hand over the oligarchs and, led by
Hamilcar Barca, they imposed a transformation of governmental
institutions. Finally, in the third phase, Hamilcar and his successor
Hasdrubal the Elder completed the process by supplementing the
revolution at home by a revolution in foreign policy, which gave
the Western Phoenicians the means of avenging their defeat, and
also gave the party in power a firm base, which was not likely to
be affected by the vicissitudes of politics at home.

It is worth noting, before we analyse these events in greater
detail, that these transformations are not only due to conditions
inherent within the Punic state, such as patriotic exasperation, the
necessity of renewing worn-out institutions, and the actions of
exceptional individuals like Hamilcar. They are also due to general
conditions within the Hellenistic world of which Carthage was a
member. The social crisis which we call the War of the Mercenaries,
was the equivalent of the Proletarian and Slave revolts of the third
and second centuries in the Graeco-Oriental world and in the
more evolved West, in Sicily and Etruria. Rostovtseff has analysed
the causes of this unrest most clearly: in the countries conquered

by the Macedonians, for instance in Egypt, the chief cause was the exploitation of the local population by the Greek colonists and the conflict was mainly between the Hellenized towns and the country-side, which had remained faithful to its own traditions. In Greece and in Western Anatolia, the conflict was within the cities them-selves, as it was in nineteenth-century Europe; the development of a vast market which was accompanied by technical progress and by the collapse of the old social pattern, resulted in a widening gap between a small but extremely rich upper class and an extremely poor but very bellicose proletariat.

Both these types of reaction took place simultaneously in Carthage which was, at one and the same time, a colonial state and a large industrial and commercial city. The evolution which was to lead from an oligarchical republic to a state that was both popular and authoritarian, governed by a monarch whose power rested in the army and in the lower urban classes, is paralleled over and over again in the case of Greek cities, and this same evolution was to take place two centuries later in Rome. We shall have occasion to note, more than once, the strong similarities between the Barcid State in Spain and the Augustan Empire.

Furthermore, there will be resemblances between the social phenomena we are studying, and those which have manifested themselves in Europe and in European colonies from the nine-teenth century onwards. Although we must not lay undue stress on these analogies, since the Ancient World knew neither mechanized industry, nor real capitalism, nor any form of socialism based on a coherant doctrine, they do however make the history of the Hellenistic period particularly fascinating for us. It is, indeed, the only time in Antiquity when we find something approaching the struggle between the classes which is such a feature of modern history.

1. THE MERCENARY WAR

The reader will perhaps be surprised to find this well-known episode viewed as a social crisis. It is, indeed, the subject of Gustave Flaubert's novel *Salammbo* where the romantic aspect is, of course, treated particularly fully following Polybius, who is our source of information, and who deals with the events as if they were a straightforward piece of military history.

The Carthaginians had to counter several mercenary revolts. One, for instance, almost took place in Lilybaeum in 250 B.C., when the city was being besieged and several Gallic leaders plotted to hand it over to the Romans. Their plans were discovered by a Greek officer named Alexon, and were foiled thanks to the diplomacy of the general Himilco and his aide Hannibal, the son of the old defender of Agrigentum. The Carthaginians were far from being the only ones to suffer from this drawback of professional armies, as we have already seen from the story of the capture of Messina by the Mamertines.

The Punic government took great precautions in order to avoid such incidents as far as possible. The Carthaginians preferred to recruit their soldiers of fortune in the Barbarian countries of the West such as Iberia, Gaul, and Liguria, instead of among the Greek *condottieri*. This method of recruiting was cheaper. Furthermore, these half-savages were completely out of their element, in the regions where they were called upon to fight, and were generally too stupid to think of forming conspiracies and, as they spoke different languages, they could not communicate easily from one group to another. The officering of these armies was carefully studied, and only the lowest ranks were supplied by the natives, and these were chosen from among the veterans who had become loyal because they loved their trade. All the other officers were Carthaginians and they received the same sort of training as their counterparts in European armies who were called upon to serve in native regiments. There were Gallic specialists such as Hannibal, son of Hannibal of Agrigentum, whose knowledge of the Gauls contributed to the failure of the Lilybaeum plot. Others studied the Libyans, the Iberians, or the Ligurians.

The Punic government was confident of the efficiency of this organization and did not, therefore, take the first signs of discontent seriously when they appeared among the troops evacuated from Sicily after the peace with Lutatius.

Gisco had been careful to repatriate the troops in small batches, and had advised that they be sent to their homes as soon as possible. First they had to be paid, however, and the treasurers of the Republic, like all conservative finance ministers, liked to economize in the payment of personnel. Thus large numbers of disbanded soldiers were allowed to accumulate in the city and, with nothing to do, these became more and more unruly. Since they soon constituted a danger to the citizens, they were sent to the confines of the Libyan territory, to Sicca Veneria, known today as Le Kef, not far from the present Algero-Tunisian frontier, an isolated fortress surrounded by independent Libyan tribes. The town was under the command of Hanno the Great, and the latter proposed paying them off, but at a lower rate than that which they had been promised. This proposal was received with indignation, and the dissenting mercenaries set out for Carthage. They settled in Tunis as Agathocles and Regulus had done before them. The government sent them Gisco, who had just returned to Africa. Many of the men, and especially the officers, had a great respect for their old leader, and they accepted him as arbitrator.

An event then took place which changed the mutiny into a revolt. Among the mercenaries there was quite a large number of 'half-Greeks', as Polybius calls them. These were mostly ex-slaves whose origins or culture were Hellenic, and who had escaped from slave-prisons in Southern Italy or Sicily. They had the intelligence and the knowledge which the Barbarians lacked. Some of them, like the Campanian Spendius, whose master was seeking him in order to crucify him, were fired with true revolutionary enthusiasm. These now combined with the Libyans, who were led by Matho since their demobilization, and who would not be able to avoid Carthaginian reprisals as their homes were not overseas.

Matho and Spendius spread propaganda throughout the camp, and succeeded in getting the other ranks to mutiny against the junior officers and N.C.O.s, who still felt bound to Carthage by ties of loyalty. In the first riot several of the latter were massacred and Gisco and his staff were arrested and held as hostages. Spendius and Matho found themselves ably seconded by a party of Gallic desperadoes who, together with their leader Autaritus, had been banished from their country because of the crimes they had committed. The relations they established with the Libyan peasantry served to aggravate the situation further, for the latter had recently been severely punished for their support of Regulus, and Hanno had increased their rent to half their crop. Seventy thousand serfs flocked to join the 20,000 mercenaries in their camp in Tunis.

Carthage would have been lost had not the conservative

governments of Rome and Syracuse realized the subversive nature of the peril with which she was threatened, and come to her assistance. As early as 265 Rome had already played the part of 'guardian of social law and order' – at the time of the Volsinian slave revolt – and she was to play the part several times more. Though the Senate did not intervene openly in the conflict, it refused to answer any calls for help from the rebels, it forbade merchants to trade with the latter, and encouraged them, on the contrary, to supply Carthage. Hieron put at the Punic city's disposal the considerable stock of food supplies and money with which his kingdom provided him.

Meanwhile, the rebels had undertaken the complete blockade of the city which was already cut off on the landward side by their occupation of Tunis. To this end they decided to obtain control of Bizerta and Utica. Hanno the Great was called upon to resist them. It is very much to his credit that he succeeded in assembling an army of citizens and mercenaries from overseas. Unfortunately he was not as able a tactician as he was an administrator; he was used to border skirmishes against undisciplined hordes of Libyan brigands and, having won an initial encounter against Spendius, who was laying siege to Utica, he had the unpleasant surprise of seeing his victory turned into a defeat.

This defeat caused discontent among the lower classes in Carthage, and resulted in Hamilcar Barca's recall. The latter had kept in the background after concluding peace with Lutatius, and he had taken no part in negotiations with the mercenaries. Gsell suggests that he may have been in disgrace. It is just as possible that he was waiting for his chance and did not wish to be compromised with the oligarchical party, whose general was Hanno, and with whom Gisco's sympathies lay. He doubtless hoped to bring the revolt to an end by negotiation as much as by force, and probably planned to use the troops to establish himself in power. This is certainly how he acted once he had been appointed commander-in-chief, with Hanno under his orders. So as to raise the morale of his own army as much as to lower that of his opponents, he first carried out a spectacular feat. Utica lies some 25 miles from Carthage, as the crow flies. A submerged, sandy causeway, which even today is almost impassable in places, closes the southern part of the bay into which the Medjerda flows. Across this spit of sand Hamilcar led his men, they surprised Spendius and further baffled him by the use of tactics which recall those employed by Hannibal at Cannae. Six thousand rebels were massacred, and the threat of a blockade by sea was removed once and for all.

Once he had established his position, Hamilcar brought to bear all the psychological pressure he could. He incorporated into his army all the prisoners who so wished, and sent the others back to their homes. He thus hoped to wreck the authority of the extremist leaders in the rebel camp, for he knew that some of the junior officers who had survived the first massacre were beginning to re-establish their influence over their men. Matho and Spendius reacted to this by imposing a rule of terror: the weaklings were massacred, and Gisco and the other prisoners were tortured to death in the most cruel way. Hamilcar was only successful with the Numidians, whose traditional chieftains were probably dissatisfied at seeing their followers associating with revolutionaries. One of these caïds called Navaras came over to the Carthaginian side, and Hamilcar promised him in recompense, the hand of one of his daughters in marriage. This rather minor gain for the Carthaginians was more than compensated by Utica, Bizerta, and the army in Sardinia rallying to the rebels. In Rome's support of Carthage lay her only hope, and Rome refused to accept Sardinia, which she had been offered by the mercenaries. The oligarchs had arguments in plenty should they wish to denounce the disastrous results of Hamilcar's policy. The conservative general, Hanno, determined to resume the power which had never been legally withdrawn from him, and share the command with Hamilcar. The latter, in the middle of the war, then launched the first of the political operations which were to cause the downfall of the aristocratic régime and eventually make him master of Carthage.

As we have seen, up to now the right to choose the generals had been the prerogative of the Elders. According to Aristotle's analysis of the Constitution, the people had the right of intervention only in the event of disagreement between the Council and the King. We can infer from Polybius that it was precisely at this moment that one of the daughters of Hamilcar married the king, Bomilcar. We can only suppose that the king participated, from now on, in Hamilcar's plans, and vetoed the Elders' nomination of Hanno, thus making popular arbitration necessary. Whatever may have been the reasons, however, we can at any rate be certain, thanks to Polybius, that the Assembly of the People was called upon to cast its vote, and decided that the army should elect whichever of the two generals it favoured. This was a truly revolutionary innovation and carried with it the seeds of a military monarchy similar to those which had ruled the East since the conquest of Alexander. As for the vacant generalship, it was to be filled by the will of the people and no longer by that of the Elders. Hanno was naturally enough the victim of this strange procedure, and the people elected, in his place, Hannibal, the son of the Hamilcar who had been victor at Paropus during the war against Rome, and who was perhaps a relation of the Barcids. The oligarchs, as was to be expected, denounced these proceedings as being highly illegal, and Hanno declared that it was force alone that prevented him from assuming the command.

Fortunately, a great victory took place just at this moment, and justified this action which approached a *coup d'état*. Hamilcar succeeded in enticing the army of Spendius and of Autaritus into the Defile of the Saw, a steep valley in the middle of the mountains of the Tunisian range. The leaders were captured and crucified, thanks to a treacherous trick, and the men were massacred. Matho, who had remained in Tunis with his Libyans, restored the balance thanks to a lucky attack which enabled him to capture the new general Hannibal, who was, in his turn, crucified. More important still, Rome considered the new order of things in Carthage as hostile to her, with the result that she reversed her benevolent policy. The Comitia, indeed, no longer favoured the Fabii, but the Cornelii, the Scipios, and the Lentuli were back in power and recommended a policy of expansion to be directed first in the direction of Corsica and Sardinia, which the members of these families had already attempted to conquer during the First Punic War. Thus in 237, the Senate accepted the 'gift' which the rebel mercenaries had already offered her the year before, and which she had then refused, namely Sardinia. This decision had no immediate practical result, but it served to demonstrate Roman ill-will.

The oligarchical party made the most of the difficult situation in which Hamilcar now found himself, and annulled part of the recent constitutional changes. The Council of State, which formed the real government of the Republic, had been shorn of most of its prerogatives, which had then become those of the generals. This Council now exerted pressure on Barca in order that he might be reconciled with Hanno and allow the latter to resume his command. Hamilcar was obliged to recognize this transaction, which, in effect, presupposed the illegality of the army's vote against Hanno. There was a public reconciliation, for form's sake, between the two rivals, and they then completed the war by crushing Matho, whom they handed over to the fury of the inhabitants of Carthage. Utica and Bizerta had to surrender, and the Libyan people were severely punished, and were once more obliged to submit to the Carthaginian yoke.

Thus, at the close of the first phase of the crisis, it looked as if the party represented by the great landowners had triumphed over social subversion and over the popular and nationalist groups in Carthage. The oligarchs were so convinced of their complete victory that they attempted to rid themselves of Hamilcar by summoning him to appear before the Council of the One Hundred and Four. Appian, indeed, tells us that he was even accused of being responsible for the Mercenary War, which his ill-considered and rash promises had caused!

2. HAMILCAR IN POWER AND THE CONQUEST OF SPAIN

The aristocrats had been too certain of their power, however. During the preceding years a People's Party had grown up in Carthage. The war with Rome had destroyed the navy, impoverished the city, and made a vast number of sailors and dockers unemployed. We can get some idea of the growing competition from the Campanian industries if we study the grave-goods of this period, which include an ever-increasing number of Italian wares. Thus the craftsmen and shopkeepers were also faced with ruin, and they made up the vast majority of Carthaginians. At first these humble folk had been afraid of the mercenaries, but they did not wish to find themselves once more under the yoke of the great landowners, whose aims and interests were in opposition to their own. They grouped themselves, therefore, round a young man called Hasdrubal, who was doubtless of aristocratic extraction but of whom we do not even know the antecedents. Hamilcar Barca must certainly have already obtained his assistance when he rid himself of Hanno. He sealed the alliance by giving him one of his daughters in marriage. In 238 Hasdrubal rushed to his father-in-law's assistance. He probably managed to get a law passed, restricting the powers of the One Hundred and Four, for from then on, there are no further examples of generals condemned by this formidable tribunal. The people once more claimed the right to elect the generals: Hanno was discredited in a propaganda campaign and was finally and definitively relieved of his command, while Hamilcar was officially proclaimed sole commander-in-chief in Africa. Hanno was not, however, proceeded against. He remained a member of the Council of Elders, where for many years he was the active leader of a bitter opposition before finally transmitting this role to his son.

Polybius tells us that at the time of the Second Punic War the citizens of Carthage had more political rights than those of Rome. In the days of Aristotle the situation had been completely the reverse. During the third century, therefore, there must have been a total reform of Punic institutions in favour of the people. This reform must have taken place after the war with Rome, for we know that aristocratic institutions were then in force. It probably took place in 237, and doubtless consisted in increasing the powers of the People's Assembly, and in transferring executive power from the permanent committees formed by the Elders, to magistrates who were elected yearly by the Assembly. It is only now, or so the present author believes, that the two suffetes, who are in future elected democratically, become the true civil leaders of the Punic Republic. The Roman consuls probably served as a model in defining their status, but they were never to command armies and so bore a closer resemblance to the Praetors, whose function was also primarily judiciary. Hamilcar was well aware of the fickleness of the Carthaginian people and so was careful not to be entirely dependent on them. Furthermore, in order to carry out his plans, he needed greater continuity than that provided by magistrates who were annually renewed. Finally, he was a soldier and not a politician. For these reasons, therefore, the constitutional reforms were but a first step in the Barcid Revolution. The second was to consist in the creation, outside Africa, of a military state of which Hamilcar would be in sole command.

The creation of this state was also a necessary preliminary to revenge against Rome. Even if Hamilcar had been able to forget his grudge against the Latin Republic, the Romans would certainly have revived the memory. As soon as peace had been re-established in Africa, Barca had obtained permission to send an expeditionary force to Sardinia. The treaty of Lutatius made such an operation perfectly legitimate. Rome had not yet taken possession of the island, which the rebel mercenaries who had sought her protection, had now evacuated. Thus the magistrates of the Phoenician cities were still exercising their power, as were the chiefs of the native tribes of the interior, who were pro-Carthaginian. Nevertheless, the Senate, with obvious bad faith, pretended to see in this action of Hamilcar's a hostile act of aggression and, without more ado, it declared war on Carthage. There was no question of fighting: Hamilcar had to renounce all his rights over Sardinia and, furthermore, he had to agree to the payment of 1200 talents in addition to the war indemnity agreed in 241.

This pitiless Roman attack was probably the most cynical act they committed during their conquests, and it was received with indignation as far afield as Greece. There is no need to describe the effect it had in Carthage. It rekindled the feelings of revenge which Hamilcar had nursed since the surrender of Eryx. The Semite's patriotic exaltation was accompanied by a mystical crisis. This took place during the famous sacrifice to Ba'al Shamim, in the course of which little Hannibal, aged nine, swore eternal hatred to the Romans. An account of this dramatic ceremony has come down to us through several sources which give us roughly the same picture and enable us to accept its perfect authenticity. Our sources are Polybius, Cornelius Nepos, Valerius Maximus, and Silius Italicus.

This impressive ceremony solemnized the inauguration of Hamilcar's great undertaking, which was going to occupy him for the rest of his life. In order to restore Carthage to her former greatness, and at the same time avenge her defeats, he decided to turn once more to Spain, which had first attracted the Tyrians to the West and finally led them to establish themselves in Africa. For more than eight centuries the Phoenicians had been exploiting the resources of the Iberian peninsula, both economically and as regards manpower. Nevertheless, these resources were on such a vast scale compared with others in Antiquity, that they were still almost intact. As we have seen, and contrary to the view generally held by historians both ancient and modern, the Carthaginians never succeeded in obtaining complete control of these resources. They had imposed their supremacy over their Tyrian colonies of the southern coast – ancient Gades, Abdera, Sexi, and Málaga. The Tartessians who lived on the coast of the Alboran Sea, had come into contact with the Phoenicians and had adopted their language and civilization, though these differed from those prevalent in Africa. The coalition which had thus been constituted had been powerful enough to drive the Greeks back into Catalonia when these had, at one stage, sought to establish their trading stations along the eastern coasts. The Greeks were now confined in Emporiae and Rhode, under the watchful eyes of hostile tribes. In the fourth century especially, Carthage had probably launched devastating raids into the interior; she had doubtless from time to time obliged the mountain landowners of the mines to hand over a large proportion of the yield which she alone had the right to export. The Iberians had never been made to submit to political or military domination, however, and so long as this type of protectorate continued to be profitable, Carthage had felt no need to assume direct administrative control such as that which she exercised in Africa.

Hamilcar could no longer afford to be content with an arrangement which his forebears had found satisfactory. The exploitation of the country's mineral resources certainly played an important part in his plan, for it was this exploitation which was to furnish the means of paying off the war indemnities which Roman avarice demanded, thus upsetting the calculations of the Italian merchants, who had hoped that by bleeding Carthage in this way, they would deal a death-blow to the Punic economy. The yield of the mines would also help to finance a new navy and siege-engines, and if this wealth were carefully distributed in Carthage, it could be used to strengthen the authority of the Barcid party. Finally, Spanish silver and gold would buy throughout the world, the political assistance necessary to isolate Rome: allies could be obtained in this way from among the independent peoples of Africa, of the Celtic world, of Greece and the East, and even of Italy. A century earlier, Philip of Macedon had shown just how far a man's ambitions could carry him if they were backed by an inexhaustible supply of money. To obtain such riches in sufficient quantities, however, it was not enough to exact a tithe of the native production. The exploitation had to be directly controlled and rational methods applied, such as had been perfected by the Macedonians in their mines near Philippi, and by the Ptolemies in Egypt. This aim could only be achieved after military conquest of the Andalusian plain and of the sierras which surround it, and by the establishment of outposts in Estremadura and La Mancha to prevent the Celtic and Celtiberian tribes of the meseta from carrying out raids into the mining areas.

It was not only in Spain, however, that Hamilcar sought the means of avoiding, in the event of another war, the economic impoverishment which had compelled Carthage to accept the peace of Lutatius. He wished, above all, to build up the necessary political and military power to enable him to carry out his plans in his own time without having to pay heed to Rome or the vicissitudes of internal politics at home, where the democratic régime was still vulnerable to oligarchical reactions. The only way of achieving this stability was through independence, by founding one of those colonial and military monarchies which had grown up all round the eastern end of the Mediterranean after Alexander's death. These monarchies had been based on the power and doctrine of leadership, by which an adventurer at the head of a devoted army could appropriate for his own use the labour of subdued populations, reduced to something approaching bondage.

Spain was particularly well suited to the realization of this ambition. The country was far enough away for the Roman Senate not to have any direct interest in it, so that it was not immediately aware of the inherent threat in the creation of this new power. For the same reason, the Carthaginian opponents of the Barcids had no easy way of controlling the legality of any action, and even if they did condemn some irregularity, the people were unlikely to worry unduly about something which had taken place so far from home. Furthermore, the two races who made up the greater part of the population of Spain at that time, the Iberians and the Celts, had long-established traditions of war and adventure. Both were used to a society based on military supremacy, and their ethics and religion praised above all, the courage and loyalty of the warrior as regards his chieftain. This loyalty was endorsed by mystical rites which compelled those who had taken part in them to die with their leader, or be dishonoured. With a little discipline and instruction, these terrible brigands, who were imbued with the spirit of chivalry, would become invincible troops. Thus the Barcid army would preserve the professionalism which had always been the chief quality of the Carthaginian army, but would be able to depend on the loyalty of its troops in the place of patriotism, and would lose the instability which had been so much in evidence during the Mercenary War.

Hamilcar had already gone a long way towards realizing his ambition when, in the middle of the Mercenary War, he had got the people of Carthage to arbitrate in his disagreement with Hanno the Great. From then onwards, the army elected its own generals while the civil authorities could only ratify the choice. Such a régime might easily have degenerated into military anarchy, such as occurred at times in both the Roman and the Ottoman Empires. There were psychological factors which prevented this happening, however, and these consisted of a careful combination of ideas, which were current throughout the Hellenistic world, with purely Phoenician traditions.

The great wars of the fourth century had put the fate of the civilized world in the hands of the soldiers of fortune, who had left their families and homes and whose only god (or rather goddess) was Fortune (Tyche in Greek). Naturally enough, most of them did not associate this with random chance, but believed that mysterious laws bestowed it on some rather than on others. Those who were favoured in this way attracted the best troops and, thanks to them, became the masters of riches and kingdoms carved out by the sword. The survivors among those who had opposed Alexander's successors were anxious to give some stability to their rule, and they therefore sought to transform these simple superstitions into a form of theology which would legitimize their success after the event. They made the most of the fashion for mystic religions, whereby the mass of aimless victims of the vicissitudes of the times sought consolation, and succeeded in persuading their soldiers and subjects that they ruled by divine right. Fortune had given them the crown according to the wish of that Providence which governed the world, and of a few associated deities. After death, this same Fortune became the inheritance of their legitimate successors. In this way a dynastic religion was born, which had at least the advantage of ensuring some sort of continuity during two or three centuries, so that the power was transmitted in a well-defined way in the monarchies which had arisen after the Macedonian Empire broke up.

Hamilcar Barca and his successors transposed these doctrines into the Punic world and adapted them to the national religion.

The Barcids probably belonged to the old Carthaginian aristocracy constituted by the descendants of the first clans. They had jealously preserved the religious traditions of the metropolis, as can be deduced from the text of the oath which Hannibal took in 216 in his undertakings with Philip V, king of Macedon (Polybius VII, 9). The pantheon which the Carthaginian then invoked was not that of his city, but rather his own or that of his ancestors.[1] Foremost in this pantheon was Ba'al Shamim, Lord of the Heavens, who was given his Greek name of Zeus and who had been supplanted in Carthage by Ba'al Hammon. The leader of the second divine triad was Heracles or Melqart, the 'King of the City', Lord of Tyre, who was very much respected in Carthage, in theory, but whose temples were not often visited, so Diodorus tells us, while his name and representation rarely occur on Punic monuments.

Ba'al Shamim and Melqart were, in fact, the great gods of the Barcids. Hamilcar sacrificed to the first of these before he left for Spain on the occasion when Hannibal swore eternal hatred to the Romans. The Lord of the Heavens appeared to Hannibal in his dreams and lent him his support on the eve of his battles. As for Melqart, as Lord of the sanctuary at Gades, he was patron of the whole Iberian peninsula and, as such, particularly useful to the conquerors of Spain.[2]

The Barcids began by rallying their soldiers to the family pantheon, thus suggesting that they were protected by the gods. They did not hesitate to go further still: on the coins which Hannibal struck at Cartagena, he and his father are assimilated to Heracles-Melqart, whose club appears alongside the representations of their heads crowned with laurels.[3] This identification of a living man with a god was entirely foreign to Semitic religion. The most the Carthaginians ever did, was admit the apotheosis of some of their dead, and particularly those who had killed themselves as a sacrifice, or victims who had been substituted for them. On the other hand, it was current usage among Greek sovereigns, and these would assimilate themselves especially to Heracles. The Barcids completely transformed the old Tyrian cult, therefore, in order that it should agree with their politics. It is probably they who dedicated to this end, in the sacred enclosure of the Temple of Gades (whose Holy of Holies contained no cult-idol), statues of Heracles in Greek style, and one of Alexander the Great, who claimed descent from Heracles. They were not worried by the fact that it was the Macedonian who had destroyed Tyre!

Once the soldiers of Spain had been well imbued with this political and religious propaganda, they could be relied upon to cast their vote every time in favour of one of Hamilcar's relations: first they elected his son-in-law Hasdrubal, and then, on the latter's death, Hannibal.

The Barcid conquest of Spain did not give Carthage a new province to replace those she had lost in Sicily and Sardinia. It caused the appearance of a new independent state in fact, if not by right, ruled entirely and solely by Hamilcar Barca and his successors. We believe that this had been Hamilcar's aim from the very beginning. It was not realized immediately, however, and was only gradually revealed as the new state became viable.

During the nine years he spent in Spain, Hamilcar had no time to develop his action on the political plane. He had to fight constantly in order to impose his authority on the natives, and he was finally killed in the course of this struggle. He had first landed at Gades and installed his headquarters there. Although the city maintained its autonomy, it was an excellent base from which to embark on the conquest of the valley of the Guadalquivir – Barca's first objective. This valley was inhabited by the Turdetani, who were the western branch of the ancient Tartessian nation which had broken up two centuries before. They do not seem to have put up much resistance, but they were doubtless very much under the influence of Phoenician propaganda already, and they do not seem to have been a very warlike people. In any case, from 235 onwards Hamilcar controlled the mines which were situated in the mountains round the upper valley of the river. It was then that the minting of silver coinage began at Gades, and its excellent quality is in marked contrast to the extremely poor African coinage issued at the end of the Mercenary War.[4] The silver which was extracted from the mines was divided into three: one part was sent to Carthage, one was given to the magistrates of Gades in recognition of their support, and with the third Hamilcar began minting his own personal coinage, which is sufficient indication of his wish for independence.

Though the Turdetani soon came to terms with the Carthaginians, the same cannot be said for the Celtiberian tribes who occupied the meseta, and who resented the fact that the neighbours they had been in the habit of raiding had now come under an authority which they had to respect. Two kings named Istolatius and Indortes came to attack the new province. They were routed, and Indortes fell into Hamilcar's hands. The Carthaginian had him lengthily tortured, had his eyes torn out, and finally had him crucified. This terrible example was supposed to indicate Hamilcar's determination to impose his law and order over the whole country by all the means at his disposal, for, according to Strabo, civilized life was impossible owing to the plundering, perfidy, and arrogance of the petty chieftains.

During this same year 235, there was a rising against the Romans in Sardinia.[5] The Byzantine historian Zonaras (18,9) adds that the Italian merchants who were in Carthage at the time were molested, and this is very probable. As we have seen, Campanian firms had been flooding the African market, since the treaty with Lutatius had abolished the protective barriers which had previously existed. Their agents must have been most unpopular. Rome, however, took a firm line, particularly so in fact, for an Atilius was consul at that time. The Carthaginian magistrates were once more threatened with war, but made their humble apologies, which were accepted. Hamilcar must certainly have counselled prudence, since nothing was more likely to upset his plans than war with Rome.

During the years that followed, Hamilcar turned his interest to the regions east of the Straits of Gibraltar. Inland from the Alboran coast lay the old Tyrian colonies of Sexi, Abdera, and Málaga, which were as old as Carthage herself and which were inhabited by Phoenicianized Tartessians whom the Romans called Bastulo-

Poeni. Another people of the same race, the Bastetani or Mastians, ruled over territory which extended as far as Murcia. They did not show much resistance and neither did their more northerly neighbours, the Deitani.

The Punic armies had thus reached the frontiers of the Iberians, a huge nation which dominated the whole Mediterranean coast of the peninsula, from Alicante to the Pyrenees and even beyond, as far as the mouth of the Hérault. They were probably closely related to the Tartessians, but were a prouder and more warlike race. Their southern tribes, especially, seem to have had a highly developed artistic sense, which enabled them to create a type of sculpture and pottery, based on Greek models, which is remarkably powerful and original. In this respect they were certainly far more gifted than the Carthaginians, and we can only deplore the fact that, by their intervention, the latter caused the death of a culture which had reached its height in the third century.

Faced by these formidable adversaries, the Punic advance was, to a great extent, slowed up, but Hamilcar did succeed in occupying the Cabo de la Nâo. In the mountainous country inland from the cape lay numerous Iberian townships. In 231 he set up his headquarters in a town which we only know as Akra Leuke or the White Headland, and which is generally thought to have stood at Albufereta, very near Alicante, where Spanish archaeologists have excavated extremely important Iberian cemeteries which contain a great number of Punic objects. This change of headquarters was intended to calm the susceptibilities of the inhabitants of Gades, as well as indicate Hamilcar's plans for driving northwards, probably as far as the Iberian frontier.

These operations could not fail to arouse the anxiety of the Greeks from Catalonia. They could not do anything themselves and so drew the attention of the Romans to what was going on, using their Marseillais compatriots as intermediaries. A mission was despatched by the Senate so that its members could see what was happening on the spot. Hamilcar welcomed them warmly, took them round the mines, and explained to the delegates that his sole aim was to provide Carthage with the means of paying the war indemnity. The Fathers returned reassured.

So far the Carthaginians had subdued only the coast. After establishing himself at Akra Leuke, however, Hamilcar decided to seek out the formidable tribes of the interior which he had already come into contact with during the attack of Indortes. He himself set out to follow the course of the Júcar inland, while his son-in-law Hasdrubal attacked from the south. Hamilcar's small army was confronted by the whole mass of the Oretani Celtiberians, who ruled over La Mancha. The Carthaginians were obliged to beat a retreat, but were surprised by the enemy as they were crossing the Júcar. Hamilcar was drowned (229 B.C.).

3. HASDRUBAL: 229–222

This catastrophe, instead of causing the collapse of Hamilcar's undertaking, had the contrary effect of showing just how well grounded and efficient his organization was. His two sons, Hannibal and Hasdrubal the Younger, were too young to succeed him. The army elected their brother-in-law, Hasdrubal the Elder, who was admiral of the fleet and therefore second in command in Spain. The people of Carthage sanctioned this choice without making any difficulties.

It will be remembered that Hasdrubal had begun his career as a politician. Although he had since been a successful commander in Spain, he had a less warlike temperament than the real Barcids. During the seven years of his governorship, he devoted himself especially to the organization of the Spanish state, ensuring its autonomy, and making it still more of a kingdom than it had been in the time of Hamilcar. He was not content with the military election that had brought him to power, but called together all the Iberian chiefs and succeeded in having himself appointed commander-in-chief of the whole nation. Just as Alexander had married a Persian princess, so Hasdrubal chose as his wife the daughter of a Spanish princeling. His most significant act was the founding of a new capital which he had the audacity to name Carthage (present-day Cartagena). This audacity was almost sacrilegious since it indicated his intention of transferring the seat of power of the Western Phoenicians to Spain. In the new city he built a palace which was based on those of oriental potentates. Hasdrubal did not hesitate, furthermore, to wear the crown, and his coins represent him with this insignia. Hasdrubal was, indeed, the first Carthaginian to have himself represented on the coins he issued, for this was a privilege of kingship which Hamilcar had not assumed. We can well imagine how these innovations were received by the more conservative element in Carthage. The Latin historian Fabius Pictor even maintained that Hasdrubal had sought to have himself accepted as king in Africa, and that, after failing in this aim, he governed Spain without paying any attention to instructions sent out by the metropolis. The second part of this statement has certainly a basis of truth: the kingdom of Spain was acting more and more as an independent power.

Spain was, however, a colonial state in which the native population was roughly treated and exploited. All positions of authority were in Carthaginian hands. The sovereign was advised by a Council, which included some members of the Carthaginian Council of State, some Elders, and generals. The native princes were obliged not only to pay tribute, but to send one of their children, and even sometimes their wives, as hostages to new Carthage. Furthermore, they were closely watched by a very active secret police, and those who were suspected of insubordination were under the constant threat of assassination, or else they disappeared and died amid terrible tortures and suffering. This was the fate of a Celtic prince of the Tagus valley, who was later avenged by one of his followers assassinating Hasdrubal. Those in more modest circumstances were no better treated, and we have good reasons for supposing that a great number of peasants were reduced to serfdom, while the workers in the mines were subject to extremely severe discipline. Indeed, the Barcid conquest caused the decline of the brilliant Iberian civilization, to which the Romans were to deal the final blow.

The Greeks of Emporiae once more drew the Romans' attention to what was happening in Spain, and the Senate was sufficiently impressed by Hasdrubal's power to force him to sign a treaty in 226, which limited his ambitions. Polybius was misinformed by his Roman sources and has completely misunderstood the significance of this event, thus leading astray most modern historians. According to Polybius, the Senate had been informed that a revolt of the Cisalpine Gauls was imminent, and therefore sought to ensure Carthaginian neutrality: they proposed an agreement to Hasdrubal whereby the Barcids might occupy the whole of Spain as far as the Ebro, which the Romans undertook not to cross. This version of the events is not only unlikely but is not borne out by later occurrences. In particular, Rome considered it a *casus belli* when, in 220 B.C., Hannibal attacked Saguntum. Now Saguntum lies some 100 miles south of the mouth of the Ebro! Carcopino has indeed shown that the river which is called Iberus in the text of the treaty of 226 is, in fact, not the Ebro but the Júcar. The treaty therefore forbade Hasdrubal from extending his empire beyond the limits which Hamilcar had reached, and rejected his claim to be the head of the whole Iberian nation. Furthermore, an analysis of the historical situation for the years 227–225 indicates that Rome was certainly not seeking to draw closer to Carthage. Rome, on the contrary, was totally unprepared for the imminent Gallic revolt, which caught her completely unawares. When this war broke out, the Roman leaders were so doubtful about Carthaginian friendship, that they stationed the greater part of their troops in Sardinia, in Sicily, and in Southern Italy, and this enabled the Celts to crush the Etruscan militia and plunder Tuscany. Some of the Roman leaders were the worst enemies of Carthage – among them the two sons of Regulus. They were resolved to check, once and for all, the growth of the Barcid state. For this reason, they did not undertake negotiations but delivered a brutal ultimatum to Cartagena; at the same time they formed a treaty of alliance with Saguntum – the most sophisticated of the Iberian towns. This treaty was negotiated by the aristocratic party which was in power in the Spanish harbour town, and was violently attacked by the popular faction. The Romans had no hesitation in intervening and the leaders of the opposition party were brutally executed.

Hasdrubal accepted the conditions of the Senate without flinching. Hamilcar would probably have been less docile, and Hannibal would certainly have shown some fight. Hasdrubal, however, had remained first and foremost a politician rather than a soldier. Whereas his father- and brother-in-law regarded Spain merely as a military base from which to launch their campaign of revenge against Rome, Hasdrubal had become extremely attached to this kingdom which he had organized and consolidated, and he did not wish to jeopardize its existence by undertaking a struggle the outcome of which was uncertain. He was depending above all on his diplomacy so as to get the better of Rome. He may also have been better informed than the Senators, and have known that the Gauls were soon intending to attack, though he did nothing to support them. We know, however, that he was in contact with Iberian princes who ruled well beyond the course of the Júcar: his agents helped Indibilis to form a federation of Catalan tribes, and Edecon to unite those of Aragon under his sceptre, and both declared themselves vassals of the Barcids. The treaty of 226 which forbade Punic armies to cross the Júcar, had not taken into account the possibility of diplomatic action of this sort. Furthermore, although the Gallic offensive did not break the might of Rome in Italy, it did nevertheless have the result of diverting Roman imperialist interests from the Mediterranean to the north. The legions undertook the methodical conquest of the Po valley and even crossed the Adriatic into Illyria, under the guidance of Fabius Maximus, the future Cunctator, and of a strange character called C. Flaminius, who was not a member of the aristocracy but whose politics often agreed with those of the Fabii, as the Italian historian Cassola has shown. Hasdrubal's wisdom seemed to bear fruit. From his palace in Cartagena he could peacefully pursue the game of intrigue which was to unite to him the peoples of the whole peninsula, thus isolating the friends of Rome in their coastal cities, hemmed in by hostile tribes. Already the Oretani were menacing Saguntum, and the agents of Indibilis were spurring on the neighbours of Emporiae and Rhode.

It was at this stage that a Celt, whose chief had been crucified by Hasdrubal's orders and who had sworn not to survive him, managed to enter into the palace and stab the Carthaginian king. The murderer was so appallingly tortured that his features were twisted by pain until they made him look as if he were laughing, like those of the Chinese who were slowly and scientifically cut to pieces by the executioners of the Celestial Empire.

4. CARTHAGE UNDER THE BARCIDS

Life in Carthage under the Barcids, from the material point of view, is fairly well documented. The township of Dar es Safi on Cap Bon near Kerkouane was destroyed by Regulus in 256. Contrary to most of the Mediterranean cities in existence at that date, it has no regular plan with straight streets crossing each other at right angles. At Dar es Safi the streets are fairly wide. The houses are, for the most part, built either of small stones set in mortar, or of mud-brick. Walls built of large stones are rare and are only used for façades. The houses are large and practical, with a central court in which there is often an altar dedicated to the household gods, decorated with red stucco. In one of these central courts stands a peristyle consisting of nine massive columns: even in Greece peristyles in private houses only become common after the death of Alexander. The fact that we find an example in Africa which dates before the middle of the third century, proves that the Hellenic fashion was quickly known and adopted. Another house has a covered section, supported on two columns only, at each end of a rectangular courtyard; the same arrangement is found at Olynthus, which was destroyed by Philip of Macedon in 348 B.C. The comfort and elegance of the houses of Dar es Safi are further enhanced by the floors, which are generally made of pink cement incrusted with small pieces of white marble, and sometimes with pieces of broken glass, to form, in several cases, the outline of the sign of Tanit, which is flanked in one example by the representation of two dolphins. We do not find this sort of mosaic in the Hellenistic world, although it was soon to spread to Italy and throughout the Western Mediterranean under the name of *pavimenta punica*. Finally, every house has its own bathroom fitted with a slipper-shaped bath and a basin. In this respect as well, the inhabitants of Dar es Safi were following the latest fashion.

The town's public buildings and temples have not yet been found. Dar es Safi owed its prosperity especially to the purple dye industry, and the broken shells of the murex, from which the dye was extracted in such quantity, are piled into great heaps along the shore. The only monument from the Dar es Safi excavations which can be said to belong to the fine arts category, is a lively sculpture of a bull which is comparable to the Iberian 'does'. Among the small finds are two rather coarse terracotta plaques representing marine deities, and one ceramic figurine of a hunting-goddess armed with two javelins.

Fine wares are almost all imported from Southern Italy or Egypt. This same predominance of imports is to be found in the cemeteries. Many tombs have been excavated on Cap Bon. In Carthage, the largest Sainte Monique cemetery, already in use in the fourth century, continued to provide a resting place for the dead until the end of the Punic Wars.

In art, Hellenistic influence is more and more marked. It can be seen in the decoration of the sacred razors, some of which are engraved with representations of Melqart-Heracles, thus bearing witness to the renewed popularity which his cult enjoyed. One of the blades is decorated on one side with a representation of a seated god, who is now indistinguishable from the Greek hero; on the other side stands a figure draped in a speckled *himation*, holding a bird and a root, who must be the faithful Iolaus, Heracles' companion, with his two talismans – the quail and the root of the *kolokasion*, a sort of water-lily which grows in the Lebanon – which helped him to revive his master after the latter's perilous fight against Typhon.

A large number of Greeks lived in Carthage, and the epitaph of a woman who had come from Cyrene was found in the cemetery near the Antonine Baths. Others lived in the Barcid court. Among these emigrés there were artists like the coppersmith Boethus of Carthage, whose signature has been found at Ephesus. Others probably came from Sicily, where they had been trained in the court of King Hieron. One of the latter was entrusted with the work of casting official portraits of Hamilcar Barca, Hasdrubal, and Hannibal. These portraits were set up in public buildings, like those of oriental potentates, and became, indeed, the centre of a cult. Those of Hamilcar and Hasdrubal are known only because of their appearance on coins – also the work of skilled engravers. Several copies in the round of Hannibal's portrait have come down to us; the finest, in bronze, was found at Volubilis in 1944, and had once formed part of the collection of King Juba II of Mauretania, who was of Barcid descent and, in the first century A.D., piously preserved the memory of his illustrious ancestors.

Greek influence was more and more apparent in religious matters. Nevertheless, children were still sacrificed on the topheth, though generally a lamb was substituted for the human victim and the horrible ceremonies seem to have lost their glamour. The Latin authors, who did their utmost to denounce Punic cruelty, do not mention human sacrifice at this period. Although the Barcids worshipped Ba'al Shamim and Melqart, they did in fact build a temple to Ba'al Hammon at Cartagena, but they never offered human sacrifices, even when times were particularly bad. In any case, there seem to have been important changes in the meaning of the moloch sacrifice. Most of the stelae seem to have been dedicated by the poorer classes: minor craftsmen, freed-men, and slaves, who now joined the people of note in 'offering' their children to Tanit and Ba'al. Under the influence of Dionysiac religion, the moloch became a sacrifice of 'salvation': the child who was offered was 'cured', that is to say, made immortal, assimilated to Shadrapa, the equivalent of Horus, Saviour, and Dionysus, whose symbols now decorate the stelae of Salammbo, side by side with the laurel wreath and emblems of victory over death.

For the most part the stelae exhibit poor workmanship. The design is still incised but the line has lost its suppleness, vigour, and flow. One of them is, however, a work of art and bears the portrait of a young man executed in the style in which Apelles had represented Alexander the Great, and which had since been used to depict Hellenistic monarchs. In this way the stele is closely related to the Volubilis bust, though the subject is different. Perhaps we have here the portrait of another member of the Barcid family, for instance one of Hannibal's younger brothers. On other stelae we find the same motifs as appear on the reverse of coins minted in Spain, symbols of the nationalist propaganda of the dynasty: galleys, war elephants, and horses and their riders representing the Punic Mars.

Gods borrowed from Greece were now particularly favoured, for instance Demeter, before whose cult-statues ex-votos were constantly being offered: terracotta incense burners in the likeness of the goddess' bust. Shadrapa was venerated in the topheth but also had his own temple. He and Melqart were more and more closely identified with their Greek equivalents, Dionysus and Heracles.

Young aristocrats of both sexes received a very complete and international education. Thanks to the lessons of their Greek tutors, Hannibal and his brothers and Sophonisba, daughter of Hasdrubal and grand-daughter of Gisco, could hold their own among the princes and princesses of the East. A great deal of time was devoted to the study of the arts – particularly in the case of the girls, who learnt music and dancing.

As far as dress is concerned, there must have been much the same variety in the streets of Carthage in those days as there is now in the streets of Tunis. Most of the male population continued to wear the long, floating Phoenician tunic, without belt or coat. To this form of dress the priests and magistrates would add head-dresses and ornaments and, in particular, the 'epitoga', which we have already discussed in Chapter III, and which was a sign of their high estate. For certain religious ceremonies the traditional costumes were still used, especially a heavy, richly ornamented and braided coat, which opened down the front to reveal a short kilt, and the conical mitres: the designs engraved on some of the sacred razors show libation scenes in which the priest is clad in this way, like a god. Those who led an active life, however, willingly adopted the short tunic with its cloak fastened on one shoulder according to Greek fashion. This was also the uniform of officers, and the armour no longer differed from that used by the Greeks. A veteran of the wars of Hannibal was buried at Ksour es Saf in Byzacenia, wearing the fine ceremonial breast-plate which he had bought at Capua. The poorer classes – and doubtless the most fortunate in hot weather – continued to wear the kilt, to which they added, on ceremonial occasions, furbelows and fringes. Women wore Greek dress – a tunic and a *pallium*.

Quite a number of the inscriptions from Carthage must date from this period. One of the most important texts is the list of regulations found at Marseilles (which was taken to that town at some unknown date) in which are set out the various dues payable by those who have come to sacrifice to Ba'al Saphon, perhaps the Carthaginian Mars. Février has shown that this tariff corresponds to a more highly developed ritual than that to which analogous inscriptions on other objects refer. He writes as follows:

'It would seem from the official ritual which is described in the so-called Marseilles tariff, that sin-offerings now form the most important part of the service, just as they had in Hebraic cult after the Exile. . . If we feel constrained to link the evolution of religious thought to specific political events – and I admit that I dislike strongly such arbitrary psychology – we might be tempted to think of the wars in Sicily as the cause of the development of sin-offerings in the Carthaginian world.'[6]

This historical hypothesis which Février so much dislikes can be confirmed to some extent by such constitutional information as the inscription contains. Two magistracies are mentioned: one is a committee of 30 people to superintend the taxes, and which is mentioned in another tariff (*CIS* 167c), and the other consists of two suffetes, Hillesbaal son of Bodastart, and Hillesbaal son of Bodesmun, together with 'their colleagues'. The mention of these dignitaries helps us to date the inscription, thus proving, incidentally, that the magistracy was renewed yearly. The reference to 'colleagues' of the eponymous suffetes has worried some people who are convinced that there were only two suffetes at any one time in Carthage. It has been suggested that they might be Elders, or members of the Council of Thirty. Both these hypotheses can be ignored, for the appointment of councillors was not limited to one year. The present author believes that these 'colleagues' cannot be other than 'minor suffetes' – a relict of the days when there had been more than two of these magistrates. Here they are subordinate to the eponymous suffetes and must have served in some auxiliary capacity. If this interpretation is correct, then the inscription must belong to a period of transition between the multiple magistracy and the diarchy, at a time, therefore, when the democratic revolution had begun but was not yet completed. The inscription could thus be ascribed to the last years of the War with Rome, or to the period of the Mercenary War. As for the Thirty appointed to 'superintend the taxes', Février identifies them with Aristotle's pentarchies, which would, he suggests, have come together to discuss questions of finance. Would it not be more plausible, however, to see in his committee the famous Council of Thirty? Aristotle does not mention the latter, while in Polybius[7] and Livy it appears as a sort of Inner Committee of the Council of the Elders, with a very wide range of powers. There is no reason, however, why this Inner Committee should not have originated, as Février suggests, as a finance control commission constituted towards the end of the fourth century – quite possibly from the fusion of six 'pentarchies'. Since it was this commission which distributed public funds as it thought fit, it could easily paralyse any action by civil or military magistrates, and furthermore it administered the temporal wealth of the Temples. It can easily be seen, therefore, how the commission could play the part of a supreme executive council without having the title.

The little which we can glimpse of the internal situation in Carthage at this period, gives the impression of a balanced régime where the equilibrium is preserved between the power of the people and the power of the aristocracy. We can add that the majority of the supporters of the Barcids were certainly among the Elders, and the Thirty. As we have seen, many of these officials collaborated closely with the leaders in Spain.

If we compare a Carthaginian text carved during the reign of the Numidian king Micipsa (139–118 B.C.) with various Latin documents, we can reconstruct to some extent, the administrative organization of Carthaginian possessions in Africa in the third and second centuries B.C. The area covered consisted first of the territory of Carthage itself, which Polybius calls *chora* and which probably included the whole of the Cap Bon peninsula. All the allied towns which were supposed to be autonomous also controlled their own *territorium*, and foremost among these were Hippo Diarrhytus (Bizerta), Utica, and Hadrumetum. The remainder of the country was divided into seven or eight districts ('RṢT, in Latin *pagi*). The district of Muxsi must have stretched to the north-west of Carthage, behind Utica and Bizerta; that of the Great Plains, with its capital at Vaga, corresponded to the fertile middle valley of the Medjerda and its tributaries. The district of Zeugei, known as Zeugitania in Roman times, has probably given its name to the modern town of Zaghouan, and must have included the mountains of the Zeugitanian Range and the fertile valley of Wadi Miliana. Immediately to the south, the valley of the Oued el Kebir doubtless formed the heart of the Gunzuzi district. That of Thusca corresponded with the Plateau of Mactar and the inland depressions of Siliana. Finally, Byzacenia comprised the whole Sahellian region with the exclusion of the large free *territorium* of Hadrumetum and of other allied cities. Each of these districts was governed by a chief administrator whose authority varied from one area to another: over peasants who were probably almost entirely reduced to bondage, or over the urban communities which enjoyed some autonomy and could elect their own town council. A general government, both civil and military, controlled the districts. There are similarities, in fact, with the Italian Confederation, with its different categories of cities subject to different régimes. There are also parallels with the administrative system of the Hellenistic kingdoms.

Notes and References

1. Cf. the present author's lecture at the Convegno di Studi Annibalici, *Accademia Etrusca di Cortone, Annuario*, XII (1964), pp. 33–35.
2. A. Garcia y Bellido, 'Hercules Gaditanus', in *Archivo Español de Arqueología*, 1964.
3. E. G. S. Robinson, 'Punic coins of Spain', *Essays in Roman Coinage presented to Harold Mattingly*, Oxford 1956.
4. A hoard of these coins was discovered at Thysdrus and was acquired by the British Museum. Cf. E. G. S. Robinson, op. cit., The owner of the hoard probably buried it during the Mercenary War or during the period of repression which followed immediately upon it.
5. Paulus Orosius, IV, 12, 2; cf. A Lippold, *Consules* (1963), p. 125.
6. *Cahiers de Byrsa*, VIII (1958–9), pp. 35–43; and *Bull. Arch. du Comité*, 1959, 1960, pp. 22–27.
7. Polybius is not very clear on this head. In I, he seems to indicate that the Council of State, which he calls *gerousia*, numbered more than thirty members. He calls the Council of Elders the *syncletos*.

6

Hannibal

1. Hannibal as a Person

HANNIBAL was born in 246 B.C. and, at the time of
Hasdrubal's death in 221, he had only just attained man-
hood, yet he succeeded to Hasdrubal and, for the next
twenty years, he dominated the whole Mediterranean political
scene. Alexander the Great was his inspiration and like him he
wielded supreme power at an age when his vitality and energy
were intact and experiences of life had not yet tempered the
audaciousness of youth.

We know what his physical appearance was from the descriptions of him in contemporary sources, though the authors of
Antiquity dwell mainly on his moral qualities; we also have his
portrait on coins struck between 221 and 219, and now definitely
identified by E. G. S. Robinson; finally we have two marble busts
of him, one in Copenhagen and one in Madrid, and one bronze
bust which was excavated in 1944 at Volubilis. These show us a
clean-shaven young man with a round head, crowned with the
royal diadem on the sculptures, and with the laurel wreath on the
coins. He had high, jutting eyebrow ridges, a long arched nose,
clearly separated from his forehead, pointed at the end with well-
defined nostrils, a small mouth which turned down at the corners,
full lips with the lower one drawn in, and a strong chin which did
not, however, stick out as far as the upper lip.[1]

In general appearance he resembled an Hellenistic prince, very
similar to Hieron II of Syracuse, for instance. His features do
reveal some 'African' characteristics, however, and these have led
specialists in the iconography of Antiquity to identify the three
busts with Juba II of Mauretania, who reigned at the end of the
first century B.C. There is a stele from the topheth of Carthage

which is carved with a rather similar portrait, and this is sufficient proof that Carthaginians could look like this in the third century B.C.

Hannibal's physical appearance agrees completely with what we know of his character, his training, and of his natural disposition. When he was born, Carthage was already deeply influenced by Hellenism; he was brought up in a kingdom which was organized according to Greek political principles; finally, in order to fight against Rome he was obliged to unite various states from all over the Mediterranean, whose only common denominator was Hellenism. That he was able to do this without losing his patriotic fervour, or rejecting any of the basic traditions of his race, makes him a universal leader in the same way that Alexander the Great was. This is how he was represented by the Greek historian Silenus of Kale Acte whose *Exploits of Hannibal* must have been an epic in prose, surrounding the hero with a mythological halo. The rationalist Polybius disapproved highly of this writer and of his imitators who, for instance, described the Punic army crossing the Alps guided by gods and supernatural heroes. Some fragments of this type of literature have been transmitted to us through Silius Italicus, who wrote his epic poem *Punica* at the end of the first century A.D., when the Romans' hatred for their great adversary had calmed down slightly, leaving some room for admiration.

This detached view was not that held by the men who fought against Hannibal in Italy and who, in several cases, have left us their account of the war. These are Fabius Pictor, Cincius Alimentus, and, especially, Ennius. For them, Hannibal was a devastating monster, pitiless and impious, whose most apparent vices were his cruelty and his perfidy. Livy, who is so often quoted in this respect, drew his portrait from these works, which, according to Polybius, he barely altered. The gods bestowed on this monster a physical appearance which reflected the blackness of his soul. It is indeed true that the handsome features of the Volubilis bust did not long survive the sufferings and exhaustions of war: the terrible winter of 218–217 especially took its toll, for Hannibal lost an eye, while the Punic army suffered from the icy dampness of the Po valley. From now on Hannibal was to appear in the pages of history as the wild Cyclops described by Juvenal: *Cum Gaetula ducem portaret bellua luscum.*

Polybius did his utmost to discover what Hannibal was really like, and listened with the same attention to excessive praise and excessive abuse. He admired Hannibal's ability to handle men, even more than his gifts as a tactician. He had been able to make a united army from a conglomeration of vastly different troops, had imbued these men from all the corners of the earth with his own patriotic passion, and had succeeded in maintaining discipline in times of failure even when all hope had to be abandoned. Polybius also examined very thoroughly the main accusations put forward by the Romans, namely Hannibal's cruelty and greed. He relied as far as possible on the evidence of witnesses who had remained uninvolved in the conflict, such as Masinissa, and came to the conclusion that Hannibal could be absolved as far as inhumanity was concerned, but was nevertheless guilty of an excessive love of money which caused him to make political and strategic mistakes.

Of all the portraits of Hannibal from Antiquity, however, the most interesting is undoubtedly that of Dio Cassius, who was a Roman senator in the third century A.D. He had originally come from Asia Minor, had had a Greek upbringing, and had lived under the rule of emperors of Punic extraction, and was therefore free from any of the prejudices which had affected the judgements of his predecessors. In addition he seems to have had access to the works of Sosylus, who was Hannibal's tutor. According to Sosylus, Hannibal was neither impulsive nor rash; he gave a great deal of thought to his plans and during his lonely meditations he would weigh them carefully and only finally reveal them at the last moment. When the opportunity occurred, however, he would seize it and go into action with the same lightning speed which had been Alexander's forte. Hannibal did not hesitate to gamble heavily then, but only when he had carefully thought the action out, basing it on sound information, and knew that the odds were in his favour. This is why he would never attack the city of Rome itself, for he knew that the town's defences were too strong for him, even after the Cannae episode. He was extremely good at adapting himself to different situations and people, and he could behave like a Gaul when he was with Gauls, and like a Greek when he was with Greeks. He was certainly no visionary – far less so, indeed, than Alexander and his successors (apart from the worthy Ptolemy) – and he was never the slave of an ideology. He never set himself up, for example, as the champion of Liberty against Roman Imperialism, or defender of Democracy against Oligarchy, even though he had the advantage of popular support in Carthage itself and in the Italian towns. Contrary to most great Semitic leaders, he does not seem to have been dominated by religious passions, and his enemies even accused him of impiety. Even his hatred of Rome, which lasted throughout his life, did not prevent him from accepting a compromise with the enemy when he was convinced that it would be impossible to carry on a war to the death.

The Ancients very much admired Hannibal's handling of men, but failed to appreciate what we imagine to be his breath-takingly original and revolutionary strategy. His famous Cannae manoeuvre was seized upon by nineteenth-century German generals who made it the model for their annihilation tactics. It consisted in withdrawing the centre of a line of attack in order to entice the enemy into the gap thus formed, when he could be surrounded and attacked from the rear; it had been unsuccessfully attempted by the Punic fleet in 246 during the first war against Rome, and had been used again by Hamilcar against the mercenaries in the battle of Utica. Hannibal himself used it only once. Certainly the sons of Hamilcar, under the tutorship of the Lacedaemonian Sosylus, had studied the treatises of military art which Greek writers had begun publishing prolifically. They had not been encouraged to specialize in a particular technique, however: Hellenistic education, especially when applied to princes, aimed to produce good all-rounders who were at one and the same time politicians, soldiers, scholars, philosophers, and artists. Hannibal, in particular, had benefited from his education, and it was thanks to it that, when he was exiled from his own country, he was able to become minister and political adviser at the courts of Antiochus III and Prusias of Bithynia, and hold his own with other Hellenized orientals.

There is one aspect of Hannibal's life, however, of which we know practically nothing: his private life. Livy and Silius Italicus tell us that he married a Phoenicianized Spanish girl from the little town of Castulo, and the poet even tells us her name: Imilike or Himilkat – a name which we often find in Punic inscriptions. We know nothing more about this marriage, though Silius Italicus maintains that they had a son before the war separated them, but since this son has left no trace in history, he may well have been a figment of the poet's imagination, created for literary purposes.

We are fairly well documented, on the other hand, concerning Hannibal's principal generals and collaborators. He followed his father's example and the old traditions of Punic monarchy, and conferred the main responsibilities on his closest relations, beginning with his two younger brothers, Hasdrubal and Mago. The former became governor of Spain and, in 207, repeated his older brother's march through Gaul in order to come to Hannibal's assistance and reverse the situation in the Carthaginian's favour. He might have succeeded and brought victory once more into the Punic camp, had it not been for the unexpected temerity of the Roman general Claudius Nero, who had not, in fact, particularly distinguished himself up till then. Mago took part in the great march of 219–218 and in the intoxicating victories which followed, but won fame for himself especially at the end of the war when he was the last Punic general to remain fighting on Italian soil. Finally, a nephew of Hannibal's, Hanno son of King Bomilcar and of a daughter of Hamilcar Barca, distinguished himself at the crossing of the Rhône, led the right wing at Cannae, and, during the last campaign in Africa, was commander of some troops against Scipio.

Side by side with the Barcids we catch glimpses of rough and proud old officers who had probably been trained under Hamilcar. Carthalo and, especially, Maharbal, who gained fame by protesting against his leader's excessive prudence after the battle of Cannae, were both experienced commanders of Numidian cavalry and had officers from allied towns under their command, for instance a certain Muttine of Bizerta or of Bône who turned traitor and finished his career in the Roman army. The rearguard and, in particular, the organization of the camps were in the hands of a man named Hasdrubal who also, on occasion, took part in actions, commanding for instance, the left wing at Cannae. There was another fierce Hannibal who was nicknamed Monomachus (Greek for 'duellist') and is supposed to have suggested that the soldiers be trained to eat human flesh, thus simplifying catering problems. Hannibal's civil and political staff consisted of delegates from the Council of Thirty and from the Elders, and we know their names thanks to Polybius, who recorded them when they were co-signatories in 215 of the treaty of alliance with Macedonia.

2. HANNIBAL'S PLAN

There can be no doubt that, as soon as he became head of the state which his father had founded in Spain, Hannibal's one wish was to join in a battle to the death against Rome. Hasdrubal may have hoped to reach a compromise which would enable the independent Barcid State of the West to flourish unimpeded. But for Hannibal as for his father, Spain was only a base which was to provide the means of revenge, and which would be sacrificed without regrets when it had served its purpose. Once the young conqueror had crossed the Alps, he turned his back completely on the country in which he had been brought up, and never thought of returning to Spain even when he was desperately seeking refuge anywhere he could find it.

Having decided on war, Hannibal must have meditated at length on the subject, weighing his chances and comparing the troops available, just as Dio Cassius describes. He must certainly have known Rome's strength. Polybius has handed down to us a famous document known as the *formula togatorum*, which gives the lists of troops for the year 225. The standing army consisted of six legions, comprising 32,000 Roman infantry and 1600 Roman cavalry with 30,000 allied infantry and 2000 allied cavalry. This army was always immediately available, was admirably trained and disciplined, and was far superior to any other army in the Mediterranean basin. A first reserve force could be mobilized extremely rapidly and was almost as large, consisting of 20,000 Roman infantry and 1500 Roman cavalry, with 30,000 allied infantry and 2000 allied cavalry. The total of Roman and Campanian citizens available for mobilization was 273,000 men, of whom 23,000 were horsemen. Furthermore, various Italic peoples had kept their militia on condition that they marched when Rome called, especially in the case of invasion. This added a further 340,000 infantry and 37,000 cavalry. These reserve troops – and particularly the latter – were of very uneven quality and their loyalty could not be entirely depended upon. In 225 the Gauls had swept aside the Etruscan militia even though the latter were fighting for their own country and homes. Nevertheless,

16

this mass of soldiers grouped around the hard Roman core could only be attacked with any hope of success by an army which was just as strongly built up and which could not afford to be much smaller. Hannibal could count on his father's Iberian veterans and on his excellent Numidian cavalry as being equal to the Roman legionaries and cavalry. He still had to find the necessary troops to counter the mass call to arms which the consuls would order.

There was another problem which was even harder to resolve, and that was the question of the sea. During the first Punic War Rome had built up the largest navy in the Mediterranean. Polybius (I, 75) has shown that it was far more powerful than any of those belonging to even the mightiest of the Hellenistic princes. Between the two wars the fear of Punic revenge had meant that the work in the shipyards had continued and several hundred ships were ready to sail at a moment's notice. Permission had been obtained for this naval development, for it involved mainly the Greek and Campanian allies of Rome rather than the Romans themselves, for the maritime glories of Etruria were but a distant memory. It so happened that Campania was at the height of her commercial and industrial prosperity. The defeat of Carthage had made all the western markets available to her merchants and their presence in a place is betrayed by the black polished vessels in which their wares were stored. Magna Graecia was affected by this competition, but still preserved a large part of the riches which she had accumulated in the fourth century. These regions could well bear the cost of the warships which would guarantee the freedom of their commercial activities. Furthermore, their leaders were eager that this should be so since, by contributing to such an extent in the maintenance of Roman power, they could have a strong say in politics, and could compel the Senate and the Italic Confederation to agree with them if argument arose.

Since this was the situation, it is surprising that Carthage should have made no effort to recover her superiority, or at least her naval equality, for this was essential to her security. There was nothing in the treaty of 241 to prevent her from doing this. Her financial situation was not so desperate as to prevent her, either: military expenditure had been greatly reduced by the loss of Sicily and Sardinia. The army in Spain paid for itself, while that in Africa probably lived off the land. The war indemnity, which was finally paid off in 221, came to less than 200 talents a year (about £50,000). The most important mines in Spain were in the Cartagena area and that of Baebelo alone produced this sum every month! Furthermore, the customs dues solely for the province of Tripolitania were so huge that 365 talents a year were paid into the state coffers.

During Hannibal's wars Carthage did manage to assemble fairly large fleets: in 213 and 212 the admiral Bomilcar had as many as 255 galleys and 700 transport ships under his command during the siege of Syracuse. At that time he had numerical superiority over the Romans but did not make use of it. Many modern historians have supposed that Hannibal was prevented from using the Carthaginian fleet for political reasons. Gsell has shown, however, that the government and public opinion in Carthage were in full support of the Barcids, and that the opposition party under Hanno only began to gain influence from 217 onwards, but without ever managing to obtain control of the state.

In order to understand why Hannibal did not attempt to attack Italy from the sea we must bear in mind that the Carthaginians no longer had a single naval base anywhere near the peninsula, and they would therefore have needed an indisputable superiority at sea in order to compensate for this initial drawback. The political situation made such a superiority impossible.

The war in Sicily had been a terrible blow to the Punic economy, it had put a stop to industrial development and had placed the African markets at the mercy of Italian merchants. Peace had not brought any improvement in this situation, and we look in vain for the products of local industry in the archaeological levels of the third century; at Hippone on Cap Bon we find only the black Campanian wares.[2] Large-scale imports from Spain had done nothing to revive local metal production. In fact it was these very riches which, by providing the means of acquiring foreign goods, prevented the local industries from getting going once more. Much the same thing was to happen in the sixteenth century of our era when gold from Peru, by its very abundance, paralysed Spanish economy and, in the long run, benefited the English and Dutch enemies of the Habsburg monarchy.

In Spain itself Hasdrubal tried to set up industries and,

in particular, shipyards, but failed completely. One large shipyard employing 2000 workmen was, however, founded at Cartagena.

In 218 the Barcid fleet was composed of 50 quinqueremes and 5 triremes, but 18 of the quinqueremes were not equipped for war. This fleet was four times smaller than the Roman in peacetime, and was not only incapable of attacking Italy, but was insufficient to protect Spain. Furthermore, when it was partly destroyed in the Battle of the Ebro, the shipyards were unable to replace the ships which had been sunk. When Scipio captured the Barcid capital in 209, he found only 18 ships in the harbour. It is probable that Hannibal cut down the subsidies for naval construction work, and he may have converted some of the workshops.

The episode in 226 served to show that, from now on, the Senate was watching the new state closely in order to prevent its getting dangerous. Hannibal had therefore reached the conclusion that a direct attack by sea along the Italian coast would be impossible. In order to vanquish Rome, he must launch a surprise attack where Rome was least expecting it.

Events in 225 had shown, furthermore, that a surprise attack could succeed if Gauls were used. The Celts of the Po valley had been carried southwards by Gallic bands from beyond the Alps; they had caught the Italians unawares and had almost succeeded in repeating the Brennus episode. The Barcids had taken note of this. Until then Carthage had regarded Gaul as a land which provided a useful supply of mercenaries. After 225, however, a mass of agents began to study the political situation in the area seriously. They had immediately concluded that this was unstable. Until the middle of the third century B.C. the Rhine had formed the axis of the Celtic dominions with Eastern France lying to the west and Southern Germany and Bohemia to the east. In about 250 the tribes of Germania, which had been pushing south for several centuries, suddenly began moving faster and drove the Celts westwards and southwards. The Belgae were the most northern tribe in this movement and were closely related to the Germanic tribes in more than one respect. They came to settle in the country between the Rhine and the Seine. The Gauls who had previously inhabited this area and Champagne, were driven to the west of the Paris basin towards Normandy and Brittany. These upheavals had their repercussions, which were felt as far afield as the Mediterranean coast. In this way, the Iberian population of the Mediterranean part of Languedoc came under the rule of the Volcae, though not without a struggle, as archaeological finds at Enserune and at Le Cayla de Maillac have shown. Soldiers of fortune known as the Gesates and among whom were some Belgae and even some Germans, poured into the Rhône valley and into Northern Italy, obviously another result of this movement of peoples. It was their arrival which was one of the main causes of the rising of the Transalpine Gauls against Rome in 225.

This situation abounded in possibilities for a leader with Hannibal's turn of mind. The whole of the West was full of uprooted peoples who were eager to find a new home and were ready to seek this as far away as possible in the countries of the south. These cruel and courageous barbarians had a terrible reputation and could provide Hannibal with the weight in numbers which he lacked, to overcome the might of Rome.

Hannibal had, indeed, the best reasons for supposing that a well-administered direct blow could shatter the foundations of what we call, rather inaccurately, the Italic Confederation.[3] This strange and complex organization had taken little more than a century to build up in an entirely empirical way and was based, in fact, on the combination of military and political strength represented by Rome, with the economic strength of Capua. This dualism is repeated exactly in the coinage of the Confederation. For her own use, and for the use of that part of Central Italy immediately under her domination, Rome minted a heavy bronze coin which looked extremely archaic and which consisted sometimes of rectangular 'bricks' and sometimes of huge round pieces (the *as libral*, which weighed 373 grammes or approximately 13 ounces). At the same time, the Campanian workshops were issuing a silver coin in the name of the Confederation, which was based on the Greek standard and was therefore valid currency throughout the whole Mediterranean.

According to the studies of the Danish numismatist R. Thomson,[4] this dualism lasted from 289 to 269. At some time between these dates there was an intermediate phase when Rome began minting silver coinage of the Greek type while still producing the *as libral*; the Campanian mint maintained its autonomy. Finally in 235 there was a radical reform: the Romano-Campanian drachmae were replaced by the *quadrigat*, which was a silver coin based on an Italic standard. Soon after, the weight and value of the bronze coinage were heavily reduced and in this way two previously independent systems became one, with the silver coins as the standard, and the bronze pieces as small coin.

These moves obviously reflect an evolution whereby Rome was seeking to usurp the economic leadership of Campania so that she might not be merely the political and military head of the Confederation. In support of this theory we have archaeological proof of the beginnings of industrial development at this time in Rome and, for instance, in the area immediately surrounding Praeneste. At the end of the First Punic War Latin literature suddenly became firmly established and almost immediately such major works as those of Ennius and Plautus began to appear. This again reflects a rapid social evolution. Finally, it would seem to be at this period, judging from what can be deduced from traditional sources, that the patriarchal framework began to crack, while the appearance of large fortunes based on agricultural, industrial, and commercial speculation led to a certain social instability.

All this naturally led to discontent and anxiety in Campanian business circles, and especially in Capua, which was virtually the capital of this prosperous region. Some of the leaders began to wonder whether union with Rome was really going to benefit their state or whether it was not more likely to have fatal consequences unless they soon determined to regain their complete independence. The leader of this faction was to draw Capua into secession, and was called Pacuvius Calavius Caecus. These men, whose wealth was based on business and not on agriculture (Livy reproached them for this in fact), were badly affected by Rome's rival economic development. The industrial crisis brought on by growing competition naturally also affected the artisans and shopkeepers who formed the bulk of the Capuan population. As a result there was social unrest which caused anxiety among the city dignitaries, and Livy tells us that Pacuvius and Virrius took the lead in this revolutionary movement from fear that it might otherwise submerge them. The same conditions were doubtless to be found in other Italic and Hellenic towns in the south of the peninsula, for instance at Tarentum, whose prosperity had begun to decline sooner than Capua's, as a result of the development of Roman hegemony.

It is legitimate to suspect that Hannibal was informed about this state of affairs. There was a sufficient number of Italian traders in the Spanish harbour towns, and similarly, enough Carthaginian merchants (or *guggas* as they were popularly known) in Italy for contacts to be easily established. As soon as Hannibal entered Italy, before he had even won his first great victory at Trebia, the commander of Clastidium handed over the fortress which he held for Rome. This officer was named Dasius and came from Brindisi, and it is very probable that his betrayal was not the result of a sudden whim but was the first consequence of the work of undermining which the Punic agents had been carrying out among the discontented allies of Rome in Southern Italy.

If all went well, that is if the united Carthaginians and Gauls could succeed in weakening Roman military power sufficiently, Hannibal could therefore depend on a large number of towns in Southern Italy leaving the Italic Confederation. The Carthaginian fleet, which would, until that time, have been carefully kept in reserve, could then play its part and use the bases which its new allies put at its disposal. Rome would then lose her mastery of the seas and would be surrounded by the invading army. She would have to accept the conditions of the victors.

At first sight Hannibal's plan seems adventurous and reckless but, on closer and more detailed examination, it becomes extremely well thought out and reasonable. At a time when soldiers and statesmen were accustomed to thinking of Fortune as the sovereign mistress of human affairs, the Carthaginian left far less to chance than Pyrrhus did, or even Alexander.

3. THE STATE OF AFFAIRS IN ROME[5]

Before this determined adversary who was in absolute command of all the means at his disposal, the leaders of the Roman Republic seem to have been divided into several parties and to have had rather different conceptions of the political line their country ought to follow.

As usual, the most traditional line was taken by the family of the Fabii, who had found a leader once more in Q. Fabius Maximus Verrucosus, whose prudent tactics during the war were to earn him the name of Cunctator or Delayer. The senatorial historians, and foremost among these his cousin Fabius Pictor, doubtless exaggerated the talents of this leader but he certainly seems to have had a strong character. A certain number of noble families grouped themselves round him together with some patrician and plebeian dignitaries, the most illustrious of whom was, without doubt, Claudius Marcellus. (He did not belong to the patrician family of the Arpii Claudii, but to a plebeian family of the same name.) The latter had earned the foremost military honour, the *spolia opima*, for killing with his own hand the Gaulish King Viridomarus at Clastidium in 222; he was to end his career by recapturing Syracuse in 212. This group depended on the votes of peasants whose importance had been increased by the re-organization of the Peoples' Assemblies. It still favoured a policy of expansion northwards and had little confidence in expeditions overseas. It would have liked to maintain peace with Carthage but its sympathies were, naturally enough, with the African land-owners led by Hanno the Great. The Fabians had been in the forefront at the end of the First Punic War and during the first few years after it. Between the years 230 and 225, however, they had been out of favour. The Gallic invasion and conquest of the Po valley had restored them to popularity. This conquest was not yet firmly established but it had already opened up a whole range of attractive possibilities for the Roman people: the countries of the West and Spain on the one hand, and Istria, Illyria, and the Balkans on the other. Already steps had been taken in the latter direction in 229. The various 'imperialist' factions seized the opportunity to attract once more the votes of the Comitia.

Among these imperialist groups was still that of the Arpii Claudii, but the foremost family was now that of the Cornelii Scipiones, whose interests traditionally lay in Sardinia and Corsica but who now looked further afield towards Spain. This illustrious family was at this time led by two brothers who were the most determined enemies of the Barcids: Publius, the father of the future 'Africanus', and Gnaeus called the Bald. Most of the Aemilii were in agreement with this policy. The expansion eastwards was especially favoured by the Valerii and by M. Livius Salinator, who was consul in 219, who was the *bête noire* of the Fabii, and who had married the daughter of the Capuan Pacuvius Calavius. These nobles no longer felt bound by traditional prejudice and did not hesitate to seek support among the rather unscrupulous merchants, most of whom had come to Rome from allied towns and were beginning to constitute themselves into a rich bourgeoisie, much to the disgust of the traditionalists.

Somewhere between these two aristocratic factions we have the 'new men', who are rather difficult to define and who have generally been unfairly and badly treated by ancient historians. Gaius Flaminius was a tribune of the plebs, censor, consul for the second time in 217, and, so Livy tells us, leader of a people's party. It does indeed seem that there was what amounted to a democratic party in Rome at this date. Cassola has shown that Flaminus' political views frequently agreed with those of Fabius Maximus, and that the two men were often colleagues. Flaminius was, indeed, a determined partisan of colonization in the north: it was he who had already divided up the Picenum, on the Adriatic coast, in 233. During his censorship in 220 he began the construction of the road which still bears his name and which played the same part in Roman relations with the north-east as the Appian way did for Campania. In 218 he obtained votes in favour of two Roman colonies at Cremona and Placentia (Piacenza) which he had himself helped to conquer during his first consulship in 223. The Gauls hated him, and he was finally speared to death by a Celtic auxiliary of Hannibal's, north of Lake Trasimene. Since Flaminius was the People's representative, he was not in favour of the merchant bourgeoisie; he presented a plebiscite in 229, through the intermediary of the tribune Claudius, which forbade the senators to trade on the high seas, and which was destined to restrict their political influence. He was not a reactionary, however, and his enthusiasm for change was restricted to the religious field: during his censorship he had caused the Circus which bears his name, to be built on the Campus Martius, and round this he organized a whole new cult centre which has been partly revealed by the excavations of the Largo Argentina. He openly despised traditionalism in politics and he treated the recommendations of the Senate and the priests with a contempt which amounted to sacrilege. Fabius Maximus did not associate himself too closely, therefore, with his dangerous ally, and conservative historians called him a scapegoat when his defeat and death on the battlefield of Trasimene seemed to be a punishment for his impiety.

Thus Hannibal's chief opponents on the Roman political field in 220 were Fabius Maximus, Marcellus, the Scipios, and Flaminius. During the second half of the war two younger men appeared on the scene: Claudius Nero and Scipio Africanus.

If war had not broken out, most of these people – with the exception perhaps of Africanus – would not have been called upon to be anything other than mediocre politicians. By 219, for instance, Fabius Maximus had already completed more than half a career which had not, so far, had anything to distinguish it particularly. From this we might deduce that the virtues of these 'great ancestors' who were praised over and over again in the centuries that followed until the end of the Empire, and have now become familiar to us in our school-books, were exaggerated or even entirely imagined by Roman panegyrists. Certainly most of these men had the good fortune to be called into the limelight at the most favourable moment of their careers: even Africanus would doubtless have made use of his gifts in vain had he been called upon, like his father and uncle, to fight against Hannibal when the latter was at the height of his career. We must concede, however, that, with the sole exception of Flaminius, whose greatest error this was, all these men were able to discipline themselves for the good of the nation, and subordinate to a large extent their private interests: at no moment was Hannibal to find a crack in the Roman front, and it was owing to this unshakeable Roman unity that his attacks failed.

4. Saguntum and the Declaration of War

There is no need to discuss at length the much disputed question of immediate responsibility for the war. As Polybius so clearly understood, the incidents which led directly to the war were only of secondary importance and were pretexts for it. There is no doubt that Hannibal systematically went out of his way to provoke a conflict, and it is equally certain that such aggressiveness was amply justified by Roman politics since the peace of Lutatius. Polybius did not, however, help to clarify matters when he misinterpreted the treaty of 226, which was a brutal act on the part of Rome and which, even more than the annexation of Sardinia, justified the young Carthaginian general in his mistrust of the Romans.

The three years between Hannibal's accession to power and the beginning of his expedition were therefore entirely concerned in counteracting the evil consequences of the concessions which Hasdrubal had had to make under duress. The campaigns of 221 and 220 were aimed at reducing to nil the strategic advantage of this agreement to Rome and her allies. The Carthaginians had undertaken not to cross the Júcar; near its mouth the river runs in a west-east direction, but further up its course it turns towards the north. Hannibal made the most of this geographical peculiarity of which the Romans probably knew nothing. He first subjected the Olcades who lived on the right bank of the river and then launched an attack northwards into Old Castile as far as the province of León, against the mighty tribe of the Vaccieni. Thus, although he kept exactly to the terms of the treaty, Hannibal reduced the territory under Roman protection to a narrow coastal belt which was from now on surrounded on all sides by the subjects of the Barcids.

These results were obtained at the cost of some hardship, but Hannibal now felt free to launch a direct attack on Saguntum. The city lay well to the north of the Júcar and was, furthermore, bound to Rome by a special treaty of alliance. Hannibal was not likely to forget, however, that a few years earlier, between 226 and 222, part of the population of the city had revolted and demanded the annulment of the treaty. Rome had intervened in force and the revolutionary chiefs had been executed. We believe that Hannibal spoke in condemnation of this action at the general congress of Iberian princes which he summoned, as Hasdrubal had done, shortly after his accession, so that they might confer on him the supreme military command of the nation which had been his predecessor's. The pro-Roman Saguntines thus appeared in the light of traitors. Furthermore, a conflict had broken out between the city and a neighbouring Iberian tribe called the Turboletae, and Hannibal, as commander-in-chief of the troops of the Iberian league, was under obligation to give them his support.

During the last eight months of the year 219 the Saguntines put up a heroic and desperate resistance, such as we find throughout Spanish history. Hannibal's first attacks failed and he therefore blockaded the city completely and lined up his siege-engines. Revolts broke out in his rear, however, in the direction of Madrid and La Mancha, and he was temporarily obliged to relax his stranglehold. The besiegers suffered heavy losses, and Hannibal himself was wounded. The town had to be fought for district by district, and improvised ramparts were built up behind the breeches. Finally the leaders of the pro-Roman party committed suicide and the remainder of the besieged asked for terms of surrender. While negotiations were under way, however, the Carthaginians took advantage of the relaxed vigilance of the guards and slaughtered the population.

This siege taught Hannibal a lesson: he never again undertook this type of warfare, for though the Carthaginians had a particular aptitude for it, it immobilized troops and exhausted them.

Before the beginning of the siege a Roman embassy had come to Hannibal and called upon him to renounce his plans. It had been contemptuously dismissed and had gone onto Carthage to demand from the Punic government the recall of their general. Although Hanno the Great backed the Roman demand (which was, in fact, presented in fairly moderate terms), the Elders answered that Saguntum was responsible for the war and that Carthage had been Rome's ally long before Saguntum was.

This first embassy had barely presented its report to the Senate when news arrived of the fall of Saguntum. There then ensued a violent argument in the Curia. The moderate faction again had its own way and new diplomatic manoeuvres were undertaken. An ultimatum was addressed directly to Carthage: the Carthaginians were to evacuate Saguntum immediately, and Hannibal and his generals were to be arrested and handed over in order that they might be tried as war criminals. The embassy came before the Elders under the presidency of the king of Carthage. The speaker who was called upon to put forward the Punic point of view, emphasized that the so-called treaty of 226 was a private agreement with Hasdrubal in which Carthage was in no way involved; Romano-Punic relations were still governed by the treaty of Lutatius in which there was no mention either of Spain or of the Saguntines. Legally speaking the logic of this argument seems irrefutable, though there is an equivocal point involved: Carthage had never officially recognized the independence of the

Barcid state, and it was also unlikely that she was unaware of Hasdrubal's actions.

There are no other examples in the history of the Republic of such a long period of inactivity and such shocking indifference, on Rome's part, to the martyrdom of her allies. The only explanation is that the political situation was particularly confused at the time, where both internal and external politics were concerned, and Hannibal was probably well aware of this.

Roman public opinion was still divided between the Fabii, who were in favour of limiting the political ambitions of the Republic to the Italian peninsula (naturally, with the Po valley and the surrounding islands included), and those who favoured a more ambitious policy. Furthermore, a great many of the latter were now turning their interests towards the Adriatic and even as far as the Balkans. The necessity of ensuring the safety of the Adriatic had carried the legions into Istria in 221 and into Illyria in this same year 219. Here the Consuls Livius Salinator and Aemilius Paulus had had to intervene in order to chase out a disloyal Roman ally, Demetrius of Pharos. Demetrius was openly supported by Macedonia, which had just re-established its hegemony over Greece at the Battle of Sellasia. The majority of the Senators could not but be doubtful about the wisdom of being involved simultaneously on two fronts, especially as the ancient kingdom of Alexander was still likely to be a fairly formidable adversary. The Fabii did not have great difficulty in advocating patience as far as Carthage was concerned, even when it was established that Hannibal enjoyed the support of his compatriots. Those who favoured a more decisive line of action did, nevertheless, succeed in having two of their number included in the first embassy which was sent to prevent the conflict. These were Valerius Flaccus, one of those responsible for the 'treaty' of 226, and Baebius Tamphilus, who belonged to the clan of the Scipios. When the first embassy failed to produce any results, the second was entrusted to the leadership of a member of the *gens* Fabia, named Buteo, and he naturally proposed making overtures to the Hannonian faction. His colleagues Livius Salinator and Baebius Tamphilus belonged to the imperialist group, however.

By now Senatorial prudence had been swamped by public opinion, which considered the fall of Saguntum to be a national disgrace. The Comitia chose as consuls for the year 218 two men who were in favour of war: Publius Cornelius Scipio (father of Africanus), and Sempronius Longus. At the same time, Fabius Buteo had realized the impossibility of reaching any sort of compromise, and he had just left a dramatic meeting of the Council of the Elders in Carthage where the latter had voted in favour of war.

This conflict, which was, perhaps, the most important in Antiquity, was therefore very much in accordance with the will of Hannibal and of his people. Rome had, however, done everything that she could in the space of one generation so as to leave no alternative to Carthage but a desperate struggle for survival, or decay.

5. THE BEGINNING OF THE WAR: THE MARCH THROUGH GAUL

In the spring of 218 Hannibal left Cartagena with an army of Iberians and Africans which Polybius estimated was 102,000 strong. He crossed the Ebro and met with strong resistance from the Iberians of Northern Catalonia, some of whom had just concluded an alliance with Rome. This first obstacle was overcome, but not without some fairly heavy losses, and the government of the conquered peoples was entrusted to a certain Hanno. Then, without bothering about Emporiae and Rhode, which were prepared to put up a defence, Hannibal crossed the Perthus. His force was already reduced to some 50,000 infantry and 9,000 cavalry. They then penetrated into the country which the Volcae had just conquered. The majority of these Celts welcomed the Carthaginians, whose arrival cannot have been entirely unexpected since Hannibal had sent agents among the Gauls several years before. A Punic garrison established itself in the *oppidum* of Enserune and several traces of its occupation have been found.[6]

Supply ships came to unload in the port of Ruscino, and the amphorae they brought have also been found.[7] A considerable quantity of coins of the Carthaginian type – a head of Demeter on the obverse and a horse under a palm-tree on the reverse – found its way throughout Gaul, and even into the hands of such northern tribes as the Parisii, who were inspired to engrave their own.[8]

The Salyes, who dominated the land behind Aix, followed the same line of conduct as the Volcae, and the Carthaginians reached the Rhône without having to strike a single blow. In order to cross the river, they were obliged to fight, however. It would seem that some of the Volcae had disassociated themselves from the policy of their compatriots and had exiled themselves so as better to be able to organize their resistance. Furthermore, the agents of Marseilles had not failed to spread their propaganda among the Celto-Ligurian tribes which came under Phocaean influence. At the same time, the leaders of the old Greek city had sent an appeal to the Consul Scipio, and the latter had just landed in the Delta. Hannibal now ran the risk of finding himself caught between the Roman legions and the fairly strong Gallic force which had grouped itself on the left bank of the Rhône, probably somewhere near Beaucaire.

For the first time, Hannibal was able to reveal himself as a tactician. He put his nephew Hanno, son of King Bomilcar, at the head of a commando of light troops and sent him to cross the river upstream. The Gauls were attacked from the rear by this force and were obliged to let the remainder of the army across. When Scipio arrived at the point where the Rhône divides to form its delta, it was to learn that the Carthaginians had gone northwards and were now in the land of the Allobroges.

This detour may seem surprising, and several modern historians, Sir Gavin de Beer, for instance,[9] have refused to accept it. Hannibal was always very well informed, however, and he knew that the Gauls of Dauphiné and Savoy were at war, and that two pretenders were disputing the throne. By intervening in this dispute, the Carthaginians would secure the goodwill of the victors whom they intended to support. This friendship was important since Hannibal could not depend on that of the Ligurian tribes of the Alps, who were wild and suspicious and who know no politics but robbery and ransom of any foreigner, whoever he might be.

Hannibal's crossing of the Alps appealed to the imagination of his contemporaries and still to-day excites the curiosity of people who are otherwise completely uninterested in Ancient History. A few years ago a repetition of the journey was even attempted, but under conditions which were far from scientific. Hannibal knew how to encourage public opinion in his favour and saw no harm in letting the 'journalists' of the day embroider and exaggerate his exploit, embellishing it with a host of invented details. The childish aspect of this propaganda irritated Polybius and later Napoleon. The latter did not hesitate to write: 'The difficulties involved in the crossing of the Alps have been exaggerated; there are none, and only the elephants could have caused him any trouble'. This sceptical attitude is also rather exaggerated. The Carthaginians probably went up the valley of the Maurienne to the Saint Bernard, and along this route they would have suffered from the cold since it was already October. They also had to transform bad tracks into something resembling a road (every schoolboy knows that they used fire and vinegar for this purpose), and they were constantly obliged to repulse the attacks of the mountain tribes. The army suffered considerable losses: of the 50,000 infantry and 9000 cavalry who had set out from Spain, only 38,000 and 8000 respectively remained at the crossing of the Rhône, though this was due, not to loss on the battle-field but to the garrisons which had been left along the route. When he arrived in Italy, however, Hannibal was left with only 20,000 infantry, 6000 cavalry, and 3 elephants! The mountains and their inhabitants had claimed almost half his troops. This reduction in the size of his army would have been disastrous if Hannibal had had to fight a strong enemy on his arrival in Piedmont. He had, however, been reassured on this head: Magil, king of the Cisalpine Gauls, had sent a messenger to Hannibal's camp on the Rhône, to inform him of a general insurrection of the Gauls. The Boii of Bologna and the Insubres of the Milan area had risen as one man and had massacred the agents of the Senate who were engaged in fixing the limits of the territory of the new colonies of Cremona and Placentia. They succeeded in cornering near Brescia the small Roman army which, under the leadership of a Praetor called Manlius, was supposed to be keeping them in order. Sempronius, the consul, who had been preparing for an invasion of Africa, had to rush to the rescue. Meanwhile his colleague Scipio had had to resign himself to abandoning a counter-offensive in Spain – the project nearest to his heart – and had sailed from Marseilles to Genoa. Furthermore, he had left the greater part of his army behind under his brother's command with instructions to pursue his project. Hannibal only had before him, therefore, an enemy who was at a loss and disorganized and whom he had already begun to move around as he pleased.

6. THE GREAT VICTORIES (218–216)

Hannibal's great fight against Rome on Italian soil can be divided into three phases. In the first, which is the shortest (218–216), he won victory after victory over the Romans and seemed to have them at his mercy. But at the very moment when success seemed to be within his grasp, Rome put up an unexpected resistance and, although she was still too weak to reverse the situation, she was nevertheless able to cancel out all the advantages which she had had to concede; this period of equilibrium lasted from 216 until 212. Finally, in the ultimate phase which lasted for ten years, Hannibal's power was neutralized and he was held in check and gradually driven back and back into Southern Italy, while the theatre of war shifted to other countries and especially to Spain and Sicily.

The first of these three phases is also the most interesting: everyone knows of the great victories of Trasimene and Cannae. The second phase is more complex and also less attractive, and only Fabius the Delayer appears in school text-books as the personification of Roman tenacity and unshakeable calm which, on their own, would have ended in the long run by defeating the Carthaginians. Nevertheless, it is this second phase which is the most decisive and which merits the most detailed examination. It is certain that, in Hannibal's carefully conceived plan, the destruction of Roman military might was only a first stage, and that it was to be succeeded by a whole series of military and, especially, political and economic moves which were to ensure the final victory. We shall have to discover why this part of the plan failed when the purely tactical preliminaries had been so overwhelmingly successful. It is sufficient here to recall the two great campaigns which put Hannibal into the forefront as one of the best tacticians of all time.

The crossing of Gaul and of the Alps had taken up the whole of the summer and autumn of 218, and the struggle for Cisalpine Gaul took place, contrary to the usual practice in Antiquity, in

17

the middle of winter. Both consuls came to meet Hannibal. Scipio arrived first but he had too small a force, and was severely wounded in a battle which took place near Vercelli. Sempronius Longus, who had returned from Sicily, was thus able to assume conduct of the operations. He was to prove himself extremely rash, and Hannibal made use of this temerity for his own ends. The legionaries were made to attack on an empty stomach, on a cold December morning, and had to ford the swollen River Trebia before climbing up a steep slope to the Punic camp. Hannibal had set a trap for them and had concealed some troops on the edge of the river: 20,000 out of 30,000 men died on the field of battle.

This set-back was serious and humiliating but did not, for all that, affect the main strength of the Roman army. In theory Hannibal was master of the Po valley but his Gallic allies were beginning to find his constant demands on them rather tedious. Furthermore, they had noticed that he sacrificed his auxiliary troops rather than endanger his old veterans. The Veneti of the Po delta were still faithful to Rome as were the Cenomani of Brescia, and even though the latter were of Celtic origin, they refused to join their compatriots. These tribes sent supplies to Cremona and Placentia, which were able to hold out. Hannibal had renounced siege warfare once and for all, however, and made no effort to enforce their submission.

Meanwhile, Rome was indulging in the game of politics and Flaminius was leading an electoral campaign in which he denounced the adventurous policies of the Scipios. He promised his peasant followers that there would be a devaluation of currency which would lighten the weight of their debts. The Comitia elected him consul for the second time, together with Cn. Servilius Geminus.

At the beginning of the year 217 Hannibal concentrated his forces on Bologna and compensated them for the prolonged campaigning of the previous year by delaying the resumption of hostilities until the end of March. The consuls did not know on which side of the Apennines Hannibal would launch his attack and Flaminius therefore centred his troops on Arezzo in order to protect Etruria, while Servilius took up his position in Rimini so as to defend the Adriatic side.

Hannibal had first thought of going down to Liguria. He could easily have made contact from there with the Carthaginians of Sardinia, who were eager to throw off the Roman yoke. The Carthaginian fleet had been released by Servilius' march northwards and was preparing to intervene, and in the Etruscan cities there were many patriots who were waiting for the time when they could once more make common cause with their traditional ally and regain their lost independence. Nature caused the first of these plans to be abandoned, but it is hard to see how the Romans could have withstood such an attack. In the spring of 217 the rains turned to floods; the Punic army was suffering from various epidemics and had to turn back, and Hannibal caught ophthalmia in the marshes and went blind in one eye.

Having gathered his army together again in Bologna, Hannibal now followed the upper valley of the Arno and came down into the plain near Fiesole where he took the road to Rome via Cortona, thereby by-passing Arezzo where Flaminius had shut himself up with his army. The consul was afraid of a direct attack on the capital and set off in pursuit without waiting for Servilius, who was coming by forced marches along the Via Flaminia. Hannibal was thus able to entice the two legions of Flaminius into a trap formed by the mountains and the shore of Lake Trasimene. On 21st June 217, the Roman column was marching along in good order when suddenly the enemy appeared at its head and on it. left flank, and began driving the Romans towards the lakes Flaminius perished, pierced by the spear of an Insubrian Gaul, together with 15,000 men. The Punic cavalry, led by Maharbal, then set off to meet the army of Servilius and destroyed its vanguard of some 4,000 men.[10]

Contrary to what many historians have believed, the victory of Lake Trasimene did not put Hannibal in a position to capture Rome. As soon as they heard of the disaster, the people of Rome had recourse to an unusual form of procedure and elected a pro-dictator. (Normally a dictator could only be chosen by one of the consuls. Of these, one was dead and the other was completely cut off from Rome.) Their choice was Fabius Maximus, who was then actively engaged in recruiting new levies and preparing the city for a state of siege. Furthermore, Hannibal had no intention of risking everything in one throw. He was now waiting for the results of the undermining work which his spies had been carrying out among the Italians, and for his victories to have their psychological effect. He had already had a partial success in this field, which, however, had been compensated for by a set-back. In Capua, Pacuvius Calavius had seized power by terrorizing the Senate with the threat of a social revolution; he still did not dare to proclaim his defection openly, however, and was waiting for the right moment. In Sardinia on the other hand, the Sardinian Hanspicora had given the signal for a national uprising. Unfortunately the Roman navy was still intact, and when the ships sent by Carthage to help the rebels appeared on the scene, they were driven back by the Romans as far as Pantellaria. Servilius Geminus first shipped off two legions from the ports of Etruria and crushed the rising, and then marched on Rome where he put his troops at the disposal of Fabius.

The six months following the Battle of Lake Trasimene are taken up by a subtle but undramatic game, with Capua as the prize.

From Etruria Hannibal set out to join Pacuvius Calavius in Campania, but he went by a very round-about way via the Adriatic coast. He had been welcomed as a liberator by the Senones Gauls of the Picenum, and had then gone on into Apulia, had re-crossed the Apennines, and had penetrated into those parts of Campania known as the Falernus Ager which had been annexed by Rome and put under cultivation on a yearly basis. As soon as Fabius had succeeded in re-assembling his troops, he had come up with Hannibal, but was content to watch and harass the enemy while avoiding a pitched battle. Hannibal was set on destroying the economic and political centres in Campania on which Roman control of the province was based. Fabius, on the other hand, was reinforcing the garrisons everywhere, particularly that of Casilinum (the site of modern Capua), for it was only a few miles away from the great city it was guarding. These tactical operations were accompanied by an equally subtle political game. Hannibal and his Italian allies awoke everywhere they went the hopes of the People's Parties. The Romans, on the other hand, were stirring up the local aristocracy to whom they had entrusted the government of their towns; in this way they had already succeeded, just after Trasimene, in avoiding a mass Etruscan defection. They also aroused the fears of the Italians by threatening that defection on their part would result in reprisals among the young men of their families who were fighting in the Roman army as auxiliaries, while also serving as hostages. Fabius seemed to be winning this game of chess. Hannibal had failed to occupy any position which could be described as strategically important, and had several times been in danger of finding himself surrounded. He finally evacuated Campania and returned to Apulia where he captured Gerunium, near Mount Gargano, where there were ample supplies and where he settled down to spend the winter of 217 to 216.

Fabius' delaying tactics were not universally approved of in Rome, however, though the election of the dictator after Trasimene had been unanimous. As he was a dictator from the conservative group, he had been given a second-in-command who was supported by the city plebs, called Minucius, who had been put in charge of the cavalry. The specific tasks of these two men had never been clearly defined and their divergent views led to embittered relations. Fabius had succeeded in re-establishing his authority over his insubordinate second-in-command, when the latter's imprudence got him into a tight corner from which he had to be rescued. The elections of 216, which were to re-establish the normal régime with the double Consulate, were influenced by the propaganda of Fabius' enemies and probably also by news from Spain. The two Scipios had, indeed, let nothing distract them from carrying out their planned Iberian counter-offensive, and their obstinacy was well justified. The first blow proved how weak the Barcid Empire was, in reality. The Scipios landed in Emporiae and succeeded, without too much difficulty, in rallying the Catalan tribes which Hannibal had conquered the year before, they defeated and captured their Punic governor, repulsed a counter-attack of Hasdrubal Barca's by destroying his fleet, they restored Saguntum, and finally caused anti-Carthaginian revolts as far away as Baetica. These successes were good for Roman self-respect and made the results obtained by Fabius' patience seem very meagre in contrast. It is not surprising, therefore, that the choice of the Comitia for the year 216 should have been Aemilius Paulus, a close friend of P. Scipio, whose son had married his daughter, and Terentius Varro, a newcomer who was a protégé of the Cornelii.

The senatorial historians maintain that the two consuls disagreed with each other but hold Varro alone responsible for what then occurred. In fact, the orders for mass mobilization decreed at the beginning of 216 prove that the two magistrates and the majority of the Senate had agreed to make a decisive move to end the war speedily. Eight legions were equipped for war, thus outnumbering Hannibal's army by two to one. Minucius, the cavalry leader who had opposed Fabius, was given an important command, while the old dictator was shorn of any responsibility.

These preparations took six months, during which time Hannibal was sitting in his fortress of Gerunium, calmly awaiting the attack. At the beginning of the summer he went down towards the rich plains of southern Apulia in order both to collect new supplies and to attract the enemy on to a battleground that was suitable for his plans. It was thus that on 2nd August 216 the two armies came face to face on the banks of the Aufidus, not far from the little town of Cannae.[11]

This is the most famous battle of all Antiquity and we shall not describe it here, since it has been extensively studied by modern tacticians. It is enough to recall that Hannibal arranged his order of battle in such a way that it formed a convex arc pointing towards the enemy. The Romans concentrated their best troops on the centre of this line, which was composed of Gallic auxiliaries who then fell back. The Romans followed them into the pocket-shape thus formed, whereupon the Carthaginian right wing, consisting of Maharbal's Numidian cavalry, swung round to surround the legionaries, who were slaughtered without mercy. According to Livy, whose figures are lower than those of Polybius and rather more credible, 46,200 Romans were killed, and among them was the consul, Aemilius Paulus. If we add to this figure those for the losses on the Trebia and at Lake Trasimene, it becomes immediately apparent that in one and a half years Rome had lost a third of her troops, and among them her most hardened campaigners. Hannibal had thus achieved his first aim: the war machine which had united Italy seemed to be shattered, and the peoples it had gathered together were now free to assume once more the control of their own destinies.

7. The Fight for the Maritime Bases: 216–211

The victory at Cannae had brought the first part of Hannibal's plan to a far more successful conclusion than even the most optimistic could have envisaged. Rome's military power was reduced by half and the Italians were now at last about to recover their liberty and open their harbours to the Carthaginian fleet, thus enabling it to reconquer its maritime supremacy. Rome would be blockaded by land and sea and would be forced to accept the peace terms proposed by her adversaries.

In fact, from the end of 216 onwards, the Romans held only a very few fortified positions in Southern Italy, and their isolated garrisons resisted without hope. Capua had been the first to welcome Hannibal in triumph. In Syracuse, old Hieron had just died and his young successor Hieronymus rallied to the Carthaginian side. Sardinia was rebelling once more, while in Cisalpina, the Gauls had slaughtered every one of the 25,000 men led against them by the consul-designate, Postumius.

Mago, Hannibal's youngest brother, had brought the news of the victory to Carthage and the city had been galvanized into activity. Troops were mobilized in order that the decisive blow might be struck. The Punic fleets, now equipped for war, were heading for Italy, Sicily, Sardinia, and Spain. It was only in this last country that fortune still smiled on the Romans. Hasdrubal had just been beaten once again at the mouth of the Ebro. However, Mago was on his way with reinforcements which were to enable the Barcids to settle their account with the Scipios, and then recruit a new army among the friendly Gauls and return to Italy in time for the final dénouement.

Finally, an extremely important diplomatic success was added to the military victories. The young king, Philip V of Macedon, had sent an embassy to Hannibal and had concluded an alliance with him: the king was to sail across the Adriatic with 200 ships. Once Rome was crushed, Carthage and Macedonia would each exercise supreme power in one of the Mediterranean basins. The complete text of the agreement has been preserved for us by Polybius, and it is one of the most important clues we have concerning Hannibal's religion and diplomatic powers, and concerning the organization of the Mediterranean world as he envisaged it after his victory: Rome was not going to be destroyed but was going to be rendered harmless by the establishment of an Italic Confederation under the presidency of Capua and recognizing Carthaginian supremacy.[12]

Hannibal held all the cards and everyone expected him to go on playing the game according to his whim until his opponent's final collapse. It was, however, exactly the contrary which took place. After Cannae the war lost the clarity and brilliance which had characterized it during the first three years; it became bogged down in a series of minor operations which are difficult to follow but in which the Romans generally appear to have gained the upper hand. It would seem that Hannibal had lost some of his genius, or had been forsaken by Fortune. This change had already been noted by the Ancients, who held Hannibal to be partly responsible for it. Some say that he knew how to win but not how to exploit his victories; others maintain that the luxuries of Capua 'softened' him. Roman historians naturally compared this weakening of their enemy with the strengthening of their own nation, whose traditional virtues had been reaffirmed by her trials.

Although this last explanation has worn very thin, it nevertheless contains more than a grain of truth. The Roman state itself had been bled almost white by the wars, but Hannibal had by-passed it and had not touched the 9000-odd square miles which formed the solid core of the state. The inhabitants were extraordinarily well disciplined. Most of them were soldier-peasants, and from now on the Republic was strongly led by men who supported the Fabian conservative party. Fabius Maximus showed himself to be an even greater statesman than he had previously seemed – even during his dictatorship. Together with his friends Claudius Marcellus and Fulvius Flaccus, he was almost always consul until the danger was passed. Most important of all – and it would seem that Hannibal had not realized the fact – Rome was no longer organized like a primitive society with its whole economy based on agriculture or war. Since the First Punic War, Rome had built up an industrial and commercial district which had already become sufficiently important to enable her to withstand the Capuan defection without suffering from an economic collapse. Indeed, the Publicani or representatives of this district first appear in the clear light of day during the second phase of Hannibal's war: they played a decisive part by organizing and financing commandos, by providing the necessary guarantees to enable the monetary system to be straightened out and the *denarius* to be created right in the middle of the war, and by seeing to the supplies in maritime theatres of operation overseas. Thanks to them, the Roman fleet remained mistress of the seas and set at nought the Punico-Macedonian alliance, the Scipios gained control of Northern and Central Iberia and turned their attention to Baetica, and the dream of a great anti-Roman marine coalition, uniting all the peoples of the Mediterranean, gradually faded away.

Faced with this Roman stability, the Italic peoples proved how incapable they were of uniting. Capua's spectacular defection was useless, for Naples, who controlled access to the sea, made her traditional hostility to the Oscans a reason for remaining faithful to the Roman alliance. The Roman and Latin colonies of Northern Campania also held their own against the enemy. For two years (216–214) Hannibal tried in vain to overcome these obstacles. He finally gave up, and left the Capuans to fight on their own until they too collapsed in 211. Hannibal turned his attention towards Tarentum, who only decided to defect in 213 and brought with her the remains of her old Italiot Confederation. M. Livius, who commanded the citadel, held out obstinately, however, and this rendered the city's strategic importance to the Carthaginians practically nil, and prevented the latter from making free use of the magnificent harbour. Meanwhile most of Sicily had finally come over to the Carthaginian side, but rather diffidently owing chiefly to the entangled state of Syracusan politics, for Marcellus had been able to organize a successful counter-offensive, and set up a total blockade of Hieron's old capital.

In the year 211 Capua and Syracuse both fell to the enemy, and the fate of Hannibal and of Carthage was sealed. From now on, unless a complete reversal took place, the initiative for the conduct of the war belonged to Rome, and she was determined that the war should end only with the complete collapse of her rival.

Carthage was offered one more chance, however, during this same year 211: this was a breach in the sacred unity of Rome. Fabius, Marcellus, and their friends were not the dedicated men Livy depicts, whose sole interest was the welfare of their nation. Victories meant tremendous opportunities of increasing personal wealth – we have only to think of what the booty of Capua and Syracuse must have represented – and those in power had no intention of dividing the spoils with those businessmen whose honesty was open to doubt and whose assistance they had contemptuously accepted during the times of greatest danger. As a result, the foremost Publicani, Postumius and Pomponius, were put on trial. These two men, on their own, had provided the Scipios with the means of conducting a war and diplomacy which the state chose to consider in the light of a private enterprise. Postumius was condemned to death, and Pomponius was killed in battle against the Carthaginians together with all his men, much to the satisfaction of the Fabiani. It was probably this that was the cause of the sudden reversal in Spain, however. In 211 the Spanish auxiliaries turned against the Romans, and the Scipios, together with the better part of their Roman troops, were massacred.

The Senate first tried to replace the Scipios with one of the young patrician Claudii called Nero. The latter was soon to reveal himself as an able commander, but he was incapable of imposing his authority on the veterans who had escaped the disaster. The young son of Publius Scipio appealed to the Comitia to entrust him with the command, in spite of the regulations. It was unfortunate for Carthage that this youth of twenty-four should have been endowed with a gift for strategy which may even have been equal to Hannibal's. Hardly had he arrived in Spain than he gave proof of this by his audacious capture of the Barcid capital of Cartagena, which the Punic generals had thought to be sufficiently far away to be safe. Phoenician prestige dropped overnight in Spain; Scipio released the hostages whom he found in the city, and the Iberian princes, out of gratitude, awarded him the royal title which they had once bestowed on Hasdrubal and on Hannibal.

Three Punic armies were still intact, however: two were under the command of Hannibal's brothers, Hasdrubal the Younger and Mago, and the third was led by Hasdrubal son of Gisco, who was no friend of the Barcids. It was then that Hasdrubal the Younger answered Scipio's audacity by an action which was even more audacious. He abandoned without regret the kingdom which his father had conquered, and which all true Barcids had always considered solely as the means towards a war with Rome. He crossed the Pyrenees at their western end – thus avoiding Catalonia, which was held by the Romans – and marched into Gaul, where he joined up with the Punic garrisons and Celtic allies who had been guarding the road into Italy for more than ten years. He spent the winter with them in 208–207, and then crossed the Alps, which were still held, on the Italian side, by the Cisalpine rebels.

This miraculous help was likely to turn the tide in Hannibal's favour. For the past two years the latter had known nothing but failure, which was only very occasionally alleviated by some lucky occurrence. One of these had taken place just as Hasdrubal was arriving – Marcellus was killed. The most bitter blow was the recapture of Tarentum which Fabius Maximus had himself secured in 209. Once this large Dorian harbour-town had fallen, the last hopes of re-establishing Carthaginian maritime supremacy had gone. It must also be admitted that admiral Bomilcar had proved himself to be totally incapable. He had allowed Syracuse to fall, and then had failed to assist Philip of Macedon, who had won some victories in Greece over the allies of Rome, though these had had no influence on the general course of the war. Once Tarentum had fallen, Hannibal had no alternative but to fall back on Calabria and transform it into a vast fortified camp, which decreased in size as time went on.

The Romans were becoming weary of the war, however, for the longer it lasted, the more evident the cost in human life became (the number of citizens had dropped from 270,000 to 137,000), and the greater became the problem of economic loss. The allies, and particularly the Etruscans, were openly rebellious; even the Latins favoured a pacifism which was almost treasonable: in 209, twelve Roman colonies out of thirty refused to pay any contribution whatsoever. The population of the Roman state was being roused by its tribunes, and was beginning to tire of the Fabii and their faction. If the two Barcid brothers had been able to meet up, public opinion would doubtless have called for peace based on a compromise, and Carthage would have had some of her power restored to her.

It was Claudius Nero, the young nobleman who had had so little success as general in Spain, who put paid to Hannibal's last chance. He was consul in 207 with Livius Salinator, a supporter of the Scipios, whom Nero detested. Livius was holding Hasdrubal off between Rimini and Ancona. Claudius was tailing Hannibal, who had heard too late of his brother's arrival and had left Bruttii and gone north into Apulia. One of Hasdrubal's scouts was captured by Nero. The latter left a mere screen of troops in Hannibal's van and hastened to rejoin his colleague on the banks of the Metaurus. The two consular armies in conjunction were too much for Hasdrubal's troops. The Carthaginians were defeated and Hasdrubal was killed; a few days later his head was sent rolling into Hannibal's camp.

There was nothing Hannibal could do but withdraw once more into his Calabrian retreat. His only hope was to prolong the war so as to increase the weariness of the Romans, and to hang on to a few important positions in Italy which would give him some bargaining power when it came to negotiations. This plan might have succeeded if Fabius had remained in power. The old Delayer was now completely eclipsed, however, by the glory of young Scipio, who had crushed the last centres of Punic opposition in Spain in 207. Hannibal's youngest brother, Mago, fled as far as Liguria, where he kept up guerrilla warfare. Scipio, meanwhile, returned to Rome to canvass for consular election in the coming year. Fabius was unable to prevent his election, but did all within his power to prevent his realizing the great project with which he had won over the Comitia: he wished to carry the war into Africa and conclude it there. Scipio's support in official circles was thus drastically reduced. He had, however, gained the extremely efficient backing of groups and districts which were anti-conservative. The fleet, for instance, was almost entirely manned by Etruscans from the towns which, only a short time before, had been so defeatist in their attitude to the war.

The invasion plan had, indeed, been carefully prepared. While he had been in Spain, Scipio had been able to obtain very accurate information as to the exact political situation in that part of North Africa which was not immediately dependent on Carthage. For about a century now,[13] a certain number of tribes from the Algerian and Tunisian Tell district had organized themselves into kingdoms. That of the Massyli Numidians consisted of the inner mountains and plains of the Tunisian Upper Tell, with Zama (Jama) and Thugga (Dougga) as principal towns. The Masaesyli Numidians occupied a district which corresponds with the province of Constantine today. Farther west lay the frontiers of the Moorish kingdoms, but these are hard to define. The organization of these little states was naturally very primitive, and they thus formed part of a Carthaginian protectorate or control zone. Peace was ensured by Punic fortresses situated in the middle of Numidian territory at such places as Sicca (Le Kef), and Carthage maintained her domination thanks to skilful diplomatic manoeuvres which made full use of rivalry between tribes and chieftains.

In 213, Syphax, king of the Masaesyli Numidians, first thought of making use of Rome in order to free himself from Punic sovereignty. To this end he had got in touch with the Scipios in Spain. Gaia, king of the Massyli, had then sent his son Masinissa to fight in that country side-by-side with the Carthaginians. In 207, however, Hasdrubal, son of Gisco, had been obliged to abandon Spain and had succeeded in bringing Syphax back into the Punic camp. He then secured his continued allegiance by marrying him to his daughter Sophonisba, who was as famous for her beauty as for her intelligence and culture. The Massyli immediately went over to the Romans. The little kingdom was surrounded by the lands of the Carthaginians and the Masaesyli and could not afford to take an independent political line, however. Gaia's death intervened at this juncture, and Syphax seized his heritage, so that Masinissa was obliged to live the life of an outlaw in the mountains of Kroumiria.

Scipio had been given Sicily as his province. He spent the first part of the year 204 in preparations which were not made any easier by the intrigues of his political adversaries, who now included, in addition to old Fabius, the young Cato. It was only towards the end of the summer that he was able to land near Utica. He established his winter quarters in a fortified camp at the mouth of the Bagradas (Medjerda), on the heights which are now crowned by Kalaat-el-Andeless. The Carthaginians first entrusted the command to Hasdrubal, son of Gisco, who obtained the support of his son-in-law Syphax. The latter thought naively that he might be of some use as a mediator. Scipio pretended to show interest in these proposals, attacked the unsuspecting Carthaginian camp, and is supposed to have killed some 40,000 men (203).

This defeat was shortly followed by another in the Great Plains region (near present-day Béja), which was fatal for both the Carthaginian and the Numidian leader. Masinissa came down from his mountains and, within a twinkling, he was once more in charge of his kingdom. He invaded the land of the Masaesyli and besieged Cirta (Constantine), its capital. When it fell in June 203,

Syphax was captured together with all his 'smala'. Among the prisoners was Queen Sophonisba, who succeeded in winning back her erstwhile fiancé, Masinissa. Laelius, Scipio's legate, was suspicious of her intentions, however, and she was obliged to take poison. Meanwhile, the father of this unfortunate princess was being held responsible by Carthage. Hasdrubal, son of Gisco, belonged to a moderate oligarchical faction, whose political views were somewhere between those of the democrats and those of Hanno the Great's ultra-conservatives. He had never been on good terms with the Barcids. The People voted him out of office and condemned him to exile, while replacing him by Hanno, son of King Bomilcar, and nephew of Hannibal. Hasdrubal continued to fight in the countryside with a band of guerrillas but ended by committing suicide in the family mausoleum.

The People's Party rested all its hopes on Hannibal's return, but the latter could not escape from Bruttii. The oligarchs proposed that negotiations should be opened, and this the Council of Thirty did. Scipio was anxious to end the war. He was afraid, and with reason, that his political enemies would succeed in having another general named in his place. Furthermore, he bore no hatred towards Carthage; the city was capable of holding out indefinitely, and the Punic navy had just defeated the Roman. The conditions which were set before the Thirty were therefore relatively moderate: Carthage must renounce all her possessions outside Africa – which she had, in fact, virtually lost already – must pay an indemnity of 5000 talents, and must reduce her fleet to twenty ships. Peace had almost been concluded when people from Hadrumetum arrived in Carthage with the announcement that Hannibal had just disembarked beneath their city walls.

After having beaten Scipio's fleet off Utica, the Punic navy had, indeed, forced the Roman blockade, and the remains of the great Barcid army had disembarked, together with their leader. This news was welcomed enthusiastically. An embassy was already on its way to Rome with the treaty in order that it might be ratified. It was torn up, however, a Roman convoy was captured, Scipio's representatives were insulted and threatened with death, and Roman propaganda once more had an opportunity of condemning Carthaginian inconstancy.

Hannibal had landed in Byzacenia for two reasons: this was

where his lands and his tenants were and he knew what resources he would have at his disposal, and he could make use of them without having to render accounts. Furthermore, there was an easy road from Hadrumetum into the heart of the Massyli lands, by five or six easy stages. Hannibal was aiming to seize Masinissa's lands, just as the latter had seized them from Syphax. If he succeeded, then the Romans would be caught between Numidia and Carthage, and their position would become untenable.

This, then, was how the fate of Carthage was decided, at the end of the summer or the beginning of the autumn of the year 202, not far from Zama, the Massylian capital, probably in the plain of Siliana, where the road from Hadrumetum (Sousse) to Sicca (Le Kef) crossed a road leading directly from Carthage along the valley of Wadi Miliana.

According to Appian, Hannibal had some 50,000 infantry, which is slightly more than the Romans commanded. His cavalry, on the other hand, was outnumbered by that of Masinissa. He was the only one to use elephants, and had 80 of them. The battle can be divided into two phases. During the first the Carthaginians vainly tried to break through the centre of the Roman line by a series of attacks, the first of which was launched by the elephants. In the second phase, the Roman cavalry put that of the Carthaginians to flight and then surrounded the Punic phalanx, which was cut to pieces. Of all Hannibal's great battles this is the one in which his genius is least apparent: he neither made use of the terrain as on the Trebia or at Lake Trasimene, nor did he try to manoeuvre as at Cannae. Scipio does not seem to have been any more imaginative, but as a result of that day's fighting he became one of the great legendary captains of all time.

On the evening of his defeat, Hannibal, accompanied by a few horsemen, set out for Hadrumetum. He covered the distance in one stage, thus once again giving proof of his extraordinary physical resilience. His moral energy did not fail either: he could no longer help his country as a soldier, but he still hoped to save it with his diplomatic and military gifts.

Fortunately, this last Punic reaction did nothing to make Scipio change his views. He did not wish to destroy Carthage, and even had he so wished, he was too sensible of the difficulties involved to risk his reputation in the attempt. The conditions which had been settled upon before Hannibal's arrival were only slightly worsened: the fleet was to consist of only ten ships and the war indemnity was doubled. Carthage kept all her African territory, however, though a clause did stipulate that Masinissa should recover all that had previously belonged to his ancestors. The Numidian king was to use this clause as a basis for constant wrangling, for the Punic territory, as defined by the 'Phoenician Boundaries', comprised such districts as that of Thusca, for instance, in which the majority of the population was Numidian, and which had only fairly recently been conquered by Carthage. At the time, however, Scipio interpreted the text of the treaty in Carthage's favour, and merely ordered the evacuation of such towns as Sicca and Theveste, which were situated beyond the Boundaries.

In this way, the great adventure which had started some seventeen years earlier, came to an end. Carthage, after the Battle of Zama, was probably no weaker than after the peace of Lutatius, but she had now definitely lost all possibility of playing a part in international politics. The best thing she could now do was live peacefully from the proceeds of her trade and agriculture, as a client city of Rome. This was obviously what Scipio intended, and his moderation can be explained by his unwillingness to weaken Punic economy too much; it was also what one section of the population wanted: old Hanno the Great was content, and so was Hasdrubal the Kid, one of the negotiators of the Treaty. One of the greatest proofs of Hannibal's intelligence and self-control is his comprehension and acceptance of the fact that it was better for his country to follow this rather inglorious but peaceful line of conduct than be exterminated.

The question remains whether it might not have been better had he realized this sooner, before he had thrown away all the advantages which his father and brother-in-law had acquired for the nation. Hannibal probably altered the course of history as much as any other single man, and, as Prof. Toynbee has recently shown, the full effect of his actions becomes apparent when seen against the background of the evolution of Rome. He contributed more than the Romans themselves towards Rome's development from a city-state to a state in the fullest sense of the word. Carthage owed him a great deal of her glory, but he certainly shortened her life-span – not so much by weakening her but by making her the object of hatred and anxiety which were finally to destroy her.

8. CARTHAGINIAN CIVILIZATION IN HANNIBAL'S DAY

Without the evidence of the texts we should find it extremely difficult to believe that Barcid Carthage was a rich city and the envy of her rivals. She was no longer the principal artistic centre of the Punic state, however. The court was now established in Spain, and it was there that Greek artists settled in answer to the summons of the princes. The presence of these Greek artists is attested by the coins, which we have already studied for their political significance. The resemblance between the portraits of Hasdrubal and those of Hieron II on the coins would seem to indicate that the engravers came from Sicily. The bronze bust of Hannibal would also seem to be the work of an artist who had been trained in the workshops of Syracuse. If, as has been suggested, this bust, which was found at Volubilis, was a copy made for King Juba II in the last few years B.C., then at least its prototype must have been made as suggested above.[14] Some of these artists must have come to Carthage when Spain was invaded, and their influence is manifest in some fine stelae from the topheth: for instance, the stele of the *strategos*, which shows us the head and shoulders of a man who is not Hannibal but whose features bear a strong resemblance to his. This work is closely related to that group of royal Hellenistic portraits which was based on those of Alexander by Lysippus and Apelles. One of these artists became world famous: this was Boethus of Carthage, whose signature was found at Ephesus. He is mentioned by Pausanias, who had seen at Olympia a bronze which had been cast by this artist and represented a seated, naked child.[15] Boethus of Carthage was the son of Apollodorus, and probably a descendent and pupil of Boethus I, the Great, who came from Chalcedon, and whose finest work – showing one Agôn crowning a Hermes – was washed up on the Tunisian coast during a shipwreck. One of these Greek craftsmen was probably responsible for the superb Shield of Hasdrubal which the Romans found in the Carthaginian baggage-train captured after Metaurus, and which they dedicated on the Capitol.

Nevertheless, Carthage must also have benefited from the Barcids' patronage of the arts, but the fire of 146 erased all trace of this, and the remains which have come down to us are not sufficient to enable us to reconstruct the city as it must have been in Hannibal's day.

Now that the cult in the topheth of Salammbo was accessible to all classes of society, it was no longer surrounded by the ceremonial which had previously attended it. There are still some fine stelae, such as those carved with portraits which we have already described, or representing some fantastic architectural form. The great majority of the ex-votos which swamp the sanctuary at this period can only be described as popular art. Most of these are flat stelae representing the façade of a cella, surmounted by a triangular pediment and acroteria, and framed by columns which are set on either side of the dedicatory inscription. On the pediment and below the text, the sculptor has attempted to fit in as many prophylactic representations as possible, regardless of any aesthetic considerations, frequently in no particular order, the most important preoccupation generally being the symbolic value of the motif depicted.

After the loss of Sicily, marble sarcophagi disappear from the tombs, the tomb furniture becomes increasingly poor, and the jewellery has no value whatsoever. The Spanish mines did indeed provide the raw materials for the bronze industry, which seems to have flourished and produced some interesting pieces. Among these are a jug decorated with winged sphinxes, and beautifully engraved razors bearing representations of sculpture from Magna Graecia or Sicily. The glass workshops produced pendants in the shape of multi-coloured masks with cork-screw curls which are very skilfully worked. They also made delicate perfume flasks. Cabinet-makers inlaid jewel-caskets and toilet boxes with small ivory plaques cut out in intricate and attractive patterns. All these objects bear witness to the wealth and good taste of their owners, but they are few and far between and we are obliged to admit that, at this period, the Carthaginians had stopped putting their more precious luxury objects in the tombs.

It would thus seem that happiness in the next world was no longer as closely linked as it had been to the 'chamber of eternity', and that the conception of life after death had evolved. Furthermore, from the middle of the third century B.C. cremation becomes more and more common in Carthage, the ashes are enclosed in

268

small stone chests without any ornament, and it would therefore seem that the after-life had lost its material character. The fashion for depositing lamps, pottery, and a few useful objects and amulets in the tomb-chambers persisted, but the works of art which adorned private houses are never included now.

The talismans of eternity, such as the razors and the stelae of moloch sacrifices, are decorated with new symbols, however. The theme running through these is no longer the gift of life on earth and in the hereafter, bestowed by the deities on their faithful servants; the theme now is that of man's victory over death, which he has achieved through his own merits. An engraved hatchet depicts a chariot driven by a winged Victory, while many others represent, as we have seen, Melqart-Heracles, who is either fighting the Cretan bull or is enjoying a hero's rest, dressed in his lion's skin and leaning on his club. Sometimes the engraver has represented, in a symbolic composition, the victory won by the heroes of the Sardinian revolt: they are represented by their eponymous god, Sardus, standing over a kneeling Roman. On the stelae from the topheth of Salammbo we find divine emblems in conjunction with laurel-wreaths and trophies consisting of a breastplate hanging from a stake. Victory over Death is no longer the privilege of the virtuous but can be achieved by all through patriotic or military exploits. For this reason, Hannibal's companions had the instruments of their victory – such as their weapons or the prows of their galleys – carved on the stelae which they dedicated to the gods of the next world: Tanit, Ba'al Hammon, and their attendant deities.

How did these victors envisage life after death? Unfortunately, no text gives us the answer. If we are to believe the Numidian stelae which date from after the fall of Carthage but which are imbued with Punic beliefs, then it would seem that a journey through the various zones of the sky was involved, the Upper Ocean was then crossed, and beyond lay eternal happiness among the Immortals. The mausoleum of Dougga, built for a contemporary of Masinissa's, is decorated with reliefs which depict this chariot journey.

Those pious men who did not participate in person in these glorious expeditions could not depict themselves in this way. They continued to belong to the religious brotherhoods which served the gods of salvation: the *marzeah* or *thiasoi* dedicated to Shadrapa-Dionysus, which we have already mentioned, and the societies which venerated the Punic Cereres or Isis. In the last years of the third century we do indeed find, on the stelae of Salammbo, the emblems of these mystic religions: a basket, the sign of Isis consisting of the disc and the uraeus, the sistrum or situla, and the Krater – symbol of faith in eternal happiness. As the fortunes of war ceased to favour Carthage, these symbols became more and more numerous.

Notes and References

1. For a discussion of these works cf. the present author's study: 'Le problème du Portrait d'Hannibal', in *Karthago*, XII (1965).
2. In connection with this site see J. P. Morel, *Bull. Arch. du Comité 1965*, séance du 20 novembre.
3. For a discussion of the Italic Confederation in the third century and its weaknesses, see A. J. Toynbee, *Hannibal's Legacy*, 1964, Vol. 1.
4. The history of Roman coinage during this period is extremely controversial. L. Breglia leads the Italian school with his *La prima fase della coniazione romana*, in which he defends the traditional dates which have come down to us through Pliny the Elder. The English school, on the other hand, would bring these dates down considerably. Thomson has adopted an intermediate position and bases his dating on the most recent archaeological evidence.
5. This question is discussed in many basic works. Among these it is worth referring to: F. Cassola, *I gruppi politici romani nel III° secolo*; A. Lippold, *Consules*; and A. J. Toynbee, *Hannibal's Legacy*, Vol. I.
6. G. Ch. Picard, *Hannibal à Enserune*.
7. The problem of Hannibal's itinerary through Gaul and the Alps was already a subject of discussion in Seneca's time. It would need a whole volume to discuss all the suggestions put forward. We shall be following the itinerary proposed by C. Jullian, which has met with the approval of both Gsell and R. Dion. Another discussion of the problem is that of F. Benoit, *Congrès Guillaume Budé d'Aix en Provence, 1963*. Another theory which has been put forward is that of Sir Gavin de Beer, *Hannibal's March*, 1967.
8. M. Maingeonnet, *Revue de Numismatique*, IV (1962), pp. 62 and 72.
9. Op. cit.
10. The topographical problems which the Battle of Lake Trasimene posed, have been solved by G. Susini, *Ricerche sulla battaglia di Trasimeno*, 1960.
11. The exact site where the battle occurred is uncertain. There have been discussions as to whether it took place on the left or the right bank of the Aufidus (the modern Ofanto). A cemetery on the right bank has been mistaken for the war cemetery for this battle, but it is in fact a necropolis of the Middle Ages. See F. Bertocchi.
12. Concerning this treaty see especially, E. Bickermann, 'An oath of Hannibal', in *Transac. Amer. Philological Assoc.*, LXXV (1944); and

'Hannibal's covenant', in *American Journal of Philology*, LXXIII (1952), pp. 1–23.

For the religious significance see also G. Ch. Picard, 'Carthage au temps d'Hannibal', in *Convegno di studi Annibalici*.

13. Concerning the Numidian kingdoms see S. Gsell, *H.A.A.N.*, Vols. V and VI; and G. Camps, 'Masinissa', in *Libyca*, VIII (1960).

14. See the present author's study on the Portrait of Hannibal in *Karthago*, XII (1965).

15. For a discussion of the different Boethoi see C. Picard, *Karthago*, XIII (1952), p. 83 ff.

7

The Death-throes of Carthage

ARTHAGE survived a little more than half a century after
Zama. This was a sad time for the unhappy Republic,
which still caused her enemies anxiety without being in a
position to offer them any resistance. Rome was anxious to erase
all memory of her period of glory, and might have succeeded, after
the death of the last survivors of the great war, had not the
Numidian problem arisen. Masinissa's attitude to the Carthaginians resembles strongly that of today's newly independent
colonies towards their former masters: bitter feelings which are
more or less justified are strangely mixed with affection for a
civilization which can no longer be dispensed with.

1. HANNIBAL'S ATTEMPT AT RE-ESTABLISHING CARTHAGE, AND HIS FAILURE

Like all states which have just conducted a lengthy war and lost
it, Carthage went through an internal crisis in about 200 B.C.

The democratic party had remained in power throughout the
war, but defeat had, it seems, caused a split in its ranks. The
extremists had been responsible for breaking off the first armistice
with Rome, and some of them wished to continue the war after
Zama: one of them had even presented his case before the
Council of the Elders. Hannibal himself had dragged him from
the rostrum, causing such indignation that he had been obliged
to apologize.

The old oligarchical party of Hanno the Great had been in
opposition for more than a third of a century and had grown
powerless. But defeat gave it a chance to play a new part. One
of its leaders, Hasdrubal the Kid, was at the head of the embassy
which signed the peace with Rome. The nobles who belonged to

this faction did not seem to be able to regain public confidence, however.

A third party had doubtless been formed, during the second part of the war, round Hasdrubal, son of Gisco. This party had ruled for a time in conjunction with the pro-Barcid party, but had finally been driven out during the dramatic events which cost its leader his life.

The constitution did nothing to help solve these problems. Like most of the peoples of antiquity, the Carthaginians had had no thought of attempting to co-ordinate institutions which had grown up at different periods to fulfil the functions of different political parties. It was the pressure of events which made one or other of these institutions temporarily the most important. The Popular Assembly maintained the right which it had acquired thanks to the Barcids, of casting the deciding vote on the most important questions which might arise. The suffetes, whom the Assembly elected every year, were its most important representatives. There were other magistrates who were less directly dependent on the People, for instance, one responsible for financial matters, to whom Livy gives the Latin title of *quaestor*. The old tribunal of the One Hundred and Four still survived. Members were recruited, as for the Roman Senate, from among ex-magistrates – especially the quaestors – who were appointed for life. 'Property, honour, and the life of all were theirs to dispose of', Livy tells us, and 'whosoever insulted one of them, brought down upon himself the emnity of the others, so that there was no lack of accusers before a prejudiced tribunal' (XXXIII, 46, 1–2). Purely political offences were now judged by the People, as at Athens. The One Hundred and Four tried bribery and embezzlement cases, however, and this gave them the means of favouring some politicians while getting rid of others.

The oligarchy therefore maintained control of finances, probably through the intermediary of the Council of Thirty, which the Marseilles Tariff mentions in connection with the control of taxes, and which we can probably equate with Livy's *concilium sanctius*. This situation had been no hindrance to the Barcids while they remained in control of the resources of their Empire, which had made them independent. They had therefore allowed the dignitaries to dispose as they wished of the ordinary state budget and, in many cases, the latter had been able to divert some of the funds into their own pockets by more or less honest means. In the present circumstances, however, Hannibal decided that Carthage could no longer afford to tolerate such practices. Furthermore, he set himself the task of completing the democratic revolution which his father had begun: all appointments were henceforward to be made by popular election, and all were to be held for a limited period of time only.

This policy naturally displeased Rome, but she was busy with affairs in the East. From 201 to 196 the Romans were fighting Philip of Macedon for control of Greece, and the victory of Cyno-cephalus (197) gave them control of the Balkans. From 222 onwards, however, Antiochus III, the Great, had given new life to the Seleucid Empire; in 198 he won Coele Syria from Egypt – an area which both states had been fighting over since their creation and which Egypt was no longer able to hold, owing to the complete decadence which had set in since the death of Ptolemy III in 221.

This meant that, all of a sudden, the Phoenicians found them-selves subjects of the Seleucids. Relations were still close between Carthage and the old metropolis – even though the latter was now almost completely Hellenized – and these relations could easily be used to forge ties between Antiochus and Hannibal. Everything was predisposed to make the two men agree: Antiochus had not the same reasons as the Barcid for hating Rome, but he could not allow her to dominate Greece. Furthermore, he had determined to seize control of that part of Asia Minor which the king of Pergamum ruled, and the latter had already put himself under Roman protection. Rome's other ally in the Greek world was the Republic of Rhodes, and if the Seleucid king had, as he intended, succeeded in gaining control of the straits, then Rhodes would have been faced with ruin. Finally, Hannibal and Antiochus were both prepared to support democratic states, while Rome lent her assistance to the oligarchical régimes.

It was unfortunate for Hannibal that he gained control of Carthage just at the time when Rome had completed her war with Macedonia and had not, as yet, embarked on her war with the Great King. We do not know what reasons prevented the Barcid from having himself elected suffete earlier. Perhaps he had had to re-establish the unity of the People's Party first, and gain the confidence of the extremists who were reproaching him for not having continued the war longer. The writers of Antiquity have produced conflicting accounts of this period which are equally unlikely: Dio Cassius maintains that Hannibal was put on trial while Cornelius Nepos tells us that he remained in supreme command of the Punic army and that the Romans had to enforce his dismissal in 200.

Thus in 196, Hannibal was elected suffete in conjunction, most probably, with a colleague who was devoted to him. Soon after his election he asked the lord treasurer of the Republic to come and give him an account of the financial situation. This move posed a serious constitutional problem. In most of the cities of Antiquity the magistrates were independent of one another, and had supreme power within the limits laid down by their office. In Carthage, the suffete was essentially in charge of justice, and had no rights as regards the public treasury. The treasurer certainly belonged to the oligarchical party, and was most probably not elected by the People, so that he had every right to regard Hannibal's injunction as an abuse of power. The Barcid was, in fact, applying a rationalist and democratic conception of things which tended to disregard established form and practice: if the People were the supreme authority, and if the suffete was the elected representative of the People, then by rights all those who held public office should obey him, he felt. Roman history produces several examples of similar conflicts. The most serious was to take place a century later when Tiberius Gracchus found that the policy which he advocated and which the People were calling for, could not be carried out owing to the constant and paralysing veto of his colleague, the Tribune Octavius; Gracchus disregarded the fact that his office was inviolate, and obtained Octavius' dismissal by the Comitia.

In the case we are discussing the quaestor refused to obey. Hannibal made use of his police powers and had him arraigned before the Assembly of the People, which had supreme authority, at that time, in matters of political jurisdiction and constitutional establishment. Hannibal therefore submitted to the Assembly a proposal for a new law whereby the judges – that is the One Hundred and Four – would be elected directly by the People and hold office for one year only. We have reason to suppose that such measures had already been instituted as regards the choice of Elders and of members of the Supreme Council. Hannibal does not, indeed, seem to have met with any opposition from either of these two bodies, but he would probably have had no hesitation in breaking their power also if he had found them hostile. The power of the aristocracy was, indeed, limited to judiciary matters and financial administration, but it felt, rightly, that it exercised by these means control over all vital issues.

There does not seem to be any good reason for supporting Gsell's suggestion that Hannibal's form of procedure before the People was not legal because the Elders had not previously been consulted. Firstly, the rules which had been in force in the time of Aristotle were certainly out of date in the second century. Secondly, the course of events proves clearly enough that the laws which were then voted, could not be attacked from the legal standpoint: Hannibal was condemned for having violated the Treaty with Rome, and not for having broken the laws of his country.

Once Hannibal had obtained control of the finances, he instituted a vast enquiry into the way these had been managed in preceding years. Those previously responsible had, in fact, presented a budget with a heavy deficit, and had called for the creation of new taxes. The report which Hannibal presented to the People's Assembly stated, in fact, that the Republic could easily pay her way and discharge her war indemnity without the necessity of establishing new taxes, on condition that the administrators who had just been deposed should pay up. Through negligence, some had allowed certain sources of income to be wasted, or had authorized unnecessary expenditure; others had arranged to have themselves paid salaries and indemnities to which they had no right, or had misappropriated state funds. The enquiry went back several years, and it would seem that those in charge of it magnified rather than minimized the scandals which they had uncovered. In any case, the result was that most of the families of the nobility were ruined and a social revolution could now be added to the political one.

Hannibal is very like Tiberius Gracchus both in his plans for social improvement and in his disregard for the law. Neither of them hesitated in attacking the interests of their own class in order to achieve their political ideals. Hannibal had already shown himself to be surprisingly enlightened when he promised his Barbarian troops that they should enjoy all the rights of Carthaginian citizenship after the victory. There was a tradition of close contact between Sparta and Carthage, and it is perhaps permissible to suggest that Hannibal, who was a pupil of Sosylus, a native of Lacedaemon, may have been inspired in his revolutionary attempts by the example of Cleomenes and Nabis: the latter had suppressed the ephorate, while Hannibal had abolished the One Hundred and Four. The kings of Sparta had also attacked the rich and had redistributed wealth both in their own town and in those they conquered. In both cases, this revolution was motivated less by the desire to improve the lot of the poor than by the wish to awaken national consciousness.

Hannibal's opponents were not going to accept this quietly, however, and, in order to escape ruin, they had no hesitation in calling for Roman intervention, and showed as little scruple as the Achaean Aratus when he called in the Macedonian army in order to stop the Spartan revolution from spreading. Livy himself tells us that Punic letters or embassies were sent to Rome to denounce Hannibal's plans for 'revenge'. Most of the Fathers were only too ready to credit such denunciations, which were not, in fact, slander. Hannibal's case found support in an unexpected quarter, however: Publius Cornelius Scipio Africanus rose in the Curia to proclaim his indignation that the mighty Roman people should pay heed to traitors, and he maintained that the independence of Carthage, which had been solemnly guaranteed, should be respected. Scipio certainly firmly and sincerely believed, together with his friend Quinctius Flaminius, the liberator of Greece, in the possibility of Rome's directing a community of free peoples. In this case as in others, however, we cannot but wonder whether he was not showing more generosity than political wisdom. It was only too certain that Hannibal was in contact with Antiochus, and the Senators were easily persuaded that this was so. They selected three of their number to go to Africa in order to rid them of Hannibal. It is true that Scipio's views on diplomacy were peculiar to himself: he did not hesitate to correspond with kings on his own authority, without reference to anyone else, even when they were at war with Rome. He ended up by feeling more at ease with these potentates than with his own compatriots, and Hannibal – in his eyes – also belonged to that 'club of heroes' who were superior to the normal run of vulgar humanity.

The Roman embassy reached Carthage in the middle of the summer of 195. Hannibal had completed his term of office,[1] but his party was so powerful that the oligarchs recommended the envoys to keep the object of their mission to themselves. They therefore maintained that they had come to arbitrate in one of the incessant frontier disputes which arose out of Masinissa's inter-pretation of the treaty. Hannibal was not deceived, however; he was afraid of being secretly assassinated and took flight in dramatic circumstances, which have been recorded in great detail by Livy.

The end of Hannibal's life is not directly linked with the history of his country. He was triumphantly welcomed in Tyre, and became an advisor to Antiochus, but he played only a minor part in the war which so rapidly showed how weak the Seleucid scare-crow was, in reality. The arrival of this famous but inconvenient and troublesome ally was viewed with a certain amount of anxiety by Antiochus' ministers; many of them successfully undertook to discredit him in the king's eyes. He was not given a land command but, rather too late, he was put at the head of a fleet, and was unable to carry out the projected landing in the West which he had proposed to the general staff. Even before Antiochus' official break with Rome, Hannibal had sought to prepare for the execu-tion of his plan by sending a secret agent to Carthage in 193. The latter was a Tyrian named Aristo, who was soon unmasked and took flight in order to avoid arrest. The only result this mission had, therefore, was to make the democrats suspect in Carthage, and the whole of Carthage suspect in Rome.

After the Peace of Apamea, which meant that he could no longer remain under the protection of Antiochus, Hannibal dragged out five more years as an exile in the courts of those Asiatic princelings who were the least dependent on Rome. Prusias, King of Bythinia, was the mortal enemy of Eumenes of Pergamum, and made use of Hannibal for a while, but eventually agreed to hand him over to the Romans. Hannibal was cornered in his castle and took poison so as to avoid imprisonment or torture (183 or 182 B.C.).

Hannibal's flight had marked the fall of his party from power. In 193, at the time of the Aristo affair, the magistrates and the majority of the Elders made it their first consideration not to compromise themselves in the eyes of Rome. This does not prove, as Gsell believed, that the constitution had been modified again, and that Hannibal's legal and financial reforms had been abolished. Certainly they cannot have been as rigorously enforced, and the noble families were able to escape complete ruin. The powers of the Assembly of the People do not seem to have been in any way restricted, however, and a few years later the suffetes were once more the leaders of the democratic party. The Carthaginian people were renowned for their violent tempers, and it is unlikely that anyone would have dared to suggest to them any reactionary undertakings for which they would have to bear the expense. In fact it would seem, as we shall see, that social differences in Carthage became less marked in the second century and Hannibal's reform must have been to some extent responsible for this.

2. THE NUMIDIAN THREAT

The defeat of Antiochus and the death of Hannibal should have meant the survival of Carthage. There was no individual or state left, throughout the whole Mediterranean, who was capable of making Rome tremble or, consequently, of making her dread a revival of her ancient rival. Memories of the war became dulled with the passage of time. The Carthaginians who now found their way to Italy, were *guggas* – cunning and picturesque merchants who were mocked and treated with suspicion, but only because of their strange form of dress, their exotic habits, and their excessive guile. Even Plautus, who at first makes us laugh at his Poenulus, finally endows his character with human sentiments and describes in touching terms the latter's joy at finding his lost daughter. Friendships between dignitaries of both nations grew up. Silanus, who was a Senator, spoke very good Carthaginian, so we are told. In fact that language must have been understood to some extent by quite a large number of Romans, for Plautus' comedy could not have been appreciated otherwise. These Carthaginians brought many tempting things with them: not only their own products from Africa, such as the fresh figs which Cato produced in the Senate one day, or the leopards which were displayed at the games, but also the trinkets, precious furniture, perfume, and sweetmeats of every sort, which came from Greece, Syria, or Egypt.

Roman officials were constantly obliged to intervene, however, in order to arbitrate in disputes between Carthage and Masinissa. It must be admitted that the latter had reason to be not best pleased with the terms of the treaty of 201, and with Scipio's interpretation of these terms. The Phoenician Boundaries, which formed the frontier between his kingdom and the Punic *territorium*, encompassed several areas which were inhabited by Libyans, who were closely related to the Numidians. Masinissa's eastern capital, Zama, lay some six miles from the frontier, while all the most fertile and best irrigated land belonged to Carthage. In an attempt to silence his complaints, doubtless, the Romans inserted a clause into the treaty which they wished him to sign, according him the right to claim anything which had belonged to his ancestors and which lay within the Punic boundary. Masinissa immediately settled down to the task of inventing genealogies for himself, proving his descent from all the Libyan princelings he could think of. At the same time, he launched a series of raids against the regions which he coveted, during the course of which he carried off booty and forced the inhabitants to accept his sovereignty.

This encroaching had begun before 195, since it was under pretext of arbitration in the Punico-Numidian conflict that the embassy sent to deal with Hannibal arrived from Rome. Two years later Masinissa sought to seize Tripolitania, and succeeded in carrying off the tribute which was supposed to go to Carthage. In the case of Lepcis alone, this tribute amounted to one talent a day (about £250).[2] The matter was taken to Rome for arbitration. The Carthaginians had a very strong case: not only had Scipio expressly stated that Syrtica was to belong to Carthage, but Masinissa himself had applied through diplomatic channels, after the peace had been concluded, for Carthaginian permission to pursue through Syrtica a rebel subject of his called Aphthir, who had sought refuge in Cyrenaica. Livy has recorded for us the speech of the Numidian delegates, which is worth quoting:

They said that the Carthaginians were lying concerning the limits set by Scipio. If the original rights of the case were to be considered, then what part of the African territory could, in fact, be said to belong to the Carthaginians? They were refugees to whom a temporary concession had been granted on which they could build a town. This was not to exceed in area that covered by an ox-hide: all that extended beyond the limits of their living-quarters in Byrsa had been acquired by violent and unjust means.

Exactly the same arguments are being used nowadays in connection with certain international problems. The Senate's answer also has a contemporary ring: a commission of enquiry was appointed which was to be presided over by Scipio Africanus. This commission decided that it would be better to suspend decision! The rights of the Carthaginians were obvious, but the Aristo episode had only recently taken place and had created a bad impression in Rome. The war against Antiochus was about to begin: Masinissa's friendship had to be maintained, and Hannibal's compatriots were treated with suspicion.[3]

During the next thirty years there are several mentions by contemporary historians of further encroaching on Masinissa's part, and of further cases taken to Rome. It would seem that every time the Senate came to a decision, it was increasingly in Carthage's favour. Certainly no important territory was lost to the enemy during this period. The king was hoping, however, to conclude the whole affair to his advantage once and for all. A party had been formed in Carthage which advocated the unification of the whole of Africa under the Numidian sceptre: Carthage would become the capital and would lose neither her autonomy nor her civilization. The members of this faction, led by a certain Hannibal the Starling, certainly did not suffer from any lack of persuasive arguments. In his kingdom Masinissa was creating or developing Phoenician towns. At Cirta, for instance, the cult of Ba'al Hammon and of Tanit – which had perhaps been introduced during Sophonisba's brief reign – was gaining in popularity in the topheth of El Hofra.[4] Numerous Carthaginians, traders, artisans, and bourgeois of all types were settling in the kingdom. Far from denying the family ties which linked him to the Barcids, the king did not hesitate to represent on his coins not only the war-horse which was the old symbol for the 'Punic Mars', but also the elephant which Hannibal had chosen as his crest.[5]

As Camps has noted, the Numidian king 'did not succeed in developing a real Numidian civilization in the towns; he favoured, on the contrary, the tremendous spread of the Punic religious cults, customs, language, and writing, which he had been brought up to in his youth'. [6] This process would naturally be greatly accelerated should Carthage decide to become part of the kingdom. It would then be possible, for instance, to make the Numidian prince abandon his suspicions as far as his Phoenician subjects were concerned, and allow them to fill political and military posts which had been reserved, up till now, for his Libyan subjects, while the Phoenicians had to be content with technical or religious appointments. Carthage would also be able to reduce the influence exercised by other foreigners such as Italians and Greeks. [7]

It would seem that Masinissa approved of this plan; he certainly allowed one of his daughters to marry a Carthaginian nobleman. The son born to this couple was called Hasdrubal, and was elected general in 149. His parents' marriage must certainly have been prior to 170, therefore, and probably took place in about 180. Even then Masinissa must have realized that Rome would set a limit to his annexation of Punic territory, and he therefore set about establishing alternative political ties. In pursuit of this aim he made contact with the principal Greek states. He was finding the part of a faithful servant of the Senate irksome.

3. CARTHAGINIAN CIVILIZATION IN THE SECOND
    CENTURY B.C.

When Scipio Aemilianus was ordered by the Senate to raze the city of Carthage to the ground, he obeyed his instructions to the letter. The ruins which were still standing after seventeen days of burning, were levelled, and the site was ploughed up and sown with salt. The same treatment was meted out to the other cities which had resisted the Roman armies. Nevertheless, Scipio's efficiency did not succeed in obliterating all trace of the town. Whereas we know only the tombs and the ex-votos of Hannibal's predecessors, we can visit the actual houses of the last defenders of the city.

The most important remains were discovered on the southern slopes of the hill of Byrsa. Scipio's legionaries destroyed the edifices on top of the plateau, and in so doing they buried the structures on the slope under débris. Later on, the builders of the Roman colony wished to increase the building-space on the top of the plateau, and a whole district of living quarters was buried in this way under nine to twelve feet of rubble and fill. In this central area land was expensive: maximum use had been made of it. The streets had been kept narrow and the size of buildings had been restricted: there was no question here of a central courtyard to give light and air – these both came exclusively from the street. The rooms were square or rectangular, and were juxtaposed without any thought for architectural effect. A certain luxury in the interior decoration proves that they were not houses belonging to the poor, however. Slender Ionic columns, covered with stucco, supported entablatures; the walls were built of mud brick or of small stones set in mortar, were supported by a vertical framework of braces, and were also decorated in stucco which imitated precious marble in accordance with the current Greek fashion. Water was obtained from numerous cisterns, and there was an elaborate system of drains. The quantity of fragments of amphorae from Rhodes, which was found among the ruins, is an indication that Hannibal's contemporaries liked their wine and were prepared to pay a high price for it. Polybius tells us that Hasdrubal, the last defender of the city, was rather too fond of good food and drink. He was certainly not the only one! The Carthaginians also spent a lot on their furniture, and Punic cabinet-makers were renowned. A few fragments of their work have come down to us. A small ivory head, found by Saumagne among the ashes of the fire of 146, was used as applied decoration on a precious piece of furniture. The thrones of gods in terracotta, decorated with Victories in the style of Alexandria, have been discovered by Dr. Carton in the chapel of Salammbo, and doubtless reproduce seats which were in more common use.[8]

This chapel of Salammbo was situated beneath the station for the electric railway, a little more than 300 yards to the west of the topheth, and is the most complete building of this period yet found. The edifice is rectangular, was built of mud brick, and was divided into two rooms, the second of which was the sanctuary. Originally this room had contained a rectangular base, decorated with stucco, which had stood opposite the doorway, against the back wall of the shrine. This was framed by four small Doric columns, which were joined to the back wall by little perpendicular partitions. At a later date, benches were built against the wall and the earlier decoration was hidden. The floor was covered with pink cement, in which were imbedded pieces of white marble. The base and the benches had been built for ex-votos and terracotta images. These represented two goddesses, seated on richly decorated thrones; one of them rests her feet on a *couchant* lion and is accompanied by two attendants; the uprights of the throne of the other goddess are decorated with representations of Victories. One at least of these goddesses is Tanit. Ba'al Hammon is represented by a head crowned with a three-tiered feather head-dress, and Demeter by several busts which were used as incense-burners. Two breast-plated torsos were probably those of the god of war, and there were also demon and Gorgon masks. Most of these images, and, indeed, architectural fragments, would not be out of place if they were found anywhere else around the Mediterranean. We must point out the increasingly war-like character of the deities, however: the goddess enthroned between two Victories, the god wearing a breast-plate. This can easily be explained by the patriotic excitement in which the last inhabitants of Carthage lived, but it also bears witness to the influence of the Hellenistic 'Victory Theologies' which the Barcids introduced.

Another, similar shrine, which may have been attached to a suburban villa, has been found to the north of Carthage in the district which is known today as Amilcar. Among other things, it contained a terracotta frieze representing members of the Dionysiac *thiasos* and is therefore yet another example of Hellenistic influence on religion.

The latest stelae in the topheth are very numerous and are in some confusion owing to re-use by the Romans when they built the colony which replaced the Phoenician city. These little monuments are, for the most part, poorly executed. They are roughly engraved – often with the representation of a sheep, which was probably sacrificed instead of the child of the person dedicating them. The chaos reigning in the upper levels of the topheth does not allow us to determine exactly the proportion of these substitution sacrifices.

The tombs from the Odeon necropolis which date from this period, also contain very poor remains.

The little city of Dar es Safi on Cap Bon was probably destroyed by Regulus and never rebuilt, but gives a good idea of small towns in the last period of Punic history. The houses were far more comfortable than those of Byrsa. They were all built round a large courtyard which was, in one case, surrounded by a portico in the Greek fashion, and all had a bathroom, which was equipped according to the latest ideas of comfort and refinement. The alterations carried out in the last occupation level would seem to indicate a lowering of the standard of living, however.

There does not seem to be any doubt that Carthage was less prosperous in the second century than she had been in the third. The coins she minted at this time are rather mediocre in quality. At the time of her destruction, however, Polybius considered her to be the richest city in the world. She still had enormous capital assets which could not all be realized – as in the case of works of art and ex-votos preserved in the shrines. The extraordinary speed with which she re-equipped herself for war, prove that Carthage's capacity for production was considerable. It seems, indeed, that her citizens, like most of their compatriots in Greece and even in Italy, were less disposed than their forebears to lavish their wealth on the gods of the dead. New forms of religion which were less demanding and more personal, and an easier and less austere way of life tended to replace the old beliefs and customs, here as elsewhere. Nevertheless, patriotism was still very much alive among the Carthaginians, as was that extraordinary tenacity which had enabled their race to survive in a hostile environment and had almost given them a world empire. The Carthaginians were about to give a final proof of these virtues by preferring mass suicide to the acceptance of submission and decadence.

4. THE DEATH OF CARTHAGE

It is a problem to know why Rome should have watched over Carthage for fifty years and then, in 150, should suddenly have undertaken an unjust, cruel, and, furthermore, a difficult war in order to crush a city which no longer constituted a threat to her existence. Gsell suggested that Masinissa was on the point of achieving his ambitions and that Rome could not tolerate the creation of a large, united African kingdom. This suggestion was accepted at the time without discussion by everyone, including the present author. The only person to take a stand against it was B. H. Warmington in 1960. The present author now believes that Warmington is right though he has been unable to explain completely the reasons for this sudden reversal of Roman policy, and he therefore seems to present the murder of Carthage as a gratuitous crime.

Gsell based his interpretation on a speech which Appian and Diodorus Siculus[9] record as having been made by a friend of Scipio Africanus – perhaps Caecilius Metellus – during the discussions which took place before the treaty of 201 was signed. As Warmington says, however, it was not necessary to destroy Carthage in order to prevent her falling into the hands of Masinissa. Hannibal the Starling's Numidian party had probably been formed somewhere round about 170, at the time when Punico-Numidian relations were slightly easier. This 'centre' party was composed of moderate aristocrats, who were halfway between the ultra-conservatives of Hanno III, the Great, and the democrats, and it seems to have been extremely popular until 155. It was then the victim of a violent explosion of popular feeling, and its leaders were exiled. Soon after, the Carthaginians declared war on Masinissa. It was thus at the precise moment when Punico-Numidian relations were at their worst that Rome is supposed to have intervened to prevent annexation, although previously, when Hannibal the Starling was in power, she had done nothing, and had, indeed, been rather well disposed towards Carthage. Gsell doubtless believed that the defeat of the Carthaginians by the Numidians had resulted in Masinissa's friends returning to power. In fact, the Democrats remained in power until it was learnt that Rome was preparing for war. It was then that the government was entrusted to Rome's real allies, the Hannonian oligarchs, and these were in charge until the political reversal which the consuls' ultimatum produced. In 150, Masinissa was 88 years old. Even if he had become the ruler of Carthage he would scarcely have had the time to organize any undertaking which might spell danger for Rome. It was easy to foresee that the struggle for his succession would be difficult to resolve, for he had three legitimate heirs and innumerable bastard sons. The heterogeneous kingdom which he had built up was most unlikely to survive him. It would be even less likely to if he succeeded in his plan to annex Carthage at the last moment, for the city would regain her independence almost as soon as she lost it, under the rule of some Numidian prince or other. This 'imminent danger' which is supposed to have brought the Romans into action, is therefore hypothetical and totally imagined.

We must add, furthermore, that the measure which Rome took to counter this threat was that most likely to increase it. At the end of a long period of terrible suspense, the Senate's decision was disclosed to the Council of Thirty by the consul. The Carthaginians were condemned to abandon their city and go and settle inland. This was the best method of ensuring that the majority of men, once they had been deprived of their means of livelihood, would go and offer their services to the Numidian king – the only man in a position to find them employment. Masinissa or his successors would therefore be surrounded by a mass of Phoenician émigrés who hated Rome and were prepared to go to any length to recover their lost land.

We must therefore give up the idea that Rome 'hastened to punish Carthage for attacking Masinissa, before Masinissa became her master and was in a position to defend her' (S. Gsell). Must we also, however, give up any hope of finding a reason for this sudden Roman fury against an enemy who was powerless? Cato was a hard man and lacked breadth of vision, but he was neither stupid nor easily excitable, and was therefore unlikely to undertake a difficult war for purely emotional reasons.

As we have had occasion to see several times already, difficulties which arise in connection with Punic history often disappear when viewed, not in isolation, but against the background of Mediterranean events generally. All chronologies indicate on the same line, under the date 146 B.C., both the destruction of Carthage by Scipio Aemilianus, and that of Corinth by Mummius. Yet the name of Corinth is not mentioned one single time in the third volume of Gsell's history.

The reasons for the destruction of Corinth are very clear. The Achaean Confederation was the main prop of Greek conservatism, and had been the faithful ally of Rome ever since the second Macedonian war. In 150 it suddenly re-orientated itself completely. The *stratēgoi* Diaeus and Critolaus adopted a nationalist policy, set about systematically freeing the slaves, and confiscated the property of the rich. They relied mainly on Corinth, which had once more become a great commercial and industrial centre containing a vast working-class population with extremely advanced ideas. As

287

Piganiol has very rightly stated, after its victory, the Senate ordered that Corinth should be razed to the ground so as to terrorize the revolutionaries.

The evolution of Achaea and of Carthage during these crucial years is exactly parallel, however. In about 155 probably, the People's party in Carthage expelled Masinissa's friends. Carthalo, one of the democratic leaders, attacked the kingdom. Appian has left us an account of these events, and maintains that Carthalo attempted to incite the Libyan farmers to revolt against the Numidians (*Lib.* 68).[10] This is an extremely interesting piece of information, for it implies that all was not well in the new state, and we know, furthermore, that Masinissa was constantly having to deal with minor revolts: first that of Aphthir, and then those of Agasis and of Soubas, who had gone over to the Carthaginians in 150. These rebels seem to have been tribal caïds who could not accept the increase in royal authority. Polybius tells us that Masinissa introduced agriculture into his kingdom, and we therefore tend to consider him as the defender of the settled people against the nomads. Camps has shown that his main preoccupation was obtaining a personal monopoly for all the developments which took place in his kingdom, and he had all the crops gathered into his own granaries, from which most of them were exported for his own profit.[11] The peasantry must have been heavily exploited, but Carthalo could not have incited them to revolt without promising to improve their lot if they joined Carthage. The democratic party must first have voted a law by which the living conditions of native cultivators on Punic soil were to be considerably bettered.

Carthalo's attack was stopped by the arrival of a Roman mission. It is surprising that the Romans did not consider then, as they did a little later, that the Carthaginians had violated the treaty of 201 when they attacked Masinissa. The latter undertook to avenge himself by claiming an enormous section of Punic territory amounting to three of the seven or eight districts which made up the Carthaginian holding. These were, from north to south, the Great Plains of the middle Medjerda, with Vaga (Béja); the district of Thusca, that is the country of Mactar with its fifty cities; and, finally, Tripolitania. Once more a Roman embassy came to arbitrate in the dispute, and once again it evaded the issue. One member of this delegation was, however, the elderly Cato, and he was worried by what he saw in Carthage. From then on he repeated constantly, at all the meetings of the Senate and whatever subject was under discussion, his proverbial *Delenda est Carthago* (Carthage must be destroyed), in spite of all the protests of the man who was then leading the clan of the Scipios, Nasica.

Up till that time, Cato had not been particularly fanatical in his anti-Punic views. He must therefore have seen something in Africa which led him to take up a radical and unyielding position. What was it? He had admired the fertility of the estates, but this cannot have been a revelation to him: he was a disciple of that agricultural expert, Mago, and knew better than any how competent the Carthaginians were in this field. There does not seem to be any reason why the fear of competition from Carthaginian speculative agriculture should suddenly lead Cato to adopt such extremist views. It is also most unlikely that he was in any way perturbed by the possible harm which the guile of the *guggas* might do to Italian trading interests.

Carthalo's lack of success did not affect the popularity of the People's Party in any way. On the contrary, a particularly radical democrat was elected suffete by the Assembly in 152. This was Gisco, son of Hamilcar. Masinissa's supporters, numbering about forty, were condemned to exile. Gisco was not satisfied with attacking the Numidians, however. His speeches aroused popular feeling against Rome itself. Other tribunes, such as Hamilcar the 'Samnite' and Hasdrubal, supported the same policy. These men obtained a vote in favour of rearmament; military arsenals and naval shipyards went through a period of feverish activity. Arcobarzane, one of the grandsons of Syphax, was said to be assembling a vast army within the Punic *territorium*, with which he was going to reconquer the lands of his fathers.

Even if we discount all the exaggerations of Roman propaganda, there is little doubt that Cato and his colleagues found Carthage in ferment, with meetings being held frequently where the name of Rome was often reviled. The nobles from Hanno's party had done nothing to conceal their anxiety: a virulent revolutionary centre was being formed on the most northern tip of Africa, close to Sicily and to Southern Italy.

It is hardly surprising that awareness of this should have caused anxiety among the majority of the Fathers. In the middle of the second century B.C., a revolutionary current was spreading through-out the Mediterranean. In Asia Minor, the last kings of Pergamum, Attalus II and Attalus III, had come to the conclusion that only direct Roman domination could preserve the established social order; the revolt was to break out in 133, led by Aristonicus. In Egypt and Syria Hellenism finally collapsed in the face of native revolutions. In Macedonia, Andriscus made himself the champion of independence and defender of the proletariat in 152. We have already mentioned the Achaean crisis. The West did not escape either: as early as 198, the *praetor urbanus* had uncovered a slave conspiracy at Setia. It is most important to note that these plotters were Carthaginians: they were the servants of Punic hostages who had been interned in the Latin colony, and they had joined up with compatriots of theirs who had been bought as slaves from among prisoners of war from Hannibal's army, and had been set to work in the fields.[12] It is very possible that this incident contributed towards Rome's determination to rid herself of Hannibal. Other slave revolts broke out in Etruria in 196 and in Apulia in 185. It would seem that the repression of the Bacchic cult, culminating in 186 in the famous *senatus consulte* of the Bacchanalia, can be attributed to a large extent to social reasons rather than to the desire to preserve religious purity. Sicily was also a prey to hordes of slaves, and the situation there was becoming explosive.

The aristocracy of Rome discovered, to its horror, that by break-ing up the established political and social framework throughout the world, and by introducing everywhere the merciless oppression of the poor by the rich who were its agents and its tax-collectors, it had liberated enormous and scarcely controllable forces which were threatening to turn the whole world into chaos. Even though there was no state capable of withstanding her, Rome realized that she had to be prepared at any moment, anywhere, and totally unpredictably, to deal with the rebellion of opponents who, though badly armed, would be desperate and innumerable.

If we take all this into account, we cannot accuse Cato of over-estimating the Punic threat. Carthage was the only great city in the Western Mediterranean basin which was not under Roman control. Her population consisted of those groups of people which are always most prone to revolt. Furthermore, she could not bring herself to forgive Rome for all the suffering and humiliation which she had endured at her hands. Her cultural and religious history, though it tended to tone down the more original aspects of Phoenician tradition, nevertheless brought the Carthaginians into closer contact with other peoples, and this facilitated the exchange of subversive ideas and projects.

Before purely and simply abolishing Carthage, the Roman government decided to give the city a last chance to transform herself. The Carthaginians were to abandon the town and were to settle wherever they wished, so long as it was at least 80 stadia (8¾ miles approximately) from the sea. When Censorinus, the consul, made known this decision to the Thirty, he accompanied it, according to Appian (*Lib*. 86) by a speech in which he urged them to accept it with good grace. At first glance, the text of this speech seems to be nothing more than a collection of platitudes. It would seem to reproduce fairly closely what the consul actually said, however. Indeed, we know from Cicero (*Acad*. II, 32, 102) that Censorinus had a tendency to Platonism. His speech in this instance reproduces, in fact, a famous theory which is developed in *Laws* (705a), and which he adapts to the case in point:

'A country's proximity to the sea gives pleasure in day-to-day life, but is a brackish and harmful thing; it makes the town suspicious and unfriendly towards itself and with regards to other men, by introducing trade and retail traffic to it, and by implanting in the soul unstable and uncertain customs.'

Plato's doctrine had been rejected by Aristotle but exercised a strong influence on the aristocracy of Rome, which had inherited a peasant morality. Quite a number of Senators must have been convinced by their own arguments and have believed that by obliging the Carthaginians to make a complete 'return to the earth', they were contributing to their moral elevation while, at the same time, rendering them harmless. Polybius tells us that most of the Senators, whose views he also held, believed that Carthage had passed from the state of political perfection, which she had enjoyed in the fourth century, to decadence. This decadence was due to the presence in the city of merchants, seafarers, and artisans who were, in all countries, the supporters of the most extreme form of democracy, 'ochlocracy', which philosophers were unanimous in condemning. Hence the reason for this strange decision, which it is wrong to regard as a goad to urge the Carthaginians into war out of sheer desperation. On the contrary, it was intended to re-integrate them into that order of things which conformed to the plans of Providence and to the laws of wisdom which Rome felt she had been called upon to establish.

Having thus satisfied their peace of mind, the Romans carried out their plan with their customary inflexibility and harshness.

We must now return to the year 150 when, as we have seen, the Carthaginians were under the rule of the People's Party and were in conflict with Masinissa. The king first sent his sons Micipsa and Gulussa into the city to demand the recall of his supporters. This mission failed, and on his return Gulussa was even attacked by one of the Carthaginian generals, Hamilcar the Samnite. War then broke out, with a city named Oroscopa as the principal stake, though we do not know where it was situated. After a first indecisive battle, the Punic army, now led by Hasdrubal, Carthalo's successor, was surrounded and finally obliged to capitulate through famine. A number of soldiers were treacherously massacred after they had handed over their weapons. Masinissa remained in control of the regions of the Great Plains, Thusca, and Tripolitania.

The news then reached Carthage that Rome was mobilizing. Consternation reigned in the city. With their customary inconstancy the Carthaginian people turned against the leaders who had been responsible for this catastrophe. Hasdrubal, Carthalo, and the other heads of the democratic party were condemned to death, though the first mentioned succeeded in escaping. Power was once more in the hands of Hanno the Great's friends, and these hastened to send an embassy to Rome to ask for pardon and forgiveness.

Then began a terrible period of suspense. The Senate gave vague and disquieting answers to the ambassadors, and recruiting continued. The people of Utica had long been jealous of Carthage and let it be known that they were on Rome's side. Manius Manilius and L. Marcius Censorinus, the consuls, were able, thanks to this, to set foot in Africa without any difficulty in the spring of 149. In the meantime another Punic delegation reached Rome and used a formula of retraction, whereby Carthage was put without any reservations whatsoever into the hands of Rome. The praetor told this delegation that Carthage would remain independent on condition that she gave hostages and obeyed the secret instructions of the consuls, which they would be told about when the right time came; some of the delegates noticed with growing anxiety that the praetor omitted to make any mention of the city itself. Indeed, Manilius soon revealed to the Thirty that the Senate had decided to destroy the city and suggested that the Carthaginians should found another city inland.

This decree roused the patriotic feelings of the Carthaginians. All friends of Rome who were unable to escape the popular fury were massacred, including the Italians who lived in Carthage. In an effort at unification, the Assembly elected as generals Hasdrubal, the ex-leader of the democrats who had been condemned to death only a short while previously, and his namesake, the grandson of Masinissa. The latter was soon accused of treason, however, and was put to death in the course of riots. All the craftsmen in the city set to work night and day in order to replace the weapons which had been handed over to the Romans shortly before; everything was done to assist them, so that daily production rose to 100 shields, 500 javelins and spears, 1000 darts for catapults, and a number of catapults themselves, which varied from day to day. The consuls could have put an end to this war effort by occupying the city, but they continued to hope for voluntary capitulation. When they finally decided to attack, however, the legionaries were repulsed.

A full-scale siege had to be undertaken, therefore. Manilius established his camp on the isthmus, before the fortification outworks which were discovered in 1949 by General Duval. These latter consisted of a ditch, which was more than 60 feet deep, and behind this was a bank crowned with a wooden palisade, and these cut across the peninsula at its narrowest point, about two and a half miles west of Byrsa. The Roman camp must have been situated near the present airport of El Aouina. Censorinus pitched his camp on the spit of land which separated the lake from the sea; he probably chose the site of the old airport, on the edge of the lagoon. He found this spot unhealthy, however, and moved down to the beach on the Khereddine side.

The Romans had thought that they were in for a military walkover; they were now involved in a difficult war. Many Phoenician towns, most of them in Byzacenia, and among them Hadrumetum, had followed the example of Utica. Most of the flatter part of the country, and the cities founded by Carthage, had remained faithful: the Libyan peasants were satisfied with Carthalo's reforms and realized that they would not gain much by changing masters. Hasdrubal the democrat had installed his army on the heights which link Cap Bon to the Zaghouan massif, thus cutting off communications with Byzacenia. While attempting to remove him, Manilius was taken by surprise in the valley of the Khanguet el Hejaj, and was only saved from disaster thanks to the skill and courage of one of his young military tribunes, who bore the great name of Scipio Aemilianus.

This young man was the son of Aemilius Paulus, the conqueror of Macedonia, and the adopted grandson of Scipio Africanus. His prestige was further increased when Masinissa finally died, at the age of ninety, and stipulated in his will that Scipio Aemilianus should settle the difficult problem of his succession as he thought best. Scipio divided the kingdom between the three legitimate sons of Masinissa – Micipsa, Gulussa, and Mastanabal. Gulussa had been appointed general and now joined the Roman camp. By this move he obliged the Libyan subjects of Carthage to join the invaders: Phamaias, the commander of the Punic cavalry, himself turned traitor together with a large number of his men.

Meanwhile, the consuls for 148 had come to relieve their predecessors. They were L. Calpurnius Piso, and L. Hostilius Mancinus, and they did not prove to be any more capable. They preferred not to attack Carthage directly, and concentrated, rather unsuccessfully, on attempting to capture the towns which had remained loyal. Bizerta and Aspis (which was now beginning to be called by its Roman name of Clupea), among others, defeated them soundly. Nevertheless, just as his term of office was coming to an end, Mancinus thought he saw a chance of ending the war at one stroke. The high cliffs of Sidi Bou Said (Megara) fall away steeply into the sea, and were therefore only slightly fortified and badly guarded. With a handful of men the consul succeeded in climbing them. He met with a strong counter-attack, however, and was only saved by the opportune and unexpected arrival of Scipio Aemilianus again.

The latter was preceded by lictors *fasces*; carrying for the Comitia had become exasperated by the general inefficiency and had finally elected Scipio to the consulship in defiance of all the rules and regulations to the contrary. Scipio arrived in Utica just in time to answer the desperate appeals for help of Mancinus. Not long after he also attacked Megara (this time probably from the La Marsa side) and succeeded in capturing it for a while. He saw how difficult it would be to attack the city from this suburb, however, and evacuated it.

Within Carthage power was now entirely in the hands of the extreme democrats under the leadership of Hasdrubal. He had succeeded in getting rid of his namesake – Masinissa's grandson – who had been struck down at a Council meeting on his orders. Hasdrubal was furious at Scipio's attack, and in order to make any possibility of compromise quite out of the question, he had the Roman prisoners put to death on the city ramparts. All those suspected of weakness or defeatism were pitilessly wiped out.

Meanwhile, Scipio methodically set about getting a stranglehold on the city. He began by blocking the isthmus off completely, by building a vast entrenched camp. He then began building a dike across the mouth of the harbour so as to prevent the ships, which continued to run the blockade, from entering, however favourable the winds. The besieged then opened up another channel so that their military harbour communicated directly with the sea. They sent out an improvised fleet which made a not unsuccessful attempt at destroying the Roman ships. Scipio succeeded, nevertheless, in gaining a foothold on the vast Salammbo platform which over-looked the entrance to the harbour. The struggle for possession of this site lasted several months. The year 147 came to an end without producing much evidence of the Romans' progress. During the winter, in defiance of all good sense, Hasdrubal tried to open negotiations, using Gulussa as intermediary. Meanwhile, Scipio succeeded in destroying a Punic army in the Khanguet region, and completed the submission of the Libyan peasantry, many of whom had remained loyal to Carthage up till then, in spite of the punitive expeditions led against them by Gulussa's cavalry.

In the spring of 146, Scipio assembled all his forces in order to launch a final attack. Before he gave the order to advance, however, he solemnly recited the magic formulae which were intended to incite the city's protective gods to abandon it, and let loose over it the powers of evil. The Carthaginians also had recourse to religion, but they no longer sacrificed their children in the topheth as in Agathocles' day. The goddesses in whom they placed their confidence were the same Demeter and Kore whom they had brought from Syracuse two and a half centuries earlier. The potters from the ceramic workshops of Dermech were hastening to complete the sacred vessels which the initiates were to carry in procession. Gauckler found them intact at the beginning of this century, still in the kilns and waiting to be fired.

One morning (we do not know the exact date), the Romans left the fortifications they had built on the dockside and stormed the walls of the military harbour. The Carthaginians were exhausted through hunger and lack of sleep, and barely had the strength to resist. The legionaries crossed over from the harbour to the nearby agora and, as they passed, they robbed the Temple of Apollo of its golden tabernacle. They then launched an attack on Byrsa, through the narrow streets with their houses rising up six stories on either side. These houses had to be burnt before they could be pulled down. The citadel held out another six days, and Scipio granted their lives to the 50,000 people who had sought refuge there. They ended their days in slavery. There were 900 deserters from the Roman army in Carthage, however, and they knew that they could expect no mercy. In order to avoid crucifixion, they barricaded themselves into the Temple of Eshmun, which was on a hill to the north of Byrsa, within the slopes of which the Roman theatre was later excavated. They set fire to the temple and threw themselves into the flames. Hasdrubal's wife had followed them with her two sons, but Hasdrubal threw himself at Scipio's feet and implored mercy. Hasdrubal's wife hurled insults at him for his cowardice, and then threw her children and herself into the flames.

Thus the life of Carthage came to an end in a tragedy which arouses a subtle combination of pity and horror. It was even the will of fate that the most learned man of his generation should have been a personal witness of the final outcome, and he recorded what he saw for those who followed after. This was Polybius of Megalopolis, who had joined Scipio when he was appointed consul. His Book XXXVIII, which contained an account of the siege, is unfortunately almost completely lost. Appian gave a fairly accurate account of it in the second century A.D., however, and even his rhetoric has not succeeded in spoiling it entirely. The destruction of Carthage is therefore one of the events of history of which we know most – not only from the point of view of material detail, but also as far as the psychology of the participants is concerned. Polybius had been Scipio's tutor and remained his friend; he was able to note and understand his most secret reactions – for instance, his romantic sorrow at the sight of his enemy's misfortune, which brings a touch of humanity into this horrifying last act of the tragedy. Hasdrubal, on the other hand, aroused the historian's dislike, for he saw in him one of those demagogic tyrants whom he abhorred. Polybius was also able to analyse, with pitiless lucidity, the drunken fury of the Romans during the street fighting; his detachment is far more moving than any oratory when he describes the martyrdom of those civilians who were burnt to death in their houses, or crushed and buried in the ruins, or dragged with hooks, while they were still alive, and thrown into pits, where they could be seen twitching for some time.

Notes and References

1. Tenure of the office at this period was, therefore, not only limited to one year but could not be renewed: Hannibal would have had himself re-elected otherwise. Here is yet another reason for not agreeing with Gsell's suggestion that the kings who ruled for periods of several years running, up till the end of the fourth century, must have been annual suffetes who had been re-elected several times.

2. Livy (XXXIV, 72) tells us in this connection that Lepcis was the only city in the area. American excavations (see above, Ch.1) have shown that Sabratha had already been founded in the fifth century. It may be that the Latin historian was giving the word *civitas* its political meaning. Sabratha would then have been a dependency of Lepcis.

3. Polybius (XXXI, 21) has recorded a different version of these events, and situates them some thirty years later; cf. S. Gsell, *H.A.A.N.*, III, p. 316 ff.

4. A. Berthier and R. Charlier, *Le sanctuaire punique d'El Hofra*, 1955; and C. and G. Ch. Picard, *Rev. Arch.*, II (1956), pp. 196–9.

5. J. Mazard, *Corpus Num. Numid.*, p. 30, No. 17. Concerning the significance of this symbol see *Karthago*, XII (1965), pp. 40–41.

6. G. Camps, *Masinissa*, p. 259.

7. The stelae of El Hofra, and Punic inscriptions on Numidian territory generally, give us the names of priests or technicians, but not of civil servants. At Mactar, after its annexation to the Numidian kingdom, and until the first century A.D., the suffetes were all Numidian. Cf. *Civitas Mactariana*, p. 61.

8. This sanctuary was excavated in 1916 but only published in 1929, after Dr Carton's death, in a booklet which contains no plan and only very poor photographs. The statues were taken to Carthage Museum. The final publication is eagerly awaited.

9. Appian, *Libyca*, 61; and Diodorus, XXVII, 13–18.
10. Τοὺς ἐν τοῖς ἀγροῖς Λίδυας ἐπὶ τοὺς Νομάδας ἤγειρεν.
11. G. Camps, *Masinissa*, pp. 209–13.
12. This episode, and the whole question in general, has been discussed by A. J. Toynbee, *Hannibal's Legacy*, II, p. 318 ff.

TRANSLATOR'S NOTE

In translating quotations from Classical sources, I have tried, as far as possible, to use a good current English translation rather than translate a French translation. Page references in my translation relate to quotations from the following works:

HOMER: *The Odyssey* – a new translation by E. V. RIEU. Penguin Classics, Harmondsworth 1945
The Iliad – a new translation by E. V. RIEU. Penguin Classics, Harmondsworth 1950
HERODOTUS: *The Histories* – translated by Aubrey de SELINCOURT. Penguin Classics, Harmondsworth 1954
JUSTIN: *Histories* – literally translated with notes and a general index by the Rev. J. S. WATSON M.A. Bohn's Classical Library, London 1853
N.B. This is the most recent English translation.
ARISTOTLE: *The Politics* – translated with an introduction by T. A. SINCLAIR. Penguin Classics, Harmondsworth 1962
PORPHYRY: *Select Works* – translated from the Greek by Thomas TAYLOR. London 1823
N.B. I could find no more recent translation.
POLYBIUS: *The Histories* – translated by S. SHUCKBURGH M.A. London 1889

I was unable to find the work by ARISTOTLE quoted in Chapter I, p. 44.

Particularly in the cases of the older translations, I have altered a word here and there to conform with Professor Charles Picard's terminology or interpretation.

Thanks are due to the publishers of the above works for permission to quote from them.

D. C.

Illustrations

LIST OF PLATES

1 *Carthage: the topheth garden-museum. The walls on which the visitors are standing, and the pillars, both belong to Roman buildings which were built above the Sanctuary. The bottom of the trench in the foreground shows the level in the eighth century B.C. The stelae which were discovered during excavation have been set up on the spoil heap behind.*

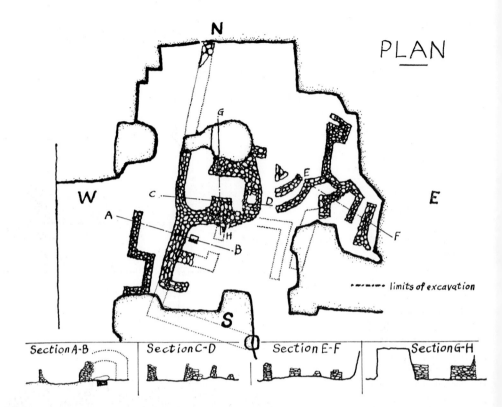

PLAN

N

W

E

S

-•—•—•— limits of excavation

Section A-B   Section C-D   Section E-F   Section G-H

2 *Above and opposite are shown the plan and sections of the excavations of the 'Cintas Chapel'*

KEY TO SECTIONS

1. Underlying bed rock
2. Natural cavity in the rock
3. Terracing built up of small stones
4. Outside walls
5. Small courtyard
6. Central vaulted chamber
7. Whitewash
8. Pavement (stone slabs)
9. Holy of Holies
10. Offerings (lamps)
11. Foundation deposit
12. Lid of 'gîr'
13. Partial collapse of the chamber
14. Fallen walls
15. What remained of the lid after the tomb's re-use
16. New deposits
17. Slab used to seal the chamber (secondary use)
18. Deposits of Punic pottery round the shrine
19. Deposit above a wall
20. Re-use of an old wall (one of the sides of the loggia containing the urn in the old wall itself)
21. The wall is broken away to make room for the deposit
22. The earlier collapse has been cleared away to make room for an offering on bed-rock
23. Level A of the sanctuary

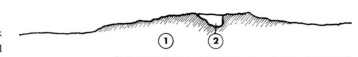

FIRST PHASE: *before occupation*

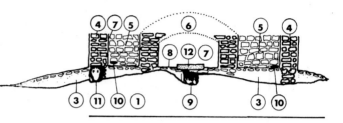

SECOND PHASE: *pre-Carthaginian building*

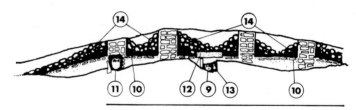

THIRD PHASE: *the building in ruins*

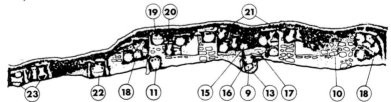

FOURTH PHASE: *the first Punic settlement, level A of the shrine of Tanit and Ba'al Hammon*

303

3 *Amphora with the twisted handles in the geometric style of the Cyclades (about 725 B.C.): found in the 'Cintas Chapel'*

4 *The entrance to a sixth-century tomb. Above the lintel are two slabs of stone, leaning up against each other and forming a relieving vault. The wall belongs to a Roman building constructed above the tomb (in the out-door museum of the Antonine Baths).*

Terracotta masks were used as phylacteries and were found in the tombs.

5 Above, *a negroid mask decorated with astral symbols and tattooing (seventh–sixth century* B.C.: *Bardo Museum)*

6 *A fifth-century mask decorated with tattoo marks. It was hung above the doorway into a tomb-chamber in the necropolis of Bou Mnijel (Bardo Museum).*

7

8

7 and **8**
Stelae shaped like thrones on which stand betyles dedicated to Ba'al Hammon. These stelae are from the topheth of Salammbo (end of sixth century B.C.).

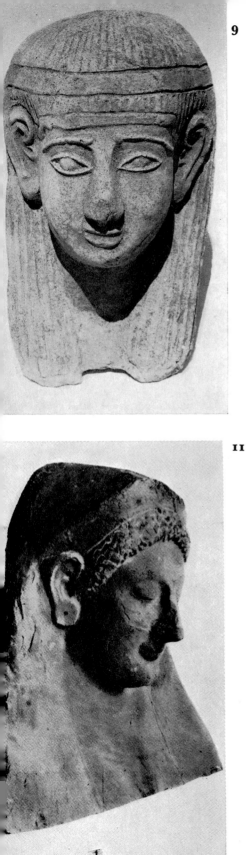

9

10

11

12

13   14

Three terracotta figurines, in the Cypriot style, which were offered to Ba'al Hammon in the topheth of Salammbo and which were found together with the sixth-century throne-shaped stelae (see Plates 7 and 8).

15

16 *Egyptian amulet, representing the god Bes, which was found in a tomb of the Dermech necropolis of the sixth to fifth century B.C.*

17 *Terracotta disc representing a god who is galloping on a horse. Between the legs of the horse runs a dog. In the field behind the rider are a sun-disc and crescent, and before him is a lotus flower. This may be Ba'al Safon, the god of storm and war.*

18 *Stele from the topheth of Salammbo which was dedicated to Ba'al Hammon, and which represents a doorway of Egyptian type decorated with the solar disc. A worshipper stands in the doorway (first years of the fifth century B.C.).*

19 *Mask of a man (belongs to the very first few years of the fifth century* B.C.: *Bardo Museum)*

20 *Terracotta statue of Ba'al Hammon, dated to the first century A.D. and reproducing a Punic model: from Thinissut (Cap Bon) (Bardo Museum)*

315

21 *The jewellery shown on this and the opposite page are from the tombs of the late sixth and early fifth centuries* B.C.: *from the cemeteries of Dermech and Borj Jedid.*

a, b Ear-rings with the Egyptian symbol of life

c–h Pendants: (d) is decorated with a sacred vessel against which lean two uraei *bearing a sun disc; another (f) shows the inverted crescent moon above a sun disc*

Opposite page (lower half)

m Gold rings

n The bezel of a ring set with a carved red carnelian depicting the two griffins on either side of a palmette

o Seal consisting of a carnelian scarab set in gold ring, the ends of which are polished round. It depicts the god Bes brandishing two lion cubs

p Signet ring with the seal-stone formed by a scarab which also depicts the god Bes.

a

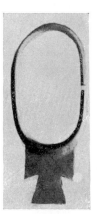

b

c

d

e

f

g

h

*i–l Tubes made to hold amulets, and decorated with a ram's
head and the head of a lioness supporting the sun disc
and* uraeus

i   *j*   *k*   *l*

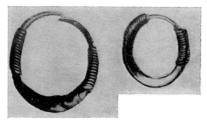

m   *n*

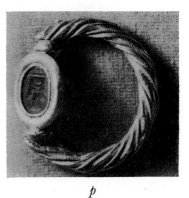

o   *p*

Plates **22–24** *show examples of bronze hatchet-shaped razors, terminating in the neck and bearing incised decoration. They were probably used for ritual shaving and were found in graves.*

22 *A razor on which are represented two worshippers (male and female) both wearing ritual dress. It was found in the necropolis of Ard el Kheraib and belongs to the last years of the fourth century* B.C. *(Bardo Museum).*

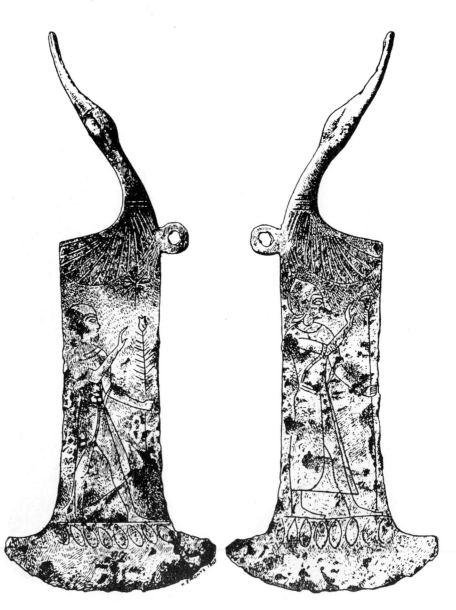

23 *A razor representing a god and his consort in attitudes of blessing above a bull and a wild boar respectively: from a tomb in the Saint Monique necropolis, belonging to the third century B.C. (Carthage Museum).*

24 *A razor in the Hellenizing style of the Barcid period. It represents a worshipper and a palm tree – the symbol of fertility of Tanit (Carthage Museum).*

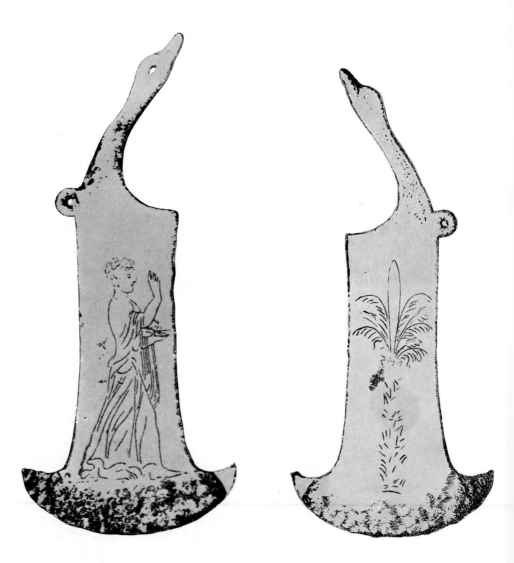

25 *A priest carrying a child which he is about to offer as sacrifice: a stele from Carthage, fourth century* B.C. *(Bardo Museum).*

26

A goddess holding a tambourine. This is probably Astarte (fourth century B.C.: Carthage Museum).

27

Tanit in the guise of the Egyptian lioness – goddess, Sekhmet. Terracotta statue of the first century A.D.: from Thinissut (Cap Bon) (Bardo Museum)

28

*Terracotta statue of Punic
Demeter: from Korba
(Cap Bon)*

Statue of a worshipper wearing Punic dress: from Utica (third century B.C.)

30 *Bronze vessel in the Hellenistic style, manufactured in Carthage. Detail of the decoration on the handle is shown in Plates 31 and 32, opposite (Bardo Museum).*

31
*Handle bottom of bronze
vessel opposite*

32
*Handle top of bronze
vessel opposite*

33 *Statue of a young woman who is wearing Punic dress in the Cypriot style: from the Dermech necropolis in Carthage (third century B.C.).*

34 *A Punic horseman at the time of the wars against Rome (perhaps the god of war)*

35 *A Punic house of the third century* B.C. *at Kerkouane*

36 *Line of the outer defences of Carthage. Excavations of General Duval and Colonel Reynier. The holes were cut into bed-rock and once contained posts which supported the defence works erected above a mound of earth. In front of this a deep ditch was dug.*

37 *Portrait of Hamilcar Barca on a coin which was struck in Spain*

38 *Portrait of Hasdrubal, son-in-law of Hamilcar Barca, on a coin struck in Spain*

39 *Prow of a galley on the reverse of the Hasdrubal coin shown in Plate 38*

40
Prow of a similar galley on a stele from Carthage

41
This representation of a merchant ship, decorated with sacred symbols, illustrates Appian's description of the ship which came to ask the Romans for peace after Zama.

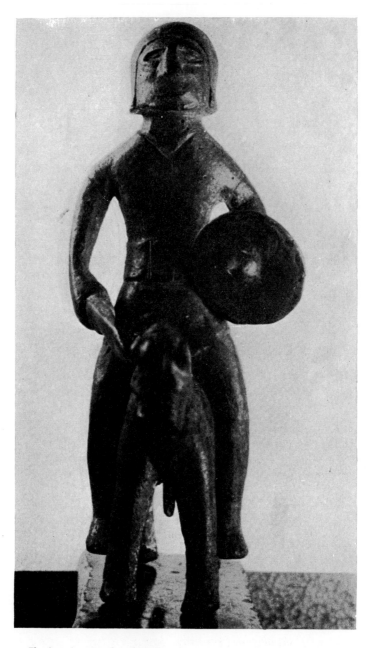

42 *Iberian bronze figurine showing a horseman of Hannibal's time*
   Courtesy of G. Nicolini

Plate 42, above, and Plate 43, opposite, illustrate the Punic armies in Spain.

43 *Low relief showing a Celtiberian soldier (Relief of Osuna in the Archaeological Museum of Madrid)*

44 *Stele from Carthage bearing the portrait of a general from the time of
the wars against Rome*

45 *Portrait of Hannibal. The bronze head of Volubilis*

46 *An episode of the Punic Wars depicted on a Roman coin of the first century* B.C. *It shows the duel of Servilius Pulex, a famous Roman champion, with a Gallic horseman of Hannibal's army.*

Hellenistic stelae from the topheth of Salammbo dedicated to Tanit Pene Ba'al and to Ba'al Hammon.

47 (left) *Decoration representing a cella in which stands the sacred vessel, shaped like a pistil supported on a stem which springs from an acanthus bush. There is a bunch of grapes in the neck of the vessel and the whole is framed by scroll ornaments. The theme is that of the sacred plant which contains burgeoning life which is born and reborn within the cella. It was inspired by the painted decoration of Italiot vessels (beginning of the third century B.C.: Bardo Museum).*

48 (right) *Flat relief with the background cut away. It shows a priestess pouring a libation on a tumulus by torchlight. Above her are the astral symbols of the lords of the topheth (end of the third century B.C.: Bardo Museum).*

49 (above) *Stele in the form of the sign for Tanit from late Carthaginian times*

50 (opposite) *The mausoleum of Dougga. The tomb of a Numidian prince of the second century B.C. built by a Punic architect. This is the only intact example of Punic architecture to have come down to us.*

Ruined mausoleums of the Punic period have been recently discovered in Tunisia and Tripolitania.

51 (opposite) *Model of a Punic temple in Hellenistic times. This chapel dedicated to Demeter was found at Thuburbo Maius (Bardo Museum).*

52 (below) *Fragments of an Ionian stuccoed column: from a second-century B.C. house on the hill of Byrsa at Carthage*

Bibliography

LIST OF ABBREVIATIONS

A.C.	*Archeologia Classica*
A.E.A.	*Archivo Español de Arqueologia*
A.J.A.	*American Journal of Archeology*
B.A.S.O.R.	*Bulletin of the American Schools of Oriental Research*
B.C.H.	*Bulletin de Correspondance Hellénique*
C.R.A.I.	*Comptes Rendus de l'Académie des Inscriptions et Belles Lettres*
H.A.A.N.	*Histoire Ancienne de l'Afrique du Nord* (St. Gsell)
J.A.	*Journal Asiatique*
M.A.L.	*Monumenti Antichi dell'Accademia Nazionale dei Lincei*
M.A.N.L.	*Memorie dell'Accademia Nazionale dei Lincei*
M.E.E.R.	*Mélanges d'Archéologie et d'Histoire de l'Ecole Française de Rome*
P.B.S.R.	*Papers of the British School at Rome*
R.A.	*Revue Archéologique*
R.E.L.	*Revue des Etudes Latines*
R.H.R.	*Revue de l'Histoire des Religions*
S.S.	*Studi Sardi*

ACANFORA, M. O. 'Panormo punica', *M.A.N.L.*, VIII, I, 1947, pp. 197–248

ACCADEMIA ETRUSCA DI CORTONA. *Studi Annibalici*, Cortona, 1964

ALBRIGHT, W. F. 'New light on the early history of Phoenician colonisation', *B.A.S.O.R.*, 83, 1941, pp. 17 *et seq.*

ALQUIER, J. and P. 'Tombeaux phéniciens à Djidjelli', *R.A.*, XXXI, 1930, pp. 1–17

AMADASI, A. *et al. Monte Sirai II*, Rome, 1965; *Monte Sirai III*, Rome, 1966; *Monte Sirai IV*, Rome, 1967

AMIET, P. 'Les intailles de la collection Chavannes à Tunis', *Cahiers de Byrsa*, VIII, 1958, pp. 13–24

ASTRUC, M. 'Nouvelles fouilles à Djidjelli', *Rev. Africaine*, XXX, 1937, pp. 199–253.

ASTRUC, M. *La nécropole de Villaricos*, Madrid, 1951

ASTRUC, M. 'Supplément aux fouilles de Gouraya', *Lybica*, II, 1954, pp. 9–48

ASTRUC, M. 'Traditions funéraires de Carthage', *Cahiers de Byrsa*, VI, 1956, pp. 29–58

ASTRUC, M. 'Exotisme et localisme', *Archivo de Preistoria Levantina*, VI, 1957, pp. 47–112

ASTRUC, M. 'Empreintes et reliefs de terre cuite', *M.E.F.R.*, 1959, pp. 107 *et seq.*

AUSEJO, S. DE. 'El problema de Tartessos', *Sefarad*, II, 1942, pp. 171–91

AYMARD, A. 'Les deux premiers traités entre Rome et Carthage', *R.E.A.*, LIX, 1957, pp. 277–93

BANDINELLI, R. BIANCHI, *et al. Leptis Magna*, Rome, 1963

BARADEZ, J. 'Nouvelles recherches sur les ports antiques de Carthage', *Karthago*, IX, 1958, pp. 45–78

BARRECA, F. *La civiltà di Cartigne*, Cagliari, 1964.

BARRECA, F. *et al*. *Monte Sirai I*, Rome, 1964

BARTOCCINI, R. 'Le antichità della Tripolitania', *Aegyptus*, VII, 1926, pp. 49–96

BELOCH, J. 'Die Könige von Karthago', *Klio*, VII, 1907, pp. 25 *et seq*.

BELOCH, J. *Griechische Geschichte*, I–IV, Berlin, 1924–31

BERNABO REA, L. *La Sicilia prima dei Greci*, Milan, 1958

BERNABO REA, L. and CAVALIER, M. 'Civiltà preistoriche delle isole Eolia e del territorio de Milazzo', *Bull. Palet. Ital.*, n.s. X (65), I, pp. 7–100

BERTHIER, A. and CHARLIER, R. *Le sanctuaire punique d'El Hofra à Constantine*, Paris, 1955

BICKERMANN, E. J. 'An Oath of Hannibal', *Trans. Am. Phil. Assoc.*, LXXV, 1944

BICKERMANN, E. J. 'Hannibal's Covenant,' *Am. J. Philology*, LXXIII, 1, 1952, pp. 1–23

BISI, A. M. 'Le stele Puniche', *Studi Semitici*, 27, Rome, 1967

BISSING, F. VON, 'Karthago und seine Griechischen und Italischen Beziehunge', *Studi Etruschi*, VII, 1933, pp. 83–134

BLANCO FREIJero, A. 'Los marfiles de Carmona', *A.E.A.*, XX, 1947, pp. 3–25

BLASQUEZ, J. M. 'Las Relaciones entre Hispania y el norte de Africa', *Saitabi*, XI, 1961, pp. 21–43

BLASQUEZ, J. M. 'El Herakleion Gaditano, un templo semita en Occidente', *Arch. Marruecos Esq.*, 1963, pp. 309–18

BLASQUEZ, J. M. 'Aportaciones al estudio del simbolismo funerario de huevo y granada en las creencias populares de las antiguas religiones mediterràneas', *Revista de Dialectología y Tradiciones populares*, XXIII, 1, 1967, pp. 132–66

BONSOR, J. *Early Engraved Ivories*, New York, 1928

BOSCH GIMPERA, P. 'Phéniciens et Grecs de l'Extrême Orient', *La Nouvelle Clio*, III, 1951, pp. 259–96

BOUCHER-COLOZIER, E. 'Les Etrusques et Carthage', *M.E.F.R.*, XLV, 1953

BOUCHER-COLOZIER, E. 'Céramique archaïque d'importation,' *Cahiers de Byrsa*, III, 1953, pp. 11 *et seq*.

BRANCOLI, I. *et al*. 'Mozia III,' *Studi Semitici*, 24, Rome, 1967

CAGIANO DE AZEVEDO, M. *et al*., *Missione Archeologica a Malta, Rapporto preliminare della campagna 1963*, Rome, 1964; . . . *della campagna 1964*, Rome, 1965; . . . *della campagna 1966*, Rome, 1967

CAMPS, G. 'Massinissa', *Lybica*, VIII, 1960

CANTINEAU, J. and LESCHI, L. 'Monnaies puniques d'Alger', *C.R.A.I.*, 1941, pp. 263–78

CARCOPINO, J. *Le Maroc Antique*, Paris, 1948, pp. 73 *et seq*.

CARCOPINO, J. 'Grandeur et faiblesse d'Hannibal', in *Profils de Conquérants*, Paris, 1961

CARCOPINO, J. *Les étapes de l'Impérialisme romain*, Paris, 1961

CARPENTER, R. 'Phoenicians in the West', *A.J.A.*, LXII, 1958, pp. 35–53

CARTON, L. *Un sanctuaire punique découvert à Carthage*, Paris, 1929

CASARIEGO, J. E. *El periplo de Hannon de Cartago*, Madrid, 1947

CASSOLA, F. *I gruppi politici romani nel IIIº secolo a.C.*, Trieste, 1952

CAVALLERO, G. 'Panormos preromana', *Arch. Stor. Ital.*, IV, 1950–1, pp. 7–182

CHIAPPISI, S. *Il Melqart di Sciacca, e la questione fenicia in Sicilia*, Rome, 1961

CIASCA, A. *et al*., 'Mozia II', *Studi Semitici*, 19, Rome, 1966

CINTAS, P. 'Le sanctuaire punique de Sousse', *Rev. Africaine*, XC, 1947, pp. 1–80

CINTAS, P. 'Fouilles puniques à Tipasa', *Rev. Africaine*, XCII, 1949, pp. 1–68

CINTAS, P. *Céramique Punique*, Paris, 1950

CINTAS, P. 'Deux campagnes de fouilles à Utique', *Karthago*, II, 1951, pp. 1–88

CINTAS, P. 'Nouvelles recherches à Utique', *Karthago*, V, 1954, pp. 89–154

CINTAS, P. *Contribution à l'étude de l'expansion carthagionoise au Maroc*, Paris, 1954

CINTAS, P. 'Tarsus-Tartessos-Gades', *Semitica*, XVI, 1966, pp. 5–37

COLOMINES ROCA, J. *Le terracuites d'Eivissa*, Barcelona, 1938

Corpus Inscriptionum Semiticarum, Pars I, Nos. 166–6068

CULICAN, W. 'Aspects of Phoenician settlements in the West Mediterranean', *Abr Nahrain*, I, 1961, pp. 36–55

DEMARGNE, P. *R.A.*, XXXVIII, 1951, pp. 44–52

DONNER, H. and RÖLLIG, W. *Kanaanäische und aramäische Inschriften*, I, II, III, Wiesbaden, 1962–6

DUNBABIN, V. *The Western Greeks*, Oxford, 1948

DUPONT-SOMMER, A. *C.R.A.I.*, 1948, pp. 12–22 (Nora inscription)

DUPONT-SOMMER, A. *J.A.*, 1964, pp. 289–302 (Pyrgi inscription)

EHRENBERG, V. *Karthago*, Leipzig, 1927

EISSFELDT, O. *Molk als Opferbegriff im punischen und hebräischen, und das ende des Gottes Moloch*, 1935

FANTAR, M. H. 'Le cavalier marin de Kerkouane', *Africa*, I, 1966, pp. 1–32

FANTAR, M. H. 'Pavimenta punica et signe dit de Tanit dans les habitations de Kerkouane', *Studi Magrebini*, I, 1966, pp. 57–65

FERRON, J. 'Le caractère solaire du Dieu de Carthage', *Africa*, I, 1965, pp. 41–58

FERRON, J. and PINARD, M. 'Fouilles de Byrsa, 1953–4', *Cahiers de Byrsa*, V, 1955, pp. 31–81; IX, 1960–1, pp. 77–170

FÉVRIER, J. G. 'Magistrature et sacerdoce puniques sur l'inscription de Gaulo', *Rev. Assyr.*, 1948, pp. 85 *et seq.*

FÉVRIER, J. G. 'A propos de Baal Addir', *Semitica*, II, 1949, pp. 21–8

FÉVRIER, J. G. 'Vir Sidonius', *Semitica*, IV, 1951–2

FÉVRIER, J. G. 'Molchomor', *R.H.R.*, CXLIII, 1953, pp. 8–18

FÉVRIER, J. G. 'Le vocabulaire sacrificiel punique', *J.A.*, CCXLIII, 1955, pp. 49–63

FÉVRIER, J. G. 'Un sacrifice d'enfant chez les Numides' in *Mélanges I. Levy*, 1955

FÉVRIER, J. G. 'A propos du serment d'Hannibal', *Cahiers de Byrsa*, VI, 1956, pp. 13–22

FÉVRIER, J. G. 'Remarques sur le grand Tarif dit de Marseille', *Cahiers de Byrsa*, VIII, 1958–9, pp. 35–43

FÉVRIER, J. G. 'Essai de reconstitution du sacrifice molek', *J.A.*, CCXLVIII, 1960, pp. 167–87

FÉVRIER, J. G. 'Le rite de substitution dans les textes de N'gaous', *J.A.*, CCL, 1962, pp. 1–10

FÉVRIER, J. G. 'La constitution municipale de Dougga à l'époque numide', *Mélanges de Carthaga*, 1964–5, pp. 85–91

FÉVRIER, J. G. 'Remarques sur l'inscription punique de Pyrgi', *Oriens Antiquus*, IV, 1965 pp. 175–80

FÉVRIER, J. G. 'Inscriptions puniques et neo-puniques' in *Inscriptions Antiques dux Maroc*, Paris, 1966, pp. 81–132

FOUCHER, L. *Hadrumetum*. Paris, 1964

349

FREZOULS, E. 'Une nouvelle hypothèse sur la fondation de Carthage',, *B.C.H.* LXXIX, 1955, pp. 153–76

GARBINI, G. 'L'espansione fenicia nel Mediterraneo', *Cultura e Scuola*, 1963, pp. 92–7

GARBINI, G. 'Scavi nel santuario etrusco di Pyrgi', *A. C.*, XVI, 1964, pp. 66–76 (the Punic inscription). Also in *Oriens Antiquus*, IV, 1965, pp. 35–52

GARBINI, G. 'Tarsis e Gen. X, 4¹, *Bibbia e Oriente*, VII, 1965, pp. 13–19

GARBINI, G. 'I Fenici in Occidente', *Studi Etruschi*, XXXIV, 1966

GARCÍA Y BELLIDO, A. *Fenicos y Carthagineses in Occidente*, Madrid, 1942

GARCÍA Y BELLIDO, A. 'Protostoria: Tartessos, colonización punica' in Ramón Menéndez Pidal, *Historia de España*, Madrid, 1960, pp. 281–492

GARCÍA Y BELLIDO, A. 'Inventarios de jarros púnico-tartessicos,' *A.E.A.*, XXXIII, 1960, pp. 44–63

GARCÍA Y BALLIDO, A. 'Deidades semitas en la España Antigua', *Sefarad*, XXIV, 1964, pp. 12–14

GARCÍA Y BELLIDO, A. 'Hercules Gaditanes', *A.E.A.*, 1964, pp. 50–80

GARCÍA Y BELLIDO, A. 'Nuevos jarros de bronce Tartessos,' *A.E.A.*, 1927, pp. 50–80

GAUCKLER, P. *Nécropoles puniques de Carthage*, I–II, Paris, 1915

GAUTIER, P. 'Grecs et Phéniciens en Sicile', *Rev. Hist.*, CCXXIV, 1960, pp. 257–274

GERMAIN, 'Qu'est-ce que le périple d'Hannon?' *Hesperis*, XLIV, 1957, pp. 205–48

GROAG, E. *Hannibal als Politiker*, I–IV, Berlin, 1929

GSELL, S. *Histoire Ancienne de l'Afrique du Nord*, Paris, 1928

HALFF, G. 'L'onomastique punique de Carthage', *Karthago*, XII, 1963–4, pp. 63–145

HARDEN, D. B. *The Phoenicians*, London, 1962

HEURGON, J. 'The inscriptions of Pyrgi', *J.R.S.*, 1966, pp. 1–15

HEUSS, A. 'Der erste Punische Krieg und das Problem des Römischen Imperialismus', *Hist. Zeitschrift*, 169, 1949

HEUSS, A. *Römische Geschichte*, Berlin, 1960

HOFFMANN, W. *Hannibal*, Göttingen, 1962

HOLM, A. *Geschichte Siziliens*, Leipzig, 1870

HOURS-MEIDAN, M. 'Les représentations figurées sur les stèles de Carthage', *Cahiers de Byrsa*, I, 1951, pp. 15–160

ISSERLIN, B. S. J. *et al.* 'Motya 1955', *P.B.S.R.*, XXVI, 1958, pp. 1–29

ISSERLIN, B. S. J. *et al.* 'Motya, a Phoenician Punic site near Marsala, Sicily: Preliminary Report of the Leeds London Fairleigh Dickinson Excavations 1961–3', *Annual of the Leeds University Oriental Society*, IV, 1962–3, pp. 84–131

JODIN, M. 'Les fouilles exécutées à Mogador en mai et juin 1956', *Bull. Arch. du Maroc*, 1957, pp. 118–25

KELSEY, J. *Excavations at Carthage: a Preliminary Report*, New York, 1926

KROMAYER, J. *Antike Schlachtfelder*, III–IV, Berlin, 1912–24

LAPEYRE, G., and PELLEGRINI, A. *Carthage Punique*, Paris, 1942

LEZIHE, A. *Architecture punique, Recueil de documents*, Paris, 1962

MAHJOUBI, A. and FANTAR, M. H. 'Une nouvelle inscription carthaginoise', *Atti Acc. Lincei*, XXI, 1906, pp. 201–10

MAUNY, R. 'Notes sur le périple d'Hannon', *Comptes Rendus de la 1ère Conf. internationale des Africanistes de l'Ouest*, II, 1951, pp. 509 *et seq.*

MAUNY, R. 'La navigation sur les cotes du Sahara pendant l'antiquité', *Rev. des Et. Anc.*, LVII, 1955, pp. 92 *et seq.*

MAURIN, L. 'Himilcon le Magonide, crises et mutations à Carthage au début du IVe siècle av. J. C.', *Semitica*, XII, 1962, pp. 5–43

MAZARD, J. *Corpus nummorum Numidiae Mauritaniaeque*, 1955

MAZZARNO, s. *Introduzione alle guerre puniche*, Catania, 1947

MERITT, E. 'Athens and Carthage', *Harvard Studies in Classical Philology*, Supp., Vol. I, 1940, pp. 247–53

MOSCATI, s. 'Il sacrificio dei fanciulli', *Rend. Pont. Acc. Rom. Arch.*, XXXVIII, 1965–6, pp. 1–8

MOSCATI, s. *Il mondo dei Fenici*, Milan, 1966

MOSCATI, s. 'La penetrazione fenicia e punica in Sardegna', *Atti. Acc. Lincei*, 5 VIII, XII, 1966, pp. 215–50

MOSCATI, s. 'Scoperte puniche in Sardegna', *Rend. Pont. Acc. Rom. Arch.*, XXXIX, 1966–7, pp. 15–32

MOSCATI, s. 'Considerazione sulla cultura fenico-punica in Sardegna', *Atti Acc. Lincei*, XXII, 8, 1967, pp. 129–52

MOSCATI, s. and PALLOTTINO, M. 'Rapporti tra Greci, Fenici, Etruschi ed altre popolazioni italiche alla luce delle nuove scoperte', *Atti Acc. Lincei*, CCLXIII, 87, 1966, pp. 1–16

PACE, M. *Arte e civiltà della Sicilia antica*, Milan-Rome-Naples, 1958

PALLOTTINO, M. 'Les relations entre les Etrusques et Carthage du VIIº au IIº siècle av. J. C.', *Cahiers de Tunisie*, IX, 1963, pp. 23–9

PALLOTTINO, M. 'Scavi nel santuario etrusco di Pyrgi', *A.C.*, XVI, 1964, pp. 58–63 ('Scoperta e prima valutazione delle lamine iscritte'); pp. 76–117 ('Le iscrizioni etrusche')

PARETI, M. 'Su i primi commerci e stanziamenti fenici nei paesi mediterranei e specialmente in Sicilia', *Arch. Stor. per la Sicilia Orientale*, XII, 1934, pp. 3–28

PELLICER CATALAN, M. *Excavaciones en la necrópolis púnica Laurita del Cerro de San Cristobál (Almuñécar, Granada)*, Madrid, 1963

PESCE, G. 'Il primo scavo di Tharros', *S.S.*, XIV, XV, 1955–7

PESCO, G. *Sardegna Punica*, Cagliari, 1961

PESCE, G. 'Il tempio punico di Tharros', *M.A.L.*, XLV, 1961, col. 333–440

PFIFFIG, A. *Uni-Hera-Astarte*, Vienna, 1965

PICARD, C. *Carthage*, Paris, 1951

PICARD, C. *Catalogue du Musée Alaoui, Nouvelle Série (Collections Puniques)*, I, Tunis, 1954

PICARD, C. 'Les oenochoes de bronze de Carthage', *R.A.*, I, 1959, pp. 29–64

PICARD, C. 'Notes de chronologie punique, le problème du Vº siècle', *Karthago*, XII, 1963–64, pp. 17–27

PICARD, C. 'Thèmes hellénistiques sur les stèles de Carthage', *Antiquités Africaines*, I, 1967, pp. 9–30

PICARD, C. 'Sacra Punica', *Karthago*, XIII, 1967

PICARD, C. 'Les installations cultuelles du tophet de Salammbo', *Rev. Studi Orientali* (in press)

PICARD, C. 'Evolution et genèse des signes de la Bouteille et de Tanit à Carthage', *Studi Magrebini* (in press)

PICARD, C. and G. C. *La vie quotidienne à Carthage au temps d'Hannibal*, 2nd edn., Paris, 1964

PICARD, C. and G. C. 'Hercule et Melqart' in *Mélanges J. Bayet* (Coll. Latomus LXX), Brussels, 1964, pp. 569–78

PICARD, G. C. *Les religions de l'Afrique antique*, Paris, 1954

PICARD, G. C. *Le Monde de Carthage*, Paris, 1956 (Eng. tr. *Carthage*, London, 1964)

PICARD, G. C. 'Les sufètes de Carthage chez Tite-Live et Cornelius Nepos', *R.E.L.*, XLI, 1963, pp. 269–81

PICARD, G. C. 'Le portrait d'Hannibal', *Karthago*, XII, 1963–64, pp. 31–41

PICARD, G. C. 'L'administration territoriale de Carthage' in *Mélanges A. Piganiol*, III, Paris, 1966, pp. 1257–65

PICARD, G. C. 'Le traité Romano-Barcide de 226 av. J. C.' in *Mélanges J. Carcopino*, Paris, 1966, pp. 747–62

PICARD, G. C. *Hannibal*, Paris, 1967

PICARD, G. C. 'La Révolution démocratique de Carthage', *Conférences de la Société d'Etudes Latines de Bruxelles 1965–6* (Coll. Latomus, LXII), Brussels, 1968, pp. 113–130

POINSSOT, L. and LANTIER, R. 'Un sanctuaire de Tanit à Carthage', *R.H.R.*, LXXXVII, 1923, pp. 32–68

ROBINSON, E. S. G. 'Punic Coins of Spain' in *Essays in Roman Coinage presented to Harold Mattingly*, Oxford, 1956, pp. 34–53

SESTON, W. 'Des "Portes" de Thugga à la "Constitution" de Carthage', *Rev. Hist.*, CCXXXVII, 1967, pp. 277–94

SOLA-SOLE, J. M. 'Tarshish y los comienzos de la colonización fenicia en Occidente', *Sefarad*, XVII, 1957, pp. 23–35

SUSINI, G. *Ricerche sulla battaglia di Trasimeno*, Cortona, 1960

TACKHOLM, U. 'Tarsis, Tartessos und die Säulen des Herakles', *Opuscula Romana*, V, 1965, pp. 143–96

TARRADELL, M. *Lixus*, Tetuan, 1959

TARRADELL, M. *Marruecos Púnico*, Tetuan, 1960

TONYBEE, A. J. *Hannibal's Legacy*, Oxford, 1965

TUSA, V. 'La questione di Solunte e la dea femminile seduta', *Karthago*, XII, 1963–4

TUSA, V. 'Testimonianze fenicio-puniche in Sicilia', *Kokalos*, X–XI, 1964–5, 599–602.

TUSA, V. *et al.* 'Mozia I', *Studi Semitici*, Rome, 1964

VAUX, R. DE. 'Les sacrifices de l'Ancien Testament', *Cahiers de la Rev. Biblique*, I, Paris, 1964, pp. 67–81

VERCOUTTER, J. *Les objets égyptiens et égyptisants du mobilier funéraire carthaginois*, Paris, 1945

VITA, A. DI. 'L'elemento punico a Selinunte nel IVº e IIIº secolo a.C.', *A.C.*, V, 1953, pp. 39–47

VOGT. J. *Rom und Karthago*, Leipzig, 1943

VUILLEMOT, G. *Reconnaissance aux échelles d'Oranie*, Autun, 1965

WALBANK, F. W. *A Historical Commentary on Polybius*, I, Oxford, 1957

WARMINGTON, B. H. *Carthage*, London, 1960

WEIL, R. *Aristote et l'histoire*, Paris, 1961

WHITE, D. 'The post-classical cult of Malophoros at Selinus', *A.J.A.*, 71, No. 4, 1967, pp. 335–52

Further Reading

Two general works contain an exhaustive bibliography of Carthage: M. Sznycer's contribution in C. Nicolet's *Rome et la Conquête du Monde Méditerranéen*: Vol. 2 (264–27 B.C.) *Genèse d'un Empire*, Paris, 1978, pp. 473–89, and W. Huss, *Geschichte der Karthager*, Munich, 1985. These two authors do not accept our doctrine pertaining to the monarchy in Carthage (M. Sznycer, ibid., pp. 545–93, particularly 565 *et seq*). We have shown (notably in the new edition of the Cambridge Ancient History, now in preparation) that monarchy and suffetes are two distinct offices which were able to co-exist.

The *I° Congresso Internazionale di studi Fenici e Punici* (3 vol. Rome, 1983) brings together the work of ninety-five scholars on the most important problems. The symposium 'Phönizier im Westen' is also of importance, edited by H. G. Niemeyer (*Madrider Mitteilungen*, Beitrag 8, 1982).

The campaign supported by UNESCO from 1972 to 1983 made headway in the study of Punic Carthage on three main fronts: the discovery and restoration of the naval base by H. Hurst's British team (published in *Antiquaries Journal*, London, 1975–9); the discovery of a quarter dating from the beginning of the third century on Byrsa by S. Lancel (S. Lancel *et al*, 'French Archaelogical Mission at Carthage': Byrsa I, 'Rapports Préliminaires des Fouilles', 1974-6, and Byrsa II, 'Rapports Préliminaires des Fouilles' 1977–8: 'Niveaux et Vestiges Puniques', Ecole Française de Rome, 1980 and 1982); and the discovery of another by F. Rakob's German mission Mitt. Deutsches Instituts, Rom, 91, 1984, pp. 1–22. A key work by H. Benichou-Safar on the Punic necropolises of Carthage is *Les Tombes Puniques de Carthage: Topographie, Structures, Inscriptions et Rites Funéraires*, Paris 1983.

From the town of Kerkouane, M. Fantar's publication adds up to nothing less than an encyclopaedia of Punic civilization in Africa; the first two tomes are devoted to architecture and town-planning and were published in Tunisia in 1984 and 1985.

Two important exhibitions devoted to Tunisian antiquities have been held recently. 'De Carthage à Kairouan', Paris, 1982, and '30 Ans au Service du Patrimoine', Tunisia, 1986–7. The catalogues, edited by archaeologists from the National Institute of Archaeology and Arts of Tunisia, are indispensable tools as well as being beautiful popular works.

An extraordinary discovery at Motya revealed a Greek statue in severe style (from the first half of the fifth century B.C.), depicting a man dressed in a long, clinging, see-through tunic; in contradiction with V. Tusa, *Archéo*, 20 October 1986, pp. 19–23 who believed it to be a charioteer, we identified it as Amilcar of Himera (see p. 284).

We have put forward our point of view on Hannibal, in the May 1986 issue of *L'Histoire*, pp. 43–8 (the Naples portrait the magazine used is not actually of Hannibal). The discovery of fragments of coinage in Andalousia depicting the elephant weakened the arguments of those who claim that the person on the right is Hannibal (A. Villaŕonga, *Studi di Numismtica Punica, Supp. Riv. Studi fenici*, Rome, XI, 1983, p. 64, pl. XXXIX, 40).

On Punic religion and the arts connected with it, C. Picard, 'Les Representations du Sacrifice Molk sur les Ex-Votos de Carthage', *Karthago*, XVII, 1973–4, pp. 67–138 and XVIII, 1978, pp. 5–116. S. Moscati, 'Scavi á Mozia, Le Stele', Rome, 1981. B. Quillard, 'Bijoux Carthaginois', I, 'Les Colliers', Louvain-la-Neuve, 1979. M. Seefried, 'Les Pendentifs en Verre a Noyau des Pays de la Mediterranée Antique', Ecole Française de Rome, 1982.

Lastly, S. Moscati, *Italia Punica*, Rome, 1986, on the Carthaginians in Italy.

INDEX

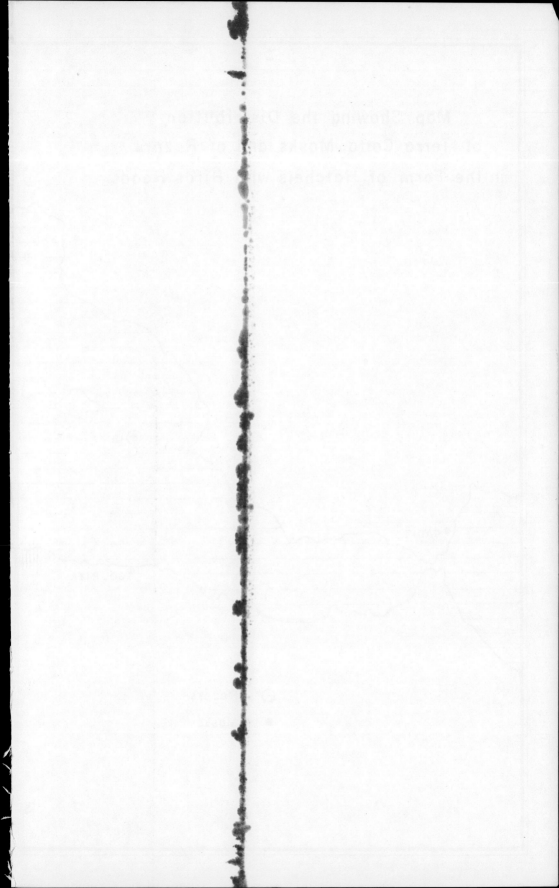

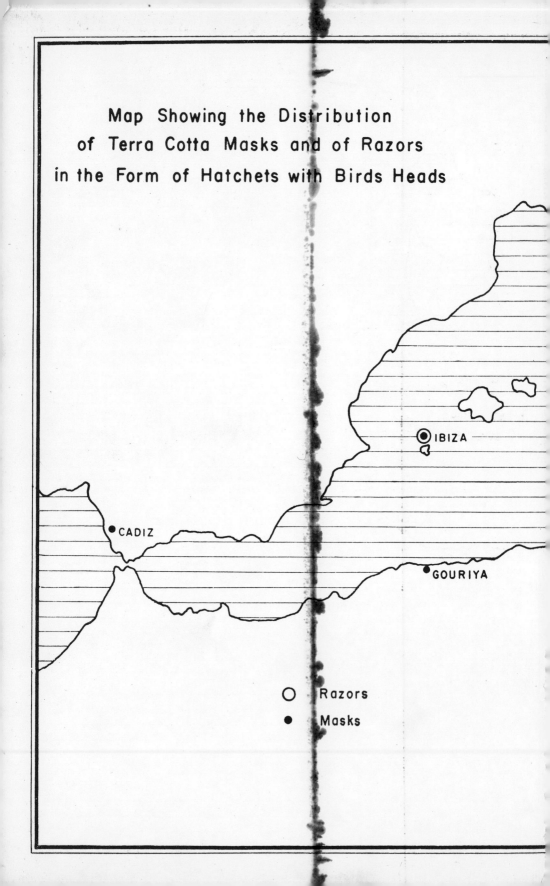

Map Showing the Distribution
of Terra Cotta Masks and of Razors
in the Form of Hatchets with Birds Heads

● CADIZ

◉ IBIZA

● GOURIYA

○   Razors
●   Masks